"In the wake of the COVID-19 pandemic, societies will need to rethink the role of a market economy in social provisioning. *Institutional Economics: Perspectives and Methods in Pursuit of a Better World* contributes to that rethinking through its fresh attention to economists such as Veblen, Commons, Polanyi, Galbraith, and Minsky. The book's distinguished contributors advance institutionalism by highlighting the importance of culture, gender, finance, the environment, citizen engagement in problem-solving, and a critical look at long-standing myths about market-based economies."

—**Alicia Girón**, National Autonomous University, Mexico

"This book presents the contemporary state of institutional economics along with new methodologies … . It is timely in that it enables economic analyses which consider not only efficiency but also pluralistic values including gender equality, worker wellbeing, and environmental protection."

—**Hiroyuki Uni**, Kyoto University, Japan

"Whalen and his contributors provide much food for thought … . Includes inquiry into instrumentalism, environmentalism, feminism, methodology, and more."

—**William M. Dugger**, University of Tulsa, USA

INSTITUTIONAL ECONOMICS

Institutional economics is a socio-cultural discipline and policy science which draws on the idea that economies are best understood through an appreciation of history, real-world institutions, and socioeconomic interrelations. This book brings together leading institutionalists to examine the tradition's most essential perspectives and methods.

The contributors to the book draw on a broad range of institutional thought, from the classic work of Thorstein Veblen, John R. Commons, and Karl Polanyi, to the newer viewpoints of post-Keynesian institutionalism, feminist institutionalism, and environmental institutionalism. Methods range from frameworks used to analyze public policy and institutional change, to modes of analysis including myth busting, historically grounded narratives, and computer-based simulations. Each chapter surveys the origins, development, key features, applications, and frontiers of a particular viewpoint, framework, or mode of analysis. Due consideration is given to both strengths and weaknesses; and woven into the chapters is attention to core institutionalist concepts, including technology, institutions, culture, and complexity.

The book provides economists with promising starting points for new research, students with contributions refreshingly in touch with the real world, and policymakers and social scientists with compelling reasons for engaging further with the institutionalist tradition.

Charles J. Whalen is Research Fellow at the Baldy Center for Law and Social Policy, University at Buffalo, USA. For over three decades he has contributed to institutional economics, national economic policy discussions, equitable regional development, and worker engagement in business decision-making. This is his fifth book.

INSTITUTIONAL ECONOMICS

Perspectives and Methods in Pursuit of a Better World

Edited by Charles J. Whalen

Routledge
Taylor & Francis Group
LONDON AND NEW YORK

First published 2022
by Routledge
2 Park Square, Milton Park, Abingdon, Oxon OX14 4RN

and by Routledge
605 Third Avenue, New York, NY 10158

Routledge is an imprint of the Taylor & Francis Group, an informa business

British Library Cataloguing-in-Publication Data
A catalogue record for this book is available from the British Library

Library of Congress Cataloging-in-Publication Data
A catalog record has been requested for this book

ISBN: 978-0-367-74945-3 (hbk)
ISBN: 978-0-367-74950-7 (pbk)
ISBN: 978-1-003-16043-4 (ebk)

DOI: 10.4324/9781003160434

Typeset in Bembo
by Deanta Global Publishing Services, Chennai, India

To the next generation of institutionalists,
inheritors of a noble tradition that helped shape
Progressivism, the New Deal, and the Great Society

CONTENTS

ILLUSTRATIONS

Figures

Tables

CONTRIBUTORS

Richard V. Adkisson is Emeritus Professor of Economics, New Mexico State University, USA.

Michele Cangiani is Associate Professor of Economic Sociology (retired), Ca' Foscari University of Venice, Italy.

Thomas Kemp is Chair and Professor of Economics, University of Wisconsin–Eau Claire, USA.

Sarah S.H. Klammer is Academic Specialist, Department of Agricultural, Food and Resource Economics, Michigan State University, USA.

Janice Peterson is Professor Emerita of Economics, California State University, Fresno, USA.

Michael J. Radzicki is Associate Professor of Economics, Worcester Polytechnic Institute, USA.

Eric A. Scorsone is Associate Professor and Director, Department of Agricultural, Food and Resource Economics, Michigan State University, USA.

William T. Waller is Chair and Professor of Economics, Hobart and William Smith Colleges, USA.

Charles J. Whalen is Research Fellow, Baldy Center for Law and Social Policy, University at Buffalo, USA.

Mary V. Wrenn is Senior Lecturer in Economics, University of the West of England, UK.

INTRODUCTION

The institutionalist tradition in economics

Charles J. Whalen

Building on bedrock

The only reason to study economics is "to make this world a better place in which to live." That was the view of Wesley C. Mitchell, economics professor at Columbia University, cofounder and first research director of the National Bureau of Economic Research (NBER), and early pioneer in institutional economics.[1] It remains a bedrock principle of the institutionalist tradition, and an ardent belief of contributors to this volume.

Institutional economics is not new. It's been part of American economics for at least a century.[2] But the mounting economic challenges of our time mean that institutionalism's past must be a springboard, launching the tradition into a new era of vibrant economic analysis and problem-solving.

The need for an economics dedicated to striving for a better world might now be greater than ever. Far-reaching economic and public-health challenges created by the novel coronavirus (COVID-19) pandemic—including the need to anticipate and cope with new waves and similar outbreaks—are only part of what must be addressed. Those challenges are layered onto already serious worldwide problems such as worker insecurity, income inequality, and global warming.[3]

This book aims to point the way forward by identifying and examining some of institutionalism's most important perspectives and methods. Its authors are thoughtful scholars and distinguished contributors to institutional thought. But, of course, this volume is just a starting point; when it comes to refashioning economics with the aim of making this world a better place in which to live, there's much more to do. While each chapter makes a constructive contribution to that end, the book's ultimate goal is to provoke a dialogue and spark innovative and practical research, not to provide a cookbook.

DOI: 10.4324/9781003160434-101

This introduction sets the stage by discussing the history of institutionalism, the timing of the book as an institutionalist research project, and the contents of the chapters.

Institutionalism

Institutional economics has a long history. It began in the United States during the tumultuous decades following the Civil War. It had considerable influence in academic and policy circles between the two World Wars. And it has continued to produce valuable research since World War II.[4]

Revolutionary beginnings

The beginnings of institutionalism can be traced to the writings of Thorstein B. Veblen and John R. Commons, who began their academic careers in the 1890s.[5] The first few decades following the Civil War were a period in which the United States was characterized by rapid socioeconomic change, including industrialization, urbanization, and corporate concentration. Those decades were also a period of revolutionary change in social thought, owing to the emergence of Darwinian evolutionary thinking, cultural anthropology, and pragmatic philosophy. All these developments were reflected in the research of Veblen and Commons, resulting in overlapping and complementary conceptions of institutional economics.

Veblen initially reflected the dynamic post–Civil War era by composing a series of essays that criticized the economics of his day for not building on the period's intellectual developments, thus failing to become a "modern" science.[6] A short time later, he wrote *The Theory of the Leisure Class* and *The Theory of Business Enterprise.* At the heart of Veblen's institutionalism is a vision of socioeconomic change as a continuing, evolutionary process, driven by pragmatic adaptation to the world of "matter-of-fact" reality and slowed by cultural or "ceremonial" resistance.

Commons focused more on studies that could contribute to social and economic reform, with special attention to the condition of workers. At the heart of Commons's institutionalism is a conception of socioeconomic evolution driven by an unending process of conflict and resolution. Throughout Commons's career, he combined research structured around that image of economic life with his goal of channeling the evolutionary process away from exploitative outcomes and toward "reasonable" solutions.

Interwar heyday

In the years between the two World Wars, institutional economics was part of the mainstream of American economics; it also had considerable influence on public policy, especially in the early days of the New Deal.[7] In addition to Veblen and Commons, leading institutionalists of the interwar period included John M. Clark, Rexford C. Tugwell, Gardiner C. Means, and Mitchell, who had been a student of Veblen at the University of Chicago. Another influential proponent of institutionalism during this period was Walton H. Hamilton, who delivered a pathbreaking paper in 1918, at the annual meeting of the American Economic Association (AEA); it boldly put forth institutional economics as superior to older economic traditions from the vantage point of both science-building and real-world problem-solving (Hamilton 1919).[8]

At the end of World War I, Hamilton and others presented institutionalism as optimistic and forward-looking. According to them, institutional economics involves the following three core elements.[9]

First, institutionalism studies the social and economic *institutions* that influence human behavior, giving particular attention to the *process* of constant change that reshapes institutions in response to developments within and external to the socioeconomic system. Moreover, because institutionalists view the economy and society as deeply intertwined, they are concerned not merely with the "conventions, customs, habits of thinking, and modes of doing" that constitute "the economic order." The scope of institutionalism encompasses examination of all the institutions that together constitute "the organization of modern industrial society" (Hamilton 1919, 311).

Second, institutionalism uses advanced *scientific methods*, enabling not only high-quality research but also a better alignment with research in other disciplines than was possible with traditional economics. For example, interwar institutionalists drew upon pragmatic philosophy to argue for theories rooted in realistic assumptions and analyses that assess theories against real-world evidence, both of which they saw as missing in conventional economics. They also drew on social psychology to argue against constructing theories by treating individuals as independent, self-interested "utility maximizers" and building on other simplistic assumptions; instead, institutionalists stressed the need to understand how social conditioning, institutions, and the past all shape human behavior. Moreover, institutionalists took seriously both observation and measurement, resulting in many empirically grounded studies and vital contributions not only to national income accounting but also to the development of financial data such as the flow-of-funds accounts.

Third, institutionalism focuses on contributing to practical *problem-solving* by offering insight into public policy formation and the reshaping of institutions in the public interest. Institutional economics in the interwar era reflected a growing awareness of the seriousness of labor problems and other economic challenges, and a realization that removing restrictions on businesses is not a universal solution to such difficulties. Thus, interwar institutionalists cast aside the false notion of a laissez-faire economy in favor of finding new and effective methods of economic management. According to the institutionalists, the state *always* shapes market activity; what's left to be determined is the form and direction of such state action.

That institutionalist approach, with its dual aims of science-building and problem-solving, was not presented as a challenge to the American economics profession. It was offered simply as a way to advance the discipline. In fact, much of the above is fully in line with the Statement of Principles crafted by founders of the AEA in the late 1880s (Ely 1885, 35–36).[10]

After World War II, institutionalism's influence within economics began to decline. That fall from prominence is the result of what Malcolm Rutherford (2009, 316) describes as a "perfect storm" with many contributing causes. They include the rise of Keynesian macroeconomics and the micro–macro neoclassical synthesis provided by Paul Samuelson's *Foundations of Economic Analysis*; the emergence of theories of imperfect competition that were incorporated into the tradition of neoclassical economics; the New Deal's achievement of many major institutionalist policy goals; diminishing public support for government activism in the economy; the willingness of institutional economists to select non-institutionalists over institutionalists when filling faculty positions; growing dissatisfaction with institutionalist theory-building; the rise of professional schools that diverted applied scholarship away from economics departments; a renewed emphasis on deduction and abstract model-building in economics; and the development of econometrics, operations analysis, and game theory.

Postwar perseverance

Over the past three-quarters of a century, institutionalism has managed to survive—and, to some extent, thrive—despite its lost influence within university economics departments across the United States. There are several reasons.

Perhaps the most important reason institutionalism has continued to exist is that conventional economics retains many of the shortcomings that attracted scholars to institutionalism long ago, especially when it comes to conducting applied research and contributing to real-world problem-solving.[11] This is what causes many institutionalists to persevere—and sometimes quip that theirs is an "ever-vanishing" breed. In fact, over time a clear pattern has emerged: interest in institutionalism surges whenever it becomes especially apparent that the economic mainstream has little to say about pressing, real-world issues (as was the case, for example, during the economic instability and stagflation of the 1970s, as well as during the global financial crisis of 2007–2009); and interest in institutionalism ebbs when real-world crises recede.

Another reason is that a few prolific and high-profile institutionalist writers—especially Robert Heilbroner and John Kenneth Galbraith—succeeded in keeping the institutionalist tradition in front of students and the general public for decades.[12] In the 1950s, Heilbroner began writing magazine articles on economics while taking graduate courses at the New School for Social Research. After editors at Simon & Schuster suggested he write a book, Heilbroner composed *The Worldly Philosophers*, which for decades was a supplementary textbook in introductory economics courses everywhere. By the time of his death in 2005,

Heilbroner had written close to two dozen books (including *An Inquiry into the Human Prospect* and *The Nature and Logic of Capitalism*), garnered four Gerald Loeb awards for distinguished journalism, and received recognition as one of the top-selling authors in the field of economics (Noble 2005).

Galbraith, for whom Heilbroner worked at the Office of Price Administration during World War II, was even more prolific (four dozen books, for example) and more explicit about his ties to institutionalism. The only staunch institutionalist on the Harvard University economics faculty for much of his career, Galbraith is perhaps best known for his trilogy on the United States economy—*American Capitalism*, *The Affluent Society*, and *The New Industrial State*—and for *The Age of Uncertainty*, which appeared as a book and television series.[13] Galbraith's last book, *The Economics of Innocent Fraud*, was published just two years before he died, in 2006, at age 97 (Noble and Martin 2006).[14]

A third reason for the survival of institutionalism is that its adherents have managed to continue providing doctoral training for interested economics students. Until the mid-1980s, The University of Texas at Austin offered the main postwar graduate program for doctoral students attracted to institutional economics.[15] Clarence E. Ayres—author of *The Theory of Economic Progress* and nine other books—was at the center of institutionalism in Austin from his arrival in 1930 until his retirement in 1969.[16] Wendell Gordon, H.H. Liebhafsky, and Ray Marshall were among those maintaining the tradition into the 1980s.[17]

Since the 1980s, students seeking graduate training in institutional economics have turned to eclectic departments at universities such as the University of Nebraska, University of Tennessee, Colorado State University, the New School, and University of Utah. In addition, an important training ground for institutionalists over the past two decades has been the University of Missouri, Kansas City (UMKC). Today, institutionalist graduates of UMKC can be found on the faculty at some of the nation's top liberal-arts institutions, including Denison University, Reed College, and Willamette University.[18]

Yet another reason for the continued existence of institutionalism is the Association for Evolutionary Economics (AFEE), which, along with the related Association for Institutional Thought (AFIT), has created a community of institutional scholars, providing them regular opportunities to present and discuss their research. AFEE was established in 1965, evolving out of an informal group of institutionalists who gathered each year at the annual meeting of the AEA. In 1967, AFEE launched the *Journal of Economic Issues* (*JEI*), a quarterly publication which has built and maintains a solid reputation within the social sciences.

Today, AFEE, which has more than 250 active members, meets each year in conjunction with the AEA annual meeting; AFIT, a smaller organization established in 1979, convenes annually in conjunction with the meeting of the Western Social Science Association. The two institutionalist organizations jointly sponsor awards that enable graduate students to present their research. In addition, AFEE bestows an award each year—named for institutionalism's founders, Veblen and Commons—to recognize significant contributions to institutional economics.

Members of AFEE and AFIT are united by a broad, shared definition of economics as well as a set of common beliefs that provide the foundation for their work. The definition comes from Allan Gruchy (1987, 21): "Economics is the science of social provisioning." Thus, the scope is much wider than market transactions. Moreover, because institutional economists stress that socioeconomic life is ever evolving, Gruchy (1987, 17) also described institutionalism as a "processual" paradigm. The common beliefs of institutionalists are summarized by Dell Champlin and Janet Knoedler (2004) as follows:[19]

- How any society provides for its economic needs is culturally and historically situated;
- The working rules of economic behavior are cultural, legal, and social rather than universal laws of nature;
- Markets are legal and cultural arrangements often characterized by relationships of conflict, power, and inequality; [and]
- Government is an integral part of the economy, and appropriate economic policy is important to ensure that the economy works in the interest of all members of society.

(Champlin and Knoedler 2004, 4)[20]

Recent developments

To close this brief summary of institutionalism's history, two recent developments must be highlighted. Both contribute greatly to the vitality of contemporary institutionalism. They are: increased engagement with other traditions in economics and the related social sciences, and internationalization of the institutionalist tradition.

Over the past few decades, institutional economists have shown more and more openness toward engaging with other economists and social researchers. While some segments of the institutionalist movement have always expressed such interest, there was also resistance from some quarters in the postwar era as recently as the late 1980s (see, for example, Gruchy 1987, 159). But that resistance has given way to a distinct and accelerating trend toward greater acceptance of pluralism among institutionalists, as well as toward building bridges—and even forging syntheses—that link institutionalism to other traditions, including post-Keynesianism, feminism, Marxism, socio- and social economics, and behavioral economics.

The internationalization of institutionalism is also an accelerating trend. To be sure, institutional economics has always included an international dimension. In the wake of the rise of fascism in Europe, for example, economists including Karl Polanyi, K. William Kapp, and Adolph Lowe came to the United States and made significant contributions to institutionalism. In addition, India's Radhamakal Mukerjee, Sweden's Gunnar Myrdal, and Japan's Hatsutaro Tanahashi were part of the institutionalist tradition in the interwar years and beyond.[21] Moreover, many American-born institutionalists have devoted much of their careers to work outside the United States, especially on subjects involving agriculture and development.

But the international dimension of institutional economics has picked up considerably since the mid-1980s. An early sign of that acceleration was the formation, with some assistance from AFEE, of the European Association for Evolutionary Political Economy (EAEPE); established in 1988, the organization currently has about 500 members. There is also a Japan Association for Evolutionary Economics (JAFEE), established in 1997, with about the same number of members as EAEPE. A more recent and even more potent development is increasingly global participation in the conferences and journals of AFEE, EAEPE, and JAFEE. That participation has led to a burgeoning of international engagement among scholars; today's institutional economists are part of a global institutionalist community.

Timing

Bringing coherence to institutional economics is not easy. "Institutionalists have been notoriously quarrelsome and independent cusses," writes William Dugger. Attempting to organize them within set parameters "is a bit like herding stray cats" (Dugger 1996, 31).

But bringing coherence to institutionalism *is* possible—and often of considerable value. In fact, Dugger himself organized a group of AFEE members that produced a number of important volumes on what he called radical institutionalism.[22] Having contributed to two of those research projects, I have a firsthand understanding of how such projects can influence research trajectories, create a community of scholars, and advance a discipline.

Another institutionalist who succeeded in trying to bring coherence to institutionalism was Marc Tool. As editor of the *JEI* in the 1980s, Tool organized two collections of solicited essays. The first collection appeared originally as "Economic Policy for the Eighties and Beyond," in the March 1984 issue of the *JEI*. The second collection, "Evolutionary Economics," appeared initially as the September and December issues of the *JEI* in 1987. Both collections were subsequently released as stand-alone books, which made them available for classroom adoption (Tool 1984; 1988). The 1987 collection was even reissued by Routledge in 2019.

Tool's collections were a huge success, especially the 1987 set. It covered nearly three-dozen topics, including the philosophical basis of institutional economics, prices and pricing, macroeconomic theory and policy, environmental economics, and regulation of industry. More than three decades later, many institutionalists continue to rely on those essays.[23]

Over the past few years, the need to update Tool's collections has been mentioned on various occasions at AFEE meetings. In the wake of the vibrant sessions and discussions that occurred at the AFFE meeting in January 2020, I had the idea for this volume. While the book is not an update of either of the Tool collections, it offers the essence of what I think is necessary as a starting point for advancing institutionalism in the years ahead: a close look at some of the tradition's most significant perspectives and methods.

Shortly after this project began, infections from COVID-19 spread across the globe. That pandemic has forced people everywhere to think perhaps more than ever about what is "the economy" and its relation to society. It has also forced a rethinking of who we value, what we value, and how we value. These issues are central to institutional economics—even when they're not telegraphed as front and center, they're still a key part of institutionalism's focus on economics as a policy science and sociocultural discipline.[24] Thus, the COVID-19 pandemic only underscores the need to reexamine and reinvigorate institutionalism.

Overview

This volume is organized as follows. Part I focuses on institutionalist perspectives. Part II examines institutionalist methods.

Institutions, reasonable value, and market society

The first three chapters in Part I examine institutionalist perspectives inspired by a trio of the tradition's "giants"—Veblen, Commons, and Polanyi. William T. Waller (Chapter 1) begins that section of the book with an assessment of how Ayres and his students turned Veblen's distinction between "institutions" and "technology," often referred to as the Veblenian dichotomy, into a device for analyzing all economic activity. Waller acknowledges that the approach is useful in a variety of ways, but concludes that it results in the unfortunate treatment of "instrumental valuation" as the only legitimate form of social valuation; distracts from focusing on the evolutionary foundations of institutional analysis; and hinders a careful consideration of key concepts, including instincts and institutions. Waller's assessment offers a fresh look at the Veblenian dichotomy and the role it should play in the future of institutional economics.

Charles J. Whalen (Chapter 2) focuses on Commons's concept of reasonable value. Whalen explains that concept and how Commons constructed his institutionalism around it, and then examines its role in the work of those associated with the branch of the institutionalist tradition that Commons established at the University of Wisconsin, a tradition that helped shape the New Deal, Great Society, and more recent progressive initiatives and proposals. Whalen also considers reasonable value in relation to instrumental value (grounded in the work of Veblen), as well as the future of reasonable value.

Michele Cangiani (Chapter 3) examines Polanyi's institutional theory of market-capitalist society. Cangiani shows that market society is, according to

Polanyi, a peculiarly "economic" society: its economy appears both autonomous and dominant, constraining the structure and evolution of other social subsystems. He also demonstrates that Polanyi's theory and method allow an explanation of the institutional transformations of market society. In the face of today's great economic difficulties, social uneasiness, and ecological distress, Cangiani presents a Polanyian institutionalism that remains a rich source of insight on humanity's challenges and possibilities.

Financialization, gender, and environmental sustainability

The other chapters in Part I present perspectives that infuse institutionalist thinking with insight from newer research traditions—post-Keynesian economics, feminist theory, and environmental science. The fusion examined by Whalen (Chapter 4) is post-Keynesian institutionalism (PKI), a perspective that developed out of the work of John Kenneth Galbraith, Hyman P. Minsky, and others working at the intersection of institutionalism and post-Keynesianism. Whalen shows that PKI has evolved into a body of research that currently focuses on the emergence and consequences of financialization, with particular (but not exclusive) attention to the United States. According to Whalen, financialization is synonymous with money manager capitalism (MMC), an era that took hold around 1980 and has been accompanied by rising economic insecurity for most Americans. The COVID-19 pandemic has exposed MMC's fundamental shortcomings, but a new, post-financialization era is not yet on the horizon.

Janice Peterson (Chapter 5) builds on the shared understanding of feminist and institutionalist economists regarding the importance of culture in social provisioning. She shows that a focus on such provisioning provides a framework for conveying the significance of gender in economic life. In particular, Peterson presents a history of feminist institutionalism, an examination of its core arguments, and a discussion of contemporary applications.

Richard V. Adkisson (Chapter 6) applies institutionalist insight to explain the formidable challenge of redirecting economic activity toward environmental sustainability. He begins by presenting an institutionalist perspective (which he calls "original" institutionalism to distinguish it from the neoclassical-oriented "new" institutionalism) on the interconnectedness of humans, technology, and the natural environment.[25] Then he underscores the role of cultural values, social beliefs, and institutional adjustment in addressing environmental issues, using case studies involving the regulation of pesticides, enactment of legislation on air pollution, and the problem of climate change. Adkisson's environmental institutionalism does not lay out a roadmap for addressing global warming; instead, it highlights the obstacles ahead and shows how similar obstacles were confronted in the course of addressing other environmental problems.

Investigational methods and impact analysis

The first two chapters in Part II begin the discussion of institutionalist methods by examining a pair of research approaches grounded in Wisconsin institutionalism. Thomas Kemp (Chapter 7) develops a set of methods based on Commons's approach to the investigation and resolution of economic problems. The first half of Kemp's chapter presents the structure and process of Commons's approach. It also highlights lessons for policy development and administration. Particular attention is given to Commons's work on civil service reform and his emphasis on administrative commissions; both offer important insights into his institutionalism. The second half of Kemp's chapter discusses Commons's view of the proper role of economists and illustrates how Commons's methods can be applied today. According to Kemp, Commons starts with a broad socioeconomic and historical perspective; strives for investigational neutrality followed by widespread public dissemination of research results (with special attention to reaching those who are or could be affected by the matter under investigation); and ends with facilitation of participatory policy development, a process that makes room for all community stakeholders.

Sarah S.H. Klammer, Eric A. Scorsone, and Whalen (Chapter 8) highlight a method devised by institutionalist A. Allan Schmid to anticipate and assess the consequences of society's policy choices. Schmid, who studied at the University of Wisconsin, called that approach the situation, structure, and performance (SSP) framework of institutional impact analysis, and argued its usefulness lies in drawing attention to how institutional choices (which are often public policy choices) affect "who gets what." Klammer, Scorsone, and Whalen explain the origin, development, and key elements of the SSP framework; demonstrate how it has been used to address real-world issues (such as regulating airspace and protecting drinking water); and discuss ongoing attempts to bolster and extend Schmid's research approach.

Myth busting, storytelling, and system dynamics

The final three chapters of Part II consider institutionalist methods through a broader examination of modes of analysis. Mary V. Wrenn (Chapter 9) focuses on institutionalists as myth busters. Wrenn demonstrates that the tools and methods of institutionalism have long included studies of economic myths and myth-making, with particular attention paid to the function and form of "enabling myths." She places special emphasis on explaining how the core tenets of neoliberalism are of a mythical character. She also stresses that the work of revealing and explaining social myths is a vital aspect of institutionalism. As Galbraith (1973, 215) observed, "The emancipation of belief is the most formidable of the tasks of reform, the one on which all else depends."

Whalen (Chapter 10) then examines economic "storytelling," including the related subject of "narrative economics," against the backdrop of a surge of attention to stories and narratives in academic and policy circles. He explores the nature and role of storytelling in institutional economics, including attention given to storytelling in work on economic methodology by Charles Wilber and Robert Harrison, economic theory by John Watkins, and real-world case studies by Deborah Figart. Whalen also offers a wider exploration of the power and pitfalls of economic narratives, and concludes by considering strategies for improving storytelling robustness.

Michael J. Radzicki (Chapter 11) completes the discussion of methods, thereby bringing the volume to a close, by surveying the role that system dynamics can and does play in institutional economics. Radzicki provides an overview of system dynamics modeling, which is described as a form of the pattern modeling approach frequently used by institutionalists. He also identifies techniques to enhance the insight generated by system dynamics model-building and use; compares system dynamics and econometric modeling; highlights the complementary usefulness of data science; and provides a balanced examination of the shortcomings of system dynamics. His chapter closes by discussing various ways that institutionalists can introduce system dynamics into their work.[26]

A better world

A common feature of this volume's chapters is insistence on the need to recognize that economic systems do not stand alone. That insistence takes many forms, including a focus on culture, concern over sustainable development, attention to the consequences of widely held social myths, and efforts to use simulation and data science to understand and control complex systems. The forms may vary, but an emphasis on socioeconomic interrelatedness, and/or the interconnectedness of humanity and the natural world, appears in every chapter.

That commonality is fitting. Gruchy recognized an emphasis on interrelatedness as an essential feature of institutional economics in 1947; it led him to brand institutionalism as "holistic economics" (Gruchy 1947, 23–28). Moreover, an appreciation of this real-world interrelatedness is what led Myrdal (1969, 10) to think of himself as an institutionalist. In the course of studying practical problems, Myrdal (1973, 141–142) concluded, "The isolation of one part of social reality by demarcating it as 'economic' is not logically feasible. In reality, there are no 'economic,' 'sociological,' or 'psychological' problems, but just problems, and they are all complex."

The complexity of the real world and its problems may be daunting, but ignoring that complexity does not make it vanish. There's also a solid reason for hope: to a very great extent, the future is ours to make. That's because socioeconomic systems are products of human action, which means they can be reshaped and reorganized. By shedding light on the world as it really is, the holistic economics at the heart of the institutionalist tradition has a key role to play in helping us move toward a better world.

Acknowledgments

The author thanks Jim Peach and Linda Whalen for comments and suggestions on an early draft of this introduction, and Deb Figart for feedback on the volume's overall structure. He also thanks the book's contributors and the editorial staff at Routledge for their collaborative spirit and high-quality work.

Notes

1 Mitchell's statement on the purpose of economics was reported by his student, Charles Gulick; see Ramstad (1989, 762).
2 According to Malcolm Rutherford (2001, 173), "The term 'institutional economics' was first brought to the general attention of the economics profession by Walton H. Hamilton" in a conference paper delivered in late 1918 and published the following year in the *American Economic Review*. But the tradition's roots go deeper, as will soon be discussed.
3 For more on such preexisting challenges, see International Labour Organization (2020); Alvaredo et al. (2018); and United Nations (2018).
4 The institutional economics described in this chapter and volume is sometimes called "original" institutional economics. In contrast, a tradition known widely as "new" institutional economics emerged in the 1970s. At first, the latter centered mainly on the work of Oliver Williamson and Douglass North, but has expanded to encompass the research of many other scholars, including Elinor Ostrom, Masahiko Aoki, and Daron Acemoglu. Unlike original institutionalism, much of the new institutionalism focuses on economic efficiency and market equilibration, and is "yoked to the model of rational [maximizing] behavior and the assumption of given individual preference functions" (Rutherford 2001, 198). For more on new institutionalism in relation to original institutionalism, see Luz and Fernandez (2018) and Spithoven (2019). Also, for an expansive look at institutional economics, which includes the original, the new, and other traditions, see Chavance (2009).
5 This discussion of institutionalism's beginnings relies heavily on Mayhew (1987).
6 Those and other related essays are collected in Veblen (1919). Some of the main points of Veblen's criticism of the economics of his day, which remain at the heart of institutionalist critiques of today's conventional economics, are as follows: economics is insufficiently grounded in institutional and historical reality; its conception of individuals (as atomistic, utility maximizers) fails to appreciate the inescapable influence of culture on human behavior; it focuses too narrowly on market mechanisms; and it rests on the unwarranted assumption that the price system is self-regulating.
7 According to Malcolm Rutherford (2011, 7), institutionalists in the interwar years "published regularly in the leading journals of economics, held positions in major research universities (dominating the economics faculty at two of the top four PhD-granting universities in the country), were highly active in the creation of institutions for research and education in the social sciences [including the NBER and the Brookings Institution], had excellent links to funding agencies, were deeply involved in economic policymaking, and became presidents of the American Economic Association and American Statistical Association." (The two economics departments referred to by Rutherford were at Columbia University, academic home of Mitchell; and University of Wisconsin, academic home of Commons.)

8 For an examination of institutionalism during the interwar period, see Rutherford (2011). See also Gruchy (1947), which examines the contributions of Veblen, Commons, Mitchell, Clark, Tugwell, and Means.

9 For more on the essential elements of interwar institutionalism, see, for example, Rutherford (2010) and Hamilton (1919).

10 Richard T. Ely (1932, 114) certainly believed that the interwar conception of institutional economics was in line with the AEA's Statement of Principles, and he was its primary author.

11 For a similar view, see Rutherford (2011, 354).

12 Robert Lekachman was another highly successful postwar economist and writer associated with the institutionalist tradition.

13 For an examination of Galbraith and his institutionalism, see Gruchy (1972, 133–176) and Stanfield and Stanfield (2011).

14 Today, James Kenneth Galbraith, a University of Texas economist, carries on in the tradition of his father. In fact, *The Predator State* (Galbraith 2008) was written at the suggestion of John Kenneth.

15 To be sure, the University of Texas was not alone. For example, the University of Oklahoma, University of Denver, and University of New Mexico (all of which had faculty members who studied in Austin) also attracted institutionalists. Among the institutionalist professors in New Mexico was David Hamilton, author of a book on institutional economics, in print since 1953, which many credit with helping to keep the institutionalist tradition alive after World War II (Hamilton 1953; Miller 2003, 53).

16 For more on Ayres and his contributions to institutionalism, see Gruchy (1972, 89–132) and Gordon (1970); see also Chapter 1 in this volume.

17 Marshall also serves to illustrate institutionalists' postwar ties to government and policy research: he served as US Secretary of Labor for President Jimmy Carter, and later cofounded the Economic Policy Institute, a nonpartisan think tank focusing on the needs of low- and middle-income workers and their families.

18 Institutional economics is also taught to graduate students in applied fields, such as agricultural economics, labor and employment relations, and public policy. At Michigan State University, for example, institutionalism remains integral to the graduate curriculum in agricultural, food, and resource economics.

19 My own early effort to outline core elements of institutionalism arrives at a similar conclusion to that of Champlin and Knoedler; see Whalen (1992). What unites institutionalists is not a set of theories or policy views; rather, they are united by a shared pre-analytic vision (the term comes from Schumpeter). For more details on the essentials of institutionalism, see Hodgson (2000).

20 For a longer statement of the tenets of institutionalism, see Association for Institutional Thought (n.d.).

21 Mukerjee (1941) was one of the first economists to write a book on institutionalism; see Gruchy (1943). For a discussion of Myrdal's contribution to institutionalism, see Gruchy (1972, 177–236); and for a brief discussion of Tanahashi, see Uni (2017, vi–viii).

22 For example, see Dugger (1989).

23 In 2018, a subset of the essays in Tool's 1987 collection were updated in the *JEI*; see, for example, Almeida (2018); Baranes and Hake (2018); and Hopkins (2018).

24 In fact, Gruchy (1947, 21) differentiates institutionalism from standard economics by describing the former as "cultural" economics and the latter as "formal" economics.

25 The theme of such interconnectedness highlights the contribution of European institutionalists such as Myrdal and Kapp, who stressed that the natural and social spheres

are all part of an interrelated "open system." Moreover, Kapp used that viewpoint as the foundation for pioneering work on environmental economics (see, for example, Kapp 1977).

26 Radzicki also discusses the "social fabric matrix," developed by institutionalists as a tool for analyzing complex systems. The matrix's framework underlies Adkisson's contribution to this volume (Chapter 6). For more on the social fabric matrix and its use, see Natarajan, Elsner, and Fullwiler (2009).

References

Almeida, Felipe. 2018. "Revisiting 'Institutions:' A Study of the Evolution of Institutional Analysis." *Journal of Economic Issues* 52 (2): 336–348. https://doi.org/10.1080/00213624.2018.1469861

Alvaredo, Facundo, Lucas Chancel, Thomas Piketty, Emanuel Saez, and Gabriel Zucman. 2018. *World Inequality Report 2018*. Paris: World Inequality Lab.

Association for Institutional Thought. n.d. "Tenets of Institutionalism." https://tinyurl.com/y54253bq. Accessed November 20, 2020.

Baranes, Avraham I. and Eric R. Hake. 2018. "The Institutionalist Theory of Capital in the Modern Business Enterprise." *Journal of Economic Issues* 52 (2): 430–437. https://doi.org/10.1080/00213624.2018.1469895

Champlin, Dell P. and Janet T. Knoedler. 2004. "Introduction." In *The Institutionalist Tradition in Labor Economics*, edited by Dell P. Champlin and Janet T. Knoedler, 3–9. Armonk, NY: M.E. Sharpe. https://doi.org/10.4324/9781315699578

Chavance, Bernard. 2009. *Institutional Economics*. New York: Routledge. https://doi.org/10.4324/9780203888582

Dugger, William M., ed. 1989. *Radical Institutionalism*. New York: Greenwood Press.

_____. 1996. "Redefining Economics: From Market Allocation to Social Provisioning." In *Political Economy for the 21st Century*, edited by Charles Whalen, 31–44. Armonk, NY: M.E. Sharpe. https://doi.org/10.4324/9781315701707-12

Ely, Richard T. 1885. "Constitution By-Laws and Resolutions of the American Economic Association." *Publications of the American Economic Association* 1 (1): 35–46.

_____. 1932. "Institutional Economics." *American Economic Review* 22 (3):105–116.

Galbraith, John K. 1973. *Economics and the Public Purpose*. Boston: Houghton Mifflin.

Galbraith, James K. 2008. *The Predator State*. New York: Free Press.

Gordon, Wendell C. 1970. "Clarence Ayres: Institutional Economist." *Journal of Thought* 5 (3): 168–176.

Gruchy, Allan G. 1943. "Review of *The Institutional Theory of Economics*, by Radhakamal Mukerjee." *Journal of Political Economy* 51 (1): 84–85. https://doi.org/10.1086/255999

_____. 1947. *Modern Economic Thought*. New York: Prentice-Hall.

_____. 1972. *Contemporary Economic Thought*. Clifton, NJ: Augustus M. Kelley.

_____. 1987. *The Reconstruction of Economics*. New York: Greenwood Press.

Hamilton, David. 1953. *Newtonian Classicism and Darwinian Institutionalism*. Albuquerque: University of New Mexico Press. In 1970, the title was changed to *Evolutionary Economics*. https://doi.org/10.4324/9780203792674

Hamilton, Walton H. 1919. "The Institutional Approach to Economic Theory." *American Economic Review* 9 (1): 309–318.

Hodgson, Geoffrey M. 2000. "What Is the Essence of Institutional Economics?" *Journal of Economic Issues* 34 (2): 317–329. https://doi.org/10.1080/00213624.2000.11506269

Hopkins, Barbara E. 2018. "Reasserting Institutionalist Insights on the Good Society: 30 Years after Petr's Call for a Mixed Economy." *Journal of Economic Issues* 52 (3): 860–868. https://doi.org/10.1080/00213624.2018.1489525

International Labour Organization. 2020. *World Employment and Social Outlook: Trends 2020*. Geneva: International Labour Office.

Kapp, K. William. 1977. "Environment and Technology: New Frontiers for the Social and Natural Sciences." *Journal of Economic Issues* 11 (3): 527–540. https://doi.org/10.1080/00213624.1977.11503460

Luz, Manuel Ramon Souza and Ramon Garcia Fernandez. 2018. "Are We Forgetting Something? Remarks on the Connection between Douglass North's Contributions and Original Institutional Economics." *Journal of Economic Issues* 52 (2): 589–599. https://doi.org/10.1080/00213624.2018.1469939

Mayhew, Anne. 1987. "The Beginnings of Institutionalism." *Journal of Economic Issues* 21 (3): 971–998. https://doi.org/10.1080/00213624.1987.11504694

Miller, Edythe S. 2003. "Evolution and Stasis: The Institutional Economics of David Hamilton." *Journal of Economic Issues* 37 (1): 51–63. https://doi.org/10.1080/00213624.2003.11506554

Mukerjee, Radhakamal. 1941. *The Institutional Theory of Economics*. London: Macmillan.

Myrdal, Gunnar. 1969. *Objectivity in Social Research*. Middletown, CT: Wesleyan University Press.

_____. 1973. *Against the Stream: Critical Essays on Economics*. New York: Pantheon.

Natarajan, Tara, Wolfram Elsner, and Scott Fullwiler, eds. 2009. *Institutional Analysis and Praxis: The Social Fabric Matrix Approach*. New York: Springer. https://doi.org/10.1007/978-0-387-88741-8

Noble, Holcomb B. 2005. "Robert Heilbroner, Writer and Economist, Dies at 85." *The New York Times* January 12.

Noble, Holcomb B. and D. Martin. 2006. "John Kenneth Galbraith, Iconoclastic Economist and Diplomat, Dies at 97." *The New York Times* May 1.

Ramstad, Yngve. 1989. "'Reasonable Value' versus 'Instrumental Value:' Competing Paradigms in Institutional Economics." *Journal of Economic Issues* 23 (3): 761–777. https://doi.org/10.1080/00213624.1989.11504937

Rutherford, Malcolm. 2001. "Institutional Economics: Then and Now." *Journal of Economic Perspectives* 15 (3): 173–194.

_____. 2009. "Towards a History of American Institutional Economics." *Journal of Economic Issues* 43 (2): 308–318. https://doi.org/10.2753/JEI0021-3624430203

_____. 2010. "Science and Social Control: The Institutionalist Movement in American Economics, 1918–1947." *Erasmus Journal for Philosophy and Economics* 3 (2): 47–71. https://doi.org/10.23941/ejpe.v3i2.55

_____. 2011. *The Institutionalist Movement in American Economics, 1918–1947*. Cambridge, UK: Cambridge University Press. https://doi.org/10.1017/CBO9780511977046

Spithoven, Antoon. 2019. "Similarities and Dissimilarities between Original Institutional Economics and New Institutional Economics." *Journal of Economic Issues* 53 (3): 440–447. https://doi.org/10.1080/00213624.2019.1594532

Stanfield, James R. and Jacqueline B. Stanfield. 2011. *John Kenneth Galbraith*. Basingstoke, UK: Palgrave Macmillan. https://doi.org/10.1057/9780230302440

Tool, Marc R., ed. 1984. *An Institutionalist Guide to Economics and Public Policy*. Armonk, NY: M.E. Sharpe. https://doi.org/10.4324/9781315495453

_____, ed. 1988. *Evolutionary Economics, Volumes I and II*. Armonk, NY: M.E. Sharpe. https://doi.org/10.4324/9781315493053

Uni, Hiroyuki, ed. 2017. *Contemporary Meanings of John R. Commons's Institutional Economics*. Singapore: Springer. https://doi.org/10.1007/978-981-10-3202-8

United Nations. 2018. *Global Warming of 1.5o C: Summary for Policymakers*. Geneva: Intergovernmental Panel on Climate Change.

Veblen, Thorstein. 1919. *The Place of Science in Modern Civilisation and Other Essays*. New York: B.W. Huebsch.

Whalen, Charles. 1992. "Schools of Thought and Theories of the State." In *The Stratified State*, edited by William M. Dugger and William T. Waller, 55–86. Armonk, NY: M.E. Sharpe. https://doi.org/10.4324/9781315487090-4

PART I

Perspectives

1

INSTITUTIONS, TECHNOLOGY, AND INSTRUMENTAL VALUE

A reassessment of the Veblenian dichotomy

William T. Waller

Introduction

The distinction drawn between "institutions" and "technology," inspired by the work of Thorstein B. Veblen, and the tradition constructed upon it by institutional economists, especially Clarence E. Ayres and his students, requires reassessment in light of the body of scholarly work addressing and employing it. This chapter provides such a reassessment, including a discussion of that distinction's future in institutionalism.

The Ayresian interlude in institutional economics is winding down. Through his teaching and writing, Ayres had a dramatic impact on institutional economics after World War II. In *The Theory of Economic Progress*, his central thesis was that economic development is a function of the increased influence of improved technology, expanding the scope of technological (instrumental) behavior and overcoming the conservative resistance created by a ceremonial cultural legacy (the norms, myths, and legends of the past) that resists change, but also structures behavior. This thesis was quite controversial among Ayres's contemporaries (Rutherford 2011, 335–338; Almeida and Goulart 2020). But it had a major influence on Ayres's students (and their students). Many in the so-called Veblen–Ayres tradition viewed this construction—which they called the "Veblenian dichotomy" between technology and ceremonial behavior or institutions—as a *methodological approach* to analysis, an interpretation encouraged by Ayres (Ayres 1935, 36–37). This chapter will discuss that development.

Ayres's attempt to address criticism that institutionalism was purely descriptive and non-theoretical seemed to take him back to Veblen (Rutherford 2011, 335). But the elements of Veblen's theorizing incorporated by Ayres were extremely selective. Ayres rejected Veblen's use of instinct psychology, upon which Veblen built his concept and theory of institutions. Ayres reconfigured

DOI: 10.4324/9781003160434-1

the definition of "institutions" and then contrasted it with technology in ways that cannot be attributed to Veblen (Hodgson 2004, 202; and especially Ayres 1935, 33).

So what did Veblen contribute? Veblen often characterized behavior in terms of two categories. But the crux of the matter is, while Veblen frequently used dichotomous categorization schemes in his theorizing and analysis, this was an *analytic* rather than a *methodological* technique.[1] Veblen neither consistently avoided dualistic constructions (in the Cartesian sense) nor developed a consistent set of dichotomies that could be coherently mapped upon one another.

The chapter focuses on reassessing Ayres's methodological turn. The reassessment will explore reservations that developed and were articulated about the provenance, internal consistency, and practical usefulness of that turn—and will explore the turn's impact, both positive and negative, on the development of institutional analysis.

Ayres's thesis (described above) was one of many theories about how Western economies developed; it also became an approach to economic analysis. The 1950s accelerated the exclusion of institutional economics from economics curricula and professional publications that began before World War II, leading to an increasing isolation of institutionalists. One response, especially by Ayresians, was the tendency to present their ideas as an oral tradition. To be sure, this characterization is an oversimplification, since many institutionalists continued to publish in journals and produce books; but with regard to many in the so-called Veblen–Ayres tradition, it is accurate enough. Ayres, his students—especially J. Fagg Foster and his students, particularly Marc R. Tool, Paul Dale Bush, and Louis Junker—and others used and constructed a historical narrative of the Veblenian dichotomy as a methodological approach.

The focus on this Veblen–Ayres approach to institutional analysis had numerous consequences that included creating community solidarity. But strangely, the Veblenian dichotomy, beyond its "methodological" elaboration, did not result in a great deal of application by its proponents—and had even less impact on institutionalism beyond this sub-community of institutionalists. In fact, it was largely ignored by institutionalists in the traditions of Walton Hamilton, John R. Commons, Wesley Clair Mitchell, Karl Polanyi, K. William Kapp, and Gunner Myrdal; by prominent post-WWII institutionalist labor economists; and, notably, by John Kenneth Galbraith. And yet, quality institutionalist research in those traditions continued.

The chapter also gives attention to the negative impacts of the Veblen–Ayres tradition. The focus on the Veblenian dichotomy resulted mainly in attention being directed to the elaboration of variations of Ayres's theory of economic change. This actually distracted institutionalists from considering other ideas on the character of evolutionary change in social institutions. Paradoxically, Ayres's approach inhibited careful consideration and scholarship on Veblen's approach, which was actually based on the role of instincts in the creation of habits leading to the formation of institutions.

The chapter also covers other ground. It demonstrates that Ayres's views challenged the very meaning of the term "institution." It also shows that a focus on "instrumental valuation" as the only legitimate form of social valuation, and the later implication that its adoption was inevitable, was dismissive of even the possibility of multiple and alternative processes of social valuation. Finally, the chapter discusses what role, if any, the Veblenian dichotomy should play in the further development of institutional economics.

Veblen gets a pass

Veblen's concept of institutions is the starting point for understanding the early formulations in which he contrasts institutions with technology. What will become clear is that scholarship since the mid-1980s shows Veblen's role was one of inspiration for the creation of categories later employed in the development of what eventually came to be called the Veblenian dichotomy.

Institutions

Veblen offers various definitions of institutions. For example:

> The institutions are, in substance, prevalent habits of thought with respect to particular relations and particular functions of the individual and of the community; and the scheme of life, which is made up of the aggregate of institutions in force at a given time or at a given point in the development of any society, may, on the psychological side, be broadly characterized as a prevalent spiritual attitude or a prevalent theory of life.
>
> *(Veblen [1899] 1934, 190)*

In another article, Veblen articulates an often-used definition, which is controversial:

> As a matter of course, men order their lives by these principles and, practically, entertain no question of their stability and finality. That is what is meant by calling them institutions; they are settled habits of thought common to the generality of men.
>
> *(Veblen [1909] 1919, 239)*[2]

Elsewhere, he writes that institutions are "of the nature of a usage which has become axiomatic and indispensable by habituation and general acceptance" (Veblen [1923] 1964, 101).

Instances in which Veblen describes the evolution of institutions include the following:

> The evolution of social structure has been a process of natural selection of institutions. The progress which has been and is being made in human

> institutions and in human character may be set down, broadly, to a natural selection of the fittest habits of thought and to a process of enforced adaptation of individuals to an environment which has progressively changed with the growth of the community and with the changing institutions under which men have lived.
>
> *(Veblen [1899] 1934, 188)*[3]

> Institutions must change with changing circumstances, since they are the nature of a habitual method of responding to the stimuli which these changing circumstances afford. The development of these institutions is the development of society.
>
> *(Veblen [1899] 1934, 190)*

> The institutions—that is to say the habits of thought—under guidance of which men live are in this way received from an earlier time; more or less remotely earlier, but in any event they have been elaborated in and received from the past. Institutions are products of the past process, are adapted to past circumstances, and are therefore never in full accord with the requirements of the present.
>
> *(Veblen [1899] 1934, 191)*

> Like all human culture this material civilization is a scheme of institutions—institutional fabric and institutional growth. But institutions are an outgrowth of habit. The growth of culture is a cumulative sequence of habituation, and the ways and means of it are the habitual response of human nature to the exigencies that vary incontinently, cumulatively, but with something of a consistent sequence in the cumulative variation that so go forward—incontinently, because each new move creates a new situation which induces a further new variation in the habitual manner of response; cumulatively, because each new situation is a variation of what has gone before it and embodies as causal factors all that has been effected by what went before; consistently, because the underlying traits of human nature (propensities, aptitudes, and what not) by force of which the response takes place, and on the ground of which the habituation takes effect, remain substantially unchanged.
>
> *(Veblen [1909] 1919, 241–242)*

Institutions play an important theoretical role in Veblen's evolutionary economics. The theoretical context for his use of the term (institutions) is as follows. For Veblen, instincts, triggered by environmental circumstances, motivate behavior for addressing problematic circumstances. Successful problem-solving leads to repeated triggering of the behavior when the same or similar circumstances arise activating the instinct again, eventually becoming habits of thought and action. These habitual behaviors are shared with other members of the social group by emulation, education, and diffusion, thus becoming community habits of thought, namely *institutions* in Veblen's terminology (see Hodgson 2006, 6–8; Waller 1982; Waller 2016; and Waller 2017b).

Dichotomous categories

Returning to the dichotomy, Veblen certainly had a tendency to distinguish between everyday employments directed at social provisioning in contrast with processes of exploit (Veblen [1899] 1934, 8); pecuniary motivated behavior was contrasted with productive provisioning behavior, thereby highlighting wasteful behavior from behavior directed at provisioning (Veblen [1899] 1934, 208). And in *The Theory of Business Enterprise*, Veblen ([1904] 1932, 20 ff) famously distinguished between making money (business) and making serviceable goods (industry). However, the characterization of this as a methodology is a much later construction.

In defense of that later construction, Tool constructs an impressive list of such distinctions in Veblen's work. The following are from Tool (2000, 70–71):

- Institutions of acquisition—institutions of production (Veblen [1899] 1934, 208);
- Pecuniary institutions—industrial institutions (Veblen [1899] 1934, 208); and
- Institutions serving invidious economic interests—institutions serving non-invidious economic interests (Veblen [1899] 193, 208).

Even more distinctions are presented by Tool (1953; 1986) and Junker (1962, 14–15):[4]

- Salesmanship—workmanship (Veblen [1914] 1946, 216ff; [1921] 1965, 105ff; [1923] 1964, 286 ff and 392 ff);
- Vested interests—common man (Veblen [1919b] 1946, 85 ff, 159ff);
- Business—industry (Veblen [1904] 1932, 20 ff; [1923] 1964, 82 ff and 320 ff);
- Ceremonial—technological (Veblen [1915] 1964, 26 ff);
- Ownership—production (Veblen [1923] 1964, 65ff);
- Free income—tangible performance (Veblen [1919b] 1946, 63ff);
- Sabotage—community serviceability (Veblen [1917] 1964, 167 ff; [1921] 1965,13 ff);
- Pecuniary employment—industrial employment (Veblen [1904] 1932, 315 ff; [1914] 1946, 221 ff; [1934] 1964, 27 ff and 280 ff);
- Invidious emulation—technological efficiency (Veblen [1899] 1934, chap XI–XIII; [1914] 1946, 217 ff);
- Competitive advertising—valuable information (Veblen [1904] 1932, 57 ff); and
- Business prosperity—industrial efficiency (Veblen [1904] 1932, 178 ff).

In "Industrial and Pecuniary Employments," Veblen ([1919a] 1961) criticizes the "classical" mainstream for using natural law in its theorizing, which allows it to treat everything that is not consumption as production. As a result, the mainstream fails to distinguish behavior that promotes only pecuniary interests from behavior that promotes the life process of the community, meaning "a process for the provision of the aggregate material means of life" (Veblen [1919a] 1961, 285). Veblen's critique is of "classical" mainstream economic methodology, which blinds such economists to a distinction that is an empirical reality. What's also important to note is that the "Industrial and Pecuniary Employments" article does not add to Veblen's earlier *methodological* arguments concerning evolutionary theorizing, cumulative causation, or cultural analysis, nor does it make any general methodological claims for this particular categorization of cultural processes.

To be sure, Veblen ([1904] 1932) employed the industrial and pecuniary categories in *The Theory of Business Enterprise*. That book is the result of Veblen's cultural analysis of business enterprise in the United States at the dawn of the twentieth century, and, in many ways, it illustrates what C. Wright Mills called "abstract empiricism"—analysis falling "between grand theory and mindless empiricism."[5] But Veblen's use of those categories in *The Theory of Business Enterprise* only underscores that while his analytic distinction between industrial and pecuniary employments appears reasonably consistent with—and may have been important in inspiring later constructions of—the Veblenian dichotomy, Veblen does *not* make any explicit argument proposing reliance on such categories as part of a methodological approach.

Other scholars have noted Veblen's theories and analyses do not support an interpretation of his categorization of social phenomenon as methodological; the categorization is, instead, an artifact of his particular theorizing.[6] For example, Geoffrey Hodgson (1998, 56–65) correctly locates the origin of the "Veblenian" dichotomy in Ayres work and demonstrates that the alleged Veblenian origins of the dichotomy are not supported by Veblen's work.[7] Oddly, Ayres himself supports Hodgson's conclusion. In a book chapter entitled "The Gospel of Technology," Ayres writes:

> Throughout the foregoing discussion I have treated the work of [John] Dewey and Veblen, the philosophy known as "instrumentalism" and the economics known as "institutionalism," as a single body of thought. I have even gone so far as to represent this body of thought as the working out in various directions of the implications of a single idea or intellectual principle: the distinction of the technological from the institutional aspects of human behavior and culture. In doing so I have of course no warrant but my own. Neither Dewey nor Veblen ever announced himself as the promulgator of any such "system" or even indicated my dichotomy as the ruling principle in his own mind, and certainly no consensus of opinion to this effect has yet developed among their avowed "followers."
>
> *(Ayres 1935, 36–37)*

In short, contemporary scholarship supports the proposition that Veblen's role in the Veblenian dichotomy was inspirational and his examples provided some of the terminology. So, we should take Ayres at his word and turn our attention to his role in its development.

Ayres's reading of Veblen

Ayres's theorizing was both inspired by *and* represents a significant break with Veblen. The two most significant breaks involved Ayres's rejection of instincts motivating behavior (which was common among institutionalists in the interwar period) and his adoption of a restrictive construction of the concept of an institution.

Rejection of instinct psychology

Ayres's rejection of instinct psychology is indisputable given his writings on the subject (Ayres 1921a; 1921b; 1958). The interwar institutionalists including Ayres adopted a vague form of behaviorism. He writes:

> I use the word "behaviorism" with quotation marks because it has been claimed as the trade name of a certain firm of psychologists. In the wider sense, however, behaviorism represents the whole trend of modern psychology, which has been without any important exception toward the correlation of behavior mechanisms with the organic structures on one side and the culture traits of civilization on the other. This synthesis is the core of the whole intellectual position which I am calling (after Dewey) instrumentalism and of the institutionalist economics. Economists trained in an older tradition have sometimes been genuinely bewildered by the insistence of some "institutionalists" that sound economics must begin with "behaviorist" psychology and of others that sound economics must begin with anthropology.
>
> *(Ayres 1935, 33–34)*

No doubt the appeal of behaviorism to Ayres and his institutionalist contemporaries was that it is empirical, whereas instinct psychology could not be explored or explained empirically at that time (see Rutherford 2011 on Samuelson, 313, 316).[8] John B. Watson, founder of behaviorism, described it like this:

> Psychology as the behaviorist views it is a purely objective experimental branch of natural science. Its theoretical goal is the prediction and control of behavior. Introspection forms no essential part of its methods, nor is the scientific value of its data dependent upon the readiness with which they lend themselves to interpretation in terms of consciousness.
>
> *(Watson 1913, 158)*

The rejection of instincts was an error created by the same desire to be considered scientific by institutionalists that pushed mainstream economics to mathematize. The consequences for both were to deprive themselves of a sensible way to understand human motivation. In the institutionalist case, it has removed the instinct-habit explanation for the motivation of behavior and creation of institutions (Waller 2016; 2017b; Hodgson and Knudsen 2010, 79, 134–135, 183–188, 227). Fortunately, this has been reversed. As one prominent example, Hodgson and Thorbjørn Knudsen (2010) have reconstructed the notion of institutions and employed it to reconstruct a Darwinian understanding of the evolution of institutions.[9]

For our purposes, however, Ayres's rejection of a clear theory of the creation of institutions allowed him to construct an alternative concept of institutions conflicting with that of his institutionalist contemporaries.[10] For Ayres, institutions became unambiguously past bound, sustained by myth and legend, and stable to the point of inhibiting any change. Thus, he saw institutions as barriers to change, which meant they could not be considered useful in overcoming social problems (Ayres 1935, 36–37). In contrast, Ayres's contemporaries, such as Hamilton (1919, 311, 313), stressed that institutions "comprise the organization of modern industrial society," and that they can change and that orchestrating such change is the key to addressing socioeconomic problems (see also Hamilton 1932; Waller 2006).

Theory of economic progress

Ayres ([1944] 1978) used his Veblenian dichotomy as the core intellectual principle of *The Theory of Economic Progress*. A central aim of that book was addressing the critiques of institutional economics as descriptive and lacking theory (Rutherford 2011, 335; Ayres [1944] 1978, 11–12). Thus, after critiquing mainstream economics, Ayres responds with a theory. According to Ayres's theory, economic development is a function of the increased influence of improved technology, which expands the scope of technological (instrumental) behavior and overcomes the ceremonial cultural legacy (the norms, myths, and legends) that also structures behavior. From Ayres's theoretical perspective, physical and cultural continuity combine to form both an empirical reality and a central analytical principle.[11]

Ayres argues the appropriate level of generalization for analysis is the cultural level. He defends his theory by establishing a cultural argument for technology and institutions. The behavior he refers to as "instrumental" is derived from behavior associated with the development of science and technology, and is said to be universal in character. The behavior he calls "ceremonial" is culturally specific behavior that he associates with the obstructionist elements of institutions.

Drawing on Veblen, Ayres emphasizes that myths, legends, and magical thinking provide the warrant for ceremonial behavior. The legends and myths *mimic* matter-of-fact causal explanations, but the underlying motive of ceremonial behavior is cultural, he argues, not instrumental.[12] Ayres writes: "Cultural phenomena (including the economic) derive exclusively from other cultural phenomena and can be explained only in terms of other cultural phenomena" (Ayres [1944] 1978, 96: see also Waller 2003).

Here Ayres's Veblenian dichotomy enters the picture. Elements of that dichotomy are considered the categories of human behavior. Ayres ([1944] 1978, 101–102) maintains that the distinction between these categories represents a dichotomy rather than a dualism, and the categories are an analytical distinction rather than "separate realms of being." He argues:

> The business of "getting a living" includes both these functions. That is, it includes activities of a technological character, and it also includes activities of a ceremonial character; and these two sets of activities not only coexist but condition each other at every point and between them define and constitute *the total activity* of "getting a living." It is the problem of economic analysis to distinguish and understand these factors, and their mutual relations, and configurations of economic activity for which they are responsible.
>
> *(Ayres [1944] 1978, 99, italics added)*

In short, Ayres has abandoned behaviorism, or any psychological explanation for human behavior, as irrelevant because social analysis should focus exclusively on cultural analysis. Additionally, his two "activities" taken together characterize all cultural processes. For Ayres this is a *methodology*; the "two sets of activities" are separate elements of reality for Ayres, not merely analytic categories.

Ayres then argues that since provisioning is the goal of the study of economics and instrumental behavior increases a culture's ability to do so, then increasing the role of instrumental behavior and minimizing ceremonial behaviors will promote economic progress. He also argues that recognizing these two sets of activities allows us to at least distinguish between better and worse policy options (given the level of knowledge and technology at a point in time). And with that, Ayres transforms his analytic categories into a process of social valuation. Thus, the "instrumental theory of value" is put forth as a universal value principle (in addition to Ayres [1944] 1978, see Ayres 1961).[13]

The instrumental theory of value is Ayres's refinement of Dewey's theory of value.[14] Recall the term "instrumental" is derived from behaviors associated with the development of the scientific process and the development of technology, and is universal in character in Ayres's system. As Anne Mayhew writes:

> Quite unabashedly, Ayres argues that the same commingling of technology and explanation (where technologically verifiable explanation is identified as science, and the commingling of tool use and explanatory reasoning is called the instrumental or technological process) represents a universally superior and progressive way of dealing with human existence.
>
> *(Mayhew 2010, 220)*

Ayres's instrumental process is considered continuous, a process whereby the evolution of knowledge, as a result of self-correction by a vigorous scientific community (via discovering new tool combinations or borrowing from other communities), improves our ability to better apply warranted knowledge to social problems. This continuous and ongoing process allows us to make judgments of better or worse changes to our practices when solving social problems, given the current state of the community's knowledge and technology. In this sense, it is a processual theory of value.[15]

In the end, Ayres accomplished much in *The Theory of Economic Progress*. He critiqued mainstream economics, showing the underlying theory of behavior was incoherent, the concept of capital was not meaningful (therefore unable to explain progress), and the mainstream value theory was tautological (and thus incapable of explaining value)—much of this originating in Veblen's critique. Ayres also constructed a general theory of progress, introduced a methodology focused on cultural analysis, and presented an alternative theory of social valuation based on the scientific-technological process. It is this framework that Ayres's students adopted and later used to produce further developments of the Veblenian dichotomy.

Foster, Tool, Junker, and Bush double down

Ayres's arguments were highly controversial among his contemporaries (Rutherford 2011, 335–338). But they greatly influenced Ayres's students and, in turn, their students as well. As a result, many in the "Veblen–Ayres" tradition viewed the dichotomization of technology and ceremony (institutions) as providing a normative standard for social analysis and a methodological approach to economics. Over time, those students (especially Foster initially, and later Tool, Junker, and Bush) would refine—in fact, redefine—elements of Ayres's analysis and arguments, and extend them theoretically.

The principle of continuity

Like Ayres, a starting point for much of the work of his students was the rejection of physical and cultural dualisms—the rejection behind Ayres's principle of continuity. But his students took the critique of dualisms much further. For example, presumably characterizing Foster's critique of the positive–normative dualism, Tool writes:

> Neither item in the paired construct is presumed to have common content or purpose with reference to the other; they are mutually exclusive perceptions of reality. Additional examples of such constructs are legion: is vs. ought, fact vs. value, objective vs. subjective, means vs. ends, economics vs. ethics, description vs. prescription, and true or false vs. good or bad … . Instrumentalists reject this divorcement of means and ends and

> perceive social value to be analytically identified in the processual and successive choosing of ends that become means, the means in turn become ends, indefinitely. Means and ends are appraised by institutionalists using the criterion of "instrumental efficiency."
>
> *(Tool 2000, 60)*[16]

Junker's (another student of Foster) dissertation on Ayres's social and economic thought, has a detailed section on Dewey's critique of the means–ends dualism. That section is motivated by Junker's statement that Ayres referred to Dewey's position approvingly (Junker 1962, 145–156). Junker follows with another section recounting Ayres's position on dualisms (Junker 1962, 156–171).

The point of discussing Tool and Junker here is to highlight the oral tradition and the fact that the source of their broad critique of Cartesian dualisms is uncertain, but likely a combination of contributions by Ayres and Foster, as interpreted by the latter's students. In any event, we come full circle back to the principle of continuity. It provides the rationale for critiquing the dualisms and converting them to a view of human experience wherein the previously separate elements of a dualism are considered the end points of a continuum of a continuous and connected characterization of human experience. In fact, the principle is crucial to Foster's reconceptualization of the Veblenian dichotomy, not only as a tool of economic analysis, but also as a device capable of use in social valuation (because the dichotomy highlights the scientific-technological process warranting instrumental behavior).

Foster's Veblenian dichotomy

Extending the principle of continuity behind the Veblenian dichotomy, Foster reconceptualizes the concept of institutions. For Foster (1981, 859), institutions are "patterns of correlated behavior" that, when they become operational, "are called institutions." Similar to Veblen, Foster (1981, 859) continues, "As institutions become firmly established, the component patterns of behavior becomes habitual—habits of thought and attitude and habits of action. … [I]nstitutions are comprised essentially of mores and folkways." Thus far, there is nothing that would contradict Ayres. But then Foster expands on his definition:

> Institutions are obviously very different in structural content, and the particular functions carried on through them may be very unlike. But those functions easily fall into two categories, both are common to *all institutions* … . On the one hand, every institution serves to bring the activities of individuals to bear in a contributory way on the instrumental function, which is the collaborative activity of the group … . It is convenient to call this category the instrumental function of the institutions … . On the other hand, every institution serves a completely different function: It serves to differentiate between persons and groups in invidious terms. The

> boss may be identified in terms of his instrumental function, but he also may be identified in terms of prestige, honor, deferential attitude, or power … . It is important to keep in mind the distinction between the instrumental and ceremonial functions of institutions.
>
> *(Foster 1981, 908, emphasis added)*

From there, Foster's students construct a very similar definition of institutions. As William Waller (a student of Junker) wrote in a 1982 article:

> In his recent book *The Discretionary Economy*, Marc Tool attributes the following definition to Foster: "The term institution means any prescribed or proscribed pattern of correlated behavior or attitude widely agreed upon among a group of persons organized to carry on some particular purpose." Another student of Foster's, Paul D. Bush, defines institution in a recent paper as "a set of socially prescribed patterns of correlated behavior." A third student of Foster's, Louis Junker, in an unpublished manuscript quoted Foster defining institution as "prescribed patterns of correlated human behavior with (a) instrumental aspects and (b) ceremonial aspects."
>
> *(Waller 1982, 764)*

The significance of the redefinition of institutions by Foster and his students is they break with Ayres's concept of institutions as separate phenomena that always inhibit progress (a perspective that, in effect, makes ceremonial behavior and institutions the same thing) and with his notion that the scientific-technological process is always instrumental in enhancing the life process and social provisioning. Instead, their redefinition acknowledges, as an analytic possibility, that institutions could both impede the provisioning process and be a source of progressive change. Thus, the redefinition reverses Ayres's break with his contemporaries on the definition of institutions.[17]

Ayres articulates the purpose of economic (and all social) inquiry as ensuring the continuity of the life process (following Veblen) and, of course, "keeping the machines running" (Ayres [1944] 1978, 223; 1949, 48). Foster's "problem solving through institutional adjustment" approach seemed more focused on Ayres's latter expression of purpose, whereas Foster's students emphasized the former. One place where Foster conjoins the Veblenian "continuity of the life process" purpose with Ayres's "keeping the machines running" purpose is in the following:

> Economics is concerned with the aspect of human experience called making a living—the production and distribution of goods and services. What, then, is value in the economic sense? … It must exist along the run of the facts in the continuum that is the economy, and the run of the facts therein is a technological process. … The existential economic realities can be considered logically only in term of their interconnectedness. And there is where value makes sense. Consider any item … . Does it add to the

> function that is called economic? If so, it has economic value; if not, it does not have economic value. Economic value is the degree of technological efficiency … . In the actual provision of the means to function as a human being, each item in the process has value in proportion as it implements that provision. That is the logical meaning of economic value; that is the *only real* meaning of economic value that permits logical treatment in economic analysis and upon which a science of economics may be built.
>
> *(Foster 1981, 895)*

According to Foster, there are ongoing social functions that must be fulfilled for the life process to continue. Foster's focus, however, is on the structures (institutions) in place ensuring the social functions are fulfilled. When a problem occurs, where a problem is defined as the difference between the way things are and the way things ought to be (the latter being conditions in which socially necessary functions are fulfilled), then the structure, which is replaceable, requires adjustment to solve the problem. Thus, the main focus of Foster's contribution to original institutional economics is a *theory of institutional adjustment*.

Valuation is inherent in the process of inquiry. A social or economic problem in a necessary ongoing function is identified—it is a difference between the way things are, and the way they ought to be. This creates a focus for inquiry to find a, or the best, or a better, pattern of correlated behavior to correct the problem. All economic analysis is a search for efficacious ways of adjusting existing institutions (patterns of correlated behavior). Hence, Foster (1981, 935) focused on what he called "the theory of institutional adjustment" (discussed below).

Instrumental value theory

For Foster (and his students) the continuity of the life process is enhanced by employing the warranted knowledge developed through the scientific-technological process. Employing that warranted knowledge, developed by a rigorous and democratic scientific community, to solve social problems of provisioning is called *instrumental behavior*. The goal is to evaluate alternative institutional arrangements, ranking them as better or worse. It is thus a valuation process. The scientific community is a cultural process, thus the warranted knowledge it constructs is culturally specific and tentative. The behavior of the scientific community, through ongoing research and critical review, is always revising and adding to the community's stock of warranted knowledge—the process has a self-correcting component. The instrumental value judgments made are context (and culturally) specific. There is no transcultural or ultimate value criteria; it is a *process* for decision-making employing the best information available in a specific time and place.

Ayres argued that a reasonable society will adopt instrumental valuational processes either consciously or unconsciously. Foster argued a stronger position: he contended that for a society to survive they must adopt instrumental valuation processes. Instrumental valuation is inevitable as a theory of valuation if a society is to survive, much less thrive. Foster articulated the "strong instrumental valuation hypothesis" in his essay, "Value and Economic Analysis." He wrote:

> [W]e are necessarily in the position of asserting that the instrumental efficiency of the economic process is the criterion of judgment in terms of which, and only in terms of which, we may resolve economic problems.
>
> *(Foster 1981, 905)*

Observations of societies employing non-rational judgmental criteria point to some interesting tendencies. A society that can produce enough goods and services to maintain survival at a socially acceptable level can tolerate a good deal of irrational behavior as long as the day-to-day business of staying alive is allowed to proceed in such a way as to sustain people in a customary manner. What Veblen called matter-of-fact knowledge—what others have called common sense, and institutionalists might now call instrumentally warranted knowledge—works whether people know why it works or not. People will use what they believe works to solve their problems. As long as enough of what they *believe* works, actually works well enough to keep them alive and reproducing, their society will persist. Societies populated by people who believe more things to be true that are actually true will have an advantage at survival and reproduction. Societies that value the palpably true over that which cannot be demonstrated to be true, and seek out such knowledge, will become better able to solve their problems (see Waller 2013). For Foster, instrumental valuational processes must be operating in a society that successfully addresses its problems through institutional adjustment.[18]

The theory of institutional adjustment

Fortunately, we have available a description of the theory of institutional adjustment by Foster (1981). He begins his description with a discussion of the nature of social scientific inquiry, and argues that scientific principles must be adhered to in social inquiry (Foster 1981, 931). The process of social scientific inquiry is not static; instead, it focuses on the continuing social functions of society that are carried out by institutions which are static structures. He continues that the adequacy of carrying out "the continuing functions" should be "the criteria of judgement" by which the institutional structures are judged. He adds, "For the solving of institutional problems necessarily involves choosing among alternatives in the form of institutional structures" (Foster 1981, 932). He then articulates three principles of institutional adjustment, to which we turn.

The principle of *technological determination* means that what the members of a community "know" is what they "know as technological or physical fact." The technological knowledge available to the community is what they can use to make institutional modifications to solve problems (which are inevitable). He notes,

> Not only is technology determinate of institutional problems in the sense that it creates such problems, but also it is determinate of the solutions in the sense that it constitutes the basic data which must be taken as given in social problems.
>
> (Foster 1981, 932–933)

The principle of *recognized interdependence* "refers to the proposition that the person whose behavior is correlated through the new structure must understand their respective patterns of participation" (Foster 1981, 941). Foster argues, "Patterns of human relationship that we call institutions are 'made up of' habitual actions and attitudes, but they are not *determined* by habit. Their determination is a matter of deliberate and guided action" (Foster 1981, 933, italics in original). Tool (2000, 93) provided essential clarification of this principle when he wrote that

> actual change in behavior can occur only when there is some recognition on the part of those affected of the need for institutional change and a willingness to accept that change as indicated by an instrumental assessment of the problematic condition to which inquiry is addressed.

The principle of *minimal dislocation* is described by Foster as a statement of fact. "All institutional modifications must be capable of being incorporated into the remainder of the institutional structure" (Foster 181, 933). He adds that institutional adjustments "must be capable of being integrated with all of the existing institutions which have not entered the comprehension of the members of the community as problematic factors" (Foster 181, 941). Again, Tool helpfully elaborates: "This principle affirms that all institutional adjustments must be capable of being incorporated into the remainder of the institutional structure without significantly disrupting instrumental functions of nonproblematic structure, if they are to be contributive to problem resolution." Tool also writes: "The minimal dislocation premise implies and affirms that communities *cannot* stop and start over" (Tool 2000, 94, emphasis in original).[19]

Foster as refined by Bush, Junker, and Tool

There is not much written by Foster (1981). We are heavily dependent upon the characterization of his work by Tool (2000). For the further elaboration of Foster's framework, we must look to the substantive work of his students, Bush, Junker, and Tool, who all focused on extending Foster's methodological and theoretical contributions.[20] All of their contributions are on interrelated aspects of the Veblenian dichotomy.

Bush and Junker wrote explicitly on the Veblenian dichotomy (Bush 1983; 1993; Junker 1982; 1983a; 1983b). Bush focused on formalizing an interpretation of the terms of the dichotomy and the interaction of the two social valuation processes manifest within ceremonial and instrumental aspects of behavior. Bush (1983, 36–37) stressed that the dichotomy contains two social valuation processes: "Values are either ceremonially warranted or instrumentally warranted. The essence of the [Veblenian] 'institutional dichotomy' is contained in this distinction between the two modes of social valuation existing within the society."

Each of the two processes has different criteria for establishing the warrant for the behavior of the respective valuation process. Bush writes:

> Accordingly, patterns of behavior correlated by ceremonial values are observed to be those social practices that manifest the use of power and coercion in the conduct of human affairs: social practices that require invidious distinctions and status relationships to justify their existence. On the other hand, patterns of behavior correlated by instrumental values are manifest in those problem-solving activities upon which the life processes of the community depend. They are subject to change and modification as the instrumental character of the problems changes or as the scientific processes produce better technology with which to address those problems.
> *(Bush 1983, 37)*

But Bush also adds the proviso that these processes are not discrete: "A particular activity or behavior may have either ceremonial or instrumental significance, or it may possess *both* ceremonial and instrumental significance" (Bush 1983, 37, emphasis in original). When an activity has both ceremonial and instrumental significance, the issue emerges: which is dominant in that activity and does it matter? To address that question, we must see how these scholars answer the question: *matter for what?*

The purpose of institutional analysis for these scholars is to solve social problems. The context for problems is important—these are problems of provisioning the community with the generic means of life, also called the life process. The community in question is embedded in a culture. The culture is continuous. Part of the culture is the accumulated knowledge of how to do things held in common by members of that culture. This is made up of their accumulated, technological, matter-of-fact knowledge, which Veblen defines as the true meaning of capital. But it also includes the myths and legends that provide the warrant for those vested interests with power and status who use their power to maintain their favored positions in that culture. This implies continuity is the community's understanding of the world and demonstrates the working of cumulative causation in that context (Junker 1982).

In the case of any particular problem, if the context of the behavior associated with addressing that problem is primarily directed to using the cultural body of matter-of-fact knowledge of the community to address the problem, then that problem-solving process is referred to by Bush as "progressive institutional change." Alternately, if the behavior associated with addressing the problem is cultural understandings built on legends and myths employed for the purpose of solving the problem in a way that does not disrupt the existing system of power and status, then that problem-solving context is said to be dominated by ceremonial valuation processes. In this latter case, both Bush and Junker refer to the matter-of-fact, technological and scientific knowledge and associated behavior as a case of "ceremonial encapsulation" of that knowledge (Bush 1983, 38; 1986, 32–37; 1994, 291–296).

When this process is so extreme that ceremonially warranted behavior is so powerful and entrenched that problem-solving necessary to adequately provision the community with the generic means of life is impossible and the very continuity of the life process is threatened, Junker identifies this as "malignant ceremonialism" (Junker 1983a; 1983b). The concept of ceremonial encapsulation has been adopted and applied in the work of many institutionalists subsequent to its introduction and elaboration by Bush. For example, Waller (1987) presents examples of the use of the concept and argues that the concept clarifies our understanding of the overall Veblenian dichotomy.

Tool gets to the same position but with greater emphasis on explicating instrumental value theory and the mechanics of institutional adjustment along the lines of Foster. Tool (1979) lays out his position systematically in his book *The Discretionary Economy*. Tool argues, following Dewey and Ayres, that knowledge, the removal of doubt, comes from warranted knowledge gained in a means–end continuum of successful social problem-solving, which generates the community's common stock of matter-of-fact knowledge through the ongoing inquiry into the ways and means of solving problems.

For Tool (1979, 39), the process of inquiry to solve social problems is a continuing process that leads to a "knowledge continuum" that is cumulative and increases "at a seemingly exponential rate." In his book, there is barely a mention of culture as more than something acquired through acculturation. The source of continuity of culture is apparently the problem-solving process. And that problem-solving process is the source of "knowledge continuum." Though based on the Dewey and Ayres means–ends continuum, in Tool (1979, 90) the technological process—with its emphasis on extensive consideration of the history of technology, the role of tool combinations principles, and cultural diffusion—is almost absent except in the discussion of defining resources for solving problems.

For Tool (1979, 108–109), the goal of social inquiry is to solve problems in the delivery of "real income;" these problems affect the ongoing social functions necessary to maintain the community. These functions are maintained through social structures. These structures are themselves completely replaceable—if they are not successful in maintaining the necessary functions, then we need to adjust or replace them through the process of institutional adjustment. Understanding the difference between instrumental functions and ceremonial (Tool used the term "invidious" after Veblen) functions is crucial to social inquiry. Tool writes, "The continuing and central task in social and economic change of the institutional fabric is one of *increasing* the degree and magnitude of *instrumental* performance and *decreasing* the degree and magnitude of *invidious* performance" (Tool 1979, 167, emphasis in original).

Solving social problems through institutional adjustment is, for Tool, the evolutionary mechanism determining how societies survive and improve their provisioning processes. Societies that do not solve their problems fail (and apparently eventually disappear, succumbing to Veblen's "triumph of imbecile institutions"). But in evaluating potential candidates for institutional change, there are also better or worse alternatives. It is social inquiry employing the knowledge continuum that allows us to evaluate the efficacy of different candidate solutions. Thus, the process of inquiry is a valuation process; it contains the matter-of-fact, technological and scientific warranted knowledge available to use in constructing potential solutions to provisioning problems of the community. Tool thus rejects the positive–normative dualism of mainstream economics; there is no value-free scientific inquiry; all scientific inquiry is inherently engaged in a self-correcting process of acquiring knowledge by making judgments about better and worse answers to questions through application of earlier scientific knowledge, which at any given time provides (always provisional) warranted knowledge.

From this view of the economic and social provisioning process, Tool articulates a strong version of instrumental value theory very similar to that of Foster. It employs the following value principle: "that direction is forward which provides for *the continuity of human life and the noninvidious re-creation of community through the instrumental use of knowledge*" (Tool 1979, 293, emphasis in original). That this is a strong version of the instrumental theory there can be no doubt when Tool continues:

> We consider the foregoing to be a criterion of judgement, a social-value principle, *which is general in its relevance to the universe of the social process*, to functional components of the process (economy, polity), and to choices among institutional forms which organize that process. We suggest further that the resolution of political and economic problems in particular (in the sense in which "resolution" can be held to have rational meaning) probably *requires the use of this criterion* in lieu of other proffered theories of value.
> *(Tool 1979, 293, emphasis added)*

Tool then describes both the explicit and implicit elements of this principle. Of the explicit elements, the first is *continuity* of both life and community. Another is that the recreation of community need be *non-invidious*, thereby not re-inscribing or creating new discriminatory patterns of access and privilege. And finally, change should be accomplished through *the instrumental use of reliable knowledge*, thereby excluding mythical, legendary, and supernatural explanations for decision-making and institutional adjustment (Tool 1979, 293–297).

Additionally, Tool introduces corollaries (implicit elements) to his value principle. One is *instrumental efficiency*, which is more than technical efficiency; it requires that the change not negatively affect the other elements of the value principle (Tool 1979, 301). He also includes *democracy* as a corollary. The process of change is inherently disruptive to ways of living. If a community is to be put through this disruption, they should be involved in the decision-making processes at every level of the solution's implementation. *Non-invidiousness* itself is a corollary in that diminishing discriminatory, exploitative behavior and differential advantages based on status is necessary for successful institutional adjustment when applying instrumental value theory (Tool 1979, 307–310). And finally, *environmental compatibility* is necessary for a change not to be self-defeating; a solution that destroys the environment cannot promote the continuity of life and the re-creation of community (Tool 1979, 310–314).

Tool describes the principles of institutional adjustment in almost the same way as Foster. Indeed, up until the publication of Foster's papers in the *Journal of Economic Issues* in 1981, Tool's book (and the unpublished dissertations of Foster's students) was the only readily available source for Foster's ideas. Foster and his students were engaged in a largely oral tradition, really more of a conversation, and all of them saw themselves as extending the "Veblen–Ayres" tradition. As it turns out, an article published in the mid-1980s by Bush (1986, 25) marks that group's first recognition of offering a distinctively different understanding of the Veblenian dichotomy, an observation he attributes to reading Waller (1982). Until then, it is not clear that Foster's students noted the distinctive differences in their own formulations of the Veblenian dichotomy and instrumental value theory.

Assessment of the "Veblenian" dichotomy in retrospect

The problem of different definitions of the term "institution" employed by institutionalists remains an issue to this day. Each generation of institutional economists has employed multiple definitions of this term. I find Walter C. Neale's (1987, 1185) process for identifying an institution operational and most satisfying. He writes: "Each constituent of an institution can be observed, or can be stated as testable predictions of [an] event sequence (1) people doing; (2) the rules, including the situations in which they are followed; and (3) the folk-views explaining the rules."

Institutions, technology, and the dichotomy revisited

In much the same vein as Neale, Hodgson's oft-cited article defends a definition of institutions "as systems of established and prevalent social rules that structure social interactions. Language, money, law, systems of weights and measures, table manners, and firms (and other organizations) are thus all institutions" (Hodgson 2006, 2). Hodgson also argues that Veblen did not have a definition of an institution because, agreeing with Tony Lawson, he argues that "settled habits of thought common to the generality of men" (Veblen 1909, 626) does not appear in its context as a definition of an institution (Hodgson 2004, n. 184). Since Hodgson's definition (elaborated in his 2006 article) systematically links instincts, habit, and institutions, it would seem a useful definition, especially since it appears consistent enough with Veblen's development of the relationship of these components to one another. That said, "habits of thought common to the generality of men" certainly isn't inconsistent with rules that structure human interaction.

Hodgson argues that Hamilton's (1932, 84) definition of an institution (not radically different than his interwar contemporaries)—"a way of thought or action of some prevalence which is embedded in the habits of a group or the customs of a people"—is preferable "as long as habits and customs are interpreted as dispositions rather than merely behavior" (Hodgson 2006, 21, n. 3). This reflects Hodgson's rejection of construing habits as behavior, in favor of the alternative view that habits are a disposition. Hodgson levels the same criticism at Foster's (1981, 908) definition of institutions as "prescribed patterns of correlated behavior." Hodgson's emphasis is on the use of "behavior" in the definition, rather than the "prescribed patterns of correlated" portion of the definition. This seems to ignore the common meaning of "correlated" as well as the focus of the definition on the "prescribe patterns," which could very well describe rules. This is important to Hodgson because he is concerned that without a shared definition, progress (and recognition in the scientific community) cannot be made in the theoretical program of institutional economics. The history of institutionalism he describes, however, suggests that the concept and definition of institutions is likely to change and evolve as the concept is used in new contexts; language usage inevitably evolves.

Ayres placed tremendous importance on tools, technology, and their role in progress. The work of Ayres's students is steeped in the history of technology literature (Hamilton et al. 2010, see especially chapters 12, 19, 20, 24, 25; DeGregori 1984). In addition, Clive Lawson (2009; 2017, 82–98, 168–176) has recently used Ayres's conception of technology, and especially the significance of tools, in a productive way in his work.

Careful scholarship by Hodgson (1998), Mayhew (2010), Floyd McFarland (1986), and Malcolm Rutherford (1981) establishes conclusively that Veblen did not intend that the distinction he used would be employed as they are in discussions of the Veblenian dichotomy. They all argue that this use can be traced to Ayres. Further, they argue that Ayres's treatment of the concept of institutions is not that of Veblen and is incompatible with that of Ayres's interwar contemporaries. Despite this, Ayres is often seen as the interwar institutional economist whose assessment of the economy was closest to Veblen's (Rutherford 2011, 14, 338). By emphasizing that all institutions have both ceremonial aspects of behavior and instrumental aspects of behavior, Foster and his students can be seen as a corrective to Ayres's conception of institutions—and a return to the interwar understanding of institutions as employed by Walton Hamilton and his contemporaries.

From within the institutional community of scholars there have been significant critiques of the employment of the Veblenian dichotomy as a methodology. Warren Samuels (1977) carefully explored a number of the problems in the Veblen–Ayres framework. Samuels's work is a generous and dispassionate evaluation of the relationship between technology and institutions. Many of the issues he puts forth as problematic were dealt with by Tool (1979). One that was not addressed, however, is the concern that the dichotomy, especially its view on the role of technology, lapses into technological determinism. Samuels writes:

> Technological determinism has been held narrow and inflexible, indeed untenable. It is a single-factor explanation at variance with the institutionalist critique of neoclassical economics which rejects narrow mechanism and urges multifactor cumulative causation. It is at variance, too, with institutionalist conceptions of systemic and institutional and evolutionary diversity. Technological determinism involves reification, hypostatization, misplaced concreteness, and the subtle intrusion of ideological or normative premises into the process channeling the role of choice in society.
>
> *(Samuels 1977, 877)*

Samuels (1977, 877, and 92, notes 30 and 31) notes the dichotomy was subject to critique on these grounds by scholars within the institutionalist community. This problem remains in the Foster version of the dichotomy in that the instrumental aspects of behavior are dependent on the Ayresian technological process (tool behavior derived by the technological-scientific process). If instrumental valuation is not only necessary, but inevitable, then users of the Foster version of the dichotomy are still making a technologically determinist argument.

Ceremonial encapsulation and the ecosystem

James Swaney (1986) introduces a co-evolutionary perspective on the dichotomy employing Bush's concept of ceremonial encapsulation. He writes:

> Bush argues that new "knowledge is either 'embodied' in instrumentally warranted patterns of behavior or 'encapsulated' within ceremonially warranted patterns of behavior." By "embodied," Bush is referring to life-enhancing uses of knowledge. Thus, when new knowledge is *embodied,* it is applied for overall human improvement, which is associated with "progressive institutional change." By "encapsulated," Bush means power-and status-enhancing uses of knowledge. Thus, encapsulated new knowledge may be put to use, but the "legitimacy of its use is held to the standard of 'ceremonial adequacy.'"
>
> *(Swaney 1986, 394)*

Introducing Richard Norgaard's concept of coevolutionary development, Swaney (1986, 395) writes, "Norgaard's concern is with the interactions between evolving socioeconomic and ecological systems." He adds:

> Unfortunately, our knowledge of the interactions between sociosystems and ecosystems is very limited, while our ignorance of the interrelationships within the global ecosystem is relatively unlimited. Ecological systems may have evolved stable equilibriums, the likes of which are never found in socioeconomic systems, except, of course, in certain economics textbooks. But there is mounting evidence that increased human well-being is realized at the expense of ecological stability.
>
> *(Swaney 1986, 396)*

Swaney asks if these two perspectives or models can be integrated and proposes both yes and no answers, but he ends up arguing that in order for it to occur, Bush's model of institutional change must be broadened to incorporate the interactions between sociosystem and ecosystem (Swaney 1986, 398). He briefly summarizes a possible integration:

> Changes which clearly provide immediate improvement in the life process cannot be unambiguously labeled "instrumental" unless they are also supportive of the ecosystem. Behaviors which meet both of these criteria are "instrumental-supportive." Changes which are instrumental in the sociosystem but disruptive to the ecosystem are "instrumental-degenerative." Such behaviors may eventually increase sociosystem service responsibilities and thereby impede further sociosystem development. On the other hand, some ceremonial behaviors will "accidentally" affect the ecosystem positively. The possibility of "ceremonial-supportive" behaviors suggests that in some cases encapsulation of new knowledge may have long-term coevolutionary payoffs. Finally, "ceremonial-degenerative" changes not only restrict the use of new knowledge for overall human improvement, thereby inhibiting sociosystem development, but also harm the ecosystem.
>
> *(Swaney 1986, 398)*

Swaney's proposed refinement of the Veblenian dichotomy, which aimed to better reflect the interconnectedness of the social-economic system and the ecosystem and to incorporate ecology into the institutionalist evolutionary perspective, was only expanded upon by a few other institutionalists (see, for example, Underwood 1998), though Swaney continued to press this argument in his later work. However, Swaney's work, like some earlier-mentioned applied work, seems to indicate that the concept of ceremonial encapsulation has been found useful by a significant number of institutionalists.

Instrumental value theory revisited

Instrumental value theory, a creation of John Dewey, is certainly separable in principle from the Veblenian dichotomy. But in any discussion of the dichotomy, that theory also requires some consideration. Once Ayres substituted instrumental behavior for technological behavior in his construction of his dichotomy, there became an inseparable cojoining of all of the following: the meaning of the term technology, tools and their associated behaviors in use, the tool-combination process, the understanding of the development of the history of technology, the problem-solving process in the context of the life process of the community, and the instrumental valuation process as a social valuation process and criterion. As Swaney (1989, 569–570) notes, many institutionalist scholars have argued against this conjoining of such disparate elements of human experience and that it led to sloppy and outmoded analysis.

Further problematizing instrumental value theory is the strong instrumentalist position argued by Foster and, on occasion, Tool. That instrumental valuation is *inevitable* if human societies are to survive, as a kind of evolutionary imperative, is simply unsupportable. While Veblen considered blind drift as a possible path for human societies, he certainly did not argue for it leading to any inevitable collapse as a result of the triumph of imbecile institutions (though such a possibility certainly exists). Any society may fail, or it may blunder about for an interminable period of time, but, as Swaney noted, it may also make instrumental judgments and fail anyway.

Also, the entire discussion of value theory in economics suffers from a lack of clarity as well as from conceit. First, it confounds individual valuation processes and social valuations processes. And second, all economic schools of thought oddly assume there is only one way to individually value or socially value.[21]

Consider, for example, that young children value things because of simple desire or appetite; students value their course work based on the effort they expended on the assignment; and skilled workers are quite adept at valuing the correct tool for a job. These are illustrations of the application of the utility theory of value, the labor theory of value, and instrumental theory of value in individual application. Note that all three of these valuation processes are used by individuals creating no conflict, confusion, or cognitive dissonance in their lives or their communities. All of these have been construed as social valuation processes by economists, all of whom have decided that one and only one of these processes determines the "real" (objective?) value of the thing or process for society. Why? This leads us to the second problem.

There is nothing in the fabric of social reality that requires that we use only one valuational process, either individually or socially. Aside from the humor in mainstream economists adopting the value criterion of spoiled small children as the single universal value of society measured by market prices, there is the obvious truth (pointed out by Veblen in *The Theory of the Leisure*

Class) that people and communities actually do value some things by their price. Similarly, we often marvel, admire, and value many human accomplishments (especially from the past) based almost solely on the magnitude of the labor involved in their construction (including, for example, the Egyptian pyramids, the Great Wall of China, and humans landing on the moon). And of course, we also socially value processes of problem-solving and instrumental valuation. Unless we have a religious or supernatural conception of the nature of value—that is, the belief that there is a "true value"—then there is no reason not to have multiple processes for assigning socially constructed value metrics.

Concluding observation

My recent research on this topic has generated the following observation. On the one hand, I find that the "Ayresian" dichotomy is much more frequently *discussed* as a methodology than it is actually *employed* as one. On the other hand, I also note that ceremonial encapsulation, a concept derived from the "Ayresian" dichotomy, is increasingly being used in actual economic analysis.

Pondering that observation, I thought of other methods, techniques, methodologies, and heuristics I use in my own work. The "Ayresian" dichotomy, similar to William Dugger's framework for analyzing power (Dugger 1980; Waller 2017c) or F. Gregory Hayden's "social fabric matrix" (Hayden 2006), is often a starting point for sorting out the overwhelming complexities of social reality. It is a first pass, that gives me a starting point for organizing my thoughts.

For example, in an analysis I conducted on bankruptcy reform, I noted two conflicting narratives: one was about the necessity of holding individuals responsible for their actions (debts) for fear of the disintegration of society; the other argued that, when the normal functioning of an economic system creates "winners" and "losers," the maintenance of social stability requires some mechanism to rehabilitate those who "lost" back into society. The "Ayresian" dichotomy did not figure in the ultimate analysis, but it did provide the place to start (Waller 2001).

So, despite the many intellectual problems that need to be addressed, the "Ayresian" dichotomy can still be fruitfully used as a starting point, but not the ending point, of institutional analysis.

Acknowledgments

I would like to thank Janice Peterson, Susan Evans, Jacob Powell, Charles Whalen, and Mary Wrenn for their comments, suggestions, and corrections that have improved the paper considerably. I would particularly like to thank Paul Dale Bush for his mentoring and support throughout my career. All errors are my own.

Notes

1 By analytic, I mean these contrasting categories were a "cut" in reality where Veblen knew these items were not distinct in reality; they were used for the purpose of analysis, but ultimately known to be part of the whole of reality. Thus the analyst carried the responsibility to repair the "cut" and reconstruct the whole of reality in the final analysis. I will be contrasting this with treating these contrasting categories as separable elements of reality as done by Ayres and some of his followers.

2 Tony Lawson (2015, 10) argues that using this particular quote as a definition is to take the fragment out of context and interpret it in a manner contrary to what Veblen is trying to explain. Lawson argues that Veblen is not here offering a definition of an institution; instead, Veblen is referring to certain principles of action, which are relatively enduring and widely recognized as such. In fact, Veblen "has been referring not to institutions per se, but rather to particular examples of social phenomena that might be called institutions." What's more, Veblen's point is that even institutions, which are relatively enduring compared to other social phenomena, are nonetheless still "subject to processes of evolutionary change or adaptation overtime."

3 Veblen's reference to "a natural selection of the fittest habits of thought" conflicts with the rest of his perspective on institutional change. Indeed, it sounds disturbingly more like Douglass North and the efficiency-oriented "new" institutionalists than Veblen. Obviously, in other works Veblen considered both "blind drift" and the triumph of imbecile institutions. See Jennings and Waller (1994).

4 A number of the citations of Veblen in Tool (1953; 1986; 2000) are incorrect and incomplete. Junker (1962) made a number of corrections and additions, which are included in this list. Additionally, I have updated some of the editions used and checked the citations to the best of my ability.

5 See Dowd (1978, xiii).

6 See note 1 for the distinction between methodological and analytical categorization.

7 Hodgson (1998) is crucial to documenting that while Veblen may have inspired Ayres and his followers' use and development of the Veblenian dichotomy, Veblen did not create it or employ it in his work. Indeed, Veblen's work is largely inconsistent with such an interpretation. Additionally, Hodgson (2004) presents an assessment essential for understanding the Ayresian interlude.

8 Much of the discussion of Ayres career and the reception of Ayres (1944) by Ayres's contemporaries is drawn from Rutherford's (2011) account of interwar institutionalism.

9 Hodgson's work is controversial. It is, however, a theory of behavior based on instincts/habits and evolutionary theory and, thus, Veblenian in character.

10 Ayres reconfigured the definition of "institutions" and then contrasted it with technology in ways Hodgson (2004, 202) argues cannot be supported as attributable to Veblen. Given the definitions of institution cited above, I think Hodgson is a bit harsh. However, I also think Ayres's reading of Veblen was highly selective.

11 There appear to be two different, albeit related, uses of "continuity" in Ayres ([1944] 1978, 91, 217). The first use asserts a continuity between physical and social behavior. It is part of Ayres's critique of dualistic thinking, that is, his critique of the suggestion that human behavior can be understood at different levels of generalization, such as the physical, chemical, biological, psychological, and cultural. By postulating the continuity of these different levels with one another, Ayres allows for the assertion that cultural phenomena should be explained by cultural processes. The second use of "continuity" seems to assert that behavior associated with the scientific-technological process is both continuous and cumulative. We will see that Foster's students make much of both of these aspects of continuity.

12 See Mary Wrenn's chapter, on the topic of enabling myths in institutional economics, in this volume (Chapter 9). Also see Galbraith (2004).

13 Dewey's pragmatism and instrumentalism were considered by many institutionalist contemporaries of Ayres. Of central importance for Ayres was Dewey's rejection

of Cartesian dualisms in understanding valuation, particularly the mean–ends dualism (Dewey 1939). Contemporaneously, Morris A. Copeland presents an alternative value position to that of Ayres. Copeland (1921, 131) writes: "Institutional value theory is genetic and functional in approach and seeks to emphasize relativity to the temporal process." And he contends: "Instead of in the objective conception of values…pragmatism finds superpersonal values in the mores, which are in perpetual conflict and evolution, through a process of institutional selection…" (Copeland 1921, 139). There are many contemporary critiques of Ayres's instrumental value framework that are beyond the scope of this work; for broadly sympathetic examinations, see, for example, Mayhew (2010), Hodgson (1998), McFarland (1986), and Rutherford (1981).

14 See Dewey (1929; 1939). Ayres has moved beyond Dewey by making instrumental value universal. Dewey treated it pragmatically.

15 See Rutherford (1981) for an excellent discussion of Ayres on instrumental valuation.

16 Tool (1979) contains a critique of the positive/normative dualism as part of an interconnected system of dualisms (278–285). For additional critiques of Cartesian dualisms in institutional economics, see, for example, Jennings (1993) and Waller and Wrenn (2021).

17 The three most important discussions of the concept of an institution that take into account original institutional economics are: Neale (1987), T. Lawson (2015), and Hodgson (2006).

18 The above is a rejection of Veblen's views. Veblen argued that there was no natural tendency toward normality or meliorative trends in the economy. He did not point to what direction was forward; instead, he argued that the direction of human affairs could be characterized by blind drift and was likely to move in the direction of the triumph of imbecile institutions. See Waller (2017a).

19 See Klimina (2020, 386) for a powerful counterexample of minimal dislocation.

20 Foster had other students who also made important contributions to institutional economics. For example, Edyth Miller made valuable contributions in the field of public utility regulation.

21 John R. Commons's concept of reasonable value is an exception to the notion that there is one valuation process applicable to individual and social valuation. Commons's reasonable value cannot be an individual valuation process. It is inherently social because it requires different people, or social groups, or their representatives, to reason together and come to a consensus. For more on reasonable value, see Chapter 2 in this volume.

References

Almeida, Felipe, and Gustavo Goulart. 2020. "Recontextualizing Clarence Ayres's *The Theory of Economic Progress* through Archival Evidence." *Journal of Economic Issues* 54 (2): 392–397. https://doi.org/10.1080/00213624.2020.1743601

Ayres, Clarence E. 1921a. "Instinct and Capacity I." *The Journal of Philosophy* 18 (21): 561–565. https://doi.org/10.2307/2939519

———. 1921b. "Instinct and Capacity II." *The Journal of Philosophy* 18 (22): 600–606. https://doi.org/10.2307/2939757

———. 1935. "The Gospel of Technology." In *American Philosophy Today and Tomorrow*, edited by Horace M. Kallen and Sidney Hook, 25–44. New York: Lee Furman.

———. (1944) 1978. *The Theory of Economic Progress*. 3rd ed., Louis J. Junker, editor. Kalamazoo: New Issues Press.

———. 1949. "The Value Economy." In *Value: A Cooperative Inquiry*, edited by Ray Leply, 43–63. New York: Columbia University Press.

———. 1958. "Veblen's Theory of Instincts Reconsidered." In *Thorstein Veblen: A Critical Reappraisal*, edited by D. Dowd, 25–37. Ithaca: Cornell University Press.

———. 1961. *Toward a Reasonable Society*. Austin: University of Texas Press. https://doi.org/10.7560/734111

Bush, Paul D. 1983. "An Exploration of the Structural Characteristics of a Veblen-Ayres-Foster Defined Institutional Domain." *Journal of Economic Issues* 17 (1): 35–66. https://doi.org/10.1080/00213624.1983.11504088

———. 1986. "The Concept of Ceremonial Encapsulation." *The Review of Institutional Thought* 3 (December): 25–45.

———. 1993. "The Methodology of Institutional Economics: A Pragmatic Instrumentalist Perspective." In *Institutional Economics: Theory, Method, Policy*, edited by Marc R. Tool, 59–107. Boston, MA: Kluwer Academic Publishers. https://doi.org/10.1007/978-0-585-29604-3_3

———. 1994. "The Pragmatic Instrumentalist Perspective on the Theory of Institutional Change." *Journal of Economic Issues* 28 (2): 647–657. https://doi.org/10.1080/00213624.1994.11505576

Copeland, Morris Albert. 1921. *Some Phases of Institutional Value Theory*. Abstract. PhD. Thesis. University of Chicago. In The University of Chicago Abstracts of Thesis. Humanities Series, Volume II.

DeGregori, Thomas R. 1984. *A Theory of Technology*. Ames: Iowa State University Press.

Dewey, John. (1929) 1960. *The Quest for Certainty*. New York: G. P. Putnam's Sons.

———. 1939. *Theory of Valuation*. International Encyclopedia of Unified Science Chicago: University of Chicago Press.

Dowd, Douglas. 1978. "Introduction to the Transactions Edition." In *The Theory of Business Enterprise*, edited by Thorstein Veblen, v–xx. New Brunswick: Transactions Publishers.

Dugger, William M. 1980. "Power: An Institutional Framework of Analysis." *Journal of Economic Issues* 14 (4): 897–907. https://doi.org/10.1080/00213624.1980.11503790

Foster, John Fagg. 1981. "The Papers of J. Fagg Foster." *Journal of Economic Issues* 15 (4): 857–1012.

Galbraith, John Kenneth. 2004. *The Economics of Innocent Fraud*. Boston, MA: Houghton Mifflin.

Hamilton, David, Glen Atkinson, William M. Dugger, and William T. Waller Jr. 2010. *Cultural Economics and Theory: The Evolutionary Economics of David Hamilton*. New York: Routledge. https://doi.org/10.4324/9780203869840

Hamilton, Walton H. 1919. "The Institutional Approach to Economic Theory." *American Economic Review* 9 (Supplement): 309–318.

———. 1932. "Institution." In *Encyclopaedia of the Social Sciences*, Vol. 8, edited by Edwin R. A. Seligman and Alvin Johnson, 84–89. New York: Macmillan.

Hayden, F. Gregory. 2006. *Policymaking for a Good Society: The Social Fabric Matrix Approach to Policy Analysis and Program Evaluation*. New York: Springer. https://doi.org/10.1007/0-387-29370-1

Hodgson, Geoffrey M. 1998. "Dichotomizing the Dichotomy: Veblen versus Ayres." In *Institutionalist Method and Value: Essays in Honour of Paul Dale Bush*, Volume 1,

edited by Sasan Fayazmanesh and Marc R. Tool, 48–73. Northhampton, MA: Edward Elgar.
———. 2004. *The Evolution of Institutional Economics: Agency, Structure, and Darwinism in American Institutionalism*. London: Routledge. https://doi.org/10.4324/9780203300350
———. 2006. "What Are Institutions?" *Journal of Economic Issues* 40 (1): 1–25. https://doi.org/10.1080/00213624.2006.11506879
Hodgson, Geoffrey M. and Thorbjørn Knudsen. 2010. *Darwin's Conjecture: The Search for General Principles of Social and Economic Evolution*. Chicago, IL: Chicago University Press.
Jennings, Ann. 1993. "Public or Private? Institutional Economics and Feminism." In *Beyond Economic Man: Feminist Theory and Economics*, edited by M.A. Ferber and J.A. Nelson, 111–129. Chicago: University of Chicago Press. https://doi.org/10.7208/9780226242088-008
Jennings, Ann and William Waller 1994. "Evolutionary Economics and Cultural Hermeneutics: Veblen, Cultural Relativism, and Blind Drift." *Journal of Economic Issues*, 28 (4): 997–1030.
Junker, Louis J. 1962. *The Social and Economic Thought of Clarence Edwin Ayres*. Unpublished Ph.D. Dissertation. University of Wisconsin.
———. 1982. "The Ceremonial-Instrumental Dichotomy in Institutional Analysis: The Nature, Scope, and Radical Implications of the Conflicting Systems." *American Journal of Economics and Sociology* 41 (2): 141–150. https://doi.org/10.1080/00213624.1994.11505610
———. 1983a. "Institutionalism and the Criteria of Development." *Economic Forum* 14 (1): 27–56.
———. 1983b. "The Conflict between the Scientific-Technological Process and Malignant Ceremonialism." *American Journal of Economics and Sociology* 42 (3): 341–351. https://doi.org/10.1111/j.1536-7150.1983.tb01719.x
Klimina, Anna. 2020. "Defining and Defending a Progressive Market Square: Bringing Institutionalist Development Discourse in Line with the Reality of Post-Soviet Transition Experiences." *Journal of Economic Issues* 54 (2): 385–391. https://doi.org/10.1080/00213624.2020.1743599
Lawson, Clive. 2009. "Ayres, Technology and Technical Objects." *Journal of Economic Issues* 43 (3): 641–660. https://doi.org/10.2753/JEI0021-3624430304
———. 2017. *Technology and Isolation*. Cambridge, UK: Cambridge University Press. https://doi.org/10.1017/9781316848319
Lawson, Tony. 2015. "Process, order and stability in Veblen." *Cambridge Journal of Economics* 39 (4): 993–1030. https://doi.org/10.1093/cje/beu045
Mayhew, Anne. 2010. "Clarence Ayres, Technology, Pragmatism and Progress." *Cambridge Journal of Economics* 34 (1): 213–222. https://doi.org/10.1093/cje/ben062
McFarland, Floyd B. 1986. "Clarence Ayres and his Gospel of Technology." *History of Political Economy* 18 (4): 617–637. https://doi.org/10.1215/00182702-18-4-617
Neale, Walter C. 1987. "Institutions." *Journal of Economic Issues* 21(3): 1177–1206. https://doi.org/10.1080/00213624.1987.11504700
Rutherford, Malcolm. 1981. "Clarence Ayres and the Instrumental Theory of Value." *Journal of Economic Issues* 15 (3): 657–673. https://doi.org/10.1080/00213624.1981.11503882
———. 2011. *The Institutionalist Movement in American Economics, 1918–1947: Science and Social Control*. Cambridge: Cambridge University Press. https://doi.org/10.1017/CBO9780511977046
Samuels, Warren J. 1977. "Technology *vis-a-vis* Institutions in the *JEI*: A Suggested Interpretation." *Journal of Economic Issues* 11 (4): 867–895. https://doi.org/10.1080/00213624.1977.11503490

Swaney, James A. 1986. "A Coevolutionary Model of Structural Change." *Journal of Economic Issues* 20 (2): 393–401. https://doi.org/10.1080/00213624.1986.11504510
———. 1989. "Our Obsolete Technology Mentality." *Journal of Economic Issues* 23 (2): 569–578. https://doi.org/10.1080/00213624.1989.11504923
Tool, Marc R. 1953. *Philosophy of Neo-Institutionalism: Veblen, Dewey, and Ayres.* Unpublished Ph.D. Dissertation. University of Colorado.
———. 1979. *The Discretionary Economy: A Normative Theory of Political Economy.* Santa Monica: Goodyear Publishing Co. https://doi.org/10.4324/9781351304887
———. 1986. *Essays in Social Value Theory: A Neoinstitutionalist Contribution.* Armonk, NY: M.E. Sharpe. https://doi.org/10.4324/9781315494616
———. 2000. *Value Theory and Economic Progress. The Institutional Economics of J. Fagg Foster.* Boston: Kluwer Academic Publishing. https://doi.org/10.1007/978-94-011-3998-4
Underwood, Daniel A. 1998. "The Institutional Origins of Crises for Economy and Ecology." *Journal of Economic Issues* 32 (2): 513–522. https://doi.org/10.1080/00213624.1998.11506059
Veblen, Thorstein B. (1899) 1934. *The Theory of the Leisure Class.* New York: M-o-d-e-r-n Library.
———. (1904) 1932. *The Theory of Business Enterprise.* New York: Charles M. Scribner.
———. (1909) 1919. "The Limitations of Marginal Utility." In *The Place of Science in Modern Civilization and Other Essays.* New York: Viking Press.
———. (1914) 1946. *The Instinct of Workmanship and the State of the Industrial Arts.* New York: The Viking Press.
———. (1915) 1964. *Imperial Germany and the Industrial Revolution.* New York: Augustus M. Kelly.
———. (1917) 1964. *An Inquiry into the Nature of the Peace and the Terms of Its Perpetuation.* New York: Augustus M. Kelly.
———. (1919a) 1961. *The Place of Science in Modern Civilization and Other Essays.* New York: Russell and Russell.
———. (1919b) 1946. *The Vested Interest and the Common Man.* New York: The Viking Press.
———. (1921) 1965. *The Engineers and the Price System.* New York: Augustus M. Kelly.
———. (1923) 1964. *Absentee Ownership and Business Enterprise in Recent Times.* New York: Augustus M. Kelly.
———. (1934) 1964. *Essays in Our Changing Order,* edited by Leon Ardzrooni. New York: Augustus M. Kelly.
Waller, William T. 1982. "The Evolution of the Veblenian Dichotomy: Veblen, Hamilton, Ayres, and Foster." *Journal of Economic Issues* 16 (3): 757–771. https://doi.org/10.1080/00213624.1982.11504031
———. 1987. "Ceremonial Encapsulation and Corporate Cultural Hegemony." *Journal of Economic Issues* 21 (1): 321–328. https://doi.org/10.1080/00213624.1987.11504612
———. 2001. "Kickin'em while They're Down: Consumer Bankruptcy Reform." *Journal of Economic Issues* 35 (4): 871–888. https://doi.org/10.1080/00213624.2001.11506418
———. 2003. "It's Culture All the Way Down: The Cultural Economics of David Hamilton." *Journal of Economic Issues* 37 (1): 35–45. https://doi.org/10.1080/00213624.2003.11506552
———. 2006. "Walton Hale Hamilton." *Dictionary of American Economists,* edited by Ross Emmett. Bristol. Thoemmes Press. https://doi.org/10.5040/9781350052505-0187

———. 2013. Research Note: "The Unreasonable Society: Foster and the Limits of Instrumental Valuation." *Journal of Economic Issues* 47 (4): 1003–1010. https://doi.org/10.2753/JEI0021-3624470410

———. 2016. "Veblen, Instincts and Exchange." In *Marx, Veblen, and the Foundations of Heterodox Economics: Essays in Honor of John F. Henry*, edited by Tae-Hee Jo and Frederic S. Lee. New York: Routledge.

———. 2017a. "A Reconsideration of William Dugger's Analysis of Power." *Forum for Social Economics* published online September 11, 2017. https://doi.org/10.1080/07360932.2017.1370603

———. 2017b. "Public Policy Adrift: Veblen's Blind Drift and Neoliberalism." *Forum for Social Economics* 46 (3): 223–233. https://doi.org/10.1080/07360932.2016.1176948

———. 2017c. "Reconsidering Thorstein Veblen's Use of Instincts." *The Anthem Companion to Thorstein Veblen*, edited by Sidney Plotkin. London: Anthem Press. https://doi.org/10.2307/j.ctt1pd2kp8.6

Waller, William, and Mary V. Wrenn. 2021. "Feminist Institutionalism and Neoliberalism." *Feminist Economics*. Published online March 12, 2021. https://doi.org/10.1080/13545701.2021.1883194. Accessed March 26, 2021.

Watson, John B. 1913. "Psychology as the Behaviorist Views It." *Psychological Review* 20 (2): 158–177. https://doi.org/10.1037/h0074428

2

REASONABLE VALUE

John R. Commons and the Wisconsin tradition

Charles J. Whalen

Introduction: reasonable value versus instrumental value

I delivered my first professional conference paper at a meeting of the Association for Evolutionary Economics (AFEE) in 1986. The call for papers invited research describing actual processes of institutional change, and, because I considered myself an institutional labor economist in the tradition of John R. Commons, I examined a business, labor, and community response to severe economic dislocation in the Buffalo region of Western New York. In particular, my paper: traced the origin and development of the Buffalo-Erie County Labor-Management Council (BELMC) and its engagement with the region's key public- and private-sector economic actors; summarized a mixed record of BELMC success as seen by the participants and as judged against the organization's aims; and highlighted some of the challenges and limitations preventing such institutional change from achieving a more vigorous economic revitalization (Whalen 1987).

Overall, the paper was well received; but a discussant puzzled me by asking how I knew that the BELMC—one of many "area labor-management committees" that emerged around the country in the 1970s—had arrived at the *right* solutions to the region's challenges. Moreover, the discussant's concern went beyond the usual worry that such institutional arrangements could lead to "corporatist" solutions, thereby failing to serve many of the region's stakeholders (a problem that could be addressed by ensuring more community engagement and increasing reliance on participative decision-making processes). For the discussant, the heart of the matter was that I hadn't introduced an external, objective standard for evaluating institutional success.

That session revealed an institutionalist fault line that I hadn't previously recognized. On one side was the "reasonable value" perspective of Commons, which he described and applied while on the faculty at the University of Wisconsin,

DOI: 10.4324/9781003160434-2

resulting in the *Wisconsin tradition* of institutionalism. On the other side was the "instrumental value" perspective that found inspiration in the writings of Thorstein Veblen, coalesced in the work of Clarence Ayres at The University of Texas at Austin, and spread (especially in the Western portion of the United States) as institutionalism's *Texas tradition.*[1] A clear and unmistakably objective standard of assessment was found only on the Texas side of the fissure.

Since I was a Texas graduate student at the time of that AFEE session, I was perplexed by having missed the Wisconsin–Texas divide. It turns out that the fault line was easy to miss. After all, Ayres (1961) described his economics as offering a path toward a "reasonable" society; Wendell Gordon (1984, 380), Ayres's successor and torchbearer of Austin's institutionalist tradition, stressed that institutionalism does not point to a "most efficient" solution or "a best result;" and institutionalists such as Glen Atkinson (1987) approached economic policy by drawing not only on the notion of instrumentalism, often found in the work of Texas institutionalists, but also on Commons's concept of reasonable value.

Nevertheless, an "instrumental value" versus "reasonable value" divide did exist in the eyes of many institutionalists, and, in an article published only a few months after my AFEE session, Atkinson zeroed-in on the crux of the disagreement. Describing the policymaking process that he saw at the center of Commons's institutionalism, Atkinson (1987, 193) wrote that the process is "complicated by the fact that we do not all share the same experience exactly. Thus, we [often] will not see the present in the same way or agree on what is possible or desirable." Then he added:

> This differs from Clarence Ayres's notion that "we have a process in which all peoples have participated, which has the same meaning for all, and which therefore constitutes a standard of valuation for all. Everyone knows what *better* and *worse* mean with reference to tools, and all peoples judge such 'betterness' and 'worseness' by the same standard."
>
> *(Atkinson 1987, 193)*

A year later, Yngve Ramstad (1989) went further than Atkinson. Devoting his entire AFEE paper to an excavation of the instrumental–reasonable divide, Ramstad concluded provocatively that the two perspectives amounted to incompatible and competing paradigms.

More than 30 years later, today's institutionalism—at least as practiced in the United States—still shows signs of having a Texas branch grounded in instrumental value theory and a Wisconsin branch grounded in Commons's notion of reasonable value. The purpose of this chapter is to explain Commons's reasonable value concept as well as the theory and applications that emerged with it, and then to show how his perspective produced a Wisconsin branch of the institutionalist tradition. The chapter closes with a summary, a brief return to the matter of reasonable value versus instrumental value, and a final comment on the future of reasonable value.

Reasonable value

Commons's notion of reasonable value is at the heart of his conception of institutional economics. He developed and refined it throughout his career, reflecting in it his reformist aims, his evolving understanding of law, economics, and related academic disciplines, and his extensive participation in resolving real-world socioeconomic problems. We begin, therefore, with a brief overview of that career. Then Commons's concept of reasonable value is presented, along with an examination of its place in his economics.[2]

John R. Commons

Commons was born in 1862, and raised in Randolph County, Indiana. His family was always financially insecure, but his mother, an Oberlin College graduate and social-justice activist, took in boarders to help support the family, saving just enough to send John R. to Oberlin.[3] Inspired by the pro-labor stance of economist Richard T. Ely, Commons studied political economy as a graduate student under Ely and other professors at Johns Hopkins University, leaving Baltimore for a teaching position at Wesleyan University when he lacked the finances to complete his doctoral thesis.

After a string of short academic appointments, the last of which was at Syracuse University, from which he was fired because his pro-worker leanings did not sit well with the university's administration, Commons worked for five years (1899–1904) as an economic researcher and mediator of labor disputes, employed by organizations such as the United States Industrial Commission and National Civic Federation. Reflecting in his autobiography, Commons (1934a, 60) writes: "My dismissal [from Syracuse] turned out to be a fortunate happening. It drove me out for five years to live in the struggles of human beings." In the wake of his firing, Commons's writing took on a softer tone, but his research focused more than ever on the problem of unemployment and other worker struggles.[4]

In 1904, Ely, who was then at the University of Wisconsin, arranged for Commons to join him on the faculty and contribute to a history of labor and industrial society; Commons made Madison his home for the rest of his career.[5] According to Paul McNulty (1984, 150–151), author of an exhaustive history of labor economics, Commons's arrival in Madison quickly established its university as the nation's leading center for labor studies. "No other single scholar turned as many graduate students in the direction of labor studies as did Commons." John Dennis Chasse (2017, 3), author of a recent biography of Commons, adds: "It would be hard to find a teacher whose students exercised as much influence on public policy." In Wisconsin, Commons and his students sponsored four reform programs of national significance: civil service reform, public utilities regulation, workers' (accident) compensation, and unemployment insurance. Commons's students then brought the Wisconsin tradition to the nation's capital, helping to shape the New Deal and Great Society.[6]

Economic value

Commons believed that economics is all about values and valuation. *Legal Foundations of Capitalism*, for example, was his attempt to work out an evolutionary and volitional theory of value (Commons 1924, vii). Thus, we start our sketch of Commons's perspective with his discussion of economic value, which traces the evolution of economic theory from use value, to exchange value, and, ultimately, to reasonable value.

Commons (1934b, 173–174) argued that Adam Smith represented a turning point in economics because although Smith recognized two types of value, "value in use" and "value in exchange," he moved beyond earlier economists' focus on use value and instead "considered that economic science had to do only with exchange value." Commons suggested that *use* value involves a relation of "man to nature" and leads to "engineering economics" and "home economics," which involves making the most efficient or productive use of land or other resources under one's control, including one's own labor (Commons 1924, 3). In this context, he frequently offered the example of "the isolated farmer," who "produces for his own use" (see, for example, Commons 1934b, 85, 439). In contrast, *exchange* value involves "a relation of man to man" and leads to a study of the "business economy" and "political economy" (Commons 1924, 3). Scarcity, not efficiency, is at the heart of an economics centered on exchange value (Commons 1950, 94).[7]

Of course, "Smith actually employed the idea of use-value in all his reasonings," Commons (1934b, 174) acknowledged; and the source of value in Smith can be traced to labor, consistent with Commons's view of use-value theories. But Smith's "productive" labor was that which "created a *vendible* commodity which could be saved and could thereafter constitute an effective demand to the extent of its use value … . A use value for him was an attribute that existed physically and could be accumulated and passed on in *exchange*" (Commons 1934b, 187, emphases added). Moreover, conventional economics eventually made the complete shift to a focus on exchange value via markets—and borrowed Smith's notion of the invisible hand as a way to argue that it all works out neatly.

Although Commons and Veblen certainly had different views and aims, Commons (1924, vii) found Veblen's criticisms of conventional economics "brilliant" and accepted his suggestion that an evolutionary theory of value must be constructed by examining the changing habits and customs of social life. Thus, it's no surprise that Commons approached standard economics, which he was trying to transcend, as a tradition grounded in what Veblen considered *ceremony*, not matter-of-fact scientific reality. In fact, Commons (1924, 2) was quite clear on this, describing as "mythical entities" not only Smith's invisible hand, but also the animating forces behind more recent economists' arguments that a market economy tends toward equilibrium.

Exchange-value economics—the standard economics of his time and our own—is what Commons (1950, 293) called *laissez-faire* economics. In that economics, government is not to interfere with market exchanges (except, perhaps, to correct for an observed market failure, such as is caused by externalities), playing an economic role only by protecting liberty and property rights, concepts that draw on yet another mythical entity—the "natural right of man" (Commons 1924, 385). In reality, however, government is *always* there, defining as well as securing liberty and property.[8]

Since rights are, in fact, afforded by the government, exchange value is strongly influenced by government action—that is, by public action that has evolved (and continues to evolve) and contains a *volitional* element. What shapes such action and the social volition expressed through it? Commons and his students dug into centuries of legal decisions to find out. They were, in other words, trying to move beyond exchange value, which obscures more than it reveals, and get the whole story that Commons described as an evolutionary and volitional theory of value. The result, they realized, was the story of capitalism's legal foundations (Commons 1924, vii–viii).

But what to call this new, more comprehensive theory of value? The answer came from Commons's research, which revealed, time and again, that the decisive factor in a court decision was whether an outcome or legal interpretation was *reasonable* (Commons 1924, vii; 1934b, 704–705). Thus, he stressed that economics had, over time, moved from a focus on use value, to the study (through a clouded lens) of exchange value, and was finally becoming a science which understands that real-world economic value is (at least in the United States and other similar societies), in fact, *reasonable* value.

The evolving meaning of property

Just as value evolved from use value to exchange value and then to reasonable value, so too has the definition of property evolved. This is easy to see from a look at US legal history. According to the Fourteenth Amendment to the Constitution (ratified in 1868), states are not permitted to deprive any person of life, liberty, or property, without due process of law. But in the United States, property meant primarily use value, not exchange value, until 1890. For example, when New Orleans butchers disputed the authority of their city to issue a monopoly franchise to a central slaughterhouse, claiming that their property was their occupation and their liberty was their right to choose and practice that occupation, the Supreme Court (in 1873) disagreed, arguing that no physical property (embodying use value) had been taken (Commons 1924, 11–12).

In 1890, however, the Supreme Court expanded the meaning of property to include exchange value. In the "Minnesota Rate Case," the court agreed with railroad owners that a state could not control rail passenger and freight rates—or regulate other businesses—without a procedure that provides for due process. The Minnesota case did not involve taking title or possession of any physical property (use value); it instead involved the state's power to alter "exchange value"—and the Supreme Court's ruling expanded and shifted the definition of property "from physical things having only use value to the exchange value of anything" (Commons 1924, 14–16).

The Minnesota Rate Case also brought reasonable value into the picture. The Supreme Court concluded that state rate controls and regulations needed to pass the judiciary's test of reasonableness—a test that, over time, eventually meant both that the purpose of government regulation must be reasonable and that the particulars (and consequences) of the regulation must also be reasonable (Commons 1924, 15, 341, 385).[9] Moreover, the judiciary's attention to the *public purpose* confirmed for Commons that law and economics are inextricably intertwined, both in reality and in his volitional theory of value: What we observe in both fields

> are the present outcome of rights of property and powers of government, which have been fashioned and refashioned in the past by courts, legislatures and executives through control of human behavior by means of working rules, directed towards *purposes* deemed useful, or just, by the law-givers and law interpreters.
>
> *(Commons 1924, 378, emphasis added)*[10]

Another way to view the evolving meaning of property involves the concepts of corporeal, incorporeal, and intangible property. The original form of property was "corporeal"—meaning "ownership of a physical body or 'corpus,' such as land, cattle, or slaves"—and "government protected those possessing such property" (Commons 1950, 79–80). Commons writes:

> Ownership [of corporeal property] consisted mainly in the expectation that the sovereign, by physical power, would not prevent physical trespass upon the "corpus" by those not deemed to be its owners. The rules adopted by the courts of England and America for preventing this trespass, and thereby permitting the owner to exercise his own free will upon the "corpus," became known as "the common law."

Over time, the growing influence of merchants led to a new form of property, a form associated with money lending. This became known as "incorporeal" property: "the duty of the debtor to pay money, known either as a credit or its equivalent debt" (Commons 1950, 80). Thus, incorporeal property, in the form of a debt that that would be recognized and enforced by courts—consistent, for example, with the US Constitution's recognition of the obligation of contracts—represents another dimension of the evolution from use value to exchange value. Moreover, reasonable value enters the picture as well because legislatures and courts have often used their authority to regulate lenders.

The meaning of property changed further with the Minnesota Rate Case mentioned above. In that case, the Court recognized that government regulation threatened to deprive businesses not of corporeal or incorporeal property but of "intangible" property—the "value of future sales" or the "expected earnings power" of their operations. The notion of intangible property was reinforced by the Court's decision in the "Adams Express Case" of 1897, which allows businesses to be assessed according to the estimated current value of their future stream of earnings—even though that intangible, capitalized value is usually many times greater than the worth of the sum of the separate pieces of tangible property. While corporeal property is tangible, and incorporeal property is the present value of payment of future debts, intangible property includes (for example) patents, trademarks, business goodwill, trade secrets, and the right to do business (Commons 1924, 18–19, 172–173; 1934b, 651–652; 1950, 80).

Transactions

Commons's theory of reasonable value is a *transactional* theory of value. It's not a use-value theory, which he relegates to the world of an isolated Robinson Crusoe "where nothing is produced for sale" (Commons 1934b, 439). But neither is it the narrow, exchange-value theory of conventional economics, which overlooks the indispensable role of government and considers only market-based exchanges. The transactional theory subsumes market exchanges and places them in their broader context (Commons 1934b, 58; 1950, 43).

Here's how Commons trains his sights on, defines, and describes transactions. First, he argues that investigations of economic activity begin with human will: "The human will is central to economic life." Next, he maintains that the place where wills meet—to produce, transfer, or define and condition property (or wealth)—is in "joint action," which Commons calls a *transaction*. Each transaction is characterized simultaneously by conflicting interests and mutual dependence, out of which some order must be fashioned; and all transactions occur in a cultural and institutional context that influences the terms agreed upon by the involved parties. Commons then identifies three types of transactions: managerial transactions; bargaining transactions; and rationing transactions (Commons 1931; 1934b, 57–62, 108–109; 1950, 21, 43).

Managerial transactions occur between managers and subordinates. They are, for example, the transactions that occur in a factory or office in the course of producing a good or service for future sale: The manager or supervisor gives the orders, and a worker performs the necessary tasks. By means of such transactions, materials are allocated within the enterprise (but ownership does not change hands) and production occurs, with the aim of production efficiency usually serving as a key consideration. The terms and conditions of employment and operations—the "working rules"—are agreed upon or otherwise established in advance (Commons 1934b, 64–67; 1950, 21).

Bargaining transactions are those involving the negotiation and transfer of ownership of property (corporeal, incorporeal, or intangible). Commons (1934b, 68) identifies the parties in such transactions as "legal equals," but he certainly doesn't assume equality of bargaining power. In fact, Commons offers a variety of reasons why some parties might be in a much better position than others to wait for more favorable terms—he even mentions that enterprises sometimes restrict the supply of their products to stabilize or boost prices. Sifting through it all, scarcity—regardless of whether attributable to chance or design—appears as a key factor in bargaining transactions: unequal power seems most often traceable to disparities in available alternatives and to other differential effects of scarcity on the negotiating parties (Commons 1924, 20–21; 1934b, 59–64, 336–348, 387; 1950, 165).

Rationing transactions are policies made by organizations to govern their overall operations. For example, they are the decisions of boards of directors of private-sector entities, as well as the legal, executive, and judicial decisions of government. They "lay down the working rules" and "apportion burdens and benefits" within each relevant organization; and the Supreme Court has the ultimate say in the context of the United States (Commons 1934b, 67–69; 1950, 43). Thus, rationing transactions provide the institutional context for—and determine what's permissible in the realm of—managerial and bargaining transactions. In the end, Commons (1934b, 58, emphasis added) argues, "[I]t is *society* that, by its rules of order, controls ownership of and access to the forces of nature."[11]

The transactional theory of value analyzes any of the aforementioned types of transactions through a five-dimensional lens. Each dimension represents one of Commons's interrelated co-determinants of value: (1) futurity (the expectational dimension), (2) efficiency (the quantity and productivity dimension), (3) scarcity (the supply-and-demand or price dimension), (4) custom (the dimension of working rules or social assumptions and practices, which create individual habits), and (5) sovereignty (the dimension of authority and its power, especially as embodied in "the state"). Commons maintained that a full understanding of any transaction requires attention to all of these dimensions or factors—each of which is subject to changing characteristics over time—as well as to how they influence each other (Commons 1934b, 45; 1950, 73–112).[12]

As an illustration, the following is a simplified example—stripped of its evolutionary component and most factor interactions—of elements to be taken into account when Commons's theory is employed to explain a bargaining transaction. Here is some of what must be considered: (a) each party has expectations concerning both the future state of the economy and the future valuations of the specific ownership rights being transferred (futurity); (b) the parties agree on a particular kind, quality, and quantity of property being transferred (efficiency); (c) they agree, operating within the context of existing customs and laws, on a price (scarcity, but also custom); (d) they may agree on an interest charge for delayed payment (futurity); (e) they agree on a method of payment (custom); and (f) the state stands ready to enforce performance of the agreement (sovereignty).

Reasonableness

Commons's transactional theory of value is a general theory of socioeconomic activity—a general theory of social provisioning. It can be applied to analyze any sort of economic system. In the real world, there is no *laissez-faire* economics, no self-regulating economy, only the *control economics* of a socially regulated economy—and such an economy comes in many forms, including assorted varieties of capitalism, fascism, and communism. Moreover, in any economic system, institutions are products of collective action, ranging from those that control individual action to those that liberate and even expand (the human capacity for) such action (Commons 1931; 1950, 293).

Common's transactional theory becomes a theory of reasonable value when the scope of inquiry narrows to a liberal, democratic market economy. That is, we find ourselves in the realm of an inquiry into reasonable value when society is characterized by features including freedom of speech, a free press, voluntary associations (freedom of association), popular elections, representative government, equal opportunity for choice, fair competition, equality of bargaining power (or at least processes and good-faith bargaining that keep inequalities in check), and a judiciary—which determines the contours of all the preceding elements—committed to due process and reasonableness (Commons 1924, vii, 15; 1934b, 63, 898, 903). Reasonable value is not a specific outcome: "Reasonable value is the evolutionary collective determination of what is reasonable in view of all the changing political, moral, and economic circumstances and the personalities that arise therefrom to the Supreme [Court] bench" (Commons 1934b, 683–684). The outcomes produced at a particular time and place are found and understood by means of academic investigation, and Commons's theory becomes relevant as a guide to such work.

To be sure, a society governed by reasonable value does not rely on reasonableness of the courts alone. Disputes have to be resolved in a reasonable manner at other levels as well—including, for example, differences between companies and labor unions, and disagreements over regulation of industry, situations that, if left to be resolved on their own, might turn entirely on the use of violence or economic or political power. Thus, Commons advocated institutional mechanisms that would enable disputants to meet, deliberate, and negotiate on an equal basis.

Consider, for example, the types of disputes just mentioned: industry and regulatory disputes. For industrywide labor disputes, Commons (1934a, 71–73, 173) advocated forums, which he called "constitutional government in industry," that would give equal voice to employers and employees and would reach collective-bargaining agreements—sometimes with the assistance of staff researchers, mediators, or even arbitrators (jointly approved, and as a last resort). For regulatory disputes, he proposed the notion of an administrative commission, which would include, via an advisory committee, representatives of all stakeholders as well as a professional staff of investigators to help identify and expand the use of "existing best practices" (Commons 1913, 395–424; 1934a, 156; 1934b, 742, 848–849; 1950, 266).

Through such institutions, Commons was seeking what he called "collective democracy" (Commons 1950, 24) and what others focusing on his work in the field of industrial relations have called "due process in industry" (Gomberg 1985, 264). As he wrote in his autobiography, "It is not revolutions and strikes that we want, but collective bargaining on something like an organized equilibrium of equality" (Commons 1934a, 73). Such institutions and their deliberative processes are at the heart of Commons's reasonable capitalism—and a key part of his attempt to "save capitalism by making it good" (Commons 1934a, 143). Writing in 1934, he was convinced this path was "the only way to save us" from communism or fascism (Commons 1934a, 73).

Commons believed there was no external, objective standard that could be used to determine reasonable value. Instead, he saw reasonable value as a social product—the result of "joint valuation" (Commons 1934b, 681). He wrote: "It is not what 'I think' ought to be, but what 'we think' ought to and can be attained, as a going concern" (by which he meant any social organization, from the smallest club to the largest corporation, nation, or international body) (Commons 1934b, 743).[13]

To be sure, Commons had his own preferences regarding economic activity, but they were primarily favored *processes*, not outcomes—processes associated with the sort of institutional mechanisms described above. For example, he favored a "consensus of opinion" between labor and management over a divided court ruling or a mandatory arbitration decision, and he preferred policy solutions modeled after "actually existent best practices" to statutes produced by political log-rolling (Commons 1900, 70; 1934b, 742–743, 846, 862, 900–901; 1950, 283–284). The common thread was that Commons wanted decisions arrived at collaboratively through investigation and deliberation, via processes that provided for the affected parties to be directly involved and even play a role in negotiating the outcomes.[14]

In Commons's view, there was something approaching "objective" (which he put in quotation marks) in a law requiring a commission to identify and insist upon existing best practice as a standard of business conduct. He also understood that such a standard led to social outcomes that were superior to regulations defining "reasonable" as "ordinary, average, or customary practices" (Commons 1934a, 155–156). As a result, beginning with his involvement in drafting workers' compensation legislation for Wisconsin in 1911, Commons sought to incorporate his preferred (best-practice–oriented) definition of reasonableness directly into the legislation he helped draft (Commons 1934b, 742–743).

But the US Supreme Court is, of course, the ultimate arbiter of reasonableness in the United States, and its definition of what is reasonable as well as its standards for assessing reasonableness were recognized by Commons as flexible and malleable, and they remain so today (Garrett 2017). In 1898, the Court gave what Commons (1934b, 683) described as a "perplexing definition" of reasonable value: each conflicting view on a case must be given "its 'due weight' under the circumstances." Yet that definition also resonated with him as "the common sense definition under which all rational and semi-rational beings [actually] operate as best they can."

The process of investigation can force us to confront and transcend our individual and collective biases, but we do not live in a utopia. "Hence reasonable value contains a large amount of stupidity, passion, and mistake," wrote Commons (1934b, 156, 699, 742). Indeed, he argued

> it is more important to know who the [people] are on the Supreme Court bench [and to know the assumptions they take for granted] than to know what the law is. The Constitution is not what it says it is—it is what the Court says it is.
>
> *(Commons 1934b, 683, 697)*

Of course, what the Court or any other deliberative body finds to be reasonable today is not set in stone for all time. Reasonableness and reasonable value are collective and dynamic; they change over time. Conditions change, new conflicts emerge, and the notion of what is reasonable evolves.

So it has been throughout history, from feudalism to the present. In each historical stage,

> new concepts of rights and reasonable practices have rapidly impinged upon the old, until we reach the present contesting concepts of reasonable value in a world that inherits the old but is compelled by economic maladjustment to evolve a future *new* out of the obsolescent *old* .
>
> *(Commons 1934b, 682, emphases in original)*[15]

Highlighting the reality of an uncertain future as both an additional social challenge and a starting point for social change, Commons continued:

> It is not a rational state of society that determines action; it is a marvelously irrational and complex set of expectations that confronts the participants in transactions. And it is a situation that changes from day to day and century to century. Within this changing complexity and uncertain futurity, they must act *now*. It is out of these complexities and uncertainties that the concepts of reasonable practices and reasonable values emerge and change the institutions themselves from day to day and age to age.
>
> *(Commons 1934b, 683, emphasis in original)*[16]

Applications and the Wisconsin tradition

Commons applied his transactional theory and conception of reasonable value to an astonishing variety of projects. This section surveys Commons's applications of his perspective as well as some of the subsequent research associated with the Wisconsin wing of the institutionalist tradition. Attention to issues involving work and employment is a main thread through much of this literature, but the full scope of topics addressed is wide: ranging, for example, from applications involving agricultural development and resource use to payday lending and other finance matters.

Commons's applications

Much of Commons's published research can be separated into two broad categories: historical accounts and problem-solving analyses. A large portion of his work is historical, including *Legal Foundations of Capitalism*, which traces how reasonable value evolved out of court decisions and "the habits and customs of social life" (Commons 1924, vii), and *Institutional Economics*, which locates his institutionalism within the history of economic thought (Commons 1934b). Working with his students, Commons also produced a masterful, ten-volume history of American industrial society as well as the classic (two-volume) *History of Labour in the United States* (Commons et al. 1918). In addition, Commons used his transactional theory and reasonable value concept to help solve real-world problems and enact policy reform in areas ranging from regulation of utilities to workplace safety. Two applications of his institutional economics are briefly summarized here as illustrations of Commons's work: his theory of the evolution of the US labor movement and his analysis of business cycles.[17]

Evolution of the labor movement

Commons's theory on the emergence and development of America's labor movement was first presented in 1909 (Commons 1909). In the following year, it was published as the preface to his history of industrial society, and in 1934 it appeared (in an updated form) in *Institutional Economics* (Commons 1934b, 763–788). The theory traces American capitalism through three stages: (1) merchant capitalism, (2) industrial capitalism, and (3) banker capitalism. In response, workers' organizations emerged, first as craft unions of skilled workers and then as industrial unions of factory workers. Details from the shoe industry keep his theory grounded in institutional reality, and the expansion of markets holds a place of particular importance in the analysis.

At the time of Commons's writing in 1934, it was not clear that labor organizations had found an innovative way to respond to banker capitalism.[18] We now know, however, that enactment of protective labor legislation (including unemployment compensation, social security, and the minimum wage) and the National Labor Relations Act of 1935 (which guaranteed private-sector workers the right to organize and bargain collectively) were key elements of the New Deal. Those developments were consistent with an observation Commons offered toward the end of his original (1909) statement on the evolution of the US labor movement: In the end, workers "resort either to private organizations equipped with coercive weapons" to defend themselves, "or else they seek to persuade or compel the government" to come to their aid. He concluded:

> In this way the contest of classes or interests enters the field of politics, and the laws of the land, and even the very framework of government, are the outcome of a struggle both to extend markets and to ward off their menace.
>
> *(Commons 1909, 79)*[19]

Business cycles

Between World War I and the start of the Great Depression, the American economy experienced several inflationary booms and deflationary busts with high unemployment. That decade is when Commons came to view business cycles as the most important of all labor problems (see, for example, Commons 1925a).[20] His investigations produced an expectations-driven, profit-margin theory of cycles as well as policy recommendations aimed at dampening and coping with them (Commons 1922, 19–20; 1934b, 508–589).[21]

Commons believed that both unemployment insurance and monetary policy had important roles to play in preventing economic downturns. His unemployment insurance proposal was designed so employers would incur a financial liability for laying off workers (Commons 1922; 1925a). He saw the liability as a factor that both employers and bankers would need to consider before allowing enterprises to expand. Thus, he believed firms would have an incentive to better regulate their growth and contraction. Meanwhile, Commons (1925b) wanted the Federal Reserve to use open-market operations, the discount rate, and moral suasion to stabilize the average price level. That, he believed, was the most effective way to stabilize the general credit situation, thereby helping to prevent an unsustainable boom.

There was even a role for an advisory committee in Commons's proposals for both unemployment insurance and monetary policy. On unemployment insurance, he wrote:

> All the state needs to do [after the insurance system is established] is to decide disputed claims for compensation, just as it does in the case of accident compensation. And in making these decisions the state umpire is aided [under proposed legislation] by representatives selected by the employees and by the employers and the trade unions, so that there may be little or no complaint of injustice.
>
> *(Commons 1922, 22–23)*

On the Federal Reserve, Commons wrote that "a powerful advisory committee"—with representatives from organizations representing manufacturers, farmers, workers, and other stakeholders—should replace the existing Federal Open Market Committee, which represents only the banking community (Commons 1950, 256–257).

However, Commons recognized that cycles could at best be tamed, not eliminated. "What is really meant by stabilization of prices," he wrote, is the avoidance of "excessive peaks and slumps" (Commons 1925b, 45). Thus, Commons saw the need for government action to cope with a downturn once it hits. Moreover, because he understood it's much easier for monetary policy to prevent an inflationary boom than to ignite a recovery and reduce joblessness in the face of low business confidence, he wrote that a more direct form of public action is needed during a recession or depression:

> In order to create the consumer demand, on which business depends for sales, the government itself must create the new money and go completely over the head of the entire banking system by paying it out directly to the unemployed, either as relief or for construction of public works, as it does in times of war.
>
> *(Commons 1934b, 589–590)*[22]

The Wisconsin tradition

Commons had a tremendous influence on his Wisconsin students and, with their collaboration and continued work even after his retirement, on public policy at the state and federal levels. Today, his institutionalist approach to economics—the Wisconsin tradition—lives on in the work of a small but intrepid band of scholars, especially in the United States, United Kingdom, France, and Japan. What follows is a survey of some of the work of those contributing to that tradition. It is meant to be illustrative, not comprehensive, and I focus on research that applies Commons's perspective and concepts to contemporary real-world problems, rather than on studies in the history of economic thought.

Wisconsin students

The Wisconsin students with a direct connection to Commons became a highly accomplished group of academics, policy advisers, government analysts, and public-sector administrators. For example, Edwin Witte, who replaced Commons when he retired at the university, served as executive secretary to the Wisconsin Industrial Commission (which oversaw the state's workers' compensation program) and advised President Franklin Roosevelt on creation of the Social Security Act. According to Chasse (1997, 943; 2017, 3), Witte—one of six of Commons's students who became president of the American Economic Association—"followed the Commons process methodically right down to the setting up of outside advisory boards." Other leading Wisconsin students from that era (all of whom are discussed in Chasse 2017) include:

- Selig Perlman, who became a distinguished labor historian;
- Kenneth Parsons, who helped Commons finish his last book and taught agricultural economics at Wisconsin;
- Elizabeth Brandeis Raushenbush and Paul Raushenbush, who shaped unemployment compensation for Wisconsin and the United States; and

- Wilber Cohen, who went to Washington to help Witte with social security legislation, became the Social Security Board's first professional employee, served as Secretary of Health, Education, and Welfare under President Lyndon Johnson, and, at the end of Johnson's term, was the last of the Wisconsin team to leave the nation's capital.

A pair of academic articles by Wisconsin graduates, one by Parsons and the other by Bruce Kaufman (who earned his Wisconsin doctorate in 1978), offer examples of how Wisconsin students have used Commons's ideas in their own work. Parsons (1986) applied Commons's ideas to agricultural policies in developing nations, resulting in three main observations.[23] The first is that achieving technical efficiency is at best only *half* the job of devising effective policies to address economic development and resource use; showing respect for and working within the context of existing procedural rules (customs), even if the goal is to nudge them in the direction of reform, is also essential to successful policymaking. Another observation is that development economists must be concerned about more than market prices; they must also be willing to foster discussions about social-value judgments, the need to create security of expectations, and "reasonable" approaches to achieving economic order. The third observation is that the work of the development economist is best aimed at achieving a coherent, productive, and participatory national economic and political order (or "commonwealth"), rather than a system of "free market" rules.[24]

Kaufman (2010) relies on Commons's institutionalism to outline four rationales for minimum-wage legislation. He argues that minimum wages: offset imperfect competition and inequality of bargaining power; promote macroeconomic stabilization and full employment; contribute to efficiency and economic growth; and account for labor market externalities and social costs of labor. Kaufman acknowledges his article's emphasis on efficiency arguments, but stresses that "normative arguments are also important" in institutionalism. He concludes: "Balance, pragmatism, progress, and human values are the leitmotivs of institutional economics (and industrial relations) in this and all other policy issues" (Kaufman 2010, 450).[25]

Ramstad, Chasse, and Atkinson

In the 1980s, a number of economists began digging into Commons's writings to interpret his economic contributions and find insight applicable to contemporary issues. Among those economists, Yngve Ramstad, John Dennis Chasse, and Glen Atkinson stand out for the quality and quantity of their research output. Here are a few examples of their applications of Commons's institutionalism.

Ramstad composed three especially noteworthy research papers applying Commons's ideas and theories. The first, published in 1987, applied Commons's theory of reasonable value to argue that US trade law "is seriously deficient" and to defend the use of import tariffs to prevent "destructive competition" harmful to workers (Ramstad 1987, 18, 22). A few years later, Ramstad (1991a, 432) demonstrated that the "negotiated economy" of Denmark represents "a pragmatic realization" of what Commons had in mind as the best way to achieve reasonable value, concluding with the suggestion that Commons's economics was of particular relevance "for those struggling with the challenges of revitalizing the economies of Eastern Europe." Then, in 2004, Ramstad and colleague Richard McIntyre coauthored a book chapter that uses Commons's analysis of the labor market to explain the business trends of outsourcing production to low-wage countries and subcontracting work to other enterprises operating in the United States. Those trends are part of what Commons called the "sweating system," and McIntyre and Ramstad (2004, 298–299) conclude by endorsing Commons's call for labor market regulation as the only viable way to reverse the growing reliance on that system.

Chasse's body of work includes two articles that focus heavily on applying Commons's theory and arguments to the problems of our time.[26] One, published in 2008, argues that trade agreements of recent decades have not benefited US workers, just as trade policies failed to help workers in Commons's time. Chasse's article then demonstrates the continuing relevance of proposals offered by Commons a century ago: an excise tax that would "create an incentive for firms to follow the most ethical employers" and a commission, with an advisory board composed of stakeholder representatives, "to keep labor law abreast of changing risks in evolving labor markets" (Chasse 2008, 1137). The other article, published in 2018, explores the correlation between union decline and erosion of support for democratic principles and institutions in the United States and abroad, showing that this is consistent with Commons's strong belief that union suppression endangers representative democracy (Chasse 2018).

Atkinson, working alone and with various colleagues, has applied Commons's economics to a variety of topics. In 1996, for example, Atkinson and Ted Oleson (1996) presented a case study of the Nevada tax system to illustrate their understanding of Commons's approach to institutionalist research. A few years later, they joined with Mark Nichols to draw on Commons's notion of the "menace of competition" (contained in his theory of the labor movement) for the purpose of understanding the evolution of the gambling industry and the development of gambling regulation (Atkinson, Nichols, and Oleson 2000, 621). Atkinson also combined insight from Commons's *Legal Foundations of Capitalism* with Hyman Minsky's financial-sector research in order to trace the evolution of US capitalism from Commons's stage of *banker* capitalism to Minsky's era of *money manager* capitalism (Atkinson 2010).[27] More recently, Atkinson has collaborated with lawyer Stephen P. Paschall and others to draw on Commons as a foundation for examining the continuing evolution of the meaning of property and the legal status of corporations (see Atkinson, Hake and Paschall 2019; Atkinson and Paschall 2011; Atkinson and Paschall 2016; Atkinson et al. 2014).

Briggs, Marshall, and Whalen

Another three institutionalists within the Wisconsin tradition are Vernon Briggs, Ray Marshall, and this author—labor economists who broadly conceive that field as encompassing all aspects of work and employment, including industrial relations and macro-labor issues such as full employment. Consistent with the perspective and work of Commons, each has considerable experience conducting field research and working with labor, management, and government practitioners.

Much of the work of Briggs and Marshall has focused on the development and use of a nation's human resources, both to ensure opportunity and security for workers and to provide a healthy economy for society overall.[28] In a 1987 article, Briggs (1987, 1209) linked that work to Commons's search for "pragmatic ways to address the inevitable human adjustment problems associated with the advances of industrialization." In a book published that same year, Marshall stressed that a major problem with business and public policy decision-making in the United States is that workers' voices are seldom heard. Building upon Commons's emphasis on collective democracy and negotiated problem-solving, Marshall sought to correct that shortcoming by encouraging the use, at all levels of economic decision-making, of what he called "consensus-building mechanisms" (Marshall 1982; 1987; 1993).[29]

My own work follows the general direction of Briggs and Marshall (who were my professors at Cornell and Texas, respectively). For example, about a decade after completing research that underscored the links between Commons's economic approach and regional labor-management partnerships in Western New York during the 1970s and 1980s (see Whalen 1988), I found myself working in that region (as part of a public service initiative) and studying its new era of partnerships as a participant observer (engaged in facilitating and conducting research to support collaborative initiatives). The result of my interviews and observations was published in 2011; in particular, I applied Commons's institutionalism to compare the labor-management initiatives of the two eras (Whalen 2011). In other work, I have drawn on Commons for other purposes, including: investigating worker insecurity; addressing the challenge of securing full employment; and outlining core concepts of institutionalist public finance (Whalen 1998; 2010; 2013; 2020a).[30]

Mansell, Mayhew, Kasper, and other recent contributors

Other scholars applying Commons's institutionalism to contemporary issues include Robin Mansell, Anne Mayhew, and Sherry Davis Kasper. Mansell, who teaches in London, draws upon Commons in her research on communications policy. In a 2006 article, for example, she relied on Commons's perspective on the origin and development of working rules to study a project of the European Commission that sought to establish an open-source Internet-based platform for small-business services (Mansell 2006). More recently, American institutionalists Mayhew (2014) and Kasper (2014) contributed papers to a symposium on how Commons's ideas are relevant to the study of economics and finance in the wake of the global financial crisis of 2007–2009: Mayhew uses Commons's lens to examine how communities might respond to mortgage crises with an innovative use of eminent domain (and how such an approach might alter the way economists analyze consumer spending and borrowing); and Kasper uses Commons's analysis of institutions, as updated by A. Allan Schmid, to examine the growth of payday lending (sometimes called fringe banking) in Tennessee.[31]

Recent contributors also include Anastasia Nesvetailova, Katherine V.W. Stone, and Agata Gemzik-Salwach. Nesvetailova (2015), a London-based professor of international politics and an expert in financial innovation, uses Commons's concept of futurity to analyze the role of shadow banking in the global financial crisis. Stone (2017), a US-based law professor, considers contemporary possibilities for achieving a legally enforceable right to employment in the United States, drawing on both Commons's support for such a right early in his career and Commons's conception of the role of the state in economic life. Gemzik-Salwach (2020), an economics professor in southeastern Poland, also draws on Commons's conception of the state in the economy, as well as his approach to institutions, to analyze the economic and social consequences of changes to Poland's banking regulations following the global financial crisis. The work of these three scholars combines with the other research discussed in this chapter to illustrate not only the continuing relevance of Commons's institutionalism, but also the ability of the Wisconsin tradition to conduct contemporary, applied scholarship in a variety of geographic locations, academic disciplines, and subject areas.

Summary and conclusions

This chapter has covered a lot of ground. It has explained the notion of reasonable value at the heart of Commons's conception of institutional economics—a notion he developed and refined throughout his career, and in which he incorporated both his own reformist aims and a deep understanding of real-world economic activity. It has explored Commons's view of the evolving meaning of property and the multifaceted nature of economic transactions, both of which highlight not only the role of social institutions, especially the state (government), in shaping socioeconomic activity, but also the longstanding use of reasonable value as an evaluative standard in the United States. And it has shown that while Commons emphasized that reasonable value must be socially determined, he also advocated using particular institutional arrangements and processes to make that determination.

The chapter has also illustrated how Commons, his students, and subsequent generations of scholars have applied his institutionalist perspective. As we have shown, that perspective has been used to analyze a wide range of socioeconomic topics. Today, Common's Wisconsin tradition continues in the work of scholars based in a variety of countries and academic disciplines.[32]

Reasonable or instrumental?

Having so closely examined Commons's reasonable value perspective, it seems useful to briefly return to the matter mentioned at the start of the chapter: reasonable value versus instrumental value. From the perspective of Commons's reasonable value, the vantage point from which I conducted the regional labor-management research described in the introduction, as long as the parties participating in the process were engaged in good-faith negotiations—involving persuasion and investigative methods, not coercion or rough methods (such as threats of violence or adversarial use of economic power)—then the committee's new initiatives and institutional changes, arrived at jointly and by consensus, were indeed the *right* solutions for those parties and their constituents, given existing conditions, current information, and the alternatives available. To be sure, it is certainly appropriate for a researcher to assess an organization's performance against its own aims, and even to recommend other policies, institutional changes, or courses of action. What *doesn't* exist in Commons's perspective, however, is an external, objective standard for evaluating institutional success.

By highlighting the gap between the reasonable value approach of Commons's institutionalism and the instrumental value perspective of the Texas tradition, Ramstad (1989) spurred a spirited discussion among institutionalists in the late 1980s and early 1990s.[33] According to Ramstad, each of these types of institutionalism has its own criterion of social value, and a fundamental difference is that the *instrumental value* approach introduces a standard of value from outside the socioeconomic phenomena being investigated (what is "good" or "right" represents "instrumental" knowledge, rooted in matter-of-fact cause-and-effect technology, whereas what is "bad" or "wrong" represents "ceremonial" behavior), while the *reasonable value* approach looks within the realm being investigated and, under the conditions described in this chapter, lets the parties decide for themselves what is good, bad, right, and wrong.[34] Moreover, Ramstad (1989, 766) argues that, for adherents to the instrumental value approach, "the instrumental criterion is equated with the human life process itself, thereby putatively providing an objective and transcultural orientation to the problem of identifying an appropriate value criterion."[35]

Having reacquainted myself with the relevant literature in preparing this chapter, I believe Ramstad (1989, 765–766) is correct: the reasonable value and instrumental value approaches are each rooted in their own criterion of value, and there have indeed been instances in which those in the instrumental value camp have seemed to offer a "normative compass" that, in their view, transcends culture.[36] I also agree with Ramstad's (1989, 766) observation that guidance from instrumental value theory seems inadequate to help an analyst choose between alternative institutional adjustments and decide "what 'instrumental efficiency' might mean with respect to the complex tradeoffs that actually exist in a specific case, other than whatever the analyst him/herself considers to be 'instrumental.'"

At the same time, however, I don't believe that the existence of two distinct social-value criteria means bridging the instrumental–reasonable divide is impossible. An approach to reconciling the two perspectives is offered by Atkinson and Reed (1990), who begin with instrumental value and then argue that concrete solutions must be negotiated in the spirit of Commons. The gap is also narrowed when we recognize that Veblen's instrumental–ceremonial dichotomy, which is at the heart of the instrumental value approach, appears in various forms within Commons's theory of reasonable value. Atkinson and Reed (1990, 1097–1098) argue that Commons incorporated ceremonial (pecuniary) aspects of economic life into his bargaining and rationing transactions, and instrumental (technological) aspects into managerial transactions. I would add that the dichotomy also appears in Commons's attempt to fashion a theory of economic value rooted in matter-of-fact reality, not mythical entities (such as the invisible hand or natural rights); and in Commons's transactional analysis, where cause-and-effect *efficiency* (Veblen's "technology") plays an integral role with the other interdependent dimensions of a transaction, including *customs* (which, for Veblen, at least according to those in the Texas tradition, would be considered ceremonial).[37]

I would even go beyond the suggestion that Veblen's instrumental–ceremonial dichotomy is incorporated in Commons's work as a *tool of analysis* and argue that the instrumental side of that dichotomy even appears in Commons's writings as *a criterion of value*. Throughout Commons's publications are calls for practices, rules, and standards that, on the basis of investigative research, have proven themselves to be the "best" that are practical under existing conditions. In that context, Commons's economics aligns squarely with Ayres's (1961, 8) suggestion that "everyone knows what better and worse mean with reference to tools." Once an end is agreed upon, there *can* be something approaching an "objective" assessment of which practice (tool) is best to achieve the task at hand (Commons 1934a, 156–160); Commons's only proviso is the practice must be shown to be feasible (practicable) (Commons 1913, 406–411; 1934b, 742).[38]

A close look at Commons and Ayres—originators of institutionalism's Wisconsin and Texas traditions, respectively—also reveals other important commonalities that suggest the possibility of instrumental–reasonable reconciliation. For example, Commons and Ayres share a common (pragmatic) conception of knowledge and truth, which holds that both concepts are determined by the community of those doing the investigating (Ayres 1961, 34; Commons 1934a, 160; 1934b, 150–156, 730). They also agree that "knowledge is always incomplete;" that "all judgments are always subject to correction;" and that human investigation and experience allow for the "slow filtration of reason" (Ayres 1961, 162; Commons 1934b, 846). Moreover, all of the bedrock values that Commons (1950, 22, 51, 97, 264) identifies in *The Economics of Collective Action*—liberty, security, democracy, justice, equality (of opportunity and treatment), and abundance—correspond to elements found in Ayres's (1961) catalogue of "genuine" or "higher" values. In short, reasonable value and instrumental value are not identical, but the gap narrows considerably once we recognize the compatibility and complementarity that comes into view when we peer across the divide.

The future of reasonable value

The title of Chasse's (2017) biography of Commons—*A Worker's Economist*—perfectly captures the essence of John R.'s career. Commons sided with workers and "the common man" from the start, never wavering in his commitment to improving worker wellbeing (see Parsons 1985, 757).[39] Early in his career, Commons believed "the weakest spot of the capitalist civilization" involved the high incidence and adverse consequences of employee accidents; so he focused on how cooperation of all stakeholders, including "plain, ordinary people," could be organized to prevent accidents, thereby promoting the public welfare. At the end of his career, Commons believed "the weakest spot remaining" involved "unemployment and [economic] insecurity;" so he and his students sought to further promote the public welfare by crafting measures to prevent unemployment, provide compensation for the jobless, and furnish income and healthcare security for seniors and others unable to earn a living (Commons 1950, 285).

Commons admired the achievements of many business leaders, but had a clear-eyed recognition that capitalism is often "oppressive, confiscatory, and exploitative" (Commons 1934b, 672). He even wrote that capitalism "thrives on the stupidity of mankind" (Commons 1934b, 846). Commons's view of capitalism as an economic system was very much like Winston Churchill's view of democracy as a political system: "it is the worst form … except for all the others" (McCoubrey 2017).

Even more important than capitalism's merits as an economic system, Commons believed it is the only system compatible with individual freedom, initiative, and expression. Thus, he aimed to save capitalism by "making it good." He did so not only by paying attention to the legal foundations of capitalism, focusing on the way those foundations shape social institutions and influence individual behavior, but also by highlighting the mutually reinforcing dimensions of capitalism and democracy. In addition, Commons sought to enlist the profit motive in pursuit of his objective. As he wrote in *Institutional Economics*, Commons (1934b, 875) intended to "appeal to the business man to get rich by making others rich, and if he does not respond, then to appeal to collective action."

But what are the current prospects for Commons's vision of a prosperous, democratic, and more humane economy? What's to be the future of reasonable value?

The challenges we face are daunting. On the economic front, we find money manager capitalism, the contemporary stage of capitalist development that is, in many ways, Commons's finance-driven "banker capitalism" on steroids (and is even more dangerous because it lacks that earlier era's private-sector efforts to stabilize the economy). In the United States, that system has been a driving force behind decades-long wage stagnation, widespread (financial, healthcare, and retirement) insecurity for working families, extraordinary economic inequality, the decline of the labor movement (which finds itself under assault despite time and again signaling a willingness to work with business and government as a problem-solving partner), and an eroded domestic manufacturing base; moreover, the adverse consequences of all these trends have been underscored recently by the coronavirus (COVID-19) pandemic. On the environmental front, we find stalled domestic and international efforts to address the planet's climate crisis, the adverse consequences of which are already evident. And on the domestic political front, we see mounting evidence of a coordinated, long-term strategy to dismantle the institutions and policies—many of which were fashioned or inspired by Commons—established during the Progressive Era, New Deal, and Great Society (see, for example, Mayer 2016; Parramore 2018).

It's important to note that the reactionary movement we see on the political front is *not* an attempt to remove the government from economic life. Even if that goal is sometimes suggested by campaign advertisements and speeches, the leaders and financial backers of this movement understand that such a removal is neither possible nor desirable. Their real aim is to marshal the power of the state and redirect it toward the corporate interests of "a private governing elite" (Parramore 2018).[40]

It's also important to note that the political movement just described focuses on society's *rules*, not just on *who* rules (though the movement definitely has a complementary strategy to elect preferred candidates and to train lawyers and future judges). The "Holy Grail" of the movement is the Constitution: "alter it [while stacking the Court with acquiescent judges] and you could increase and secure the power of the wealthy in a way no politician could ever challenge" (Parramore 2018). In other words, a formidable and well-financed segment of right-wing America understands the economics of John R. Commons. That group has just chosen to turn Commons's argument on its head. The result is a playbook for further concentrating economic power, and further weakening democracy.[41]

Thus, despite the daunting challenges we face on the economic, environmental, and political fronts, it is now more important than ever for progressive economists to understand and reorient Common's institutionalism in the direction he intended. That direction—which requires investigation and experimentation, and may be our only way to avoid severe sociopolitical turmoil in the coming years—is toward what Commons (1950, 294) envisioned as "a reasonably successful world of fairly equal opportunities for everyone." In short, it is the direction of *reasonable value*.[42]

Acknowledgments

The author wishes to thank John Dennis Chasse, Tom Kemp, Kota Kitagawa, Sarah Klammer, Kim Kowalewski, Jim Peach, Eric Scorsone, Linda Whalen, Tim Wunder, and Hiroyuki Uni for comments and suggestions.

Notes

1 Key contributors to this tradition include Ayres's student J. Fagg Foster, and Foster's students, Marc R. Tool and Paul Dale Bush.

2 Commons left no definitive or introductory statement of his theories, requiring readers to make their own interpretations of ideas that even his closest students and colleagues often said they didn't understand.

3 "John R." is what most people called him throughout his life. Early on, it likely helped differentiate him from his father, John A.

4 As an illustration of his change in tone, compare Commons (1899) to Commons (1900).

5 Commons retired in 1932, finished *Institutional Economics* and his autobiography, *Myself*, in 1934, and moved two years later to a trailer park in Fort Lauderdale, Florida. However, he soon felt rejuvenated, began writing again, and returned to Madison each spring for a number of years to teach a spring course and conduct a fall lecture series. Then, less than a year before his death in 1945, Kenneth Parsons, a former student of John R., visited him in Florida to help complete the book that was eventually released as *The Economics of Collective Action*. All of this is discussed in Chasse (2017, 225–233).

6 Wilbur Cohen, a student of Commons who contributed to writing the Social Security Act, serves as one illustration of Commons's legacy: Cohen "oversaw the creation and implementation of Medicare, the Elementary and Secondary Education Act, the Civil Rights Act, and a host of Social Security amendments" (Chasse 2017, 3). In 2007, the Social Security Administration Building in Washington, DC, was renamed the Wilbur J. Cohen Federal Building.

7 Commons's language often displays the male-centeredness common to the academic writing of his era. I will try to avoid it where possible, but will sometimes use his statements as written to support my interpretation of his viewpoint. I will also try to avoid making a direct reference to Commons in every sentence of my interpretation; and when a view is my own (not merely my interpretation of Commons's views), I will indicate that to the reader.

8 Commons (1924, 385) writes that government's role of granting rights to individuals and then protecting those rights worked "so smoothly," especially in England starting in the eighteenth century, "that the rights which it afforded came to be looked at as a natural right of man—in the sense, not as an ideal that man ought to have by aid of government, but in the sense of something which he previously had by nature and was deprived of by government."

9 Reasonableness also requires (as suggested by the discussion of due process above) a right to appeal to the courts, a notion Commons incorporated into his own policy proposals (see, for example, Commons 1913, 391–392).

10 Drawing on the industrial relations literature (see, for example, Kochan, Katz, and McKersie 1986), most of which can be traced to Commons, I often find it useful to look at his "working rules" as a bundle of institutional structures, strategies, practices, and processes.

11 For further discussion of managerial, bargaining, and rationing transactions, see Commons (1950, 43–57), which includes attention to the alternatives facing sellers and buyers.

12 Commons (1950, 104–109, 126) also suggested that all economic activity has four stages: expectation, negotiation, transaction, and administration.

13 Here Commons was unquestionably influenced by the pragmatic philosophy of Charles S. Peirce, who wrote: "The opinion which is fated to be ultimately agreed to by all who investigate is what we mean by truth" (Commons 1934b, 152).

14 Consistent with this emphasis on *process* is a statement Commons made during a University of Wisconsin lecture in 1939: "I have no system. I have an administrative process" (Dorfman 1959, 390).

15 As John Kenneth Galbraith (1958, 13) wrote in *The Affluent Society*, "The enemy of the conventional wisdom is not ideas but the march of events."
16 For a discussion of Commons's notion of futurity, see Atkinson and Whalen (2011).
17 For a comprehensive look at Commons's body of research, including the controversial *Races and Immigrants in America*, see Chasse (2017). Also, for more on his policy-oriented research, see Thomas Kemp's Chapter 7 in this volume.
18 Some might argue the labor movement is still trying to find an effective response to finance-driven capitalism. Commons, however, anticipated enactment of New Deal labor legislation; see Commons (1934b, 888).
19 The short summary above is based largely on Commons's 1934 presentation; for a more detailed summary of the theory in its early form, including a discussion of organized labor's evolving methods, see Chasse (2017, 101–104).
20 To be sure, Commons was troubled by the problem of unemployment, which, in the mid-1920s, he described as "the outstanding defect of capitalism" (Lewisohn et al. 1925, 152). But he also saw other adverse consequences of the business cycle for workers. In particular, Commons (1934b, 794, 903) wrote that the business cycle demoralizes laborers on the upturn of prices, pauperizes them on the downturn, and coerces them by lack of jobs during the early stages of recovery.
21 Commons's insight into macroeconomics provided John Maynard Keynes with the basis for *The General Theory of Employment, Interest and Money*; see Kates (2011).
22 For a discussion by Commons and his colleagues on the usefulness of public works, see Lewisohn et al. (1925, 121–151).
23 Another publication worth examining for its application of Commons's ideas to the realm of agriculture is Kazmierczak and Hughes (1996), which draws on the notion of reasonable value to call for negotiated regulations, mediated by government agencies, to resolve resource-use and environmental disputes. This approach was first proposed for US federal regulations—across a wide range of agencies and departments—during the 1970s; see Harter (2009).
24 For a discussion of how A. Allan Schmid, one of Parsons's students, incorporated the Wisconsin tradition into his own work, see Chapter 8 in this book.
25 Three other Wisconsin graduates are worth mentioning briefly: Harry Trebing, Thomas Kochan, and Lawrence Mishel. Trebing carried on the Wisconsin institutionalist tradition in his work as a practitioner and scholar on the regulation of public utilities (see, for example, Stevenson 2016). Kochan, a graduate of the Wisconsin industrial relations program established by Edwin Witte, is a leading scholar in the field of work and employment relations (see, for example, Kochan 2016). Mishel served until recently as president of the Economic Policy Institute, a non-profit, pro-worker think tank, about which I recall him saying at a recent meeting of the American Economic Association, "EPI is institutionalist."
26 Another article by Chasse (1997) mixes historical analysis with a discussion of how Commons's view on special interests remains relevant today.
27 For my own contributions to this linkage, see Whalen (2001; 2008).
28 Marshall and Briggs have also devoted much research attention to the challenges facing workers in low-wage labor markets (see, for example, Briggs 1980), immigration policy, and policies to combat employment discrimination.
29 In 1986, Marshall, who served as US Secretary of Labor during the administration of President Jimmy Carter, helped establish the Economic Policy Institute, a think tank that in many ways resembles the American Association for Labor Legislation, a center for policy research and advocacy (which operated from 1905 until 1943) that Commons helped to create.
30 See also the research on capitalist evolution cited in note 27.
31 For additional applications associated with that symposium, see Chiong, Dymski and Hernandez (2014); Ashton (2014); and Maclachlan (2014). For Schmid's analysis, see Chapter 8.

32 For the pre-analytic vision and method that combine with Commons's reasonable value and transactional analysis to round out his institutionalist perspective, see Whalen (forthcoming). Also see Chapter 7 in this book for a discussion of how Commons conducted economic investigations and viewed the role of the economist.
33 See, for example, Atkinson and Reed (1990; 1991); and Ramstad (1991b).
34 Of course, researchers adopting Commons's approach can still criticize or even denounce outcomes not in keeping with the spirit of the reasonable-value process, especially in cases where decisions adversely affect parties excluded from the process; and researchers are also free to step away from the reasonable-value framework and introduce their own value premises and assessments.
35 As indicated in the introduction to this chapter, Ayres referred to instrumental values as "a standard of valuation for all" (Atkinson 1987, 193).
36 To be sure, it could be argued that Commons also offers a normative compass as a standard of value for all—one focused on process, not outcomes. I would concede this is one way to look at Commons's reasonable-value approach. However, that criterion is still distinctly different from the one that Ramstad identifies as the instrumental-value approach.
37 In Commons, instrumental and ceremonial dimensions of socioeconomic life are always intertwined (see, for example, Commons 1934b, 672–673). But that interconnectedness also appears as an opportunity to reconcile instrumental value and reasonable value, for Ayres (1961, 9, 15–19) clearly recognized that all human practices contain a mix of instrumental and ceremonial elements.
38 Of course, Commons also would not want a solution imposed on parties; rather, as this chapter has emphasized, Commons strongly preferred problem-solving in which all stakeholders (through representatives of their own choosing) have a voice. This does not merely build broad support for the solution selected; it also ensures consideration of the widest range of consequences, including those that might only be anticipated when looking at the matter from certain stakeholder perspectives. As this chapter has shown, for Commons there is no route to "objective" knowledge except via "joint valuation."
39 According to Parsons (1985, 757), "[Commons's] interest matured...into a lifetime devoted to an understanding of the US economy in ways that could support the humanization and stabilization of [that] economy, without...impairing the productivity of the system."
40 Lynn Paramore (2018) writes: "Despite the rhetoric..., shrinking big government is not really the point. The oligarchs require a government with tremendous new powers so that they can bypass the will of the people. This, as historian Nancy MacLean points out, requires [for example] greatly expanding police powers 'to control the resultant popular anger.'"
41 For an eye-opening look at the erosion of American democracy that remains relevant nearly three decades after it was published, see Greider (1992).
42 For a further discussion of contemporary obstacles to reasonable value and how they might be overcome, see Whalen (2020b).

References

Ashton, Philip. 2014. "The Evolving Juridical Space of Harm/Value: Remedial Powers in the Subprime Mortgage Crisis." *Journal of Economic Issues* 48 (4): 959–979.

Atkinson, Glen. 1987. "Instrumentalism and Economic Policy: The Quest for Reasonable Value." *Journal of Economic Issues* 21 (1): 189–202. https://doi.org/10.1080/00213624.1987.11504604

_____. 2010. "The Legal Foundations of Financial Capitalism." *Journal of Economic Issues* 44 (2): 289–299. https://doi.org/10.2753/JEI0021-3624440202

Atkinson, Glen and Ted Oleson. 1996. "Institutional Inquiry: The Search for Similarities and Differences." *Journal of Economic Issues* 30 (3): 701–718. https://doi.org/10.1080/00213624.1996.11505832

Atkinson, Glen and Stephen Paschall. 2011. "Citizens United v. Federal Election Commission: The Return of Substantive Due Process?" *Journal of Economic Issues* 45 (2):439–446. https://doi.org/10.2753/JEI0021-3624450221

_____. 2016. *Law and Economics from an Evolutionary Perspective*. Cheltenham, UK: Edward Elgar. https://doi.org/10.4337/9781785361302

Atkinson, Glen and Mike Reed. 1990. "Institutional Adjustment, Instrumental Efficiency, and Reasonable Value." *Journal of Economic Issues* 24 (4): 1095–1107. https://doi.org/10.1080/00213624.1990.11505104

_____. 1991. "Rejoinder." *Journal of Economic Issues* 25 (4): 1136–1140. https://doi.org/10.1080/00213624.1991.11505238

Atkinson, Glen and Charles Whalen. 2011. "Futurity: Cornerstone of Post-Keynesian Institutionalism." In *Financial Instability and Economic Security After the Great Recession*, edited by Charles Whalen, 53–76. Cheltenham, UK: Edward Elgar. https://doi.org/10.4337/9780857934840.00012

Atkinson, Glen, Eric Hake, and Stephen Paschall. 2019. "Evolution of the Corporation in the United States: Stabilized Scarcity and Vested Interests." *Journal of Economic Issues* 53 (1): 1–25. https://doi.org/10.1080/00213624.2019.1556998

Atkinson, Glen, Mark Nichols, and Ted Oleson. 2000. "The Menace of Competition and Gambling Deregulation." *Journal of Economic Issues* 34 (3): 621–634. https://doi.org/10.1080/00213624.2000.11506297

Atkinson, Glen, Stephen Paschall, Brian Bonnefant, and Frederick Steinmann. 2014. "Ignorance Is Not Bliss: Asymmetric Information in the Residential Mortgage Market." *Journal of Economic Issues* 48 (2): 507–514. https://doi.org/10.2753/JEI0021-3624480226

Ayres, Clarence E. 1961. *Toward a Reasonable Society*. Austin, TX: The University of Texas Press. https://doi.org/10.7560/734111

Briggs, Vernon M. 1980. *Youth Employment Programs in the Southwest*. Austin, TX: Bureau of Business Research, University of Texas at Austin.

_____. 1987. "Human Resource Development and the Formulation of National Economic Policy." *Journal of Economic Issues* 21 (3): 1207–1240. https://doi.org/10.1080/00213624.1987.11504701

Chasse, John Dennis. 1997. "John R. Commons and the Special Interest Issue: Not Really Out of Date." *Journal of Economic Issues* 31 (4): 933–950. https://doi.org/10.1080/00213624.1997.11505985

_____. 2008. "Trade Agreements and Labor Problems: The Current Bearing of a Commons Proposal." *Journal of Economic Issues* 42 (4): 1123–1144. https://doi.org/10.1080/00213624.2008.11507205

_____. 2017. *A Worker's Economist: John R. Commons and his Legacy from Progressivism to the War on Poverty*. New York: Transaction Publishers. https://doi.org/10.4324/9781315107165

_____. 2018. "How Necessary are Unions? Insights from John R. Commons." *Journal of Economic Issues* 52 (2): 413–421. https://doi.org/10.1080/00213624.2018.1469888

Chiong, Melody, Gary Dymski, and Jesus Hernandez. 2014. "Contracting the Commonwealth: John R. Commons and Neoliberal Financial Crises." *Journal of Economic Issues* 48 (4): 927–947.

Commons, John R. 1899. "Discussion of the President's Address." In *Supplement to Economic Studies, Vol. 4, No. 2. Hand-book of the American Economic Association together with the Report of the Eleventh Annual Meeting*, 111–112. New York: Macmillan.

_____. 1900. "Discussion of the President's Address." In *Publications of the American Economic Association*, Third Series, *Vol. 1, No. 1. Papers and Proceedings of the Twelfth Annual Meeting*, 62–80. New York: Macmillan.

_____. 1909. "American Shoemakers, 1648–1895: A Sketch of Industrial Evolution." *Quarterly Journal of Economics* 24 (1): 39–84. https://doi.org/10.2307/1886057

_____. 1913. *Labor and Administration*. New York: Macmillan.

_____. 1922. "Unemployment Prevention." *American Labor Legislation Review* 12 (1): 15–24.

_____. 1924. *Legal Foundations of Capitalism*. New York: Macmillan.

_____. 1925a. "The Stabilization of Prices and Business." *American Economic Review* 15 (1): 43–52.

_____. 1925b. "The True Scope of Unemployment Insurance." *American Labor Legislation Review* 15 (1): 33–44.

_____. 1931. "Institutional Economics." *American Economic Review* 21 (4): 648–657.

_____. 1934a. *Myself*. New York: Macmillan.

_____. 1934b. *Institutional Economics: Its Place in Political Economy*. New York: Macmillan.

_____. 1950. *The Economics of Collective Action*, edited by Kenneth H. Parsons. New York: Macmillan.

Commons, John R., David J. Saposs, Helen L. Sumner, Edward B. Mittleman, Henry E. Hoagland, John B. Andrews, and Selig Perlman. 1918. *History of Labour in the United States*, 2 volumes. New York: Macmillan.

Dorfman, Joseph. 1959. *The Economic Mind in American Civilization*, Volume 4. New York: Viking.

Galbraith, John K. 1958. *The Affluent Society*. Boston, MA: Houghton Mifflin.

Garrett, Brandon L. 2017. "Constitutional Reasonableness." *Minnesota Law Review* 102 (1): 61–126. https://doi.org/10.2139/ssrn.2903598

Gemzik-Salwach, Agata. 2020. "Institutional Analysis of Banks and Personal Loan Companies: Lesson from Poland." *Journal of Economic Issues* 54 (1): 142–163. https://doi.org/10.1080/00213624.2020.1720570

Gomberg, William. 1985. "The Historical Roots of the Democratic Challenge to Authoritarian Management." *Human Resource Management* 24 (3): 259–269. https://doi.org/10.1002/hrm.3930240303

Gordon, Wendell. 1984. "The Role of Institutional Economics." *Journal of Economic Issues* 18 (2): 368–381.

Greider, William. 1992. Who *Will Tell the People: The Betrayal of American Democracy*. New York: Touchstone.

Harter, Philip J. 2009. "Collaboration: The Future of Governance." *Journal of Dispute Resolution* 2009 (2): 411–488.

Kasper, Sherry D. 2014. "Payday Lending: The Case of Tennessee." *Journal of Economic Issues* 48 (4): 905–925.

Kates, Steven. 2011. "Subverting Say's Law: Harlan McCracken and the Commons-Keynes Connection." In *Financial Instability and Economic Security after the Great Recession*, edited by Charles Whalen, 15–27. Cheltenham, UK: Edward Elgar. https://doi.org/10.4337/9780857934840.00010

Kaufman, Bruce E. 2010. "Institutional Economics and the Minimum Wage: Broadening the Theoretical and Policy Debate." *Industrial and Labor Relations Review* 63 (3): 427–453. https://doi.org/10.1177/001979391006300304

Kazmierczak, Richard F. and David W. Hughes. 1996. "Reasonable Value and the Role of Negotiation in Agriculture's Use of the Environment." Louisiana State University Agricultural Center, Staff Paper 96-09. Baton Rouge, Louisiana.

Kochan, Thomas A. 2016. *Shaping the Future of Work*. New York: Business Expert Press.

Kochan, Thomas A., Harry C. Katz, and Robert B. McKersie. 1986. *The Transformation of American Industrial Relations*. New York: Basic Books. https://doi.org/10.7591/9781501731693

Lewisohn, Sam A., Ernest G. Draper, John R. Commons, and Don D. Lescohier. 1925. *Can Business Prevent Unemployment?* New York: Alfred A. Knopf.

Maclachlan, Fiona. 2014. "Repurchase Agreements and the Law: How Legislative Changes Fueled the Housing Bubble." *Journal of Economic Issues* 48 (2): 515–522. https://doi.org/10.2753/JEI0021-3624480227

Mansell, Robin. 2006. "Collective Action, Institutionalism, and the Internet." *Journal of Economic Issues* 40 (2): 297–305. https://doi.org/10.1080/00213624.2006.11506907

Marshall, Ray. 1982. "Government, Markets, and Consensus-Building Mechanisms." *National Productivity Review* 1 (4): 445–450. https://doi.org/10.1002/npr.4040010412

_____. 1987. *Unheard Voices: Labor and Economic Policy in a Competitive World*. New York: Basic Books.

_____. 1993. "Commons, Veblen, and Other Economists." *Journal of Economic Issues* 27 (2): 301–322. https://doi.org/10.1080/00213624.1993.11505418

Mayer, Jane. 2016. *Dark Money*. New York: Doubleday.

Mayhew, Anne. 2014. "The Backward Art of Thinking about Consumer Spending." *Journal of Economic Issues* 48 (4): 949–958.

McCoubrey, Carmel. 2017. "Don't Quote Them on It." *The New York Times*. February 14.

McIntyre, Richard and Yngve Ramstad. 2004. "Not Only Nike's Doing It: 'Sweating' and the Contemporary Labor Market." In *The Institutionalist Tradition in Labor Economics*, edited by Dell P. Champlin and Janet T. Knoedler, 297–314. Armonk, NY: M.E. Sharpe. https://doi.org/10.4324/9781315699578-20

McNulty, Paul J. 1984. *The Origins and Development of Labor Economics*. Cambridge, MA: MIT Press.

Nesvetailova, Anastasia. 2015. "A Crisis of the Overcrowded Future: Shadow Banking and the Political Economy of Financial Innovation." *New Political Economy* 20 (3): 431–453. https://doi.org/10.1080/13563467.2014.951428

Parramore, Lynne. 2018. "Meet the Economist Behind the One Percent's Stealth Takeover of America." Institute for New Economic Thinking. May 30. https://tinyurl.com/y5kdjnlk.

Parsons, Kenneth H. 1985. "John R. Commons: His Relevance to Contemporary Economics." *Journal of Economic Issues* 19 (3): 755–778. https://doi.org/10.1080/00213624.1985.11504414

_____. 1986. "The Relevance of the Ideas of John R. Commons for the Formulation of Agricultural Development Policies." *Journal of Economic Issues* 20. (2): 281–296. https://doi.org/10.1080/00213624.1986.11504500

Ramstad, Yngve. 1987. "Free Trade versus Fair Trade: Import Barriers as a Problem of Reasonable Value." *Journal of Economic Issues* 21 (1): 5–32. https://doi.org/10.1080/00213624.1987.11504596

_____. 1989. "'Reasonable value' versus 'Instrumental Value:' Competing Paradigms in Institutional Economics." *Journal of Economic Issues* 23 (3): 761–777. https://doi.org/10.1080/00213624.1989.11504937

_____. 1991a. "From Desideratum to Historical Achievement: John R. Commons's Reasonable Value and the 'Negotiated Economy' of Denmark." *Journal of Economic Issues* 25 (2): 431–439. https://doi.org/10.1080/00213624.1991.11505176

_____. 1991b. "Reasonable Value versus Instrumental Value: A Reply to Klein and Atkinson and Reed." *Journal of Economic Issues* 25 (4): 1127–1133. https://doi.org/10.1080/00213624.1991.11505236

Stevenson, Rodney. 2016. "Economics, Ethics, and the Long Arc of Public Utilities: A Paper in Honor of Harry M. Trebing." *Journal of Economic Issues* 50 (2): 503–509. https://doi.org/10.1080/00213624.2016.1179057

Stone, Katherine V.W. 2017. "A Right to Work in the United States: Historical Antecedents and Contemporary Possibilities." In *The Right to Work: Legal and Philosophical Perspectives*, edited by Virginia Mantouvalou, 275–290. Portland, Oregon: Hart Publishing. https://dx.doi.org/10.5040/9781474202077.ch-015

Whalen, Charles. 1987. "Consensus Mechanisms and Community Economic Development: The Buffalo Experience." *Journal of Economic Issues* 21 (2): 763–774. https://doi.org/10.1080/00213624.1987.11504668

_____. 1988. *Beyond Neoclassical Thought: Economics from the Perspective of Institutionalists and Post Keynesians*. Doctoral dissertation, University of Texas at Austin. Available from UMI, Ann Arbor, Michigan.

_____. 1998. "Economic Insecurity and the Problem-Solving Approach of John R. Commons." In *Proceedings of the Fiftieth Annual Meeting, Industrial Relations Research Association*, edited by Paula Voos, 320–327. Madison, Wisconsin: Industrial Relations Research Association.

_____. 2001. "Integrating Schumpeter and Keynes: Hyman Minsky's Theory of Capitalist Development." *Journal of Economic Issues* 35 (4): 805–823. https://doi.org/10.1080/00213624.2001.11506415

_____. 2008. "John R. Commons and John Maynard Keynes on Economic History and Policy: The 1920s and Today." *Journal of Economic Issues* 42 (1): 225–242. https://doi.org/10.1080/00213624.2008.11507123

_____. 2010. "Full Employment with Liberty: John R. Commons's Perspective and Its Continuing Relevance." *Journal of Economic Issues* 44 (2): 559–568. https://doi.org/10.2753/JEI0021-3624440229

_____. 2011. "Union Engagement in Western New York Economic Development: An Institutional Analysis." In *Advances in Industrial and Labor Relations*, Volume 18, edited by David Lewin, Bruce Kaufman, and Paul Gollan, 177–213. Bingley, UK: Emerald. https://doi.org/10.1108/S0742-6186(2011)0000018009

_____. 2013. "Core Concepts of Institutionalist Public Finance: Problem Solving, Institutional Analysis, Strategic Choice, and Stakeholder Engagement." *Forum for Social Economics* 42 (4): 359–378. https://doi.org/10.1080/07360932.2012.727360

_____. 2020a. "John R. Commons and Government as Employer of Last Resort: Three Paths to a Progressive Right to Work." *Journal of Economic Issues* 54 (2):434–431. https://doi.org/10.1080/00213624.2020.1752525

_____. 2020b. "The 'Middle Way' of John R. Commons: Pursuing Reasonable Value in the Age of Unreason." *Journal of Economic Issues* 54 (4): 1161–1173. https://doi.org/10.1080/00213624.2020.1835130

_____. Forthcoming. "The Institutionalist Method and Vision of John R. Commons." *Journal of Economic Issues*.

3

MARKET SOCIETY AND THE INSTITUTIONAL THEORY OF KARL POLANYI

Michele Cangiani

Introduction

Karl Polanyi's (1886–1964) life and work are characterized by a tight weaving of civic responsibility and commitment to knowledge. His institutional approach developed gradually yet coherently, influenced not only by contact with different political and cultural environments, but also by the dramatic historical changes from the *belle époque* to the period following World War II (WWII). Indeed, Polanyi was able to transform his own migrations into opportunities. The rise of fascist regimes forced him to move from Budapest to Vienna in 1919, then to England in 1933. He wrote *The Great Transformation* (Polanyi [1944] 2001) between 1941 and 1943, at Bennington College in Vermont; and his 1947 appointment at Columbia University in New York allowed him to recognize and more fully practice his own institutionalism. *Trade and Market in the Early Empires* (Polanyi, Arensberg, and Pearson 1957)—a collection of essays by Polanyi and his colleagues and students—marked a turning point in anthropological and historical studies, and more generally in the methodology of social sciences.

In addition to those two books, the posthumous *The Livelihood of Man* (Polanyi 1977) and other writings on ancient and primitive economies are indispensable for understanding Polanyi's institutional approach and his views on social problems. His historical and anthropological research is aimed at creating a general method for comparative studies of economic systems. He regarded this method as necessary for deepening and supporting his critique of the market-capitalist system and of conventional economic and social theories.

As is typical of the institutional approach, he was aware of the inherent normativity of knowledge. Indeed, *The Livelihood of Man* explicitly underlines that the goal of his studies on societies of the past was "to yield answers to some of

DOI: 10.4324/9781003160434-3

the burning moral and operational problems of our own age," through a non-fallacious comparative analysis of social systems (Polanyi 1977, XXXIX). And, a few pages later he reaffirms that the purpose of his work, "in a period of perilous transformation," was "to enlarge our freedom of creative adjustment, and thereby improve our chances of survival." To this end, "the problem of man's material livelihood should be subjected to total reconsideration" (Polanyi 1977, XLIII).

In the following sections, after a rapid survey of Polanyi's intellectual biography, considered from the point of view of the formation of his institutional position, the most general achievements of his holistic and comparative method are expounded. His theory of the market-capitalist institutional setup and his critique of the method of economics are subsequently considered. A concluding note briefly deals with Polanyi's analysis of the institutional "transformation" of the market society.

From Budapest to New York

Gyula Pikler, professor of philosophy of law and history of institutions at the University of Budapest, was violently attacked by reactionary students in 1907. Polanyi, a student of his, continued his law studies at the University of Koloszvar (today Cluj, Romania), because he had been expelled for having defended Pikler together with other students. The following year he participated in creation of the Galilei Circle (*Galilei Kör*) in Budapest and became its first president. The Circle's mission was to oppose not only the conservative character of university teaching, but also dogmatic science as well as religious, ethnic, and class prejudices. It organized lectures and courses for adults, workers in particular, and published the journal *Szabádgondolat* (*Free Thought*), for which Polanyi became co-director in 1913.[1]

The Hungarian phase

In his 1897 book, *A jog keletkezéséről és fejlődéséről* (*On the Origin and Evolution of Law*), Pikler presents institutions as cultural ways of adaptation that are historically contingent (Congdon 1976, 171). Such an attitude—condemned as "relativist" by Budapest academics and political reactionaries—calls to mind Thorstein Veblen's "evolutionary" approach, and is likely a root of Polanyi's historical-institutional method.

But it was not the only root. "New roads" were also opened by "the epistemology of Ernst Mach and the psychology of William James," writes Polanyi ([1929] 2016, 206). In fact, he translated, with a Preface (Polanyi [1910] 2016), the first three chapters of Mach's *Die Analyse der Empfindungen* (*The Analysis of Sensations*, written in 1886) for the Hungarian edition of 1910, absorbing important ideas along the way.

An important aspect of the Hungarian phase in the formation of Polanyi's thought is his critique of "scientific *Weltanschauung*" (Polanyi [ca. 1920] 2005), addressed against Spencerian sociological positivism and Second-International Marxism. Mach's epistemology was influential in this regard, characterized as it is by rejection of all metaphysics and the combination of empiricism with the constructive function of knowledge.[2] In that view, an analysis of functional relationships and mutual interactions should replace the mechanistic, Newtonian cause–effect relationship. Furthermore, the interdependence between subject and object, which Mach's method implies concerning natural sciences, is unavoidable when the subjects of investigation are human activities and relationships, the constitution of society, and its historical development. Generalizations about society, for Polanyi, should not be construed as natural-essential characteristics determining historical dynamics, but spelled out instead in cultural-ethical terms. The "facts" of social sciences are human deeds, which cannot be separated from mental representations of the actors and their vision of the world. History is built by human beings, by their ideas and activities, by their creativity and moral responsibility.

In his Preface, Polanyi ([1910] 2016, 45) points out the relevance of Mach's book beyond Europe: a similar tendency "has recently been created in America under the name of 'pragmatism.'" Here is another bridge across the Atlantic Ocean, in addition to that between the German Historical School and American institutionalism (Dorfman 1955). The latter was influenced by James's psychology and pragmatist philosophy, by John Dewey's "cultural naturalism" in particular. Knowledge, for Dewey, is to be conceived as an aspect of cultural evolution, addressed to the adaptation of humankind among all the other natural species living on Earth. In a similar manner, Veblen ([1898] 1994, 71) defines institutions as "settled habits of thought," which are the effect of "human knowledge, skill and predilection," and are subject to evolution for the sake of adaptation. According to Polanyi ([1944] 2001, 262), "Institutions are embodiments of human meaning and purpose," aimed at improving "our chances of survival" (Polanyi 1977, XLIII).

The similarity of Polanyi's political prospect to that of the young György Lukács and Ervin Szabó (1982), respectively a friend and a cousin of his, attests the influence on him of the so-called Hungarian Marxism (Gabel 1975). For Polanyi, socialism primarily means ethical-institutional progress, through individual freedom, creativity, and responsibility. Lukács too insists on "morality"; his perspective of communism, in those years, is grounded on the free expression of individuals who act and interact voluntarily, convinced as they are of the interdependence between their own interest and what is good for society. In this kind of social organization, "freedom of morality will take the place of legal compulsion in the regulation of all behavior" (Lukács [1919] 1972, 48). Lukács will later accept that a temporary dictatorship of the proletariat could be imposed—with the purpose, however, of overcoming any apodictic and repressive legal constraint. Though taking some distance from that position, Polanyi continued to reflect on the question that he and Lukács used to raise in their Budapest years: "*How can we be free in spite of the fact of society?*" (Polanyi [1925] 2006, 317, his emphasis). "The true significance of freedom in a complex society" will be the central theme of the last chapter of *The Great Transformation* (Polanyi [1944] 2001, 262), as well as of later manuscripts, in particular those inspired by the philosophy of Jean-Jacques Rousseau.[3]

The period preceding World War I (WWI) was marked by social unrest, both in Europe and America, and more or less successful and lasting revolutionary attempts followed. They were an important aspect of the definitive crisis of liberal nineteenth-century capitalism. Polanyi (1919) saw the Great War as a radical break, whereby not only capitalism, but also Marxist positivist epistemology and determinist philosophy, are questioned. The crisis stimulated innovative analyses and plans of societal reorganization, including such diverse proposals as Walther Rathenau's (1918) "new economy," Otto Neurath's (1919) "natural economy," Bertrand Russell's (1918) socialist and anarchist "roads to freedom," and Otto Bauer's (1919) "road to socialism."

After the Great War

In those times of inspiring turmoil, Polanyi found new theoretical perspectives and political motivations. After the Great War and the end of the Empire, Vienna became the seat of memorable debates and social achievements, which are remembered with lucidity and emotion in the note "Speenhamland and Vienna" appended to *The Great Transformation* (Polanyi [1944] 2001, 298–299). In so-called Red Vienna, Polanyi's acquaintance with economists of the Austrian School and socialists of an Austro-Marxist tendency helped improve his theoretical background and better define his political philosophy. He felt at ease in the Austrian socialist milieu, which was characterized by the refusal of dogmatism and opposition to both Second-International economism and Bolshevist methods of seizing power.

In the situation where democracy seemed acquired and "socialization" of the economy was on the agenda, Polanyi felt the need to go beyond criticism of the "scientific *Weltanschauung*" in the name of individual liberty, moral engagement, and human creativity. A new theory was necessary to explain why the old society should be overcome and how a new one could be built. Institutions matter—and the fact that they simultaneously constitute a limit and an opportunity for freedom would thenceforward be the subject of Polanyi's theoretical research and political philosophy.

The purpose of Polanyi's ([1922a] 2016) essay on "Socialist Accounting" is to contribute to the development of a theory of a socialist economy reflecting the ideas of both British Guild Socialism—to which he dedicates two articles (Polanyi [1922b] 2016; [1923] 2016)—and Austrian Otto Bauer's "functional socialism." The essay, opposing theses that Ludwig von Mises stated in the same journal, tries to demonstrate the plausibility of a non-centrally planned socialist economic system, where both "productivity" and "social right" would be safeguarded. These requirements turn out to be inadequately confronted and even contrasted in the capitalist system.

As to the first requirement (productivity), Polanyi draws on socialist theories concerning monopolistic concentration, economic crises, unproductive expenditure, the slowing down of technological development, and the preservation of relatively unproductive businesses. Arguments of this kind can also be found in the work of institutional economists, especially in Veblen's analysis of various forms of "sabotage" and "competitive waste."

As to the second requirement (social right), to which Polanyi ([1922a] 2016, 405) also refers with the expressions "social utility" and "social productivity," he points out "the organic indifference of the capitalist mode of production to the requirements of orienting production toward higher social utility." Not only does capitalism's evaluation on the side of demand remain individual, but, on the side of supply, the aim of orienting production "in a sense useful to the community" is subordinated to the aim of profit. Social assessments, then, may not be taken into account, nor the painfulness of work and "the repercussions of the production process on community life." Indeed, individuals' needs are "led astray by artificially stimulating false needs." Capitalist production follows its own path, welcoming the needs of its human and social environment only to the extent that they meet its own purposes: as if it lacked the "sensory organ" to do otherwise. "Finally, the capitalist economy fails completely where economic goals intersect with *general human goals*, like international assistance and peace."

It is worth noting that the way Polanyi presents what today would be called the "self-referential" tendency of the economic system as well as the process of "circular cumulative causation" (Gunnar Myrdal) seems to announce the subsequent development of systems theory. The problems he identified, however, were not new. The strategies business carries out—Veblen writes ([1901] 1994, 298–299)—are congruent with the fact that the basis of its survival "in the competitive pecuniary struggle … is fitness for pecuniary gain, not fitness for serviceability at large," not "the convenience of the community."

In his subsequent Vienna years, Polanyi continued to debate with Mises on "socialist accounting" and, correspondingly, to reflect on political philosophy.[4] His interest in freedom evolved, beyond the moral-philosophy criticism of scientist attitudes, by taking the historical-institutional context into consideration. How is freedom made possible and, at the same time, repressed in the present conjuncture and, more in general, in modern society, given its market-capitalist organization? What kind of organization could be designed that would better correspond to the modern promise of freedom? To begin with, key aspects of the *necessity* which socialism should overcome are "the historical laws of the capitalist economy, which operate as the natural laws of present society" (Polanyi [1927] 2018, 16). In order to define those laws, Polanyi felt the need to continue his study of economics and to resume his reading of Karl Marx.

The long crisis of liberal capitalism, and its acme in WWI, marked a turning point not only in Polanyi's formation, but for economics in general, forced as it was to reconsider its postulates, insofar as they were linked to the competitive market model. A way out was sought in two opposite directions. One tendency is the abstract formalism of "economic analysis," so defined by Joseph Schumpeter (1954): a pure "toolbox," suitable for the analysis of any reality. In fact, as Thomas Balogh (1982, 32) maintains, in this way economic theory becomes "a tale of evasions of reality." Having denied "vast changes and vital problems … in order to be able to produce a 'scientific' system," it condemned itself to "irrelevance."

On the contrary, the starting point of the other tendency—to which Polanyi belongs—is the analysis of the economic system as a historical process. In Europe, major contributions can be ascribed to socialist thinkers and "heretical" economists.[5] In the United States, the most influential current was that of institutional economists. For the latter, a fundamental point of reference was Veblen's criticism of classical and neoclassical economics, which addressed not only the substance of their method, but also the fact that they are ideologies in the Marxian sense: they represent—argues Veblen ([1898] 1994, 65)—"the standpoint of ceremonial adequacy," insofar as they transfigure "the accepted ideal of conduct" into "laws of the normal or the natural."

Institutionalists also drew lessons from the War, especially about taking institutions and their mutation into consideration. For example, Wesley Mitchell (1924, 21) maintained that WWI left us an example of "bolder action in the common interest" and planning. He believed the same attitude could now be usefully applied to such problems as controlling the business cycle and large enterprises, organizing innovation in agriculture and industry, conserving natural resources, and addressing industrial relations and income distribution.

Such after-war institutional attitude was notoriously influential during the New Deal, and it is from this perspective that Polanyi analyzed that period of American history, writing several articles on the subject in the years 1935–1937 for the Viennese weekly *Der Österreichische Volkswirt*. In 1924, he had become a member of the editorial staff of that magazine, for which he published some 250 articles on various economic and political issues—until 1938, when it was forced to close as a consequence of the *Anschluss*. Day-by-day investigations required for that work contributed to Polanyi's theoretical improvement, which in turn enriched his commentary.

In England, where he resided from 1933 to 1946, Polanyi taught in courses for adult learners organized by the Workers' Educational Association (WEA).[6] His lectures and seminars were dedicated to the history of capitalism and the current world situation. Two British historians influenced his theoretical approach and political mind: Richard Tawney, who was president of the WEA, and G.D.H. Cole, who prefaced his pamphlet on European history from WWI to the Spanish Civil War (Polanyi 1937).

In the second half of the 1930s, Polanyi participated in the activities of a group belonging to the British movement of the Christian Left. Taking part in its internal debates helped prepare Polanyi for lectures and conferences for a wider public. He also guided a group reading of Marx's *Economic and Philosophical Manuscripts of 1844*, published for the first time in 1932. Several of Polanyi's articles and manuscripts of those years are the outcome of his study of Marx's works, as well as of discussions within the group.

In short, the analysis of the origin, nature, and vicissitudes of the market society that Polanyi carries out in *The Great Transformation* rests on the background of his previous experience, jobs, and studies. But Polanyi also conceived his research at Columbia University as a means to widen and strengthen that analysis. This broader task implied a further critique of conventional social sciences.

The "market system" and the "place of the economy"

Polanyi's research on "Origins of Economic Institutions" at Columbia University began in 1948.[7] His proposals, memorandums, and semi-annual reports range from that year to 1962.[8] In those documents, since the beginning, he clarifies the aim of the project: "primarily, to inquire into the origins of trade, money and markets; secondarily, to ascertain the place of the economic system in human society, in general." The relevance of the research for understanding contemporary society and facing its problems is immediately stated: its purpose is the explanation of "the singular position occupied by the market system in society." In those documents, Polanyi points out that also for Max Weber the focus of the study of "economic history in general" is "the institution of the *market*" and its peculiarity as a fundamental institution of our society—a *market society*, precisely because of the *place* the market holds in it. Weber sees the establishment of a market economy as "part of a more comprehensive process of 'rationalization' in all major spheres of human activity." However, Polanyi continues: regarding "the inherent rationality of market institutions," we should be even more skeptical than was usual in Weber's times.

Principles of behavior in The Great Transformation

Working at Columbia, Polanyi's vast review of anthropological and archaeological literature supplied new evidence to the comparative theory already laid down in *The Great Transformation*, where the problem addressed was "the entirely unprecedented nature" of modern society, owing to being "dominated by the market pattern." In all previous societies, on the contrary, economic activities were "submerged in social relationships" and "run on noneconomic motives" (Polanyi [1944] 2001, 45, 46, and 48). Bronislaw Malinowski—a primary source for Polanyi—summarizes the result of his own research on the economic life of Trobriand Islanders in this way:

> Economic elements enter into tribal life in all its aspects—social, customary, legal and magico-religious—and are in turn controlled by these … . Customary and legal norms, magical and mythological ideas, introduce system into their economic efforts and organize them on a social basis.
>
> *(Malinowski 1921, 7, 15)*

To explain how production and distribution could be organized, not only in small and "primitive" societies, but in all premodern societies, Polanyi's *The Great Transformation* introduces "two principles of behavior not primarily associated with economics: *reciprocity* and *redistribution*" (Polanyi [1944] 2001, 49). Those principles are respectively supported by the "institutional patterns" of *symmetry* (relationships between groups linked by mutual obligations) and *centricity* (a central agency collects goods for successively redistributing them, totally or partially, in accordance with various criteria).

Polanyi also adds a third principle, *householding*, supported by the pattern of the "closed group" (i.e., of *autarchy*). Concerning this principle, Polanyi ([1944] 2001, 55–56) makes reference to Aristotle, who insisted on "production for use as against production for gain as the essence of householding proper," thereby prefiguring the opposite essence of our society, the production for gain (in general for a monetary revenue, in particular for profit). All economic systems, including Europe "up to the end of feudalism," "were organized either on the principle of reciprocity or redistribution, or householding, or some combination of the three" (Polanyi [1944] 2001, 57).[9]

Another principle introduced by Polanyi is *barter*. The corresponding pattern, the *market*, applies to relationships aimed at exchanging goods according to equivalences or prices, which can be either pre-established or contracted in the occasion of the exchange. Later, in the essay "The Economy as Instituted Process," Polanyi (1957) deals with the most general methodological implications of *Trade and Market in the Early Empires* and of the research from which it originated. In that essay, he substitutes the term "form of integration" (i.e., of organization of the economic activity) for "principle," and the term "exchange" for "barter." Thus, the "principle of barter" becomes the "form of integration of exchange."

Comparative method

Polanyi's comparative method involves a holistic approach to cultures, considered as a whole, in their historical specificity. The "place of economy in society"—the way the economy is "integrated" or socially organized—is the key question. The study of the shifting place occupied by the economy in society, Polanyi (1957, 250) explains, "is no other than the study of the manner in which the economic process is instituted at different times and places."

The "forms of integration" are "tools" for his study. Although diverse forms may, and normally do, coexist in the same society, one turns out to be dominant.

The dominance "is identified with the degree to which [that form of integration] ... comprises land and labor," that is, the factors of production (Polanyi 1957, 255). Clearly, then, the institutions included in that form are the principal "place" where the economic function is performed.[10] In small societies studied by anthropologists, the dominance of reciprocity corresponds to the dominant role of ties of kinship as to "the integration of land and labor into the economy"; in contrast, land and labor in floodwater empires are "distributed" by a center, "by temple or palace" (ibid.).[11]

It is important to notice that "forms of integration" are very abstract models. A further theoretical step is required: the definition of the specific "culture traits" of each society (Polanyi [1944] 2001, 55), and particularly of the "definite institutional conditions" (Polanyi 1957, 251) concerning its productive organization. Only such definition makes it possible to say how the forms of integration actually exist and function in any given social system, as a specific whole within which the various aspects of social life are instituted and then meaningful. Thus, for instance, the redistribution may be accomplished by such different institutions as the Melanesian "big man," the Polynesian king, the Egyptian pharaoh, and the modern state: the institutional specificity is to be the object of explanation.

Theory of market society

Polanyi's comparative method provides the grounding for his theory of the "market society." For that purpose, he points out that the principle of barter (i.e., the form of integration of exchange) "is not on a strict parity with the three other principles" (Polanyi [1944] 2001, 59–60). In fact, the pattern corresponding to it, the market, "being related to a peculiar motive of its own, the motive of truck or barter, is capable of creating a specific institution, namely, the market" (ibid.). In other words, the peculiarity of the *market* compared to the other patterns is that of being not merely a general model of relationships, but also a socially-historically determined institution. Thus, the question is: what are the *features* of this institution in each society?

In premodern societies, "[t]he presence or absence of markets or money does not necessarily affect the economic system" (Polanyi [1944] 2001, 61), which is fundamentally organized by institutions not belonging to the form of integration of the exchange, but to the other forms. In this sense, Polanyi says that "the economic system was absorbed in the social system" and markets were mere "accessories of economic life" (ibid., 71). Even in the era of mercantilism, "markets were merely an accessory feature of an institutional setting controlled and regulated more than ever by social authority" (ibid., 70).

A radical change as to *all* preceding societies occurred in the "next stage in mankind's history," with the setting up of the market system. Now markets no longer draw their meaning, function, rules, and limits from other institutions. On the contrary, the system of price-making markets becomes itself a general "cultural trait," that is, the institution by which the economic activity is in general organized. Instead of *markets* in a subordinated and "accessory" position, there is now a *market system*, constituting the "institutional setup," the "definite institutional conditions," on which "the control of the economic system" and "the societal effects of individual behavior depend" (Polanyi 1957, 251).

What is the specific difference connoting the market system as a way for socially organizing—instituting—economic activity? What matters is its difference from all previous organizations. As a consequence, as Polanyi explains in a memorandum on his research at Columbia, comparison is unavoidable; and the hypothesis that the present form of the market, the *market system*, comes from a "simpler, embryonic form" must be discarded in favor of research on the separate origin and independent institutionalization of the three "constitutive elements" of the "institutional definition" of the market system: trade, money, and market. Polanyi names these three elements the "catallactic triad," with reference to the fact that, in the market system, they are typically interrelated.[12]

Anthropological and historical evidence shows that "forms of trade, money uses, and market elements" do exist in most, if not all, societies. However, in each society, they have peculiar origins, functions, and relationships to each other and to the whole social system. The market system is unique:

> Since trade is directed by prices and prices are a function of the market, all trade is market trade, just as all money is exchange money. The market is the generating institution of which trade and money are the functions. … Viewed as an exchange system, or, in brief, catallactically, trade, money and market form an indivisible whole. Their common conceptual framework is the market.
>
> *(Polanyi 1957, 256–257)*

In Polanyi's view, the market system is the institution enabling the exchange as a "form of integration" to acquire a dominant position. The "market pattern" undergoes an "evolution," from local and "accessory" markets to "price-making markets" and the "attempt to set up one big self-regulating market" (Polanyi [1944] 2001, 70). All economic activities become or require market transactions of commodities. Labor, land, and money become commodities, called "fictitious" by Polanyi, in the sense that this is an unprecedented institution. The money becomes "all-purpose money"—measure of value, means of exchange, object of hoarding. Like Marx in Part One of *Capital*, Polanyi explains modern money as the consequence and integral part of the generalized process of exchange of commodities.

Polanyi (1968, 121) mentions the proposal of the name "'catallactics,' or science of exchanges," for economics by Archbishop Richard Whately (1787–1863) in a note for his teaching at Columbia, where he outlines two distinctions. The first one regards the place of the economy in society, that is, "the separateness or the embeddedness" of economic institutions (ibid., 122). The second distinction regards two alternative approaches—societal or economistic—in the history of economic thought. The "societal approach"—from Montesquieu to Smith and Marx—raises the question of the place of the economy; the "economistic" approach—from Townsend to neoclassical economics—does not.

Polanyi is, obviously, a radical supporter of the societal approach. The relevance of his conception of the "catallactic triad" is that it reveals that the institution of the market has acquired a dominant role in carrying out the economic function in all its aspects. The peculiarity of the market society, its specific difference, is that the way its economy is instituted gives it a place of its own: the result is an "economically" instituted society. Polanyi, on the basis of the Weberian "rationalization," to which, as we have seen, he makes reference, connotes the market economy as institutionally differentiated, no longer "embedded" in society. It tends, then, to be autonomous (i.e., able to determine its own norms), and thereby dominant. In fact, he writes:

> The control of the economic system by the market is of overwhelming consequence to the whole organization of society: it means no less than the running of society as an adjunct to the market. Instead of the economy being embedded in social relations, social relations are embedded in the economic system. ... For once the economic system is organized in separate institutions, based on specific motives and conferring a special status, society must be shaped in such a manner as to allow that system to function according to its own laws. This is the meaning of the familiar assertion that a market economy can function only in a market society.
>
> *(Polanyi [1944] 2001, 60)*

In short, Polanyi's theory of the market system constitutes the conceptual core of the explanation of the modern (market and capitalist) society and its dynamics. The fact that the market economy is "economically" instituted raises the question of the relationship between the economy and other aspects of the organization of social life. While in all preceding societies the economy was "embedded"—in the sense that the economic function was carried out by diverse non-economic institutions, generally traditional, and prevalently concerning kinship, politics or religion—the peculiarity of market society is that the economy is "disembedded."

A critique of political economy

Polanyi's "market society" coincides with "capitalism." "Market-capitalist society" would be the appropriate expression, as pointed out by J. Ron Stanfield (1977), an early and reliable interpreter of Polanyi.[13] The evidence thereupon is widespread and clear in Polanyi's works. Suffice it to mention the relevance of the issue of the institution of labor market in *The Great Transformation* and the following passage of *The Livelihood of Man*:

> Within a generation—say, 1815 to 1845 ... —the price-making market ... showed its staggering capacity for organizing human beings as if they were

> mere chunks of raw material and combining them, together with the surface of mother earth, which could now be freely marketed, into industrial units under the command of private persons mainly engaged in buying and selling for profit. ... The commodity fiction, as applied to labor and land, transformed the very substance of human society.
>
> *(Polanyi 1977, 9)*

An epochal break

The issue of capitalism was normally the subject of social scientists in Polanyi's time; and Weber held a similar view. In Weber's *General Economic History*, the part on capitalism begins by stating that its establishment as a *specific social system* cannot be dated before the first half of the nineteenth century, when capitalist production provided for the greater part of livelihood in limited areas of the world. According to Weber ([1923] 1961, 208), it was an epochal break, presupposing such institutional conditions as the modern entrepreneur, the "commercialization" of the economic life, and the free laborer—i.e., legally free, but forced to sell his labor on the market by the "whip of hunger."[14]

A further implication of Polanyi's "societal" and holistic approach confirms his closeness to Weber. For him, the market-capitalist system is not the result of a teleological evolution, but is qualitatively, as a whole, different from preceding societies; it marks a historical *caesura*, "a violent break" (Polanyi 1977, 10). "Market-economy ... created a new type of society," in which "fear of starvation with the worker, [and] lure of profit with the employer, would keep the vast establishment running" (Polanyi [1947] 2018, 200). "Hunger and gain" have acquired a role in the organization of the economic system "through the need of 'earning an income'" (ibid., 201), obviously in the market. When "the market mechanism became determinative for the life of the body social," Polanyi ([1947] 2018, 200) points out, the result "was an 'economic' society to a degree previously never approximated." Common people were forced to adopt "a utilitarian outlook;" economists were trapped into an "economistic" ideology.

The market-capitalist societal setup happens, in fact, to be represented in a "catallactic" way: hunger and gain appear as "economic" motives per se; the "economizing" attitude appears as economic activity in general; and the market appears as the *natural* device by which the system works. From Whately to Mises (1949) and Friedrich Hayek, "economics" and "catallactics" appear as interchangeable terms.[15]

Formal versus substantive definitions of economic activity

For Polanyi, there is an important difference between economic activity in general and the "economizing" form it acquires in the market society. The latter form, if it is not specifically institutionally explained, suggests a falsely general definition of the economy, based on the "formal [neoclassical] meaning of economic." Such definition "refers to a definite situation of choice, namely, that between the different uses of means induced by an insufficiency of those means," which implies the need to "economize" them, Polanyi writes (1957, 243). To this definition, he opposes his own "substantive definition":

> The substantive meaning of economic derives from man's dependence for his living upon nature and his fellows. It refers to the interchange with his natural and social environment, in so far as this results in supplying him with the means of material want satisfaction.
>
> *(Ibid.)*

Why does Polanyi call his definition *substantive*? He seems to allude to the real function and historical organization of the economic activity, as opposed to "the logical character of the means-ends relationship." Besides, "substantive" may be understood in the Aristotelian sense of "essence" of a thing. Polanyi's definition, in fact, can be applied to any economic system. It is the definition of the set whose elements are all economic systems—differing from each other as to the way they are socially instituted and thereby related to the natural environment.

It is in the market system that an "economic" (economizing) attitude guides individual choices about the use of scarce means for alternative ends. The formal (conventional) definition is fallacious because it generalizes specific features of this system. As a consequence, while those features are projected onto differently organized societies, *also* our society is not defined as a whole, as a specific system. The relation means/ends, needs/resources is dealt with as if it would pertain to individuals, immediately, that is, without any social-institutional mediation. For example, neoclassical economist Lionel Robbins, at the beginning of his *Essay on the Nature & Significance of Economic Science*, mentions Robinson Crusoe, alone in the desert island, as representative of his standpoint. The fact that Robinson belongs to a society, has a culture, and behaves "like a good Englishman" (Marx [1867] 1976, 170), is simply ignored.

Repression of the social

Chapter 10 of *The Great Transformation* deals with the "discovery of society," which is a fundamental aspect of the modern condition of human beings, who conceive themselves as individuals and, correspondingly, see society as a problem to be faced. The paradox pointed out by Polanyi is the prevailing of naturalism over a "societal approach." In that prevailing view, society appears to be governed by general-natural laws, such as Malthus's law of population and Ricardo's law of diminishing returns. Moreover, as a consequence of neoclassical economics, Adam Smith's "propensity to truck, barter, and exchange" has evolved into the formal laws of individual, economizing behavior. The market system is thereby considered the natural result of the natural behaviors of individuals exercising their full liberty, not as a historical social form that shapes and constrains individual attitudes and choices.

The repression (in a psychoanalytic sense) of the social form, of the social institution of society and the social nature of human beings, is the ground on which the "economistic fallacy" grows. In *The Livelihood of Man*, Polanyi (1977, 6) explains it as a "logical error." A "broad, generic phenomenon"—human economy—is "somehow taken to be identical with a species with which we happen to be familiar."

Anthropological studies support Polanyi's thesis of the cultural-contingent nature of the *homo œconomicus*, who belongs to the market society. That contingent nature refutes both the idea of an inherent "economizing" rationality of human behavior and the notion of "scarcity" as a general condition shaping choices. Scarcity becomes *systemic* only in the market society: only in such society does it acquire an *institutional* reality as a constituent element of the social system. It is only in this society that needs are not culturally predefined: their satisfaction depends instead on purchasing power on the demand side, and, on the supply side, on the profitability of "pecuniary employments" (Veblen). In the realm of the "never enough," needs and capitalist accumulation have no limits. Besides, both meeting needs and making profits are uncertain. Money seems the only certainty in a situation where the "cash nexus" (money as the universal social medium) is a key factor of the functioning and reproduction of the system. However, money is per se scarce because it is merely quantitative worth; besides, spending it makes it disappear.

The formal-economistic approach conceals the institutional meaning of scarcity within the general concept of scarcity, referring to the need human beings have to get bread by the sweat of their brow. Polanyi's point is, on the contrary, that only in the market-capitalist society does economic behavior *systematically* consist in "economic" choices taken in conditions of scarcity. There is anthropological and historical evidence that, in pre-capitalist societies, scarcity used to have other, various causes. Resources could even be overabundant in relation to culturally limited needs and technology—a limitation not ethnocentrically reducible to "backwardness," insofar as it was devised to maintain a successful adaptation to the natural environment, a steady social equilibrium, and individual well-being.

"The Original Affluent Society" is the title of the first chapter of *Stone Age Economics*, by Marshall Sahlins, who explicitly recognizes his debt to Polanyi. According to Sahlins (1972, 36), in comparison to hunter-gatherer societies, modern society "is the era of hunger unprecedented. Now, in the time of the greatest technical power, is starvation an institution." Such is the strange—indeed, paradoxical—case of the market society: hunger and scarcity are *problems* that the organization of the economy is supposed to solve, and, at the same time, they are *institutions* of this organization.

There is no room here to show how consistently Polanyi founds his political philosophy on his theory. He shares a modern ideal of individual liberty with Hayek, but does not accept Hayek's "liberal credo" about the market system as the natural and most efficient way of realizing that ideal. On the contrary: the liberal (and neoliberal) "negative" conception of freedom is illusionary, because it represses what Polanyi calls the "reality of society," both in general and in its present market-capitalist form. As this form becomes invisible, its constraints become unquestionable. Individuals are thereby deprived of the higher, "positive" level of freedom, including conscious and responsible participation in social choices concerning both the operation of social institutions and their change.[16]

Divides in anthropology and history as well as economics

Given Polanyi's reliance on anthropological insight to criticize economics, an ironic development is that the influence of conventional neoclassical economics has led some anthropologists to adopt an "economistic approach." In this case, analyses are carried out with reference to a given, general model of economy, the formal-economizing model. Melville Herskovits, for example, makes reference to scarcity and rational choice to propose an economic anthropology aimed at understanding "the intercultural implications of the process of economizing" (Herskovits 1952, 4). The specificity of each economic system is then ascribed to its degree of "development," and to the cultural environment within which economic behavior takes place. However, the "economic" as such tends to be defined by means of "formal" (market-centric) categories—as if cultural-institutional diversity would not concern it.

The application of an economic theory drawn from a particular form of society—modern capitalism—to different societies is criticized by Daniel Fusfeld (1957). He shows that the rational-choice model only allows for a generic and distorted picture of economic systems, which, in reality, are based on relationships and motivations belonging wholly and directly to each specific socio-cultural organization. Consistent with Fusfeld's Polanyian criticism of the method of economic anthropology is the method of "anthropological economics" proposed by Sahlins (1969), that is, the study of the economic implications of cultural diversity—the reverse of Herskovits's approach.

Harry Pearson's (1957) also follows Polanyi's path, and in particular his critique of "economic determinism," regarding the false generalization of the concept of "surplus." He argues that the meaning and very existence of surplus depend on the institutional traits of each society. Only in the market society does the surplus—in the form of profit—become institutionally determinant for the allocation of resources, the division of labor, and social relations. It therefore acquires a general meaning, often improperly employed in the analysis of differently organized economic systems, and is treated as the essential, natural premise of all social changes.[17]

Polanyi's institutional-holistic definition of the specificity of the market system and its connection to capitalism created a divide also among historians. The reaction of those influenced by neoclassical economics shows that he hit the mark. For example, Paul Veyne (1976) declares his disagreement with Polanyi at the beginning of *Le Pain et le Cirque*, in connection with his methodological statement on the appropriateness of dealing with the economy of ancient Rome in terms of individual conduct motivated by self-interest and a rational use of means for given ends. In a similar manner, Fernand Braudel (1979, 195) dedicates some pages to refutation of "Polanyi's notion of the 'self-regulating market,'" which, in his opinion, being devoid of empirical evidence, "stems from a theological taste for definition." Braudel tends, in fact, to extend in the "long run" a "catallactic" approach: trade existed in antiquity as well, the bill of exchange was invented in the Middle Ages, the chair-mender offering his service in the streets of medieval towns was already an entrepreneur, markets developed gradually, etc.

Finally, Douglass North (1977) contrasts Polanyi's method with that of the "new" economic history he supports. According to North, not only does economic behavior follow constant norms and motives of its own, but premodern institutions—e.g., the ports of trade—and their evolution can be explained, fundamentally, in relation to their function of keeping "transaction costs" relatively low and opening up new opportunities for economic development.

These examples of criticisms addressed to Polanyi, as well as his opposition to the "formalist" tendency in economics and the social-historical sciences it influences, confirm the basic principles of his method:

- The social system, as a whole and in its historical-institutional specificity, is the priority subject of the analysis.
- The economy is defined by its "place" in society, that is, by the way it is instituted, specifically in each social system.
- The market system and capitalist relations of production are the fundamental institutions of contemporary market society and its economy.
- Such institutional theory supplies "good abstractions" (compared to the "bad abstractions" of conventional economics) that are the prerequisite for more specific analyses of market-capitalist society's complex functioning in diverse times and places.

Conclusion: Transformations of the market society

In *The Great Transformation*, different analytical levels are intertwined. The more general one concerns the market system in the sense of the market-capitalist form of society. We could say that, at this level, the market system is considered from an ethnological viewpoint, involving the comparison with other forms of society. Concepts elaborated at this level are the theoretical background for the explanation at a more specific level of analysis: that of market system in the sense of the particular institutional structure initially assumed by capitalist society.

This is, in fact, the principal subject of *The Great Transformation*: nineteenth-century liberal capitalism—also called "Victorian" by Polanyi, with reference to British hegemony.

Liberal capitalism rested on the four institutions mentioned on the first page of that book: the balance of power between European states, the gold standard, the self-regulating market, and the liberal state. Each of these institutions lived a contradictory life until the final catastrophe: imperialistic rivalries led to WWI. Interventions by central banks, customs protectionism, and price controls prevented the gold standard from fulfilling its function of forcing the readjustment of the economic system within each country. Such interventions affected, in general, the self-regulation of the market, which was also hampered by industrial cartels, monopolistic concentrations, and wage and normative achievements of the working classes. Finally, with the generalization of suffrage, a basic requirement of the liberal state disappeared: the control of political power by the same class holding the economic power.

A fundamental contradiction can be found since the beginning, and persists beyond crises and transformations of the market-capitalist system. "The trading classes," writes Polanyi ([1944] 2001, 139), "fulfilled their function by developing an all but sacramental belief in the universal beneficence of profits"; being devoid, however, "of organs to sense the dangers involved in the exploitation" of human and natural resources.

The "liberal creed," supported by conventional economic theories, sought a consistent fulfillment in the four basic institutions of liberal capitalism, presumably capable of assuring the optimum allocation of resources. However, Polanyi maintains, this was a utopia, as he shows by more specific analyses of the historical events of liberal capitalism. Intervention was inevitable, as a consequence of the increasing political and administrative functions required by economic development itself, and of the need to protect society from the negative, even fatal consequences of such development. Another contradiction, particularly concerning the nineteenth-century institutional setup, grew, then, aside the above-mentioned fundamental one. On the one hand, politics was formally separated from an economy instituted as a self-regulating market; on the other hand, the unavoidable political intervention undermined the functioning of this kind of economic organization.

The contradictory evolution of liberal capitalism is analyzed by Polanyi as a "double movement": the expansion of the market system and the "counter-movement"; the latter was aimed at defending the human and natural environment of the economic system, and economic activities themselves. Polanyi's methodological teaching lies in his constant reference to historical evidence. The "double movement" is not a generic, passe-partout category, in itself explanatory: its meaning results, instead, from the analysis of different contexts (such as the times of the Poor Laws or the Depression of 1873–1886), different exigencies (such as customs protection for producers or protection of workers' health), and different political sources (such as imperial rivalries or workers' struggles).

The growing political power acquired by workers—thanks to their organizations and the conquest of parliamentary representation—made, so to say, the "double movement" go beyond itself. The fundamental institutions of the market-capitalist system in general were now at stake: not only its nineteenth-century institutional setup. Polanyi ([1944] 2001, 228) writes: "Into this final phase of the fall of market economy the conflict of class forces entered decisively." Actually, the radical turning point taking place around WWI did not lead away from the market economy in general, as Polanyi hoped, but only from its nineteenth-century institutional shape. Polanyi happens to use the same terms—market economy, market system, market society—at two analytical levels, whose distinction is, actually, a fundamental trait of his thought. The utopian, *nineteenth-century* "self-regulating market" should not be confused with the general characteristics of the market society all along its history: the peculiar "place" of the economy, its market-capitalist system, and that system's autonomy.

The transformation of the market society from one institutional setup to another, from liberal to neoliberal-corporative capitalism, is, in fact, the main subject of Polanyi's writings from the 1920s onwards.[18] The purpose of *The Great Transformation* is to counter neoliberalism, that is, the ideology which, by restyling liberalism, intended to reproduce its basic theoretical and political features—even after WWI, the Great Depression, fascism, and WWII. In the interwar period, Polanyi was already aware that it was not merely a question of the nineteenth-century "double movement" of the contradiction between "self-regulation" and "social protection," but of the twentieth-century conflict on the governance of the overall social system, on different projects of societal organization. In this sense, he explains also the international situation as a global "civil war" opposing not only democracy and fascism, but also capitalism and socialism.[19]

After WWII, Polanyi continued to point out that the alternative is between "a truly democratic society [where] the problem of industry would resolve itself through the planned intervention of the producers and consumers themselves" and a society "more intimately adjusted to the economic system"—a system keeping its most general characteristics unchanged ([1947] 2018, 210–211). Here, and elsewhere, he was able to outline the essential traits of neoliberalism. The economy—in its market-capitalist form—continues to be dominant. However, at a less general level, there is an institutional change, a transformation of the market society after the definitive crisis of the liberal nineteenth-century setup. The goal is no longer the "institutional separation" between economy and politics, but the reverse: the "marketization" of society and politics, the control over the environment of economic activity. "Authoritarian liberalism," presently considered to be inherent in neoliberalism (Wilkinson 2019), corresponds to the decay of democracy Polanyi analyzed in the 1930s and continued to fear after the war. This was, in his view, the inevitable outcome, insofar as the attempt at reintegrating the economy into society through democratic politics was given up in favor of its opposite, the "adjustment" of society to its economic system.

Acknowledgments

The author wishes to thank Jamie Peck and David Zalewski for their precious suggestions, and Charles Whalen for editorial input.

Notes

1 For further biographical information beyond what is presented in this chapter, see Polanyi-Levitt and Mendel (1987).
2 On the influence of Mach on Polanyi, cf. Dale (2011, especially 151 and 153).
3 "Jean-Jacques Rousseau, or Is a Free Society Possible?" three manuscripts, dated from 1943 to 1953, Karl Polanyi Archive (KPA), container 18, folder 24. (See Polanyi (n.d.).) The last one has been published (Polanyi 2018, 167–176).
4 Cf. Polanyi (2018, Part I: the manuscript "On Freedom," and the articles "The Functionalist Theory of Society and the Problem of Socialist Accounting" and "New Reflections Concerning our Theory and Practice").
5 The reference is to the book by John Hobson (1938), and obviously to his previous writings.
6 On Polanyi and adult education cf. Mendell (1994).
7 Polanyi's appointment at Columbia was supported by two institutional economists, Carter Goodrich and Robert MacIver, recalls Walter Neale (1990, 150). He adds that "many of us…who gathered around Polanyi in the late 1940s and in the 1950s regarded ourselves as institutionalists." Neale and Daniel Fusfeld, both contributors to *Trade and Market in the Early Empires*, and Anne Mayhew, deeply interested in Polanyi's thought, became presidents of the Association for Evolutionary Economics (AFEE). The favorable climate for Polanyi's work within Columbia University was paralleled by worries and obstacles due to the general political situation after the onset of the Cold War and the second "Red Scare" (see Dale 2016, chapter 7). Because of that situation, Polanyi's work was "somewhat impeded," writes his wife, Ilona Duczynska (2006, 312); they had, in fact, to settle near Toronto, because she, as a former communist militant, was banned from the United States.
8 All are kept in KPA, container 31, folder 15. See Polanyi (n.d.).
9 Later, in Polanyi (1957), features of householding are absorbed into the principles of reciprocity and redistribution.
10 A precedent of Polanyi's approach can be found in Marx. A brilliant example of such comparative-institutional method is Marx's ([1939] 1973, 471–514) analysis on the "Forms which precede capitalist production."
11 Walter Neale (1964) interestingly develops this point. In his contribution to *Trade and Market…*, Neale (1957) analyses the traditional Indian economy—based on the caste system and the religious-political culture inspiring it—in terms of reciprocity and redistribution.
12 Again, see KPA, container 31, folder 15; see Polanyi (n.d.).
13 The enormous growth of literature on Polanyi in the epoch of triumphant neo-liberalism has mostly taken different paths. On the contrary, in my view, the present situation enhances the theoretical and political relevance of Stanfield's work on "original" institutionalism, which incorporates his interpretation of Polanyi's thought (cf. e.g., Stanfield 1980; 1986; and 1999). My debt to Stanfield is, I think, noticeable.
14 Polanyi's viewpoint is also substantially similar to that of Veblen; see (Veblen [1909] 1994, 245).
15 "The Market Order or Catallaxy" is the title of Chapter 10 of Hayek's *Law, Legislation and Liberty* ([1976] 1982, vol. 2, 107). The verb καταλλάσσω in ancient Greek means "to exchange," but also "to make an enemy a friend" and "to admit

into the community." The difference with the modern economistic meaning of the term is revealing.

16 Cf. in particular Polanyi ([1927] 2018) and the last chapter of Polanyi ([1944] 2001).

17 The contribution of Polanyi and scholars influenced by him in economic anthropology (such as Fusfeld and Pearson) has been innovative and lasting; see, for example, Neale and Mayhew (1983); and Dalton and Köcke (1983).

18 See Cangiani (2011).

19 See the above-mentioned pamphlet, published in the times of the Spanish Civil War (Polanyi 1937).

References

Balogh, Thomas. 1982. *The Irrelevance of Conventional Economics*. New York: Liveright Publishing.

Bauer, Otto. 1919. *Der Weg zum Sozialismus*. Berlin: Freinet.

Braudel, Fernand. 1979. *Civilisation matérielle, économie et capitalisme, XVème-XVIIIème siècles*. Vol. 2, *Les jeux de l'échange*. Paris: Armand Colin.

Cangiani, Michele. 2011. "'A Staggering World.' Karl Polanyi's Contribution to *Der Österreichische Volkswirt*." In *The Beginnings of Scholarly Economic Journalism*, edited by Jürgen G. Backhaus, 1–14. New York: Springer. https://doi.org/10.1007/978-1-4614-0079-0_1

Congdon, Lee. 1976. "Karl Polanyi in Hungary, 1900–19." *Journal of Contemporary History* 11 (1): 167–183. https://doi.org/10.1177/002200947601100108

Dale, Gareth. 2011. "Positivism and 'Functional Theory' in the Thought of Karl Polanyi, 1907–1922." *Sociology Compass* 5 (2): 148–164. https://doi.org/10.1111/j.1751-9020.2010.00348.x

———. 2016. *Reconstructing Karl Polanyi*. London: Pluto Press.

Dalton, George and Jasper Köcke. 1983. "The Work of the Polanyi Group: Past, Present and Future." In *Economic Anthropology. Topics and Theories*, edited by Sutti Ortiz, 21–50. Lanham and London: Society for Economic Anthropology.

Dorfman, Joseph. 1955. "The Role of the German Historical School in American Economic Thought." *American Economic Review* 45 (2): 17–28.

Duczynska, Ilona. 2006. "I first met Karl Polanyi in 1920…." In *Karl Polanyi in Vienna*, edited by Kenneth McRobbie and Kari Polanyi Levitt, 302–315. Montréal, QC: Black Rose Books.

Fusfeld, Daniel B. 1957. "Economic Theory Misplaced: Livelihood in Primitive Society." In *Trade and Market in the Early Empires*, ed. Karl Polanyi, Conrad M. Arensberg and Harry W. Pearson, 342–356. Glencoe, Ill.: The Free Press & The Falcon Wing Press.

Gabel, Joseph. 1975. "Marxisme hongrois, 'hungaro-marxisme' et école de Budapest." *L'Homme et la Société* N°. 35–36: 47–61. https://doi.org/10.3406/homso.1975.1572

Hayek, Friedrich A. (1976) 1982. *Law, Legislation, and Liberty*. Vol. 2, *The Mirage of Social Justice*. London: Routledge & Kegan Paul.

Herskovits, Melville J. 1952. *Economic Anthropology*. New York: Knopf.

Hobson, John A. 1938. *Confessions of an Economic Heretic*. London: George Allen & Unwin.

Lukács, György. (1919) 1972. "The Role of Morality in Communist Production." In Id. *Political Writings, 1919–1929*, edited by R. Livingstone, 48–52. London: New Left Books.

Malinowski, Bronislaw. 1921. "The Primitive Economics of Trobriand Islanders." *The Economic Journal* 31 (121): 1–16. https://doi.org/10.2307/2223283

Marx, Karl. (1939) 1973. *Grundrisse. Foundations of the Critique of Political Economy.* London: Penguin.

———. (1867) 1976. *Capital*, Volume One. New York: Vintage Books.

Mendell, Marguerite. 1994. "Karl Polanyi and Socialist Education." In *Humanity, Society and Commitment. On Karl Polanyi*, edited by Kenneth McRobbie, 25–42. Montréal, QC: Black Rose Books.

Mises, Ludwig. 1949. *Human Action*. New Haven, CT: Yale University Press.

Mitchell, Wesley C. 1924. "The Prospects of Economics." In *The Trend of Economics*, edited by Rexford G. Tugwell, 3–34. New York: Alfred A. Knopf.

Neale, Walter C. 1957. "Reciprocity and Redistribution in The Indian Village: Sequel to Some Notable Discussions." In *Trade and Market in the Early Empires*, edited by Karl. Polanyi, Conrad M. Arensberg, and Harry W. Pearson, 218–238. Glencoe, Ill.: The Free Press & The Falcon Wing Press.

———. 1964. "On Defining 'Labor' and 'Services' for Comparative Studies." *American Anthropologist* 66 (6): 1300–1307. https://doi.org/10.1525/aa.1964.66.6.02a00050

———. 1990. "Karl Polanyi and American Institutionalism: A Strange Case of Convergence." In *The Life and Work of Karl Polanyi*, edited by Kari Polanyi-Levitt, 145–151. Montréal, QC: Black Rose Books.

Neale, Walter C. and Anne Mayhew. 1983. "Polanyi, Institutional Economics, and Economic Anthropology." In *Economic Anthropology. Topics and Theories*, edited by Sutti Ortiz, 11–20. Lanham and London: Society for Economic Anthropology.

Neurath, Otto. 1919. *Durch die Kriegswirtschaft zur Naturalwirtschaft*. München: Georg D. W. Calwey. (Partial translation in Otto Neurath. *Empiricism and Sociology*, edited by Marie Neurath and Robert S. Cohen. Dordrecht and Boston: D. Reidel, 1973).

North, Douglass. 1977. "Markets and Other Allocation Systems in History: The Challenge of Karl Polanyi." *Journal of European Economic History* 6 (4): 703–716.

Pearson, Harry W. 1957. "The Economy Has No Surplus: Critique of a Theory of Development." In *Trade and Market in the Early Empires*, edited by Karl Polanyi, Conrad M. Arensberg and Harry W. Pearson, 320–341. Glencoe, Ill.: The Free Press & The Falcon Wing Press.

Polanyi, Karl. n.d. Karl Polanyi Archive, Concordia University. https://www.concordia.ca/research/polanyi/archive.html. Accessed November 22, 2020.

———. 1919. "Weltanschauugskrise." *Neue Erde* 31–32: 458–462.

———. 1937. *Europe To-Day*. London: Workers' Educational Trade Union Committee.

———. 1957. "The Economy as Instituted Process." In *Trade and Market in the Early Empires*, edited by Karl Polanyi, Conrad M. Arensberg and Harry W. Pearson, 243–270. Glencoe, Ill.: The Free Press & The Falcon Wing Press.

———. 1968. *Primitive, Archaic and Modern Economies*, edited by George Dalton. Garden City, NY.: Anchor Books–Doubleday.

———. 1977. *The Livelihood of Man*, edited by Harry W. Pearson. New York: Academic Press.

———. (1944) 2001. *The Great Transformation*. Boston, MA: Beacon Press.

———. (ca. 1920) 2005. "Wissenshaft und Sittlichkeit" (Science and Ethics), ms. In Id. *Chronik* der *großen Transformation*-Band 3, edited by Michele Cangiani, Kari Polanyi-Levitt and Claus Thomasberger, 172–199. Marburg: Metropolis-Verlag.

———. (1925) 2006. Letter to a friend. In *Karl Polanyi in Vienna*, edited by Kenneth McRobbie and Kari Polanyi Levitt, 316–318. Montreal/New York/London: Black Rose Books.

———. (1910) 2016. "Preface to Ernst Mach's The Analysis of Sensations." In Id. *The Hungarian Writings*, ed. Gareth Dale, 45–48. Manchester: Manchester University Press.

———. (1922a) 2016. "Socialist Accounting." In Johanna Bockman, Ariane Fischer and David Woodruff. "Socialist Accounting" by Karl Polanyi: with preface "Socialism and the embedded economy." *Theory and Society* 45 (5): 385–427. https://doi.org/10.1007/s11186-016-9276-9

———. (1922b) 2016. "Guild Socialism." In Id. *The Hungarian Writings*, ed. Gareth Dale, 118–120. Manchester: Manchester University Press.

———. (1923) 2016. "Guild and State." In Id. *The Hungarian Writings*, ed. Gareth Dale, 121–122. Manchester: Manchester University Press.

———. (1929) 2016. "The Galilei Circle: A Balance Sheet." In Id. *The Hungarian Writings*, ed. Gareth Dale, 204–208. Manchester: Manchester University Press.

———. (1927) 2018. "On Freedom." In Id., *Economy and Society. Selected Writings*, ed. Michele Cangiani and Claus Thomasberger, 15–40. Cambridge: Polity.

———. (1947) 2018. "Our Obsolete Market Mentality." In Id., *Economy and Society. Selected writings*, ed. Michele Cangiani and Claus Thomasberger, 197–211. Cambridge: Polity.

———. 2018. *Economy and Society. Selected Writings*, edited by Michele Cangiani and Claus Thomasberger. Cambridge: Polity.

Polanyi, Karl, Conrad M. Arensberg and Harry W. Pearson, ed. 1957. *Trade and Market in the Early Empires. Economies in History and Theory*. New York & London: The Free Press.

Polanyi-Levitt, Kari and Marguerite Mendell. 1987. "Karl Polanyi: His Life and Times." *Studies in Political Economy* 22 (1): 7–39. https://doi.org/10.1080/19187033.1987.11675572

Rathenau, Walter 1918. *Die neue Wirtschaft*. Berlin: G. Fischer Verlag.

Russell, Bertrand 1918. *Roads to Freedom: Socialism, Anarchism, and Syndicalism*. London: Allen & Unwin.

Sahlins, Marshall. 1969. "Economic Anthropology and Anthropological Economics." *Social Sciences Information* 8 (5): 13–33. https://doi.org/10.1177/053901846900800504

———. 1972. *Stone Age Economics*. Chicago, IL: Aldine Atherton.

Schumpeter, Joseph A. 1954. *History of Economic Analysis*. New York: Oxford University Press.

Stanfield, James Ronald. 1977. "Institutional Economics and the Crises of Capitalism." *Journal of Economic Issues* 11 (2): 449–460. https://doi.org/10.1080/00213624.1977.11503455

———. 1980. "The Institutional Economics of Karl Polanyi." *Journal of Economic Issues* 14 (3): 593–614. https://doi.org/10.1080/00213624.1980.11503767

———. 1986. *The Economic Thought of Karl Polanyi*. London: Macmillan. https://doi.org/10.1007/978-1-349-18434-7

———. 1999. "The Scope, Method, and Significance of Original Institutional Economics." *Journal of Economic Issues* 33 (2): 231–255. https://doi.org/10.1080/00213624.1999.11506154

Szabó, Erwin. 1982. *Socialism and Social Science. Selected Writings of Ervin Szabó*, edited by György Litván and János M. Bak. London: Routledge & Kegan Paul. https://doi.org/10.4324/9780203802366

Veblen, Thorstein. (1898) 1994. "Why Is Economics Not an Evolutionary Science?" In Id. *The Place of Science in Modern Civilization. And Other Essays*, 56–81. London: Routledge/Thoemmes Press.

———. (1901) 1994. Industrial and Pecuniary Employments. In Id. *The Place of Science in Modern Civilization. And Other Essays*, 279–323. London: Routledge/Thoemmes Press.

———. (1909) 1994. "The Limitations of Marginal Utility." In Id. *The Place of Science in Modern Civilization. And Other Essays*, 231–251. London: Routledge/Thoemmes Press.

Veyne, Paul. 1976. *Le Pain et le Cirque*. Paris: Éditions du Seuil. https://doi.org/10.14375/np.9782020045070

Weber, Max. (1923) 1961. *General Economic History*. New York: Collier Books.

Wilkinson, Michael. 2019. "Authoritarian Liberalism." In *The Crisis Behind the Eurocrisis: The Eurocrisis as a Multidimensional Systemic Crisis of the EU*, edited by Eva Nanopoulos and Fotis Vergis, 101–121. Cambridge, Cambridge University Press. https://doi.org/10.1017/9781108598859.006

4

GRAPPLING WITH AN EVER-CHANGING ECONOMY

The evolution of post-Keynesian institutionalism

Charles J. Whalen

Introduction

According to Hyman Minsky, economies are evolving systems. Indeed, Minsky (1993, 104) stressed that "societies are evolutionary beasts which cannot be frozen in time and reduced to static mathematical formulations." Moreover, the process does not end: "[H]istory does not lead to an end of history."

Minsky attributed the same view to John Maynard Keynes: Every state of the economy is transitory and changes in response to both endogenous and exogenous factors. This dynamism was most evident in Keynes's view of business cycles, but Minsky saw it from a broader perspective. "We live out our lives in transition: there is no final solution to the problems of organizing economic life," he wrote when concluding his 1975 book that reinterpreted Keynes (Minsky 1975, 168).

In early 1996, less than a year before his death, Minsky received the Veblen-Commons Award, the highest honor bestowed by the institutionalists' Association for Evolutionary Economics (AFEE). On that occasion, Minsky (1996a, 357) began his remarks by mentioning a letter that Keynes sent to institutionalist John R. Commons, which highlighted the affinity between their economic perspectives. As it turns out, Commons's analysis of an ongoing transition in economic history had an influence on Keynes ([1926] 1932, 334, for example), so Minsky's reference to Keynes's letter helps draw attention to the fact that Keynes and the institutionalists were both grappling with an ever-changing economy.

That effort continues today in the work of post-Keynesian institutionalism (PKI), a strand of the institutionalist research tradition that builds on institutionalism's compatibility and complementarity with post-Keynesian economics. Like the capitalist system it studies, PKI is constantly evolving, and this chapter traces that evolution—from the early days of the US economic expansion following

DOI: 10.4324/9781003160434-4

World War II, when PKI was foreshadowed in a pair of essays by institutionalist Allan Gruchy (1950a; 1950b), to the present phase of PKI research, which began in response to the global financial crisis of 2007–2009, with its focus on financialization and rising economic insecurity in an era dominated by institutional investors (Minsky 1993, 111). Along the way, the chapter offers suggestions for future research, and its conclusion looks with optimism toward PKI's future.

The postwar boom and PKI foreshadowed

PKI fuses the institutionalist tradition—which emerged out of the early twentieth-century work of American scholars such as Thorstein Veblen, Wesley Mitchell, and Commons—with the insight and contributions of Keynes and those he inspired who call their work post-Keynesian economics. Given the considerable common ground in the work of Keynes and the early institutionalists, such a fusion is not surprising. Indeed, in 1927, Keynes ([1927] 1982) wrote the following to Commons (in the letter mentioned in Minsky's Veblen-Commons address): "There seems to me to be no other economist with whose general way of thinking I feel myself in such genuine accord."

No sure thing

In fact, however, the development of PKI was not a sure thing in the wake of Keynes's *The General Theory of Employment, Interest, and Money.* According to Philip Klein (1998, 44), many institutional economists "failed to appreciate the commonalities and some were … hostile to Keynes." In addition, Malcolm Rutherford and Tyler Desroches (2008, 31) provide a detailed examination of institutionalists' reaction to *The General Theory,* which concludes that "the institutionalist response to Keynes was a varied one, and involved some substantial criticisms … on methodological, theoretical, and empirical grounds"—criticisms that were mostly an outgrowth of institutionalists' own active research agendas on monetary economics and the business cycle in the 1920s and 1930s.

Nevertheless, early in the boom era following World War II, PKI was foreshadowed in essays by Gruchy on similarities and contrasts of Keynes and the institutionalists. At the end of those essays, Gruchy (1950a; 1950b) concluded not only that institutionalism and the economics of Keynes have much in common, but also that their differences are mostly complementary:

> In spite of all the differences in their interests and opinions, the economic studies of Keynes and the institutionalists have contributed much to a synthesis of the economics of the individual firm, to studies of the flow of national income, and to investigations into the nature of the economic order. Such synthesis seems to be, and may very well turn out to be, the major contribution of [economics in] this century.
>
> *(Gruchy 1950b, 125–126)*

In fact, Gruchy saw Keynes-institutionalist compatibility in two other areas—economic methodology and economic policy—in addition to the fields hinted at above.

Methodology, theory, and policy

In Gruchy's essays, a shared Keynes-institutionalist methodology—preconceptions serving as the foundation for an alternative to both neoclassical and Marxist economics—emerges from his discussion of the definition, scope, methods, and values of economics. According to Gruchy, Keynes and the institutionalists define economics as the study of all aspects of human culture that relate to providing the goods and services that satisfy human needs and wants. Theirs is a broad and "holistic," problem-solving science, which: views the economy as an interwoven and constantly evolving part of the social whole; believes theories should be fashioned around empirical generalizations relevant to the "concrete reality [of] the economic system in which we live and work"; and recognizes that social values and "service values" (derived from goods or services in use) often diverge from the valuations generated by market-based transactions (Gruchy 1950a, 97–100; 1950b, 108–111, 120).

Gruchy also saw compatible and complementary views on theory and policy. He argued that institutionalism's microeconomic contributions and Keynes's macroeconomics both stem from giving attention to money as a vital factor in industrial capitalism, with institutionalists emphasizing the emergence and consequences of oligopolistic corporations and Keynes emphasizing the determination of national income and employment (Gruchy 1950a, 104–105; 1950b, 110–114). On the nature and evolution of economic order, Gruchy (1950b, 115–120) maintained that Keynes focused on the demand side (such as a weak inducement to invest), while institutionalists concentrated on the supply side (including changing economic conditions). Acknowledging differences on policy details, Gruchy (1950b, 120–121) highlighted a shared rejection of laissez-faire and a "strong reformist drive." He also found a common goal: to experiment, in various ways, with "a wider use of collective action" for the purpose of "giving greater expression to the individual."

The Great Stagflation and the bimodal economy

By the time the postwar boom gave way to the Great Stagflation of the 1970s, the neoclassical interpretation of Keynes was under attack not only in academia but also in the world of policymaking. While an assault from Milton Friedman and other monetarists received much of the attention, a growing group of progressive scholars believed neoclassical "Keynesianism" had omitted the most significant aspects of the economics of Keynes, leading them to band together in the early 1970s under the post-Keynesian label. A discussion of the origins and history of this group demonstrates that it was a fluid network—whose early members included (among others) Joan Robinson, Alfred Eichner, Paul Davidson, and Minsky—with varied and evolving economic ideas (Lee 2000).

Peterson's presidential address

Although Gruchy wrote optimistically in 1950 about a synthesis of insight from Keynes and the institutionalists, little movement in that direction took place within the institutionalist camp until the mid-1970s. A watershed moment was when Wallace Peterson (1977) devoted his presidential address before AFEE to core ideas he saw as the foundation of both post-Keynesianism (which he called the "economics of Keynes") and institutionalism, and concluded that economists of both traditions would be best able to understand and address real-world problems by building a common analytical framework. Peterson's presentation highlighted a shared emphasis on uncertainty, institutions (especially financial institutions), power relations, economic change, macroeconomic instability, and the need for public action to address concentrations and abuses of private power (even as private power was acknowledged to often have a grip on public power).[1]

In the wake of Peterson's address, a number of institutionalists showed interest in exploring the compatibility and complementarity of institutionalism and the emerging post-Keynesianism. Brazelton (1981), for example, stressed institutionalism's compatibility with elements found in the post-Keynesianism of Sidney Weintraub, including an emphasis on mark-up pricing, attention to the institutional determinants of wage setting, and rejection of the assumption that economic processes are inherently self-equilibrating. Keller (1983) added that the two camps complemented each other because institutionalism had more fully considered the conceptual underpinnings to active state involvement in the economy, while post-Keynesianism had more fully developed analyses of problems such as inflation. Moreover, Marshall (1983) pointed to the policy failures of Keynesianism and Reaganomics, and insisted the time was right for an alternative economic analysis and policy agenda based on a synthesis of institutionalism and post-Keynesianism.

Wilber and Jameson's post-Keynesian institutionalism

As if on cue, Charles Wilber and Kenneth Jameson (1983) published *An Inquiry into the Poverty of Economics*. It explicitly offered PKI as an alternative to other economic paradigms. The book laid out the methodology of PKI, described the structure and operation of the US economy and its relevance to the problem of stagflation, and closed with policy recommendations aimed at a set of clearly stated economic goals.

According to Wilber and Jameson (1983, 151–157), PKI seeks to understand and resolve real-world problems from a vantage point that sees the economy as not only constantly evolving, but also holistic and systemic. In other words, from the perspective of PKI, the economy is not neatly separable from other social spheres: interdependencies are pervasive, and society's various institutions shape economic life. Moreover, PKI rejects universal economic laws in favor of "empirical generalizations that are historically specific and must be revised as culture and institutions change." Thus, Wilber and Jameson argued that a guiding principle of the methodology of PKI is "look at the world, then theorize."

Stagflation in the bimodal economy

To fashion their PKI view of the economy and its relevance to analyzing stagflation, Wilber and Jameson drew on the work of many of that era's institutionalists and post-Keynesians. But at the heart of their analysis was John Kenneth Galbraith's (1973) notion of the bimodal economy. The focus on Galbraith was appropriate not only because of the usefulness of his work for studying the problem at hand, but also because of his stature in the profession. Galbraith—who held a faculty position at Harvard University and served as president of the American Economic Association (in 1972)—was the most prominent institutionalist of the day and recipient (in 1976) of AFEE's Veblen-Commons Award. But he was also an early supporter of the post-Keynesian movement, played an instrumental role in establishment of the *Journal of Post Keynesian Economics*, and contributed an essay on post-Keynesian economics for that journal's inaugural issue (Galbraith 1978).

According to Wilber and Jameson (1983, 168–194), the US economy of the postwar era was a bifurcated system. The dominant force was what Galbraith referred to as the "planning" sector of about a thousand large corporations, operating in an oligopolistic fashion and wielding considerable economic power; and on the periphery was a "market" sector containing millions of small firms with "little or no control over the economic environment." Planning-sector firms, which Eichner (1976) called "megacorps," aimed for steady growth and profits, using an "administered" mechanism to set prices as a markup over the sum of direct costs (such as labor, materials, and rent), a target rate of return, and the funds needed for reinvestment. However, since investment decisions rest on a volatile foundation of profit expectations, the rate of economic expansion (or contraction) is always subject to change, and business cycles are recognized as an ordinary part of capitalism.

After developing the broad contours of their synthesis of institutionalism and post-Keynesianism, Wilber and Jameson (1983, 174–176, 207–217, 223–226) applied it to what they identified as the most pressing economic problem of the day: stagflation. According to their analysis, higher inflation was triggered by the wage increases of labor unions in the planning sector, combined with oil-price increases and a slowdown of productivity growth—and rising prices subsequently fueled inflationary expectations throughout the economy. The federal government responded by aiming to reduce inflation with conventional macroeconomic tools, but contractionary fiscal and monetary policies had been rendered counterproductive by planning-sector power. Relying on evidence that planning-sector firms raised prices as recessionary pressures mounted, the authors argued that conventional macroeconomic management exacerbated inflation even as it increased joblessness.

The final chapter of Wilber and Jameson's (1983, 230–263) book offered a number of policy ideas. Stagflation is part of what they sought to address, but they aimed even further and discussed three broad socioeconomic goals: enhancement of life-sustenance; promotion of self-worth, human dignity, and opportunities for fellowship; and individual freedom, which involves meaningful autonomy for consumers, workers, and citizens. Specific recommendations included establishment of "indicative" planning mechanisms to promote genuine full-employment budgeting; use of incomes policies to directly contain inflation; and measures to promote workplace democracy.

The Great Moderation and the financial instability hypothesis

Although its PKI foundation was well-constructed, *An Inquiry into the Poverty of Economics* failed to receive much attention because the book appeared just as inflation was being beaten down. Wilber and Jameson identified an important, real-world problem, but, ironically, their book was a casualty of the economic change process they placed at the heart of PKI. Their analysis was too tied to stagflation; to advance further, the analyses of PKI would need a more dynamic focus.

Turning toward Minsky

The economics of Minsky provided the necessary focus: the study of economic instability, with an emphasis on the interaction of finance and macroeconomics. In the mid-1980s, Minsky's ideas featured prominently in two special issues highlighting institutional economics for AFEE's *Journal of Economic Issues* (*JEI*). In the first, Fazzari and Minsky (1984) critically examined monetarism and outlined an alternative to conventional economic theory and policy. Their perspective was organized around the notion that capitalism is inherently unstable, and their alternative was formed by combining insight from Keynes with a deep appreciation of the importance of institutional realities. A few years later, Dillard (1987, 1642) identified Minsky's analysis of financial instability as a "major contribution" to understanding money as an institution of capitalism; and, in the same issue of the *JEI*, Peterson (1987, 1613) highlighted Minsky's work as "a promising and imaginative start" toward incorporating the key institutions of modern capitalism into macroeconomics.

Minsky, who for many years called himself a "financial Keynesian," welcomed institutionalists' interest in his ideas and embraced the work of helping to bridge different traditions in economic thought. He was accepted by his colleagues as both a post-Keynesian and an institutionalist, and openly discussed how his views were rooted in both camps. Moreover, he used receipt of AFEE's Veblen-Commons Award as an opportunity to stress the *continuing relevance* of the affinity between Keynes and the institutionalists (Minsky 1996a, 357).[2]

Paradigm and hypothesis

A key starting point for Minsky (1975) was that capitalism is prone to financial crises, economic instability, and bouts of high unemployment. In other words, he began with the perspective of Veblen, Mitchell, Commons, and Keynes, which saw business cycles as endogenously generated, not extraordinary events caused merely by factors external to the economic system. He also started with the Keynes-institutionalist view of the centrality of money and finance, which some have called a monetary theory of production (a perspective recognizing not only that production precedes marketplace exchange but also that finance precedes production). In particular, Minsky offered a "Wall Street paradigm" as an alternative to the "barter paradigm" that he saw at the root of conventional economics: In Minsky's economics, the underlying image is of a world shaped largely by corporate and financial-sector decisions regarding investments and financial portfolios. That alternative enabled Minsky to focus on how individuals and organizations manage cash flows and debt in a world in which production takes time and where the future is uncertain.

Building on that foundation, Minsky (1977) developed his "financial instability hypothesis" (FIH), which can be seen as an alternative to the efficient market hypothesis (EMH) of conventional economics and finance. In contrast to the EMH—which argues that financial markets are efficient and stable, and that financial-market participants are not (as a group) predisposed to overconfidence and other biases—the FIH accommodates herd behavior (but does not require "irrational" decisions) and sudden changes in expectations, and argues that the financial structure of capitalist economies tends to become more fragile over a period of prosperity. Minsky (1977; 1986a, 206–213) described that process as the recurrent evolution from conservative to more and more risky forms of financing. Fragility reaches its peak when some firms (usually those borrowing merely to make interest payments) cannot sustain themselves, sending shockwaves through the economy in the form of falling business expectations, deleveraging, and perhaps even debt deflation (as an asset selloff causes asset prices to plummet).

Relevance

Minsky initially placed his FIH at the heart of an investment-oriented theory of business cycles (see, for example, Minsky 1975; 1977); over time, however, he began to emphasize its longer-term relevance—as a way to explain the evolution of finance in the United States after World War II (see, for example, Minsky 1980; 1986a; 1986b). According to that broader perspective, the first two postwar decades were relatively tranquil because the memory of the Great Depression caused enterprises to operate on sizable margins of safety. But prosperity eventually led to an erosion of those margins and spurred institutional innovations in finance; as a result, the financial system became more fragile. The credit crunch of 1966—the first in the postwar era—signaled a new era of "contained turbulence," during which the solvency of financial institutions was protected by Federal Reserve intervention and business profits were sustained by government deficit spending.

The FIH provided PKI with a powerful approach to analyzing not only the US economy but also financial crises elsewhere. Applied to the United States, it could account for the Great Depression, the postwar boom, and the return of US financial instability (which had been a serious problem for several decades leading up to the Great Depression). As part of Minsky's overall macroeconomic framework—which was spelled out in *Stabilizing an Unstable Economy* (Minsky 1986a) and had many elements in common with Wilber and Jameson (1983)—the FIH also helped account for the Great Stagflation and for the abatement of inflation during the era of Reaganomics (owing to an erosion of union power and a flood of imported goods). Then, in the 1980s and 1990s, many economists (Cypher 1996, for example) also used the FIH to shed light on financial and economic crises in various parts of the world, ranging from Mexico to Russia.

To be sure, PKI's turn toward the FIH in the mid-1980s had its own element of irony. It occurred just when the US economy entered an era that mainstream economists would later call the Great Moderation because of low inflation and modest business cycles. But, of course, that 1984–2007 period was far from tranquil. It included: the largest single-day percentage drop in stock-market history (October 19, 1987); a savings and loan crisis that lasted about a decade (roughly from 1985 until 1995, involving the failure of over 1,000—one-third—of the nation's thrift institutions); the dot-com boom and collapse (from which the Nasdaq index took 15 years to recover); and "jobless" recoveries (characterized by sluggish job growth) following business-cycle troughs in 1991 and 2001. In addition, Minsky's discussions of "contained turbulence" clearly identified and highlighted the institutions and interventions that reined in downside instability, though he also worried that "the further evolution of our financial structure" would "diminish our ability" to contain such instability (see, for example, Minsky 1986b, 352). In fact, Minsky (1986c) warned as early as 1986 that financial innovations such as securitization of financial assets would eventually lead to an international financial crisis.

Linkages, applications, and extensions

A number of contributions to PKI during the Great Moderation addressed post-Keynesian and institutionalist linkages, while many others offered applications and extensions. For example, Wray (1992) contrasted the "endogenous" approach to money and interest rates—embodied in both institutional and post-Keynesian economics, and consistent with Minsky's approach to finance and macroeconomics—with other approaches including that of conventional economic theory. Wray (1994; 1998; 2002) also applied the FIH to the financial instability of the 1980s and early 1990s; elaborated on Minsky's proposal for government to ensure full employment by serving as "employer of last resort" (a recommendation also advocated by generations of institutional economists); and offered a Minskyan perspective on the US economy's public and private balance sheets following the collapse of the dot-com boom on the eve of the new millennium. At the same time, Whalen (1992; 1996) sketched the linkages that unite institutionalism and post-Keynesianism at the level of methodology, analysis, and policy, giving a central place to the FIH and macroeconomic instability; and Whalen and Wenger (2002) applied the FIH to call for shoring up the US economy's fiscal stabilizers.

Other contributors to the FIH literature in that period included Carter (1989), Dymski (1997), and Kregel (1997; 1998). Carter extended the FIH by reviewing financial innovations of the 1980s and examining how they contributed to a more fragile financial structure. Dymski offered a deeper understanding of the FIH by clarifying key aspects of the underlying Wall Street paradigm. And Kregel focused on the role of margins of safety in generating financial fragility, as well as on how the Asian financial crisis (1997–1999) was compatible with Minsky's hypothesis.

Additional contributors focused on the FIH's implications for financial-sector regulation. Phillips (1997) presented the case for Minsky's "cash-flow oriented approach" to rethinking bank examinations. Tymoigne (2007) and Brown (2008) drew on insight from the FIH to highlight the worsening condition of household finances just prior to the global financial crisis and to call for greater financial regulation. Perhaps the most prescient of all those applying the FIH, however, was McClintock (1996), who warned—a decade before the global financial crisis (but still a decade after Minsky's warning in the mid-1980s)—that rapid evolution of the financial derivatives market had caused the international financial system to become troublingly fragile, and that significant national and supranational policy intervention would be required to cope with the coming crisis.

Others also introduced considerations that place the FIH in a global context. For example, Wolfson (2002) identified important features of the global institutional setting and addressed their consequences for Minsky's analysis, concluding that "financial crises and debt deflations will be the continuing legacy" of attempts to deregulate global financial markets. Rima (2002) offered a similar conclusion, emphasizing how information technology contributed to the globalization of finance as well as how venture capital fueled the technology sector (thus becoming an important new financial component of the economy for PKI to consider). And an ambitious article by Niggle (2006) linked Minsky's ideas with those of other institutionalists and post-Keynesians to forge a synthesis with "more explanatory power and more usefulness in the design of macro policy" than conventional macroeconomics.[3]

The global financial crisis and money manager capitalism

When US house prices fell sharply in 2007, triggering a global financial crisis and the Great Recession, Minsky became an overnight sensation. Despite having been dead since 1996, Minsky was featured on the front page of the *Wall Street Journal* (Lahart 2007). Economist Robert Pollin (2008) declared "We are all Minskyites now"—and Paul Krugman (2009) chose to speak about Minsky in a lecture organized to celebrate Krugman's receipt (in 2008) of the Nobel memorial award in economics. The ideas of PKI were receiving widespread interest; but the focus of PKI was about to change.

A spotlight, but also a new phase for PKI

As that crisis unfolded and then receded, a flurry of economists (such as Barbera 2009; and a number of contributors to Tavasci and Toporowski 2010), including some associated with PKI (such as Fernandez, Kaboub, and Todorova 2008; Prasch 2010; and Whalen 2007), applied the FIH to that crisis and to others that emerged in the developing world during the previous decade or so. But those most familiar with Minsky's work soon recognized that the FIH was not a sufficient device for analyzing the global crisis; Minsky's conception of money manager capitalism (MMC), a product of the theory of capitalist development to which he devoted considerable attention during the last decade of his life, was also relevant. Whalen (2008a; 2010) and Wray (2009; 2010) were the first to highlight this element of the crisis, signaling a new phase of PKI research in which MMC became the main focus.

In this new phase—which continues to the present—the FIH remains relevant, but must be integrated with MMC, which Minsky saw as the latest stage of capitalist development. Writing in the early 1990s, Minsky (1993) used the term "money manager capitalism" to highlight the dominant position that pension-fund managers and other institutional investors came to hold in the US economy beginning in the 1980s, a position they used to influence both corporate decision-making and public policy. Then, in early 1996, less than a year before his death, Minsky (1996a) applied his theory not only to discuss how the US economy evolved in the decades after World War II from a system driven by corporate managers (a stage he called "managerialism") to one controlled by money managers, but also to highlight the problem of worker insecurity, which had been growing more and more widespread for years because of MMC.

Two sides of the same coin—and then crisis

In the decade between Minsky's death and the financial turmoil that culminated in the global financial crisis of 2007–2009, his work on capitalist development and MMC received limited attention, mostly from Whalen (1997; 2001; 2002; 2008b), Van Lear (2001; 2002), and Zalewski (2002; 2004; 2005). Whalen focused mainly on: fleshing out Minsky's theory of stages (including the evolution from one stage to another); underscoring how MMC and the spread of worker insecurity are two sides of the same coin; and updating Minsky's analysis (in the wake of the dot-com boom and later on the eve of the Great Recession). Van Lear drew on Minsky's analysis to show that widespread institutional equity ownership inhibits economic growth as well as to argue that MMC is incompatible with fundamental American principles such as a commitment to liberty, representation, and enterprise. Zalewski explored economic insecurity in the age of MMC (owing to erosion of worker retirement benefits, for example), along with possibilities for constructive policy reform.

In Minsky's theory of capitalist development, the financial system is always significant because finance influences business activity and financial structures are especially prone to innovation (in response to both the demands of businesses and the entrepreneurialism of financing organizations). But finance became even more important after the shift from managerial capitalism to MMC because institutional investors, the new pivotal source of financing, are driven by the sole aim of maximizing shareholder value. As a result, business leaders grew increasingly sensitive to short-term profits, and, along with fund managers, those executives and their bankers became eager to pursue initiatives that might boost stock-market values. Such initiatives included, for example, introduction of corporate reorganizations (such as mergers, corporate divestitures, and leveraged buyouts), use of unconventional financial practices (such as stock buybacks and creative use of off-balance-sheet commitments), and adoption of innovative financial products (such as the commercial paper of finance companies, mortgage-backed securities, and credit default swaps) (Whalen 2008b).

Economic insecurity for workers is the flipside to MMC's drive for stock-market returns. Under pressure from money managers, corporate executives went on the offensive against labor unions, downsized in-house operations, and relied increasingly on job outsourcing and offshoring. In addition to job insecurity for those in "permanent" positions, the emergence of MMC meant that growing numbers of employees (including professional workers and managers) faced workplaces in which productivity pressures and contingent (contract-based) work were on the rise, while wage gains stagnated and retirement and other workplace benefits and opportunities (such as training and job ladders) were curtailed or eliminated. As MMC took hold, labor became increasingly viewed by enterprises as just another "spot market" commodity, to be employed or discharged as dictated by conditions that could change overnight (Whalen 2008b).

Then, in 2007, US real estate prices began to fall, leveling a financial house of cards that was global in scope and built around mortgage securitization, the investment of choice for many of the era's managed-money funds; it was all as Minsky (1986c) had warned. In the wake of the crisis, two books analyzed its causes, consequences, and policy implications from the perspective of economists associated with PKI: *Financial Instability and Economic Security after the Great Recession* (Whalen 2011) and *The Rise and Fall of Money Manager Capitalism* (Tymoigne and Wray 2014). Both books are grounded explicitly in a Minskyan perspective linking FIH and MMC, and complement each other in a variety of ways. For example, while *Financial Instability* highlights the link between the early stages of Minsky's theory of capitalist development and the work of Commons (thereby situating Minsky's approach firmly in the PKI tradition) and includes an examination of the impact of MMC on emerging market economies, *The Rise and Fall* digs more deeply into the evolution from managerial capitalism to MMC, and provides a more detailed look at financial fragility in the era of MMC.

PKI today: core elements, research themes, and new directions

This penultimate section summarizes some core elements and vital research topics and themes in PKI today. Additional directions for future research are also suggested.

Core elements

The core elements of PKI begin with economic methodology. According to Dugger (1996), institutionalists define economics as the study of ever-evolving, real-world processes of social provisioning, and that definition provides their economics tradition with its methodological underpinnings. Dugger also adheres to the holism of Gruchy and Wilber and Jameson (whose foundations remain relevant), which holds that boundaries between the economy and other social spheres are always imprecise. Today's PKI builds on the same perspective. The following are some implications of that foundation: (1) PKI theorists are more interested in analyses built on realistic assumptions (recognizing, of course, that all theories are an abstraction from reality) than on construction of formal models; (2) people are recognized as acting in a world of uncertainty, which means not only that they are understood to rely heavily on habits and social conventions and that lessons are learned through experience (which often involves unmet expectations), but also that ends and means are subject to constant reconsideration; (3) human wants are shaped by culture and corporate advertising, which means that investigations of want creation are within the scope of economics; and (4) PKI sees institutions, not impersonal forces or universal laws of nature, as the balancing wheel of the economy.[4]

Because PKI is the product of scholars aiming to better understand the problems surrounding them, its research centers mainly on the study of economic life under contemporary capitalism. A core element here is recognition that, as Commons (1934a, 766) writes, "Capitalism is not a static or single concept." In such research, PKI emphasizes endogenous socioeconomic evolution and market dynamics that involve cumulative causation and path dependence. Real-world markets may not rapidly or fully adjust to price signals in the near term, and, in any event, market "equilibrium" is never more than a moving target.

PKI also rests on Minsky's Wall Street paradigm (in place of the barter paradigm of standard economics) and on the notion of the state as a creative entity (an alternative to the neoclassical perspective of the state as a body that corrects market failures). Building on the Wall Street paradigm, other core elements include the FIH (including the associated theory of endogenous business cycles) and Minsky's theory of capitalist development, which in our time means a focus on MMC. Meanwhile, PKI views the government as deeply and unavoidably involved in shaping the economy by fashioning institutions and making and enforcing rules that are always evolving. PKI also recognizes that government's creative effort can be constructively directed toward any of a variety of conceptions of efficiency (including, for example, allocative, macroeconomic, or adaptive efficiency) and that public policy is often shaped by other considerations as well (such as social justice).[5]

Methodology as a research area

Turning to research topics and themes, we also begin with methodology. In the area of economic methodology, current PKI research themes include both the further integration of post-Keynesian and institutionalist methodological contributions and the assimilation of insight from psychology and other disciplines into PKI.

Examples of such work include recent contributions by Tauheed (2011) and Fernández-Huerga (2008). Tauheed proposes an innovative approach to policy deliberation that combines elements from post-Keynesian system dynamics with a heuristic framework of analysis from institutionalism. While Tauheed builds bridges within economics, Fernández-Huerga draws on neurosciences and psychology to highlight the influence of habits and social institutions upon human motivation, cognition, reasoning, and decision-making, and to outline a post-Keynesian institutionalist model of human economic behavior that is more realistic than the model implicit in conventional economics. Institutionalism has long borrowed from other traditions and disciplines; continuing to engage in such efforts can only strengthen PKI.

Financial instability

As the global financial crisis of 2007–2009 demonstrated, financial instability has not disappeared in the era of MMC; the context is just different than in earlier eras. Thus, it's not surprising that financial instability remains a prevalent research topic in the institutionalist literature. In fact, in AFEE's *JEI*, Minsky's FIH was discussed in 19 articles published from the beginning of 2010 through September 2020—and 68 articles gave at least some attention to the notion of financial instability.

Three contributions from that literature are especially noteworthy because each represents a research stream that will likely continue to help advance the economic and policy analyses of PKI for some time. The first contribution is a pair of articles by Ülgen (2018; 2020) that rest on an "institutionalist Minskyan" view of financial instability and call for macro-prudential financial-sector regulation that takes a skeptical look at financial innovation and involves tight supervision of financial markets. Since economists holding such a perspective seem to be constantly swimming against the stream in academic and policy circles, PKI will need to continue sharpening its instability analyses and recommendations for the foreseeable future.

The other notable contributions are Scott and Pressman (2019) and Tokucu (2014). Scott and Pressman continue a recent and important stream of PKI research that extends the FIH (which focused originally on businesses) to analyze the economic consequences of household debt, consumer spending, and income inequality.[6] Tokucu continues a different strand of important FIH research, which applies that analysis to developing nations (whereas Minsky focused heavily on the United States), in this case shedding light on economic developments threatening the financial stability of Turkey's economy.

Money manager capitalism

Analyzing the characteristics, consequences, and evolution of MMC is at the heart of contemporary PKI. Between the start of 2010 and September 2020, MMC was addressed in 27 diverse articles in the *JEI*. For example, they include an examination of household agency over stages of US capitalism (Cardwell and Todorova 2016); exploration of similarities between MMC and the economic stage (often called finance capitalism) that preceded the Great Depression (Van Lear and Sisk 2010); and investigation of financial crises and institutional changes in Latin America since the 1980s, including a discussion of how those changes cleared the way for an expansion of MMC (Correa 2014).

At the core of MMC research (in the *JEI* and beyond), is the matter of MMC's implications for overall economic activity and performance. For example, focusing primarily on corporate behavior, Prasch (2014) argues that MMC established financial instability, business myopia, and predatory financial practices as the "new normal." In a more recent publication focusing on economic outcomes, Whalen (2020b) shows that MMC has slowed technological progress, increased financial fragility and instability, intensified and widened worker insecurity, and fueled rising income inequality—just as Minsky warned decades ago.

Minsky's periodization of capitalist development and the continuing evolution of MMC are also recent and ongoing subjects of research in PKI. Diop (2016) and Toporowski (2020) each offer valuable contributions that aim to improve Minsky's periodization.[7] Ongoing work highlights how the COVID-19 pandemic reveals and compounds significant US economic weaknesses traceable to MMC (see, for example, Liang and Whalen 2022). Such work will need to continue as the economy continues to evolve.

Other streams of research in PKI need to consider financial markets and business enterprises under MMC. Within the financial sector (which Minsky saw as an especially dynamic part of the economy) are numerous institutions, tools, and practices—ranging, for example, from private equity and hedge funds to more obscure forms of shadow banking (on the latter, see Nesvetailova 2014)—that have emerged as significant in the era of MMC. At the same time, the focus on shareholder value within corporations, mixed with the evolution of finance and the law, has altered the nature and use of capital assets by corporations and in many other ways reshaped business structures, strategies, and practices. All of this is currently being studied from the lens of MMC (see, for example, Atkinson, Hake, and Paschall 2019; Baranes and Hake 2018; Dean 2018; and Jo and Henry 2015), and such work, including further updates to institutionalism's long history of research on capitalism's legal foundations, will need to continue.[8]

Since widespread worker insecurity is the flipside to enterprises driven by shareholder value, the topics of employment and worker well-being (including the economic status of those seeking a job and those who have retired) are also key parts of the research of PKI. A major theme since the start of MMC research (see, for example, Minsky, and Whalen 1996) has been rising economic insecurity—the dimensions of which include income insecurity (owing to wage stagnation and elimination of job ladders that once provided a route to income gains), retirement and healthcare insecurity (owing to erosion of pensions and other employee benefits), and job insecurity (owing to downsizing, outsourcing, contingent work, and other changes to the employment relationship). At first, much of this insecurity seemed to fall largely on blue-collar industrial workers, but it quickly became a reality for more and more workers and their families, squeezing those in the middle of the income distribution and causing many to reconsider the viability of what they considered a "middle class" existence (Greenhouse 2008).

PKI has a long research tradition to draw upon when it comes to employment and worker well-being. Those topics have interested generations of institutionalists and post-Keynesians, resulting in valuable analyses of the labor market (including Fernández-Huerga, García-Arias, and Salvador 2017; Prasch 2004; and Seccareccia 1991) and employment policies (see, for example, Levin-Waldman 2018). There has also been important recent work done by a diverse group of scholars and journalists with an interest in employment and workers (including Appelbaum and Batt 2014; Case and Deaton 2020; Kessler 2018; and Weil 2017). The task for PKI is to keep abreast of such research, incorporate its contributions into an understanding of MMC, and, when possible, advance that literature with investigations of the changing world of employment and its consequences for working families.

Greater income and wealth inequality are also a consequence of MMC that needs attention from PKI. Such inequality contributes to economic insecurity among middle- and low-income households. It also drags down economic growth, exacerbates financial and economic instability, and threatens social and political stability (Costantini and Seccareccia 2020; Galbraith 2012; Stiglitz 2012).

Government and public policy

PKI recognizes the inescapable and pivotal role played by the state in economic life. Two ongoing research streams stand out in this literature: work focusing on the creative state, and work on the predator state. In reality, the state is and will likely continue to be a mixture of the two—a creative force for good and an instrument of predation by those seeking private gain. The state is, after all, terrain in which competing groups "assert the legitimacy of their rights and freedoms" (Brown 1992, 13).

The notion of the creative state offers much for PKI to consider at the conceptual and analytical levels—that is, it has relevance to discussions about the relationship between the state and the economy (see, for example, Schmid 1999) as well as to analyses that seek to anticipate the effects of policy changes on socioeconomic life (see, for example, Chapter 8 in this book). But equally important is that viewing the state as a creative entity can help us reimagine socioeconomic institutions and practices so as to improve economic performance and advance the public interest. Thus, this side of the state appears in vital post-Keynesian institutionalist research designed to find constructive policy solutions (such as Tcherneva 2018).

Recognizing, exploring, and devising ways to curtail the predatory side of the state, which has become more visible and consequential in the MMC era, are also essential elements of contemporary PKI. James Galbraith (2008) offered a major contribution to this literature, explaining public-sector predation as a situation in which government officials do not recognize the public interest and instead manage the public sector to serve private interests. Of course, it comes as no surprise that deregulation of the financial sector is one illustration offered by Galbraith: MMC didn't just emerge on its own; it was helped along as financial elites used their influence to shape public policies in ways that furthered their own private interests.

Financialization, gender, and race

In addition to the topics and themes mentioned so far, PKI will need to put financialization, gender, and race on its research agenda. Financialization is a hot topic among researchers in a variety of fields of study. But the study of financialization is in many ways just a different way of referring to the study of MMC. In fact, while financialization contains a number of research strands, Minsky's work on MMC represents a contribution to all of them—and in some cases, he anticipated much of the work done in recent decades (Whalen 2020). Going forward, PKI needs to build bridges with scholars engaged in financialization research (including some within the ranks of institutional economics); greater engagement across this terminological divide can only strengthen our understanding of the economy and its evolution—and may better enable us to devise institutional reforms that achieve shared social goals.[9]

Because PKI has focused heavily on macroeconomic matters, it has tended to reflect the macro field's lack of attention to gender and race. Some researchers have sought to point the way to a feminist PKI, including Jennings (1994) and Todorova (2009), while Girón (2015) places gender at the center of an analysis that looks at micro-finance institutions in the context of MMC. In fact, the work of such researchers suggests that gender considerations are relevant at the level of methodology, economic analysis, and public policy. Much less has been written to guide greater attention to race (but see Shulman 1996 and Tauheed 2008); PKI will need to grapple with both gender and race in the years ahead.

Global reach and planetary sustainability

PKI is deeply rooted in American institutionalism and began with a focus on the US economy; today, however, it is a tradition with global reach. Its contributors come from around the world, and its concepts are applied to study not only a wide variety of economies, but also the interplay among nations.

In 1990, Minsky (1990, 71) observed that MMC was already international in terms of the managed-money funds and their assets. He also argued that more and more countries would be drawn into the MMC orbit over time, leading to greater global financial integration and requiring coordinated international policy responses to crises. Today, the economics literature shows (as indicated above) that researchers find it useful to draw on PKI to study not just the most advanced market economies but also Argentina, Turkey, Chile, and other emerging market economies. In fact, some draw on PKI to analyze the state capitalism of Russia and China (Girón 2018; Klimina 2013; Poirot 2001).[10]

Of course, only part of the reason for the global reach of PKI stems from worldwide concerns about financial instability and from a recognition of the global scope of the institutions of MMC. International interest in PKI also comes from recognition of inequality and worker insecurity as global problems. Moreover, as economist Raghuram Rajan recently warned, capitalism "is under serious threat" because it currently fails to provide opportunity for most people (BBC News 2019). That suggests the current need for scholarship rooted in PKI becomes as urgent as the work of Commons and Keynes was in their time, when very real threats from authoritarianism of various sorts created the need to "save capitalism by making it good" (Commons 1934b, 143).

Meanwhile, most urgent is the need for scholars in all fields to help address global warming, which threatens sustainability of life on Earth (United Nations 2018). Within economics, PKI may be in a particularly strategic position to address this matter—institutionalism has long been better able than conventional economics to recognize and accommodate the issue of sustainability (see Greenwood and Holt 2016), and the relentless and single-minded drive for shareholder value at the heart of MMC represents perhaps the greatest challenge to moving toward sustainability.

A final observation: back to Gruchy

This chapter has documented the considerable progress made by PKI as a research tradition in economics. Although PKI was foreshadowed early in the US economic expansion following World War II, the notion of a synthesis of institutionalism and the economics of Keynes languished until the mid-1980s. Since then, though, this strand of institutional economics has begun to blossom. In his 2005 presidential address to AFEE, Waller (2005) made it clear he considers himself both an institutionalist and post-Keynesian, as did two more recent AFEE presidents (see Whalen 2019; and Zalewski 2020).

Considering the role Minsky's ideas have played in fashioning PKI, it is tempting to give him the last word by closing with his reminder: "As capitalism evolves, so too should economic theory and policy" (Minsky 1996b, xiii). But recalling that Klein (1978, 271)—who supported the development of PKI—ended his AFEE presidential address by observing that the more things change, the more they stay the same, we return to Gruchy's early postwar essays (on Keynes and the institutionalists) for a final observation. In those essays, Gruchy (1950a; 1950b) did not merely foreshadow the shape of the coming PKI; he also foreshadowed its evolution.

That Gruchy foreshadowed the methodological foundation of PKI is clear from the historical narrative provided above, but he also (unexpectedly, indeed inadvertently) anticipated PKI's evolution when he ended those essays by identifying the following as key aspects of a promising institutionalist-Keynes research synthesis: the economics of the firm; analyses of the flow of national income; and inquiries into the nature and evolution of economic order. As it turns out, research on the economics of the firm (including related examinations of the structure of industry) is what led to the notion of the bimodal economy, providing the core of PKI in the era of the Great Stagflation. Then, in the 1980s, the focus of PKI shifted to the FIH and related macroeconomic analyses, research fully in line with what Gruchy called analyses of the flow of national income. After the global financial crisis of 2007–2009, the focus shifted again, this time to the evolution of capitalism that brought us the economic order we now call MMC.

Today's focus of PKI—capitalist development, with an emphasis on the current order—is fitting for three reasons. First, this phase of PKI incorporates all of the key subject matter of the earlier periods—especially corporations and industry structure (and their consequences for workers), and finance and macroeconomics, respectively—and places it in an integrated and evolutionary framework. Second, it underscores PKI's crucial methodological features of socioeconomic holism, evolution, and institutional balance. Third, it is fitting because Gruchy (1950b, 121–125; 1987, 152) considered a theory of capitalism—capable of accounting for both the current order and economic change—to be institutionalism's most essential contribution to economics.

Writing at the end of his essays in 1950, Gruchy (1950b, 126) might have miscalculated with his timing, but, advanced to our era, his closing words may still prove correct: In economics, PKI—a synthesis of institutionalism and the economics of Keynes that constantly grapples with an ever-changing economy—may indeed turn out to be "the major contribution of this century."

Acknowledgments

The author wishes to thank Deb Figart, Marc Lavoie, John Marangos, Jim Peach, Jan Toporowski, Linda Whalen, and Tim Wunder for comments and suggestions. He also dedicates this chapter to the memory of Allan Gruchy, Alfred Eichner, and Hyman Minsky, each of whom provided inspiration and encouragement at precisely the right moment.

Notes

1 Those core ideas do not just link institutionalism and post-Keynesianism; they also distinguish post-Keynesianism from the "Keynesianism" of the neoclassical synthesis (Peterson 1977).
2 Another economist with a foot in both the institutionalist and post-Keynesian camps was Eichner, who died unexpectedly in 1988 at the age of 50. Had he survived, Eichner would have certainly played a central role in PKI. While Eichner's research was far-reaching, his student Fred Lee (1996) continued Eichner's work on price setting by businesses, resulting in an empirically grounded pricing model consistent with many aspects of post-Keynesian and institutional economics.
3 The FIH applications and extensions discussed above are illustrative, not comprehensive.
4 This chapter's brief discussion of core elements draws on the extended discussions in Whalen (2013, 16–21; 2020a, 78–79).
5 Of course, as Peterson (1977) recognized, the state can be used for good or ill, and private power often has a hold on public power.
6 Lavoie (2020) identifies Minsky's neglect of households as one of a number of FIH weaknesses; addressing the other weaknesses identified by Lavoie must also be part of the research agenda of PKI.
7 Toporowski also extends the analysis beyond the United States.
8 For an updated look at administered pricing in the age of MMC, see Jo (2016); and for work that incorporates such pricing into an explicitly post-Keynesian institutionalist model (constructed using system dynamics), see Nichols, Pavlov, and Radzicki (2006).
9 Like financialization, "modern monetary theory" (MMT) has received considerable attention over the past several years and has aspects that overlap with PKI. For a contribution to the growing literature on MMT and its relationship to institutional and post-Keynesian economics, see Nesiba (2013).
10 An interesting question for future research from the perspective of PKI is what China's belt-and-road initiative means for MMC and subsequent capitalist development.

References

Appelbaum, Eileen and Rosemary Batt. 2014. *Private Equity at Work*. New York: Russell Sage.

Atkinson, Glen, Eric Hake, and Stephen Paschall. 2019. "Evolution of the Corporation in the United States: Stabilized Scarcity and Vested Interests." *Journal of Economic Issues* 53 (1): 1–25. https://doi.org/10.1080/00213624.2019.1556998

Baranes, Avraham and Eric Hake. 2018. "The Institutionalist Theory of Capital in the Modern Business Enterprise." *Journal of Economic Issues* 52 (2): 430–437. https://doi.org/10.1080/00213624.2018.1469895

Barbera, Robert. 2009. *The Cost of Capitalism*. New York: McGraw Hill.

BBC News. 2019. "Raghuram Rajan Says Capitalism Is 'Under Serious Threat.'" *BBC News*, March 12. https://www.bbc.com/news/business-47532522. Accessed December 12, 2019.

Brazelton, W. Robert. 1981. "Post Keynesian Economics: An Institutional Compatibility?" *Journal of Economic Issues* 15 (2): 531–542. https://doi.org/10.1080/00213624.1981.11503874

Brown, Douglas. 1992. "The Capitalist State as a Terrain of Rights." In *The Stratified State*, edited by William Dugger and William Waller, 13–34. Armonk, NY: M.E. Sharpe. https://doi.org/10.4324/9781315487090-2

Brown, Christopher. 2008. *Inequality, Consumer Credit, and the Saving Puzzle*. Cheltenham: Elgar. https://doi.org/10.4337/9781848443808

Cardwell, Laura. and Zdravka Todorova. 2016. "Evolution of US Household Agency Over Stages of Capitalism." *Journal of Economic Issues* 50 (2): 542–548. https://doi.org/10.1080/00213624.2016.1179062

Carter, Michael. 1989. "Financial Innovation and Financial Fragility." *Journal of Economic Issues* 23 (3): 779–793. https://doi.org/10.1080/00213624.1989.11504938

Case, Anne and Angus Deaton. 2020. *Deaths of Despair*. Princeton, NJ: Princeton University Press. https://doi.org/10.1515/9780691217062

Commons, John R. 1934a. *Institutional Economics*. New York: Macmillan.

———. 1934b. *Myself*. New York: Macmillan.

Correa, Eugenia. 2014. "Institutional Changes in Financial Crises: Lessons from Latin America." *Journal of Economic Issues* 48 (2): 323–330. https://doi.org/10.2753/jei0021-3624480205

Costantini, Orsola and Mario Seccareccia. 2020. "Income Distribution, Household Debt and Growth in Modern Financialized Economies." *Journal of Economic Issues* 54 (2): 444–453. https://doi.org/10.1080/00213624.2020.1752537

Cypher, James M. 1996. "Mexico: Financial Fragility or Structural Crisis?" *Journal of Economic Issues* 30 (2): 451–461. https://doi.org/10.1080/00213624.1996.11505809

Dean, Eric. 2018. "The Going Enterprise Paradox: Stability and Instability Under Money Manager Capitalism." *Journal of Economic Issues* 52 (4): 1084–1108. https://doi.org/10.1080/00213624.2018.1527591

Dillard, Dudley. 1987. "Money as an Institution of Capitalism." *Journal of Economic Issues* 21 (4): 1623–1647. https://doi.org/10.1080/00213624.1987.11504717

Diop, Samba. 2016. "Minsky's Analysis of Capitalist Development: A Critical Assessment and Perspective." *Review of Radical Political Economics* 48 (2): 201–216. https://doi.org/10.1177/0486613415591808

Dugger, William. 1996. "Redefining Economics: from Market Allocation to Social Provisioning." In *Political Economy for the 21st Century*, edited by Charles Whalen, 31–43. Armonk, NY: M.E. Sharpe. https://doi.org/10.4324/9781315701707-12

Dymski, Gary. 1997. "Deciphering Minsky's Wall Street Paradigm." *Journal of Economic Issues* 31 (2): 501–508. https://doi.org/10.1080/00213624.1997.11505940

Eichner, Alfred S. 1976. *The Megacorp and Oligopoly*. Cambridge: Cambridge University Press. https://doi.org/10.1017/cbo9780511895647

Fazzari, Steven and Hyman Minsky. 1984. "Domestic Monetary Policy: If Not Monetarism, What?" *Journal of Economic Issues* 18 (1): 101–116. https://doi.org/10.4324/9781315495453-5

Fernandez, Louisa, Fadhel Kaboub, and Zdravka Todorova. 2008. "Democratizing Financial Turmoil: A Minskian Analysis of the Subprime Crisis." Working Paper No. 548. Levy Economics Institute of Bard College. https://doi.org/10.2139/ssrn.2334056

Fernández-Huerga, Eduardo. 2008. "The Economic Behavior of Human Beings: The Institutional/Post-Keynesian Model." *Journal of Economic Issues* 42 (3): 709–726. https://doi.org/10.1080/00213624.2008.11507175

Fernández-Huerga, Eduardo, Jorge García-Arias, and Ana Salvador. 2017. "Labor Supply: Toward the Construction of an Alternative Conception from Post Keynesian and Institutional Economics." *Journal of Post Keynesian Economics* 40 (1): 576–599. https://doi.org/10.1080/01603477.2017.1338968

Galbraith, James K. 2008. *The Predator State*. New York: Free Press.

———. 2012. *Inequality and Instability*. New York: Oxford. https://doi.org/10.1093/acprof:osobl/9780199855650.001.0001

Galbraith, John K. 1973. *Economics and the Public Purpose*. Boston, MA: Houghton Mifflin.

———. 1978. "On Post Keynesian Economics." *Journal of Post Keynesian Economics* 1 (1): 8–11. https://doi.org/10.1080/01603477.1978.11489090

Girón. Alicia. 2015. "Women and Financialization: Microcredit, Institutional Investors, and MFIs." *Journal of Economic Issues* 49 (2): 373–396. https://doi.org/10.1080/00213624.2015.1042738

———. 2018. "Is China Living a Minsky Moment? Between the 'Lender of Last Resort' and the Chinese Shadow Financial System." *Journal of Economic Issues* 52 (2): 445–454. https://doi.org/10.1080/00213624.2018.1469900

Greenhouse, Steven. 2008. *The Big Squeeze*. New York: Knopf.

Greenwood, Daphne and Richard Holt. 2016. "Sustainable Development in Affluent Countries and the Neo-Institutionalist Synthesis." *Journal of Economic Issues* 50 (3): 647–666. https://doi.org/10.1080/00213624.2016.1210363

Gruchy, Allan. 1950a. "Keynes and the Institutionalists: Some Similarities." In *Economic Theory in Review*, edited by C. Lawrence Christenson, 96–105. Bloomington, IN: Indiana University.

———. 1950b. "Keynes and the Institutionalists: Important Contrasts." In *Economic Theory in Review*, edited by C. Lawrence Christenson, 106–126. Bloomington, IN: Indiana University.

———. 1987. *The Reconstruction of Economics*. New York: Greenwood Press.

Jennings, Ann. 1994. "Toward a Feminist Expansion of Macroeconomics: Money Matters." *Journal of Economic Issues* 28 (2): 556–565. https://doi.org/10.1080/00213624.1994.11505568

Jo, Tae-Hee. 2016. "What If There Are No Conventional Price Mechanisms?" *Journal of Economic Issues* 50 (2): 327–344. https://doi.org/10.1080/00213624.2016.1176474

Jo, Tae-Hee and John F. Henry. 2015. "The Business Enterprise in the Age of Money Manager Capitalism." *Journal of Economic Issues* 49 (1): 23–46. https://doi.org/10.1080/00213624.2015.1013877

Keller, Robert. 1983. "Keynesian and Institutional Economics: Compatibility and Complementarity?" *Journal of Economic Issues* 17 (4): 1087–1095. https://doi.org/10.1080/00213624.1983.11504189

Kessler, Sarah. 2018. *Gigged*. New York: St. Martin's Press.

Keynes, John M. (1926) 1932. "The End of Laissez-Faire." In *Essays in Persuasion*, edited by John M. Keynes, 272–294. New York: Harcourt, Brace. https://doi.org/10.1007/978-1-349-00807-0_21

———. (1927) 1982. Letter to John R. Commons. April 26, 1927. Reproduced in John R. Commons Papers, microfilm edition. Madison: State Historical Society of Wisconsin.

Klein, Philip. 1978. "American Institutionalism: Premature Death, Permanent Resurrection." *Journal of Economic Issues* 12 (2): 251–276. https://doi.org/10.1080/00213624.1978.11503527

———. 1998. "Normative Macroeconomics: Conjoining Keynes and Institutionalism." In *Institutionalist Theory and Applications*, edited by Sasan Fayazmanesh and Marc Tool, 44–65. Cheltenham: Elgar.

Klimina, Anna. 2013. "Placing the Analysis of Contemporary State Capitalism within an Evolutionary Discourse." *Journal of Economic Issues* 47 (2): 545–554. https://doi.org/10.2753/jei0021-3624470228

Kregel, Jan. 1997. "Margins of Safety and Weight of the Argument in Generating Financial Fragility." *Journal of Economic Issues* 31 (2): 543–548. https://doi.org/10.1080/00213624.1997.11505945

———. 1998. "Yes, 'It' Did Happen Again: A Minsky Crisis Happened in Asia." Working Paper No. 234. Levy Economics Institute of Bard College.

Krugman, Paul. 2009. "The Night They Re-read Minsky." June 10, London School of Economics. Video recording no longer available online (last accessed December 1, 2009).

Lahart, Justin. 2007. "In Time of Tumult, Obscure Economist Gains Currency." *Wall Street Journal* August 18. p. A1.

Lavoie, Marc. 2020. "Was Hyman Minsky a Post-Keynesian Economist?" *Review of Evolutionary Political Economy* 1 (1): 85–101. https://doi.org/10.1007/s43253-020-00002-7

Lee, Frederic S. 1996. "Pricing and the Business Enterprise." In *Political Economy for the 21st Century*, edited by Charles Whalen. Armonk, NY: M.E. Sharpe. https://doi.org/10.4324/9781315701707-16

———. 2000. "The Organizational History of Post Keynesian Economics in America, 1971–1995." *Journal of Post Keynesian Economics* 23 (1): 141–162. https://doi.org/10.1080/01603477.2000.11490275

Levin-Waldman, Oren. 2018. *Restoring the Middle Class Through Wage Policy*. Cham, Switzerland: Palgrave Macmillan. https://doi.org/10.1007/978-3-319-74448-3

Liang, Yan and Charles Whalen. 2022. "Money Manager Capitalism and the Coronavirus Pandemic." In *A Modern Guide to Post-Keynesian Institutional Economics*, edited by Charles J. Whalen, chapter 4. Cheltenham: Elgar.

Marshall, F. Ray. 1983. "Comments on the Institutionalist view of Reaganomics." *Journal of Economic Issues* 17 (2): 503–506. https://doi.org/10.1080/00213624.1983.11504134

McClintock, Brent. 1996. "International Financial Instability and the Financial Derivatives Market." *Journal of Economic Issues* 30 (1): 13–33. https://doi.org/10.1080/00213624.1996.11505764

Minsky, Hyman P. 1975. *John Maynard Keynes*. New York: Columbia University Press. https://doi.org/10.1007/978-1-349-02679-1

———. 1977. "The Financial Instability Hypothesis: An Interpretation of Keynes and an Alternative to 'Standard' Theory." *Nebraska Journal of Economics and Business* 16 (1): 5–16.

———. 1980. "Capitalist Financial Processes and the Instability of Capitalism." *Journal of Economic Issues* 14 (2): 505–523. https://doi.org/10.1080/00213624.1980.11503759

———. 1986a. *Stabilizing an Unstable Economy*. New Haven: Yale University Press.

———. 1986b. "The Evolution of Financial Institutions and the Performance of the Economy." *Journal of Economic Issues* 20 (2): 345–353. https://doi.org/10.1080/00213624.1986.11504505

———. 1986c. "Global Consequences of Financial Deregulation." *Marcus Wallenberg Papers on International Finance* 2 (1): 1–19.

———. 1990. "Schumpeter: Finance and Evolution." In *Evolving Technology and Market Structure*, edited by Arnold Heertje and Mark Perlman, 51–74. Ann Arbor, MI: University of Michigan Press.

———. 1991. "The Rationale for the Conference: An Agenda for the Good Financial Economy." Remarks prepared for delivery at Restructuring the Financial Structure for Economic Growth, a conference held at the Levy Economics Institute of Bard College, 21–23 November 1991. Photocopy.

———. 1993. "Schumpeter and Finance." In *Market and Institutions in Economic Development*, edited by Salvatore Biasco, Alessandro Roncaglia, and Michele Salvati, 103–115. New York: St. Martin's Press. https://doi.org/10.1007/978-1-349-22526-2_7

———. 1996a. "Uncertainty and the Institutional Structure of Capitalist Economies." *Journal of Economic Issues* 30 (2): 357–368. https://doi.org/10.1080/00213624.1996.11505800

———. 1996b. "Foreword." In *Political Economy for the 21st Century*, edited by Charles Whalen, xi–xiv. Armonk, NY: M.E. Sharpe.

Minsky, Hyman and Charles Whalen. 1996. "Economic Insecurity and the Institutional Prerequisites for Successful Capitalism." *Journal of Post Keynesian Economics* 19 (2): 155–170. https://doi.org/10.1080/01603477.1996.11490102

Nesiba, Reynold F. 2013. "Do Institutionalists and Post-Keynesians Share a Common Approach to Modern Monetary Theory?" *European Journal of Economics and Economic Policies: Intervention* 10 (1): 44–60. https://doi.org/10.4337/ejeep.2013.01.05

Nesvetailova, Anastasia. 2014. "A Crisis of the Overcrowded Future: Shadow Banking and the Political Economy of Financial Innovation." *New Political Economy* 20 (3): 431–453. https://doi.org/10.1080/13563467.2014.951428

Nichols, Mark, Oleg Pavlov, and Michael Radzicki. 2006. "The Circular and Cumulative Structure of Administered Pricing." *Journal of Economic Issues* 40 (2): 517–526. https://doi.org/10.1080/00213624.2006.11506931

Niggle, Christopher. 2006. "Evolutionary Keynesianism: A Synthesis of Institutionalist and Post Keynesian Macroeconomics." *Journal of Economic Issues* 40 (2): 405–412. https://doi.org/10.1080/00213624.2006.11506918

Peterson, Wallace C. 1977. "Institutionalism, Keynes, and the Real World." *Journal of Economic Issues* 11 (2): 201–221. https://doi.org/10.1080/00213624.1977.11503432

———. 1987. "Macroeconomic Theory and Policy in an Institutionalist Perspective." *Journal of Economic Issues* 21 (4): 1587–1621. https://doi.org/10.1080/00213624.1987.11504716

Phillips, Ronnie. 1997. "Rethinking Bank Examinations: A Minsky Approach." *Journal of Economic Issues* 31 (2): 509–516. https://doi.org/10.1080/00213624.1997.11505941

Poirot, Clifford S. 2001. "Financial Integration under Conditions of Chaotic Hysteresis: The Russian Financial Crisis of 1998." *Journal of Post Keynesian Economics* 23 (3): 485–507.

Pollin, Robert. 2008. "We're All Minskyites Now." *The Nation*. November 17, 5–7.

Prasch, Robert. 2004. "How is Labor Distinct from Broccoli?" In *The Institutionalist Tradition in Labor Economics*, edited by Dell Champlin and Janet Knoedler, 146–158. Armonk, NY: M.E. Sharpe. https://doi.org/10.4324/9781315699578-10

———. 2010. "Bankers Gone Wild." In *Macroeconomic Theory and Its Failings*, edited by Steven Kates, 184–206. Cheltenham, UK: Edward Elgar. https://doi.org/10.4337/9781849803397.00018

———. 2014. "The Rise of Money Manager Capitalism and Its Implications for Economic Theory and Policy." *Journal of Economic Issues* 48 (2): 559–566. https://doi.org/10.2753/jei0021-3624480232

Rima, Ingrid. 2002. "Venture Capitalist Financing: Contemporary Foundations for Minsky's 'Wall Street' Perspective." *Journal of Economic Issues* 36 (2): 407–414. https://doi.org/10.1080/00213624.2002.11506484

Rutherford, Malcolm. and Tyler Desroches. 2008. "The Institutionalist Reaction to Keynesian Economics." *Journal of the History of Economic Thought* 30 (1): 29–48. https://doi.org/10.2139/ssrn.905613

Schmid, A. Allan. 1999. "Government, Property, Markets ... In That Order ... Not Government versus Markets." In *The Fundamental Interrelationships between Government and Property*, edited by Nicholas Mercuro and Warren Samuels, 233–237. Stamford, CT: JAI Press. https://doi.org/10.4324/9780203484654.ch18

Scott, Robert and Steven Pressman. 2019. "Financially Unstable Households." *Journal of Economic Issues* 53 (2): 523–531. https://doi.org/10.1080/00213624.2019.1603765

Seccareccia Mario. 1991. "An Alternative to Labour-Market Orthodoxy: The Post-Keynesian/Institutionalist Policy View." *Review of Political Economy* 3 (1): 43–61. https://doi.org/10.1080/09538259100000004

Shulman, Steven. 1996. "Racial Inequality and Radical Institutionalism: A Research Agenda." In *Inequality*, edited by William Dugger, 251–271. New York: Greenwood Press.

Stiglitz, Joseph E. 2012. *The Price of Inequality*. New York: W. W. Norton.

Tauheed, Linwood. 2008. "Black Political Economy in the 21st Century." *Journal of Black Studies* 38 (5): 692–730. https://doi.org/10.1177/0021934707310292

———. 2011. "A Proposed Methodological Synthesis of Post-Keynesian and Institutional Economics." *Journal of Economic Issues* 45 (4): 819–838. https://doi.org/10.2753/jei0021-3624450404

Tavasci, Daniela and Jan Toporowski, eds. 2010. *Minsky, Crisis and Development*. Basingstoke, UK: Palgrave Macmillan. https://doi.org/10.1057/9780230292321

Tcherneva, Pavlina. 2018. "The Job Guarantee: Design, Jobs, and Implementation." Working Paper No. 902. Levy Economics Institute of Bard College. https://doi.org/10.2139/ssrn.3155289

Todorova, Zdravka. 2009. *Money and Households in a Capitalist Economy: A Gendered Post Keynesian-Institutional Analysis*. Cheltenham, UK: Edward Elgar.

Tokucu, Erkan. 2014. "Appraising the Effectiveness of the Recent Turkish Monetary Policy: A Minskian Perspective." *Journal of Economic Issues* 48 (3): 787–820. https://doi.org/10.2753/jei0021-3624480310

Toporowski, Jan. 2020. "Financialisation and the Periodisation of Capitalism: Appearances and Processes." *Review of Evolutionary Political Economy* 1 (2): 149–160. https://doi.org/10.1007/s43253-020-00005-4

Tymoigne, Eric. 2007. "A Hard-Nosed Look at Worsening US Household Finance." *Challenge* 50 (4): 88–111. https://doi.org/10.2753/0577-5132500406

Tymoigne, Eric and L. Randall Wray. 2014. *The Rise and Fall of Money Manager Capitalism*. London: Routledge. https://doi.org/10.4324/9780203717295

Ülgen, Faruk. 2018. "Collective Action and the Institutionalist Approach to Financial Regulation." *Journal of Economic Issues* 52 (2): 541–549. https://doi.org/10.1080/00213624.2018.1469934

———. 2020. "An Institutionalist Framework for a Consistent Financial Regulation." *Journal of Economic Issues* 54 (2): 436–443. https://doi.org/10.1080/00213624.2020.1752528

United Nations. 2018. *Global Warming of 15° C: Summary for Policymakers*. Geneva: Intergovernmental Panel on Climate Change.

Van Lear, William. 2001. "Macroeconomic Implications of Institutional Equity Ownership." *Challenge* 44 (6): 108–117. https://doi.org/10.1080/05775132.2001.11034105

———. 2002. *A Populist Challenge to Corporate Capitalism*. Singapore: World Scientific.

Van Lear, William and James, Sisk. 2010. "Financial Crisis and Economic Stability." *Journal of Economic Issues* 44 (3): 779–793. https://doi.org/10.2753/jei0021-3624440310

Waller, William. 2005. "Accidental Veblenian, Intentional Institutionalist, and Inevitable Feminist." *Journal of Economic Issues* 39 (2): 326–334. https://doi.org/10.1080/00213624.2005.11506809

Weil, David. 2017. *The Fissured Workplace*. Cambridge: Harvard University Press. https://doi.org/10.4159/9780674726123

Whalen, Charles. 1992. "Schools of Thought and Theories of the State." In *The Stratified State*, edited by William Dugger and William Waller, 55–85. Armonk, NY: M.E. Sharpe. https://doi.org/10.4324/9781315487090-4

———, ed. 1996. *Political Economy for the 21st Century*. Armonk, NY: M.E. Sharpe. https://doi.org/10.4324/9781315701707

———. 1997. "Money-Manager Capitalism and the End of Shared Prosperity." *Journal of Economic Issues* 31 (2): 517–525. https://doi.org/10.1080/00213624.1997.11505942

———. 2001. "Integrating Schumpeter and Keynes: Hyman Minsky's Theory of Capitalist Development." *Journal of Economic Issues* 35 (4): 805–823. https://doi.org/10.1080/00213624.2001.11506415

———. 2002. "Money-Manager Capitalism: Still Here, But Not Quite As Expected." *Journal of Economic Issues* 36 (2): 401–406. https://doi.org/10.1080/00213624.2002.11506483

———. 2007. "The US Credit Crunch of 2007: A Minsky Moment." *Public Policy Brief*, No. 92. Levy Economics Institute of Bard College.

———. 2008a. "Understanding the Credit Crunch as a Minsky Moment." *Challenge* 51 (1): 91–109. https://doi.org/10.2753/0577-5132510106

———. 2008b. "Post-Keynesian Institutionalism and the Anxious Society." In *Alternative Institutional Structures*, edited by Sandra Batie and Nicholas Mercuro, 273–299. London: Routledge. https://doi.org/10.4324/9780203894439-17

———. 2010. "An Institutionalist Perspective on the Global Financial Crisis." In *Macroeconomic Theory and its Failings*, edited by Steven Kates, 2325–259. Cheltenham: Elgar. https://doi.org/10.4337/9781849803397.00021

———, ed. 2011. *Financial Instability and Economic Security after the Great Recession*. Cheltenham: Elgar. https://doi.org/10.4337/9780857934840

———. 2013. "Post-Keynesian Institutionalism after the Great Recession." *European Journal of Economics and Economic Policies: Intervention* 10 (1): 12–27. https://doi.org/10.2139/ssrn.2062469

———. 2019. "Institutional Economics and Chock-Full Employment: Reclaiming the 'Right to Work' as a Cornerstone of Progressive Capitalism." *Journal of Economic Issues* 53 (2): 321–340.

———. 2020a. "PostKeynesian Institutionalism: Past, Present, and Future." *Evolutionary and Institutional Economics Review* 17 (1): 71–92. https://doi.org/10.1007/s40844-019-00150-4

———. 2020b. "Understanding Financialization." In *Alternative Approaches to Economic Theory*, edited by Victor Beker, 185–206. London: Routledge. https://doi.org/10.4324/9780429021510-9

Whalen, Charles and Jeffrey Wenger. 2002. "Destabilizing an Unstable Economy." *Challenge* 45 (6): 70–92. https://doi.org/10.1080/05775132.2002.11034179

Wilber, Charles and Kenneth Jameson. 1983. *An Inquiry into the Poverty of Economics*. Notre Dame, IN: University of Notre Dame Press.

Wolfson, Martin 2002. "Minsky's Theory of Financial Crises in a Global Context." *Journal of Economic Issues* 36 (2): 393–400. https://doi.org/10.1080/00213624.2002.11506482

Wray, L. Randall. 1992. "Alternative Approaches to Money and Interest Rates." *Journal of Economic Issues* 26 (4): 1145–1178. https://doi.org/10.1080/00213624.1992.11505365

———. 1994. "The Political Economy of the Current US Financial Crisis." *International Papers in Political Economy* 1 (3): 1–51.

———. 1998. "Zero Unemployment and Stable Prices." *Journal of Economic Issues* 32 (2): 539–545. https://doi.org/10.1080/00213624.1998.11506062

———. 2002. "What Happened to Goldilocks? A Minskian Framework." *Journal of Economic Issues* 36 (2): 383–391. https://doi.org/10.1080/00213624.2002.11506481

———. 2009. "The Rise and Fall of Money Manager Capitalism: A Minskian Approach." *Cambridge Journal of Economics* 33 (4): 807–828. https://doi.org/10.1093/cje/bep024

———. 2010. "Minsky, the Global Money-Manager Crisis, and the Return of Big Government." In *Macroeconomic Theory and Its Failings*, edited by Steven Kates, 260–280. Cheltenham, UK: Edward Elgar. https://doi.org/10.4337/9781849803397.00022

Zalewski, David. 2002. "Retirement Insecurity in the Age of Money Manager Capitalism." *Journal of Economic Issues* 36 (2): 349–356. https://doi.org/10.1080/00213624.2002.11506477

———. 2004. "Wealth and Power: Ethical Implications of Executive Power Since the 1980s." In *The Institutionalist Tradition in Labor Economics*, edited by Dell Champlin and Janet Knoedler, 286–296. Armonk, NY: M.E. Sharpe. https://doi.org/10.4324/9781315699578-19

———. 2005. "Economic Security and the Myth of the Efficiency/Equity Tradeoff." *Journal of Economic Issues* 39 (2): 383–390. https://doi.org/10.1080/00213624.2005.11506815

——— 2020. "Confronting the Trilemma: Culture, Institutions, and Macroeconomic Disequilibria." *Journal of Economic Issues* 54 (2): 295–315.

5

CULTURE, GENDER, AND FEMINIST INSTITUTIONALISM

Janice Peterson

Introduction

The roots of feminist inquiry in institutional economics run deep. The foundational work of Thorsten Veblen in the late nineteenth and early twentieth centuries contained important insight on the status of women and significance of gender in economic relationships. Yet, in the late twentieth century, some scholars noted a conspicuous lack of gender analysis in institutionalist inquiry as it had grown and developed after Veblen. Scholarship to address this shortcoming provided a foundation for development of a distinct feminist institutionalist approach to economic analysis.[1] This chapter examines the origins, evolution, and key elements of feminist institutionalist thought, concluding with observations on applications to current challenges and new frontiers.

Origins

In the 1970s and 1980s, four scholars highlighted the origins of feminist institutionalism by exploring and extending Veblen's gender analysis and its significance for feminism and economics: Edythe Miller (institutional economist), John Diggins (historian), Barbara Ryan (sociologist), and Daphne Greenwood (institutional economist). Each contributed important insights that helped pave the way for feminist economic scholarship over the following decades.

Edythe Miller

Writing in 1972, Miller saw a close parallel between Veblen's analysis of the role of women in society and the "women's liberation" movement of her day. She also linked that analysis to his criticism of orthodox economics, arguing that Veblen's

DOI: 10.4324/9781003160434-5

"refusal to accept the traditional view of the role and function of women was an integral part of his refusal to accept either the assumptions or the methodology of the economic orthodoxy of the day" (Miller 1972, 78). Thus, for Veblen, as for many contemporary feminist economists, orthodox economics is seen as incapable of addressing the inferior status of women.

Miller (1972) identifies analyses of the devaluation of women's work, the treatment of women as objects, and belief that a "woman's place" is in the home as key components of Veblen's gender analysis. She writes that Veblen established the framework for his analysis of the concept of "women's work" by tracing its origin in primitive societies, where the devaluation of such work reflects his fundamental distinction between "work and exploit." In this context, the differences in the type of work considered "appropriate for the sexes" are due far more to "cultural conditioning" than to differences in "original endowments." Veblen contended that the tasks of "women's work" were not unimportant in themselves, but "they became viewed as such because they did not involve the requisite element of prowess." Miller (1972, 79–80) writes: "[T]he resultant invidious comparison between the occupational activities of the sexes remains. The work women do is considered less honorific, and women are less 'worthy' than men." In Veblen's work, Miller locates a core feminist economic contention that "women's work" is valued less because women do it.

Miller (1972, 81–82) also sees similarities with the feminist issues of her day in Veblen's writings on women as objects (in the form of property and display) and "woman's place" in the home. Veblen traced the institution of ownership to the capture of women, valued as property for the "repute their possession confers upon their possessor." Over time, women are valued for their roles in supporting male conspicuous consumption and conspicuous leisure—providing proof of a man's "pecuniary ability to maintain persons of no use whatsoever"—thus relegating women to "essentially and normally a vicarious life." Veblen also noted the importance of the belief that a woman's proper place is in the home—a household with a male head—and the close association of a "woman's place" in the home with femininity.

John Diggins

While Miller underscored the closeness of Veblen's analysis to the arguments of the women's liberation movement, historian Diggins (1978) begins his discussion of Veblen's work on "the barbarian status of the women" by noting Veblen's absence from the feminist studies of that same era, including *The Feminist Papers* by Alice Rossi (1973). Diggins introduces Veblen's work by contrasting it with that of liberal commentator John Stuart Mill. In *The Subjection of Women* (1869), Mill argued the goal of female equality remained "the unfinished political commitment of liberalism itself, a commitment that could be fulfilled when women were granted the political rights that had been available to men in the progress of history" (Diggins 1978, 142). Veblen's perspective, informed by the anthropology of his day, saw women's oppression stemming more from the persistence of social rituals, customs, and the continuity of habit than the absence of political rights (Diggins 1978, 143). The argument that equal political rights alone will not fully emancipate women becomes an important one in feminist institutionalism.

Like Miller, Diggins (1978, 144) places employment, ownership, and marriage at the core of Veblen's analysis of the status of women. Diggins argues that Veblen's unique perspective enabled him to "see in human evolution the descent of woman as well as the ascent of man" as society passed from the era of "peaceable savagery" to "barbarism." As tools make possible the existence of a surplus and the ability to make weapons, distinctions between the sexes begin to develop with respect to economic activities. Two types of employment emerge: the "honorific," calling for "masculine strength"; and the "humiliating," calling for "feminine diligence." Thus, to men fall the activities of "predation and exploit" (defending the tribe, conquering and plundering the enemy), while to women fall the activities of "industry and drudgery" (the everyday work of the community). Further, Veblen identifies the "coercive ownership marriage system"—where over time the practice of capturing women as trophies gives rise to a "conventionally recognized marriage relation"—as the basis for both private property and the patriarchal family.

Diggins (1978, 168) argues that Veblen's analysis of employment, ownership, and marriage illuminates the reification of coercion and power in socially accepted customs and practices, a particularly important concern for feminist inquiry. In addition, again like Miller, he sees Veblen's analysis of women's status as part of a critique of orthodox economics: Veblen rejected the orthodox economic equation of value with market relations, and expressed what he saw to be the true source of value—serviceability and provisioning—in the distinction between male and female occupations. Diggins (1978, 146) argues that when Veblen rejected "the mystique of economic man" it was "not only because of its individualist premises but also because of its masculine bias."

Barbara Ryan

Ryan (1982, 43) begins her discussion of Veblen's feminism by noting not only his absence from sociology, but also the broader male bias in Veblenian research, which largely "repressed or ignored" Veblen's feminist principles. Ryan (1982, 29) argues that Veblen's work presents class divisions under capitalism as "outward manifestations of the desire for dominance in order to gain self-esteem and prestige." While the division between "pecuniary and industrial occupations" was Veblen's primary illustration of this process, Ryan (1982, 33) argues that for Veblen, "the first and most important division from which all others follow is the division between the sexes." The lower status "industrial employments" are an outgrowth of "what was classed as women's work in the primitive barbarian community." Ryan (1982, 35) emphasizes, however, that the important question for Veblen was not so much how this division of labor came about, but "why women's work suffered loss of esteem."

Ryan (1982, 37) also sees Veblen's analysis of women in society going well beyond the liberal "equal rights" position. She notes, for example, Veblen's recognition that differential status levels are perpetuated by promoting the entrance of women into the work force yet still maintaining "a lowered evaluation of them as human beings." Ryan (1982, 44) argues that Veblen saw "a detrimental masculine framework generalized throughout society," making his views consistent with contemporary feminist calls to "reconsider the goal of 'equal rights' within the present institutionalized setting and instead to use sex equality as the first step in changing the entire socio-economic structure."

Daphne Greenwood

Greenwood raised a number of issues and arguments of relevance for feminist institutionalism in two articles published in 1984. In the first, Greenwood (1984a, 457) addresses "the institutional inadequacy of the market in determining comparable worth" and considers the implications for value theory. "Comparable worth" refers to a call for "equal pay" for work that is "equally valuable to the firm." Drawing on Veblen's analysis of "exploit" versus "industry," Greenwood (1984a, 461) argues that the essence of "comparable worth" is that much of women's work is of equal value to men's work, but is treated as less valuable because it is performed by women. Thus, contrary to orthodox economics, value is not determined by measurements of output but "by the status of the person providing the inputs." Greenwood (1984a, 462) concludes that in calling for a revaluation of the worth of jobs traditionally held by women "the comparable worth strategy raises the larger question of how to correctly determine value."[2]

In her second article, Greenwood (1984b, 663) addresses the economic significance of "woman's place" more broadly. She begins with the observation that while institutional economics sought to distinguish itself from mainstream (neoclassical) economics, "in its treatment of women and their economic roles, institutionalism has not made that important differentiation." While mainstream economists have "long ignored differences in economic behavior and reward based on gender," institutionalists "have not proposed an alternative paradigm." She argues that "this vacuum is the more remarkable since the founder of institutionalism, Thorstein Veblen, made significant strides toward establishing a theory of economic behavior in which the unique role of women … played an integral part."[3]

Greenwood (1984b, 667) argues that the way institutional economics defines the economic problem and approaches problem-solving makes it better suited for the analysis of the economic status of women than mainstream economics, and begins with a discussion of Veblen's work to make this case. She views Veblen's analysis of the social and economic position of women as the foundation for further theorizing because he deals with it as "basic to the nature of the economic system." Unlike many economists, Veblen "did not view 'woman's place' as a special topic to which economic theory might be applied, but as an intellectual window through which there may be deeper insights into the values dominant in society."

Extending Veblen's work, Greenwood (1984b, 673) notes institutionalists agree that market exchange does not reflect the full economic reality, and "value" is something that arises from the unfolding of the life process. She argues that this ("instrumental") conception of value—with its emphasis on the life process, nurture, and purposeful activity—by its nature takes account of non-market labor. The traditional woman's role, defined by "woman's place," is the most important example of this labor. Greenwood (1984b, 675) stresses that "rather than remaining an implicit conclusion of institutionalist theory, this should become explicit."

Greenwood (1984b, 675) also argues that an institutional economic analysis of the household should begin with the recognition of patriarchal marriage as a "long-standing habit of mind" that "obscures a great deal of the labor in the economy" that takes place outside the market. In this context, power relationships become important for understanding economic behavior. Occupational choice—particularly with respect to performing market versus non-market work—is "both consequence and determinant of family relationships." In addition, Greenwood (1984b, 675) argues that it is a "fundamental error" to view households as purely centers of consumption when they actually produce much of the output consumed by people and reproduction (both biologically and culturally) is the "first and foremost kind of production."

Consequently, the status of women in the patriarchal household is inseparable from their status in the paid labor market. Greenwood (1984b, 667–678) argues that labor market discrimination reflects a "segregation of women into traditional non-market work as much as out of the more prestigious areas of market work." Further, the inferior status of women in the paid labor market is an extension of the low value placed on their traditional non-market work (including the nurture of children), particularly in traditional female occupations.

Greenwood (1984b, 677) argues that attempts to alter "woman's place" in society cannot be achieved through limited liberal reform, but will "necessarily change other values and relationships in society," such as attitudes toward the status of manual versus managerial work. In addition, she argues that institutionalism must confront sexism to address fully the questions of value and invidious distinction in its inquiry. She concludes: "The elimination of sexism is intertwined with the acknowledgement of the innate desire of humans to do purposeful work, and the triumph of industry over exploit" (Greenwood 1984b, 678).

Evolution

Since publication of Greenwood's articles, institutionalist scholarship has made considerable progress not only in understanding and addressing the absence of feminist thought in institutional economics, but also in sketching out a new "feminist institutionalism." Drawing on Veblen's work, and influenced by feminist economics and radical institutionalism, a number of institutionalists made important formative explorations in the 1990s. Then, building on those explorations, feminist institutionalism has made further developments through insightful research in the new millennium.

Feminist economics

Feminist economics calls for "rethinking economics through a feminist lens" (Strober 1994); it addresses both the status of women in real-world economies and gender bias in the discipline of economics. Among its distinctive features are the importance of gender as an analytical category, a critique of the conventional definition of economics as "the science of choice" and the study of "rational economic man," and an alternative definition of economics as the "study of social provisioning." The social provisioning definition of economics encompasses feminist economists' concerns regarding the devaluation of unpaid work, the adequacy of traditional measures of economic well-being, the explicit recognition of values, and the importance of methodological pluralism (Beneria, Berik, and Floro 2016; Nelson 1993; Power 2004). Feminist economics is a pluralistic field of study, with practitioners drawn from different schools of thought within both economics and feminism. For many feminist economists, intersectional analysis—attentive to differences among women (and men) based in distinctions such as "class, caste, race/ethnicity, national origin, sexual orientation, and age"—is an integral part of feminist economics (Beneria, Berik, and Floro 2016; Strober 1994).

Feminist analysis in economics has a long history, but it was only in the early 1990s that feminist economics gained recognition as providing "a distinct set of new perspectives" (Strassmann 1999, 360). The first professional association for feminist economics (the International Association for Feminist Economics) was founded in 1992, and the association's journal (*Feminist Economics*) was launched in 1995 (Shackelford 1999). Many of the core ideas of feminist economics were explored at conferences and in papers published in edited volumes such as *Beyond Economic Man* (Ferber and Nelson 1993) and *Out of the Margin* (Kuiper and Sap 1995). The 1990s saw a flourishing of published feminist economic research across a wide range of fields within the discipline and on a variety of topics and issues (Peterson and Lewis 1999). In the first two decades of the twenty-first century, the feminist economics community has grown globally and the scope of feminist economic research has continued to expand (see, for example, Agenjo-Calderon and Galvez-Munoz 2019; Figart and Warnecke 2013; Kuiper 2008).

Radical institutionalism

Radical institutionalism is a processual, critical approach that seeks to describe accurately the "working of an economic system with the intent of purposefully altering the system toward more democratic and participatory social structures and practices" (Waller 1989, 39). It is a paradigm rooted in the work of Veblen, and focused on "changing the direction of cultural evolution and changing the outcome of social provisioning in order to promote the full participation of all" (Dugger 1989,126).[4]

While radical institutionalism had a long history in Veblenian analysis, contemporary explorations of this approach began in earnest following publication, in 1989, of *Radical Institutionalism*, edited by William Dugger. That volume both articulated the enduring "core concepts" of radical institutionalism derived from Veblen's work and identified places where "modernization" was desirable. In particular, Dugger (1989, 112–113) argued that while Veblen's distinction between behavior that is self-serving ("pecuniary") and behavior that is socially useful ("industrial") remained relevant, it needed to be refocused to address "the burning issues of our time"—"racism, sexism, and imperialism."[5]

The call for radical institutionalism was not a condemnation of original institutional economics, but a call for it to return to its radical, Veblenian roots. Embracing Veblen's feminism was seen to be central to this cause. Dugger (1989, 125) argued that, "like Veblen, the radical institutionalists are feminists even though very few of us—so far—are women." As explorations of radical institutionalism unfolded, bringing feminist insights into the analysis and developing a feminist institutionalism became important parts of radical institutionalism's research agenda. In addition, outreach to female institutionalist scholars to participate in the radical institutionalist project added women's voices to the discussion.

Formative explorations

During the 1990s, institutionalists' explorations of radical institutionalism and feminist economics led to many of the core concepts and arguments in feminist institutionalism. Following publication of *Radical Institutionalism*, conferences and scholarship associated with three additional edited volumes on aspects of radical institutionalism were particularly consequential for the development of feminist institutionalist analysis: the Hobart and William Smith Conference on the Institutionalist Theory of the State (August 1989) generated *The Stratified State* (Dugger and Waller 1992); the Northern Arizona University Conference on Radical Institutionalism and Gender (August 1991) generated *The Economic Status of Women Under Capitalism* (Peterson and Brown 1994); and *Inequality* (Dugger 1996a) completed the series.

The Stratified State

The conference at Hobart and William Smith Colleges led to three chapters on the significance of gender in relation to the meaning, role, and theory of the state (see Dugger and Waller 1992, Chapters 6, 8, and 9). Taken together, they illustrate how feminist institutionalist principles evolved by taking gender seriously in the development of broader theoretical constructs. For example, Ann Jennings (1992), building on feminist discussions of the historical and cultural separations of public and private spheres, developed a framework showing how both the family and the state had been defined as "not the economy," imposing artificial restrictions on the activities of both. This mythical "double dualism," embedded in conventional economics, is shown to support both the mainstream economic principle of laissez-faire and the traditional definition of women as familial, non-economic persons because of their association with the family.

Jennings' conception of the "double dualism" becomes an important framework for further feminist institutionalist analysis, and the interrogation of cultural dualisms becomes a key element of feminist institutionalism. In an article extending the ideas within Jennings's chapter, William Waller and Jennings (1990, 613–614) identify the rejection of dualistic constructions as a shared methodological foundation for feminism and institutional economics. Consequently, they conclude that the observed omission of gender and feminist concerns from institutional analysis was not explained by "epistemological and methodological incompatibility," but did underscore the need for institutional economists to "consciously reconstruct our intellectual tools" (Waller and Jennings 1990, 618).

The Economic Status of Women Under Capitalism

The conference at Northern Arizona University in 1991 focused on the question of how institutional economics can provide a more feminist economics, drawing on institutionalism's feminist roots in the work of Veblen and radical institutionalism. The scholarship produced by that conference illustrates how feminist institutionalism evolved through serious engagement with feminist theory, identification of methodological commonalities, revision and extension of core concepts and understandings, and applications to real-world analyses of the status of women.

The first two sections of *The Economic Status of Women* (Peterson and Brown 1994) explore connections between institutionalism and feminism, and offer constructive critiques and extensions. For example, Dugger (Chapter 1) applies Veblen's framework to the study of gender inequality, a serious concern for radical institutionalists because it distorts the direction of cultural evolution away from democratic politics and participatory economics. Waller (Chapter 4) examines the meaning of "technology" and illustrates how dualistic, hierarchical distinctions shaped the way this vital institutionalist concept was defined and understood. Paulette Olsen (Chapter 5) and Jennings and Dell Champlin (Chapter 6) address how the practice of universalizing the experiences of white Europeans to all people has marginalized women in the Global South and Black women in the United States. The final section, focused on the contemporary economic status of women, illustrated the importance of: carefully considering our categories of analysis; appreciating the culturally defined significance of gender;

understanding that increased labor force participation is not equal to women's liberation; and recognizing changing family structures.[6]

Inequality

In *Inequality*, Dugger's chapter, "Four Modes of Inequality," is particularly relevant to feminist institutionalism because it presents "a common framework and vocabulary for understanding inequality as process" (Dugger 1996a, xii). He identifies four interrelated processes or modes of inequality—gender, race, class, and nation—and explains each in terms of the practices of inequality, the myths that justify it, and the antidotes to counteract it. In this context, he defines gender inequality as the domination of women by men through a series of gendered practices, supported and justified by enabling myths that rationalize privilege, blame the victim, and create fear of change. This construction of gender inequality is important in the evolution of feminist institutionalism because it clearly demonstrates the role of socially constructed power relations. Further, by situating gender inequality in an interrelated web of processes associated with other modes of inequality, it provides a framework for exploring inequality's multidimensional and intersectional aspects (Dugger 1996a, 21–39).

Insight for the twenty-first century

The centennial of publication of Veblen's *The Theory of the Leisure Class* at the end of the twentieth century invited reflection on the significance of his work for the twenty-first century (for example, Brown 1998). The global economy of the late twentieth century differed significantly from the world observed and dissected by Veblen, presenting women with new realities and challenges. Veblen's relevance for addressing the status of women in the new century was seen to be rooted in his holistic analysis centered on gender and the value of women's work (paid and unpaid), and in a recognition that strategies to combat gender inequality must be more than enabling entry of women into the labor force. His framework for studying the nature of institutions and societal change was seen to have lasting relevance, as was his insight into how institutions and processes thought to be emancipatory (such as higher education) may actually embody invidious distinctions and reinforce the "otherness" of women (Brown 1998, Chapters 7–10).

In the first two decades of the twenty-first century, feminist economists across different traditions worked to deepen and extend feminist inquiry, embrace new theoretical and methodological questions, explore new fields of study within economics, and address contemporary economic problems and challenges. Among feminist institutionalists, that work included further exploring the contributions of different traditions within institutionalism as well as incorporating insights of other heterodox schools of thought—including social economics, Marxian political economy, and post-Keynesian economics (for example, Figart, Mutari, and Power 2002; Todorova 2009). It also meant engaging in important economic policy debates, including (in the US context) welfare reform (for example, Peterson 2003) and the provision of non-invidious employment (for example, Figart 2003).

Over the course of both decades, feminist institutionalism has remained relevant to an ever-evolving economy. As the first decade of the new century came to a close, feminist economists made important contributions to broadening the analysis of economic crisis and recovery (Fukuda-Parr, Heintz, and Seguino 2013; Karamessini and Rubery 2013). In its analysis of the US Great Recession and recovery, feminist institutionalism provided a robust framework for understanding the gendered outcomes and interrogating the gendered narratives that captured popular attention and dominated media discussions (Peterson 2012; 2016). As the second decade of the twenty-first century came to a close, feminist institutionalists joined other heterodox economists in challenging narratives of the "strongest economy in US history" and "historic US prosperity" in light of not only the economic insecurity gripping many individuals and families but also ongoing efforts to limit the federal government's role in social provisioning (Peterson 2020).

Key elements

Seven core concepts of feminist institutional economics emerge from the discussions above: culture, gender, dualism, social provisioning, institutions, inequality, and care. Focusing on these key elements enables discussion not only of feminist institutionalism's essential contributions to (and "starting points" for) economic inquiry, but also its contemporary arguments and analyses.

Culture, gender, and dualism

Institutionalists and feminists both begin with an understanding of the importance of the concept of culture and the influence of cultural patterns and constructions on the social provisioning process. Culture may be defined as a "system of symbolic interpretation that unites human thought and action" (Jennings 1993, 113). The concept of culture grounds a conviction that "human behavior must be understood as part of a system of ongoing social processes and social meanings, all of which evolve and change over historical time" (Jennings 1992, 117). In this context, gender is understood as a cultural phenomenon; it is a social construction with tremendous significance for both the roles women play in provisioning processes and how their contributions are valued.[7]

Anne Mayhew (1999, 479–480) identifies the "centrality of focus on the analytic concept of 'culture'" as the core idea of institutional economics that has most set institutionalists apart from other economists while also providing an important point of commonality with feminists. She argues that the emphasis on historically influenced cultural patterns, and their impact on the processes of provisioning, *shifts the focus* of economic analysis, providing opportunities for a fuller understanding of gender roles and the status of women in different societies. To illustrate, Mayhew (1999, 491) contrasts explanations for differences in female labor force participation based on neoclassical assumptions of "rational" choice with those derived from the ethnographic, historical, and statistical methods of institutional analysis. She argues that the tools of cultural analysis employed by institutionalists allow for "discovery of patterns of female participation and entitlement in different times and places" that reveal insights about the significance of gender in different historical and cultural circumstances that have nothing to do with "rational" choice.[8]

Mayhew also argues that institutionalists and feminists share an understanding of the role of power in the social construction of gender roles. That is, "not only are gender roles socially constructed, but so are the economic advantages and disadvantages, entitlements and penalties associated with those gendered roles in the economy" (Mayhew 1999, 484). Recognizing the importance of culture also means recognizing that "patterns of behavior and beliefs—such as prejudices about women and their role in the economy—are not innate, but learned in a particular culture and therefore changeable" (Mayhew 1999, 479). Thus, the concept of culture both refocuses the analysis on social provisioning and provides a framework for thinking about social change.[9]

Jennings (1992; 1993; 1994) also emphasizes the centrality of the concept of culture in institutional economics, and the increasing attention to cultural constructions in feminist inquiry as an important point of commonality with institutional economics. Jennings (1993, 114) articulates several of the connotations culture has for institutionalists, including the rejection of universal categories and embrace of historical and interdisciplinary methods. Perhaps most fundamentally, "culture implies an essential continuity of all human social activity as necessary to viable and coherent social arrangements." Consequently, institutionalists view "theories that posit the separateness of any sphere of endeavor as cultural defenses of existing social distinctions," and instead "understand all behavior as multi-dimensional and complex, having various economic, political, and reproductive aspects that cannot be separated" (Jennings 1993, 114).

The "continuity of the cultural process" grounds the rejection of dualisms, introduced earlier in this chapter. As Waller and Jennings (1990, 616–617) have argued, institutionalists "have long rejected the division of social reality into dualistic categories." While the intellectual act of creating dualisms is "one way that human beings conceptualize and systematize their understanding of the world," the problem is that dualisms become reified. With the reification of dualisms, the "unified reality ceases to be the object of inquiry and instead the bifurcated conceptual apparatus becomes the reality" (Waller 1995, 167–168).

One consequence of the emphasis on continuity in institutionalist thought is "a strong resistance to the notion that any significant portion of human behavior is private, in the sense of being untouched by cultural norms and values" (Waller and Jennings 1990, 619). In particular, dualisms that separate "public" from "private" realms of human activity are viewed as "central to defining and constructing social hierarchy in our culture" (Waller 1995, 169). This is particularly significant for the relationship between institutionalism and feminism, because for many feminists "the cultural conception of some spheres of life as private, as disconnected from social life, is integral to the subordination of women in modern western culture" (Waller and Jennings 1990, 619).

According to Waller (1995, 171), the construction of women's roles and identities in our culture as simultaneously "familial" and "non-economic" has had profound consequences because our pecuniary society determines an individual's "social status, identity and value" by where they are located in the "economic sphere." These consequences include limitations of women's economic opportunity and ability to participate fully in economic society, as well as the "devaluation of the activities prescribed by women's non-economic designation." Jennings (1992; 1993) traces the emergence of the public/private split in US history to the nineteenth-century ideology of "separate spheres" and the "cult of domesticity." She also finds that the strong influence of public/private distinctions on gender norms does not, in fact, derive from their historical accuracy. Women were not absent from economic activity to the degree suggested by this ideology, and the extent to which women's activities did not conform to their "proper roles" was largely a function of social class and/or race-ethnicity.[10]

Recent analyses and applications of the public/private dualism by Waller and Mary Wrenn (2021) emphasize, as noted by Jennings, the historic fluidity of such distinctions and increasingly dynamic nature of gender dualisms. They argue that "recognition that power relationships operate on multiple dimensions" is particularly significant and highlights the importance of intersectional analysis to address the "inseparable simultaneity of multiple axes of oppression."[11] Waller and Wrenn also argue that the critique of dualistic constructions of reality developed in feminist institutional work should be seen as a necessary step in the development of intersectional analysis because of "the cultural importance of enabling myths that justify this system of dualistic constructions."

Social provisioning, institutions, and inequality

The belief that economics is the study of social provisioning is a shared conviction of feminist and institutional economists, and is one of the cornerstones of feminist institutionalist inquiry. Grounded in Veblen's approach, a focus on social provisioning leads to a broad understanding of economic activities that includes caring and other actions that cannot be understood entirely in terms of individual choices and market outcomes (Todarova 2009; Waddoups and Tilman 1992).

For institutional and feminist economists, a focus on social provisioning both frames the critique of neoclassical economics and provides analytical "starting points" for inquiry that strives to capture the complexities and conflicts of social provisioning in the real world (for example, Dugger 1996b; Power 2004). Drawing on institutional and feminist economics, such starting points for feminist institutionalism may include:[12]

- Accepting the centrality of the concept of culture and the rejection of public/private dualisms (as well as analytic frameworks resting on them) and the devaluation of unpaid work;
- Rejecting the notion of a "value-free economics" and recognizing that all knowledge—including economic knowledge—is socially constructed;
- Accepting economic inquiry as "values-driven" with the objective of enhancing the life process and elevating outcomes associated with well-being;
- Shifting the focus of economic analysis from individual rational choice and equilibrium to processes and power relationships, recognizing that evolving economic forces give rise to conflict and thus to the need to interrogate domination in all its forms (including sexism, racism, and classism); and
- Replacing a reliance on abstract mathematics and methodological individualism with a historical-empirical approach and methodological holism.

Institutional economists seek to observe and understand the various processes of social provisioning in the context of institutions. For Veblen, institutions were part of an analysis of behavior at the cultural level and characterized as "settled habits of thought" (Waller 1982, 759–760). In institutional economic analysis, "culturally specific and culturally shared patterns of behavior" constitute institutions and shift the focus away from rational, individual choice (Mayhew 1999, 479–480).[13] The institutions of a society are complex and embody processes that may have ceremonial (based in predation) as well as instrumental (based in workmanship) aspects (Todorova 2009, 5). Societal institutions are also consequential in the roles they play in distributing power (Stanfield 1989, 4). Institutional economics' recognition of socially constructed norms and power relationships embedded in economic relationships has resonated with feminist economists (Beneria, Berik, and Floro 2016, 50) and informed feminist institutionalist applications.

Irene van Staveren and Olasunbo Odebode (2007, 904–905), for example, note Veblen's recognition of the influences of gender norms and patriarchy on the provisioning process, as well as Dugger's recognition of power relations (including patriarchy) in his analysis of different "modes of inequality" (Dugger 1996a). In this context, van Staveren and Odebode (2007, 908) argue that it is important to characterize gender as an "asymmetric institution." That is, to characterize gender as "a complex, multi-dimensional institution shaped unequally for men and women, with men generally benefiting more than women in terms of access to control over resources, the household division of labor, the distribution of rewards, and decision-making power." They also argue that because norms and institutions are often related, the expression of gender norms are mediated through other institutions, which become "bearers of gender."[14]

Households and labor markets are institutions with particular significance as "bearers of gender" in feminist institutional economics. Veblen identified patriarchal marriage and the patriarchal household—and the myths supporting both as natural—as central to the subordination of women in the leisure class society of his time. Greenwood (1984b) identified the continuing ramifications of these belief systems as central to women's association with low-status, unpaid familial work and to their inferior occupational status and pay in the labor market.

Jane Wheelock (1994, 333–334) has argued institutional analysis provides special insights into households as gendered institutions, as well as their relationship to labor markets. In particular, the focus on power relations moves institutionalist analyses of the household away from individual choice, allowing gender to be taken seriously. In addition, she argues that the focus on cultural processes and the social construction of knowledge encourages questions about the decisions households make with respect to work strategies and allocating time to paid and unpaid work. Finally, recognizing the process of evolutionary change encourages analysis of the ways in which the relationship between the household and the economy changes over time, to better understand the influence of the household/family life-cycle as well as structural economic changes.

Economic analyses of labor markets typically attempt to explain how wages and employment are determined. Feminist economists have responded to traditional labor market theories with "concerns about their underlying assumptions, implicit gender biases, and their applicability to women's experiences" (Jennings 1999, 510). Feminist institutionalist analyses of labor markets are grounded in the recognition of the labor market as a social institution, where wages and employment are not determined in the abstract, but in the context of a society's laws, traditions, ideologies, and power relationships. Wages do more than merely allocate scarce resources among competing ends; they are closely linked to status, defining the place of individuals relative to others in society (Peterson 1990, 607–610).

Deborah Figart, Ellen Mutari, and Marilyn Power (2002, 4–5) identify three "implicit wage theories" in the debates leading to regulations and policies regarding wages over the twentieth century: wages as a price, wages as a living, and wages as a social practice. They argue that the dimension of wages "as a social practice"—which shapes as well as reflects gender, class, race-ethnicity, and cultural understandings of workers' appropriate "place"—has largely been ignored by both mainstream and heterodox economists, leading to an incomplete analysis of labor market issues. This includes the analysis of labor market discrimination, which typically focuses narrowly on wages as a price (Figart, Mutari, and Power 2002, 211–212). Figart proposes a feminist definition of labor market discrimination that incorporates all three aspects of wage setting: "a multidimensional interaction of economic, social, and political forces both in the workplace and the family, resulting in differential outcomes involving pay, employment and status" (Figart 1997, 7; 1999, 112).

Inequality—a central concern for feminists and institutionalists—brings together many of the concepts and issues discussed in this section, and Dugger's "modes of inequality" framework is helpful for this integration. Dugger (1996a, 21) defined a "mode of inequality" as a social process where a powerful group reaps benefits for itself at the expense of a less powerful group. Different modes of inequality—such as gender, race, class, and nation—overlap and reinforce each other. Each mode of inequality has an associated set of practices, which allow the powerful to take advantage of the powerless, and "enabling myths" that culturally enforce the practices and make them "seem fair." Each mode of inequality also has a "focal point," the particular institution where the "myths justifying it are learned and the practices realizing it actually take place." There is also an "antidote" for each mode of inequality, a set of "values, meanings, and beliefs that can debunk the enabling myths."

In this framework, Dugger (1996a, 22–26) defines gender inequality as the domination of women by men through a series of gendered practices, supported by sexist myths of female inferiority and male superiority. This domination has an "institutionalized focal point" in the patriarchal family, where the cultural values and beliefs that support male domination are taught. The dualistic separation of public and private activities associated with men and women supports sexist myths of women's "otherness" and reinforces their inferior status. The antidote for gender inequality in this framework is feminism. Because gender inequality is part of a whole complex of different modes of inequality, the intersectionality of feminist analyses becomes critically important for feminism to serve this role.

Feminist economist Kanchana Ruwanpura (2008) provides a discussion and application of "multiple discrimination," a concept that is consistent with Figart's feminist definition of discrimination and Dugger's modes of inequality framework. Ruwanpura (2008, 88–90) centers her analysis in the recognition that "social categories are constructed and contested, as they may vary from context to context." She notes a "vicious cycle" of discrimination that is rooted in the historical process, particular institutional arrangements, and social relationships. She argues that this helps to explain "the diverse forms of discriminatory practices, and particularly that of multi-discrimination." Her work illustrates how, in a stratified society, inferior status is assigned differently to different groups, and the practices and experiences of dominance can be very different.

Care

Attention to "care" is a hallmark of feminist economics, where it has been widely discussed and analyzed.[15] Contemporary institutional economic analyses of care are more recent, but have drawn inspiration from Veblen and reflect many elements of institutional thought. Veblen's characterization of social provisioning and his distinction between activities based in pecuniary values and those based in serviceability provides not only valuable insight into the status of women in the leisure class society of his time, but also a starting point for thinking about care, its complexities, and how it is valued in pecuniary societies.

Zdravka Todorova (2009) addresses care in her exploration of the ceremonial (pecuniary) and instrumental (serviceable) aspects of households in the social provisioning processes of twenty-first-century pecuniary culture. She demonstrates, for example, that the ceremonial aspects of the household manifest through a hierarchical gender division of labor, while the instrumental aspects of the household manifest as concern for the continuation of the life process, through both "material provisioning" and "care" (Todorova 2009, 88, 108). Material provisioning includes activities that provide nourishment and clean living spaces ("housework"), while care, reflecting the parental bent, involves "not only tending to physical needs, and developing capabilities, but also a sense of recognition and personal worth" (Todorova 2009, 88, 109).[16]

Todorova (2009, 108–109) notes further that while the activities of material provisioning are necessary for the continuation of human life, they may also take on aspects of invidious distinction that are "masked as instrumental." Further, she argues, the instrumentality of care should not mask the ceremonial effects of gendered childrearing within a hierarchical household division of labor. Todorova (2016, 113–114) also notes that while care may be organized as monetary production in modern society, the fact that money enters into the provision of care does not mean that individuals delivering care are exclusively governed by pecuniary concerns. She argues, however, that "the richness of human relations" does not "nullify the centrality of economic compulsion to sell one's labor and the dependence on money to access paid care."

Andrew Cumbers, John Davis, and Robert McMaster (2015, 584) also begin with Veblen in their analysis of care. They emphasize the significance of the parental bent (defined as "other-regarding" behavior) in Veblen's work, as well as his recognition that "institutions can encourage the dominance of particular instincts over others through the cumulative effect of habit." Thus, they argue that care has both "instinctive and socially constructed properties," with social institutions, roles, and values predicating (at least partially) the human ability to care.

Cumbers, Davis, and McMaster (2015, 584) expand on Veblen's framework with the work of care theorist Joan Tronto (2013), who introduced the concept of a "caring deficit" where "the needs of care are greater than human abilities to provide care." Cumbers, Davis, and McMaster (2015, 589) illustrate "caring deficits" with an example from the 2008 financial crisis and the austerity programs that followed (in response to increasing fiscal deficits), which "only served to increase the need for care, while reducing the capacity for care" (thus increasing "caring deficits"). They conclude: "From a Veblenian perspective, the cumulative effect of over three decades of neoliberal economic hegemony has crowded care out to the detriment of all."

Anna Zachorowska-Mazurkiewicz (2015) also addresses the importance of social institutions, gender roles, and values in the provision of care, and the significance of care for the economy and society. She argues that neoliberal values have shaped policies related to the provision of care in ways that are detrimental to the implementation of a progressive care agenda. She concludes:

> There is a need for a new social contract that not only redefines gender relations, but also takes into consideration the role of the state. Responsibility for ensuring that caring work does not lead to poverty and social exclusion should be taken out of the private sphere and reframed as a collective responsibility.
>
> *(Zachorowska-Mazurkiewicz 2015, 409)*

Wrenn and Waller (2017) investigate neoliberalism as an ethical system and its relationship to an "ethic of care." They argue neoliberalism postulates that individuals are "self-interested and proceed in the service of this self-interest in atomistic, individualistic terms," a characterization of human nature that precludes caring. Neoliberalism requires the dualistic separation of activities in private and public realms, assigning all caring responsibility to the private sphere and ignoring the relational character of caring and other human relationships. Neoliberalism, as an ideology, "valorizes autonomy as a state of being and as an ethics of self-interest and personal responsibility exclusively." As such, neoliberalism "crowds out an ethic of care" (Wrenn and Waller 2017, 495–496, 499).

Waller and Wrenn (2021) extend this analysis, situating their investigation of neoliberalism and care in feminist institutionalism. They note that Jennings (1993) prescribed a solution for the influences of cultural dualisms that elevate the market economy over the state (political processes) and the family (familial processes): "the dissolution of the divides between work, home, and the state." That is, the "re-embedding of the productive sphere into and within the reproductive and political spheres would integrate and validate all human activities" (Waller and Wrenn 2021). Waller and Wrenn argue that today the demystification of such dualisms would "render the policy prescriptions of neoliberalism untenable," meaning that:

> Care work could be prioritized and valorized for its contribution to human survival and flourishing and made a social priority, rather than another human need turned over to the market for allocation to those with the means to pay for it. Occupations historically cast as feminine—teaching, nursing, and parenting—could be supported and the opportunities therein expanded to reflect their critical roles.
>
> *(Waller and Wrenn 2021, 20)*

Feminist institutionalism offers a path forward for debunking the enabling myths preventing establishment of an ethic of care.

Conclusion: current challenges and frontiers

This chapter closes by discussing the relevance and significance of feminist institutionalism for framing an analysis of the economic impacts of the COVID-19 crisis (as it is unfolding in the United States) and thinking about steps forward for a better future.

Precariousness and inequality before the crisis

In recent years, feminist institutionalists have shared the interest and concern of other heterodox economists with regard to the changing structure and growing precariousness of employment, and the seemingly contradictory situation of individuals and households reporting high levels of economic vulnerability and stress in the context of a highly touted "strong economy." Popular discussions of the economy have addressed these issues as well. For example, in May 2019, Jacob Hacker argued in *The New York Times* that this situation reflects how the changing structure of employment has shifted risk once shared by workers and employers onto workers alone—leaving many with work that had been "gig-ified" (Hacker 2019). Further, research studies documented that the growing economy was leaving many low-wage workers behind in work that is precarious, unpredictable, and with no or few benefits (Escobari 2019), and that people of color and women were overrepresented in the low-wage workforce (Ross and Bateman 2019). In early February 2020, an opinion essay by Steven Rattner (2020) characterized the US economy as "not as good as it looks," with its subdued real wage growth and record income inequality.

The COVID-19 crisis

With the onset of the COVID-19 pandemic, the US economy plunged from being "not as good as it looks" into historic crisis, exposing the invidious distinctions and enabling myths that have shielded serious economic problems from appropriate attention. The COVID-19 crisis has exposed the precarious lives of low-wage workers who lack fundamental employment protections (Hund-Mejean and Escobari 2020). It has debunked the myth that "gig work" and other forms of alternative employment serve as a "safety net" for workers, as "non-traditional workers" have been found to be particularly at risk for both negative employment and health outcomes in the current crisis (Nunn and O'Donnell 2020).

Most fundamentally, and despite the popular slogan "we're all in this together," COVID-19 and the economic impacts associated with it have laid bare the stark inequality—across many dimensions—plaguing the US economy. This is evidenced in numerous news stories and editorials on the impacts of the crisis, where a multitude of inequalities are seen to both contribute to the current hardship experienced by many and threaten to make the recovery more difficult (Leonhardt and Serkez 2020). Further, an early study by the Levy Institute argued that the most vulnerable segments of US society would disproportionately bear the (health and economic) costs of the COVID-19 pandemic, likely exacerbating income, racial, and gender inequality in the United States (Nassif-Pires et al. 2020), something that is proving accurate as the crisis continues to unfold.

Feminist economic insights

Drawing on feminist economics, we can also see that the COVID-19 crisis shines a bright light on the critical importance of care and caring labor (paid and unpaid)—illuminating the severe consequence of caring deficits for individuals, society, and economic recovery. The crisis has fostered consideration of an expanded definition of (paid) caring labor, to encompass all those who are "essential workers" (Folbre 2020). A sharp focus on the care economy also reveals its long-standing hierarchies and the poor circumstances of many essential workers. Working under intense and potentially unsafe conditions, many of those workers who were lauded as "heroes" at the onset of the crisis continue to experience low status and low pay (Kinder 2020).

The crisis also brings explicit attention to the critical importance of unpaid care work and the enormous subsidy it provides to the economy and society. With "stay at home" mandates and "work from home" policies, a great many of life's activities returned to the home. For workers with the privilege and ability to work from home, it becomes the site of both unpaid and paid work interacting closely. For households with children, unpaid caring labor may expand to include home schooling. In households with two adults, the household division of labor may take new forms and/or become newly contested terrain. In households where a family member (or members) must work outside the home to keep their job, the lack of appropriate health protections at work, safe transportation, and/or childcare can mean tremendous stress and difficult decisions. As the crisis continued, for example, there were increasing reports of women leaving the labor force because of the increased strain of work in the home. These challenges illustrate the complexities of the relationship between unpaid labor and paid employment that are not addressed adequately in traditional models of labor supply, and require deeper consideration of the meaning of "work-family balance."

Moving forward

Moving forward from the COVID-19 crisis will require attention to the economic vulnerability and precariousness faced by many Americans, the historic levels of inequality that existed prior to the crisis, and the economic impacts of the crisis itself and associated policy responses. Feminist institutionalism—guided by a focus on social provisioning—has much to contribute to framing these necessary discussions, beginning with the recognition of the importance of historical context. In that context, this crisis reveals the legacy of decades of neoliberalism and failure to value care and unpaid work in the home or community, as well as centuries of racism and structural inequality. Feminist institutionalism is well situated to frame and promote the necessary discussions, which include addressing caring deficits, multidimensional inequality, precarious employment, and the increasingly complex labor force participation and employment decisions facing many women—to name only a few of the critical issues. As the crisis and recovery continue to unfold, there will be trends to identify and explain, and policies to develop and evaluate. The need for holistic, feminist, reality-based research has never been greater; we are in an important moment for feminist institutionalism to step up and make a difference.

Acknowledgments

The author wishes to thank Dell Champlin, Deborah Figart, William Waller, and Charles Whalen for their helpful comments.

Notes

1 Feminist institutionalism can be viewed as a distinct approach within both institutional economics and feminist economics. This chapter focuses on feminist institutionalism within institutional economics; for a discussion focused on its place within feminist economics, see Mutari (2021).
2 The analysis of "comparable worth" (or "pay equity") policies has been important for feminist institutionalists; see, for example, Peterson (1990); Mutari and Figart (1997).
3 See also Greenwood (1988) for further discussion of institutionalism's need to focus more on gender.
4 Not all of the institutional economic scholarship contributing to the early development of feminist institutionalism was part of the radical institutionalist explorations discussed here. The radical institutionalist project was, however, significant in identifying aspects of original institutionalist economics particularly conducive to feminist thinking, recognizing concepts and arguments in need of updating, and encouraging such work.
5 Veblen's distinction between self-seeking and socially useful behavior was formalized by later institutionalists as the "Veblenian Dichotomy" and structured as "ceremonial" versus "technological" and/or "ceremonial" versus "instrumental" behavior (see Dugger 1989, 7, 112–113; Stanfield 1989, 84–86; Waller 1982; Waller 1989, 41–44). For further discussion of that dichotomy in institutional economics, see William Waller's contribution to this volume (Chapter 1).
6 See Waddoups and Tilman (1992) for their discussion (presented at the conference) of Veblen's understanding of social provisioning as a process that integrates the economy and culture, explicitly including provisioning activities that occur in the family.
7 Waller (2005, 331) identifies gender as a "cultural category," which essentially labels "groups of people with some similarity on the basis of that commonalty," and "treats their common characteristics as having social significance and values it either positively or negatively in that particular culture."
8 Mayhew (1999, 481) illustrates with an example from ethnographic work by Eiman Zein-Elabdin that revealed how women play very different roles in the provisioning processes in different parts of the world, and challenged the current discourse on economic development, gender, and the environment.

9 For example, Mutari and Figart (2015) draw on feminist, institutional, and social economics, as well as detailed interviews with Atlantic City casino workers, to construct a definition of "good jobs" based on the lived experiences of these workers, and then conduct an analysis of "good jobs" in this industry based on this definition. Their work provides a framework for thinking about job quality in many industries, and identifying possibilities for change.
10 Williams (1993, 151–152) argued that the domestic ideology surrounding this public/private split was "a very race specific discourse. Thus, the economy/family dualism anchors gender, but in a racialized fashion."
11 See for example, Ruwanpura (2008).
12 The "starting points" presented here draw ideas and inspiration from the institutionalist "implications" and "fundamentals" presented in Dugger (1996b) and Petr (1984), the feminist economic "starting points" presented in Power (2004), and the contributions of feminist economics and radical institutionalism discussed in this chapter.
13 This understanding of institutions is distinct from that in the "new institutional economics," where such patterns are seen to derive from individual choices (Mayhew 1999, 479).
14 Elson (1999) referred to labor markets as "bearers of gender" in her analysis of labor markets as gendered institutions; van Staveren and Odebode (2007) apply the concept to households.
15 Waller and Wrenn (2021) document the extensive attention to care in feminist economic scholarship. See also, for example, Folbre and Nelson (2000); Folbre (2012).
16 Todorova (2009, 106) defines "parental bent" as "an instinct that secures the renewal of the social group through intergenerational communication of methods of associated living."

References

Agenjo-Calderon, Astrid and Lina Galvez-Munoz. 2019. "Feminist Economics: Theoretical and Political Dimensions." *American Journal of Economics and Sociology* 78 (1): 137–166. https://doi.org/10.1111/ajes.12264

Beneria, Lourdes, Günseli Berik, and Maria S. Floro. 2016. *Gender, Development, and Globalization: Economics As If All People Mattered*, second edition. New York: Routledge. https://doi.org/10.4324/9780203107935

Brown, Doug, ed. 1998. *Thorstein Veblen in the Twenty-First Century: A Commemoration of the Theory of the Leisure Class (1899–1999).*Cheltenham, UK: Edward Elgar.

Cumbers, Andrew, John Davis, and Robert McMaster. 2015. "Theorizing the Social Provisioning Process Under Capitalism: Developing a Veblenian Theory of Care for the Twenty-First Century." *Journal of Economic Issues* 49 (2): 583–589. https://doi.org/10.1080/00213624.2015.1042806

Diggins, John P. 1978. *The Bard of Savagery: Thorstein Veblen and Modern Social Theory.* New York: The Seabury Press.

Dugger, William M., ed. 1989. *Radical Institutionalism: Contemporary Voices.* New York: Greenwood Press.

———, ed. 1996a. *Inequality: Radical Institutionalist Views on Race, Gender, Class, and Nation.* Westport, CT: Greenwood Press.

———. 1996b. "Redefining Economics: From Market Allocation to Social Provisioning." In *Political Economy for the 21st Century*, edited by Charles Whalen, 31–43. Armonk, NY: M.E. Sharpe. https://doi.org/10.4324/9781315701707-12

Dugger, William M. and William T. Waller Jr., eds. 1992. *The Stratified State: Radical Institutionalist Theories of Participation and Duality*. Armonk, NY: M.E. Sharpe. https://doi.org/10.4324/9781315487090

Elson, Diane. 1999. "Labor Markets as Gendered Institutions: Equality, Efficiency and Empowerment Issues." *World Development* 27 (3): 611–627. https://doi.org/10.1016/s0305-750x(98)00147-8

Escobari, Marcela. 2019. "The Economy Is Growing and Leaving Low-Wage Workers Behind." Brookings, December 19. https://tinyurl.com/ugqh23w. Accessed October 9, 2020.

Ferber, Marianne A. and Julie A. Nelson, eds. 1993. *Beyond Economic Man: Feminist Theory and Economics*. Chicago, IL: University of Chicago Press. https://doi.org/10.7208/chicago/9780226242088.001.0001

Figart, Deborah M. 1997. "Gender is More Than a Dummy Variable: Feminist Approaches to Discrimination." *Review of Social Economy* 55 (1): 1–32. https://doi.org/10.1080/00346769700000022

———. 1999. "Discrimination, Theories of." In *The Elgar Companion to Feminist Economics*, edited by Janice Peterson and Margaret Lewis, 107–112. Cheltenham, UK: Edward Elgar.

———. 2003. "Policies to Provide Non-Invidious Employment." In *Institutional Analysis and Economic Policy*, edited by Marc R. Tool and Paul D. Bush, 379–409. Boston, MA: Kluwer. https://doi.org/10.1007/978-1-4615-0261-6_13

Figart, Deborah M., Ellen Mutari, and Marilyn Power. 2002. *Living Wages, Equal Wages: Gender and Labor Market Policies in the United States*. London: Routledge. https://doi.org/10.4324/9780203994139

Figart, Deborah M. and Tonia L. Warnecke, eds. 2013. *Handbook of Research on Gender and Economic Life*. Cheltenham, UK: Edward Elgar.

Folbre, Nancy. 2020. "Are We All Care Workers Now?" Care Talk, April. https://blogs.umass.edu/ folbre/2020/04/04/are-we-all-care-workers-now/. Accessed April 10, 2020.

Folbre, Nancy, ed. 2012. *For Love and Money: Care Provision in the United States*. New York: Russel Sage.

Folbre, Nancy and Julie A. Nelson. 2000. "For Love or Money?" *Journal of Economic Perspectives* 14 (4): 123–40. https://doi.org/10.1257/jep.14.4.123

Fukuda-Parr, Sakiko, James Heintz, and Stephanie Seguino. 2013. "Critical Perspectives on Financial and Economic Crises: Heterodox Macroeconomics Meets Feminist Economics." *Feminist Economics* 19 (3): 4–31.

Greenwood, Daphne. 1984a. "The Institutional Inadequacy of the Market in Determining Comparable Worth: Implications for Value Theory." *Journal of Economic Issues* 18 (2): 457–64. https://doi.org/10.1080/00213624.1984.11504245

———. 1984b. "The Economic Significance of 'Woman's Place' in Society: A New-Institutionalist View." *Journal of Economic Issues* 18 (3): 663–80. https://doi.org/10.1080/00213624.1984.11504269

———. 1988. "A Comment on *Evolutionary Economics I: Foundations of Institutionalist Thought*." *Journal of Economic Issues* 22 (1): 249–251. https://doi.org/10.1080/00213624.1988.11504746

Hacker, Jacob S. 2019. "The Economy Is Strong. So Why Do So Many Americans Still Feel at Risk?" *The New York Times*, May 21. https://www.nytimes.com/2019/05/21/opinion/trump-economy.html. Accessed May 22, 2019.

Hund-Mejean, Martina and Marcela Escobari. 2020. "Our Employment System Has Failed Low-Wage Workers." Brookings, April 28. https://tinyurl.com/y9sh428s. Accessed October 9, 2020.

Jennings, Ann L .1992. "Not the Economy: Feminist Theory, Institutional Change, and the State." In *The Stratified State*, edited by William M. Dugger and William T. Waller Jr., 117–149. Armonk, NY: M.E. Sharpe. https://doi.org/10.4324/9781315487090-6

———. 1993. "Public or Private? Institutional Economics and Feminism." In *Beyond Economic Man*, edited by Marianne A. Ferber and Julie A. Nelson, 111–129. Chicago, IL: University of Chicago Press.

———. 1994. "Feminism." In *The Elgar Companion to Institutional and Evolutionary Economics*, edited by Geoffrey M. Hodgson, Warren J. Samuels, and Marc R. Tool, 225–228. Aldershot, UK: Edward Elgar. https://doi.org/10.4337/9781843768661.00046

———. 1999. "Labor Markets, Theories of." In *The Elgar Companion to Feminist Economics*, edited by Janice Peterson and Margaret Lewis, 511–521. Cheltenham, UK: Edward Elgar. https://doi.org/10.4337/9781843768685.00068

Karamessini, Maria and Jill Rubery, eds. 2013. *Women and Austerity: The Economic Crisis and the Future for Gender Equality*. London: Routledge. https://doi.org/10.4324/9780203066294

Kuiper, Edith and Jolande Sap, eds. 1995. *Out of the Margin: Feminist Perspectives on Economics*. London: Routledge.

Kuiper, Edith. 2008. "Feminism and/in Economics." In *The Elgar Companion to Social Economics*, edited by John B. Davis and Wilfred Dolfsma, 188–206. Cheltenham, UK: Edward Elgar. https://doi.org/10.4337/9781848442771.00021

Kinder, Molly. 2020. "Essential But Undervalued: Millions of Health Care Workers Aren't Getting the Pay or Respect They Deserve in the COVID 19 Pandemic." Brookings, May 28. https://tinyurl.com/y7esb2nb. Accessed October 9, 2020.

Leonhardt, David and Yaryna Serkez. 2020. "America Will Struggle After Coronavirus. These Charts Show Why." *The New York Times*, April 10. https://www.nytimes.com/interactive/2020/04/10/opinion/coronavirus-us-economy-inequality.html. Accessed April 10, 2020.

Mayhew, Anne. 1999. "Institutional Economics." In *The Elgar Companion to Feminist Economics*, edited by Janice Peterson and Margaret Lewis, 479–486. Cheltenham, UK: Edward Elgar. https://doi.org/10.4337/9781843768685.00063

Mill, John Stuart. 1869. *The Subjection of Women*. London: Longmans, Green, Rader, and Dyer.

Miller, Edythe S. 1972. "Veblen and Women's Lib: A Parallel." *Journal of Economic Issues* 6 (2/3): 75–86. https://doi.org/10.1080/00213624.1972.11503031

Mutari, Ellen. 2021. "Feminist Institutional Economics: A Cross-Fertilization of Congruent Approaches." In *Routledge Handbook of Feminist Economics*, edited by Günseli Berik and Erbu Kongar, 43–52. London: Routledge.

Mutari, Ellen and Deborah M. Figart. 1997. "Markets, Flexibility, and Family: Evaluating the Gendered Discourse Against Pay Equity." *Journal of Economic Issues* 31 (3): 687–705. https://doi.org/10.1080/00213624.1997.11505960

———. 2015. *Just One More Hand: Life in the Casino Economy*. Lanham, MD: Rowman & Littlefield.

Nassif-Pires, Luiza, Laura de Lima Xavier, Thomas Masterson, Michalis Nikiforos, and Fernando Rios-Avila. 2020. "Pandemic of Inequality." *Policy Brief No.149* (April). Levy Economics Institute of Bard College. http://www.levyinstitute.org/pubs/ppb_149.pdf. Accessed May 1, 2020.

Nelson, Julie A. 1993. "The Study of Choice or the Study of Provisioning? Gender and the Definition of Economics." In *Beyond Economic Man*, edited by Marianne A. Ferber and Julie A. Nelson, 23–36. Chicago, IL: University of Chicago Press.

Nunn, Ryan and Jimmy O'Donnell, J. 2020. "Unpredictable and Uninsured: The Challenging Labor Market Experiences of Nontraditional Workers." Brookings, May 7. https://tinyurl.com/y3yjjftz. Accessed October 9, 2020.

Peterson, Janice. 1990. "The Challenge of Comparable Worth: An Institutionalist View." *Journal of Economic Issues* 24 (2): 605–612. https://doi.org/10.1080/00213624.1990.11505059

———. 2003. "Welfare Reform." In *Institutional Analysis and Economic Policy*, edited by Marc R. Tool and Paul D. Bush, 157–182. Boston, MA: Kluwer. https://doi.org/10.1007/978-1-4615-0261-6_6

———. 2012. "The Great Crisis and the Significance of Gender in the US Economy." *Journal of Economic Issues* 46 (2): 277–290. https://doi.org/10.2753/jei0021-3624460203

———. 2016. "The Well-being of Working Women in Times of Economic Crisis and Recovery: Insights from the Great Recession." In *Handbook on Well-being of Working Women*, edited by Mary Connerley and Jiyun Wu, 517–539. New York: Springer. https://doi.org/10.1007/978-94-017-9897-6_30

———. 2020. "Welfare Policy and Precarious Lives: 'Welfare Reform' Revisited." *Journal of Economic Issues* 54 (2): 377–384. https://doi.org/10.1080/00213624.2020.1743589

Peterson, Janice and Doug Brown, eds. 1994. *The Economic Status of Women Under Capitalism: Institutional Economics and Feminist Theory*. Aldershot, UK: Edward Elgar.

Peterson, Janice and Margaret Lewis, eds. 1999. *The Elgar Companion to Feminist Economics*. Cheltenham, UK: Edward Elgar. https://doi.org/10.4337/9781843768685

Petr, Jerry L. 1984. "Fundamentals of an Institutionalist Perspective on Economic Policy." *Journal of Economic Issues* 18 (1): 1–17. https://doi.org/10.1080/00213624.1984.11504216

Power, Marilyn. 2004. "Social Provisioning as a Starting Point for Feminist Economics." *Feminist Economics* 10 (3): 3–19. https://doi.org/10.1080/1354570042000267608

Rattner, Steven. 2020. "The Economy Is Not As Good As It Looks." *The New York Times*. February 5. https://www.nytimes.com/2020/02/05/opinion/trump-economy-election.html. Accessed February 5, 2020.

Ross, Martha and Nicole Bateman. 2019. "To Lift the American Economy, We Need to Understand the Workers at the Bottom of It." Brookings, November 14. https://tinyurl.com/y4zazlt4. Accessed October 9, 2020.

Rossi, Alice. 1973. *The Feminist Papers: From Adams to de Beauvoir*. New York: Columbia University Press.

Ruwanpura, Kanchana. 2008. "Multiple Identities, Multiple-Discrimination: A Critical Review." *Feminist Economics* 14 (3): 77–105. https://doi.org/10.1080/13545700802035659

Ryan, Barbara E. 1982. "Thorstein Veblen: A New Perspective." *Mid-American Review of Sociology* 7 (2): 29–47. https://doi.org/10.17161/str.1808.4930

Shackelford, Jean. 1999. "International Association for Feminist Economics (IAFFE)." In *The Elgar Companion to Feminist Economics*, edited by Janice Peterson and Margaret Lewis, 486–489. Cheltenham, UK: Edward Elgar. https://doi.org/10.4337/9781843768685.00064

Stanfield, James Ronald. 1989. "Recent US Marxist Economics in Veblenian Perspective." *Radical Institutionalism*, edited by William M. Dugger, 83–104. New York: Greenwood Press.

Strassmann, Diana. 1999. "Feminist Economics." In *The Elgar Companion to Feminist Economics*, eds. Janice Peterson and Margaret Lewis, 360–373. Cheltenham, UK: Edward Elgar. https://doi.org/10.4337/9781843768685.00048

Strober, Myra H. 1994. "Rethinking Economics Through a Feminist Lens." *The American Economic Review* 84 (2): 143–147.

Todorova, Zdravka. 2009. *Money and Households in a Capitalist Economy: A Gendered Post Keynesian–Institutional Analysis*. Cheltenham, UK: Edward Elgar.

———. 2016. "A Further Veblenian Articulation of a Monetary Theory of Production." In *Marx, Veblen, and the Foundations of Heterodox Economics: Essays in Honor of John F. Henry*, edited by Tae-Hee Jo and Frederic S. Lee, 102–122. London: Routledge.

Tronto, Joan. 2013. *Caring Democracy: Markets, Equality, and Justice*. New York: New York University Press.

van Staveren, Irene and Olasunbo Odebode. 2007. "Gender Norms as Asymmetric Institutions: A Case Study of Yoruba Women in Nigeria." *Journal of Economic Issues* 41 (4): 903–925. https://doi.org/10.1080/00213624.2007.11507080

Waddoups, Jeffrey and Rick Tilman. 1992. "Thorstein Veblen and the Feminism of Institutional Economics." *International Review of Sociology* 3 (3): 182–204. https://doi.org/10.1080/03906701.1992.9971127

Waller, William T. 1982. "The Evolution of the Veblenian Dichotomy: Veblen, Hamilton, Ayres, and Foster." *Journal of Economic Issues* 16 (3): 757–771. https://doi.org/10.1080/00213624.1982.11504031

———. 1989. "Methodological Aspects of Radical Institutionalism." In *Radical Institutionalism*, edited by William M. Dugger, 39–49. New York: Greenwood Press.

———. 1995. "Compulsive Shift or Cultural Blind Drift? Literary Theory, Cultural Rhetoric, Feminist Theory and Institutional Economics." In *Institutional Economics and the Theory of Social Value: Essays in Honor of Marc. R. Tool*, edited by Charles M.A. Clark, 153–178. Boston, MA: Kluwer. https://doi.org/10.1007/978-94-011-0655-9_10

———. 2005. "Accidental Veblenian, Intentional Institutionalist, and Inevitable Feminist." *Journal of Economic Issues* 39 (2): 327–334. https://doi.org/10.1080/00213624.2005.11506809

Waller, William and Ann Jennings. 1990. "On the Possibility of a Feminist Economics: The Convergence of Institutional and Feminist Methodology." *Journal of Economics Issues* 24 (2): 612–622. https://doi.org/10.1080/00213624.1990.11505060

Waller, William and Mary V. Wrenn. 2021. "Feminist Institutionalism and Neoliberalism." *Feminist Economics*. Published online March 12, 2021. https://doi.org/10.1080/13545701.2021.1883194. Accessed March 26, 2021.

Wheelock, Jane. 1994. "Household, the Economics of." In *The Elgar Companion to Institutional and Evolutionary Economics*, edited by Geoffrey M. Hodgson, Warren J. Samuels, and Marc R. Tool, 332–338. Aldershot, UK: Edward Elgar. https://doi.org/10.4337/9781843768661.00069

Williams, Rhonda. 1993. "Race, Deconstruction, and the Emergent Agenda of Feminist Economics." In *Beyond Economic Man*, edited by Marianne A. Ferber and Julie A. Nelson, 144–153. Chicago, IL: University of Chicago Press.

Wrenn, Mary V. and William Waller. 2017. "Care and the Neoliberal Individual." *Journal of Economic Issues* 51 (2): 495–502. https://doi.org/10.1080/00213624.2017.1321438

Zachorowska-Mazurkiewicz, Anna. 2015. "The Concept of Care in Institutional and Feminist Economics and Its impact on Public Policy." *Journal of Economic Issues* 49 (2): 405–413. https://doi.org/10.1080/00213624.2015.1042747

6

ENVIRONMENTAL SUSTAINABILITY IN SOCIAL CONTEXT

An original institutionalist perspective

Richard V. Adkisson

Introduction

Knowledge about environmental sustainability is imperfect, but there is ample evidence to suggest that human interactions with the natural environment can have negative impacts. Some argue that our planet is now in the Anthropocene epoch wherein global human activity is the dominant influence over geologic/environmental change (Lewis and Maslin 2015). Humans have acted to mitigate some human-caused environmental damage, but in other cases have struggled to act decisively on environmental issues. At the extreme, some humans deny the existence of environmental problems. Why is this? The quick and simple answer is that environmental damage—and correction—happens in a social context.

Achieving environmental sustainability will require social change and governmental policy actions. In democratic systems, these actions require public support, which comes easier when proposed government actions satisfy social criteria. Building on the foundation of original institutional economics (OIE), a research tradition tracing its roots to Thorstein B. Veblen and John R. Commons, this chapter examines the role of national culture and social beliefs on the evolution of environmental problems and policy. After a brief discussion of original institutionalism, attention turns to three case studies of environmental issues. The cases show how social beliefs have shaped environmental problems and policies over the years and provide insight into the prospects for environmental policy. Though many environmental issues demand international or global action, this chapter will focus on the United States.

DOI: 10.4324/9781003160434-6

Natural environment? Sustainability?

The introduction uses the words "natural environment" and "sustainability" as if they have clear and universal meanings. Here, the natural environment represents the system of processes that would continue in the absence of human-developed and accumulated technology. Humans could exist in this environment, but their lives would be much like life in the state of "mere nature" as described by Thomas Hobbes:

> In such condition there is no place for industry, because the fruit thereof is uncertain: and consequently no culture of the earth; no navigation, nor use of the commodities that may be imported by sea; no commodious building; no instruments of moving and removing such things as require much force; no knowledge of the face of the earth; no account of time; no arts; no letters; no society; and which is worst of all, continual fear, and danger of violent death; and *the life of man, solitary, poor, nasty, brutish, and short.*
>
> *(Hobbes 1651, 78, emphasis added)*

Even in that state of mere nature, the natural environment would not be static. Biogeochemical cycles would continue, largely unhindered and untapped by humans, but the natural environment would still experience volcanic eruptions, earthquakes, floods, fire, storms, etc. Humans are not the only cause of environmental disruption.

As used here, environmental sustainability implies patterns of human/social activity that allow the natural environment to reproduce, evolve, and heal itself in much the same way as it would without the burden of modern human activities. Long-term human existence and quality of life rely on the ongoing ability of nature to continue its processes.

The original institutionalist economics foundation

There are multiple ways to think about economies. Although economies have many facets, they are ultimately systems that societies use to provide for themselves, regardless of the level of development or one's preferred ideology. Human provisioning involves nature. As they provide for themselves, humans, like other living organisms, look to nature to deliver inputs and to process wastes. Unlike other living organisms, humans have developed, and continue to develop, technologies to assist them in providing for themselves (Ayres [1944] 1962). In a state of mere nature, humans have little advantage over other organisms. With technology, humans have the potential to survive, extract inputs, and discard wastes at rates far beyond those of other species. The process of human provisioning places demands on nature far beyond those of other life forms.

Explaining economic coordination: the importance of a worldview

Through the economic process, humans "transform that which is available (resources) into that which serves society by providing goods and services" (Adkisson 2009, 27). How the economic process plays out depends on the generosity of nature, the state of technology, the needs and perceived wants of humans, and their worldviews (Matutinović 2007). Like any other research starting point, the OIE paradigm employed in this chapter has an underlying worldview.

OIE sees the economic system as embedded.[1] "The term 'embeddedness' expresses the idea that the economy is not autonomous, … but subordinated to politics, religion, and social relations" (Block 2001, xxiii–xxiv). OIE is pluralist. OIE uses ideas, theories, and methods from multiple disciplines (Hodgson 2014). Swaney (1987, 1744) identifies three elements of the OIE worldview that guide the OIE approach to environmental issues: "preconceptions, values, and a fundamental approach to solving problems (methodology)."

OIE worldview: preconceptions regarding the natural environment and human activity

Michael Colby (1989) outlines five paradigms of environmental management. These range from Frontier Economics to Deep Ecology. Frontier Economics sees nature as infinite in potential and thus not permanently harmed by human activity. Swaney refers to this as the "quiescent Earth" mentality. Deep Ecology envisions lives closer to the state of mere nature. Between these extremes are three intermediate paradigms: Environmental Protection, Resource Management, and Eco-Development. The OIE view lies somewhere in the middle:

> Generally, institutionalists recognize that the biosphere—life on earth and the physical elements on which it depends—is composed of innumerable interacting, interdependent, complex, evolving ecosystems. Some of these systems are very resilient, while others are very fragile. When altered by human activity some evolve into new stable ecosystems favorable to human habitation, while others degenerate.
>
> *(Swaney 1987, 1746)*

OIE worldview: preconceptions regarding economic coordination and institutions

History reveals three basic ways to coordinate economic processes: markets, command, and tradition (Heilbroner and Milberg 2012). The real world is one of mixed economies where a combination of markets, command, and tradition work together. OIE views all economies as mixed economies and studies them as such (Petr 1987). Although they do not completely reject markets or capitalism (Hodgson 2014), institutionalists are sympathetic to the need for some social control of the economic process (Swaney 1987).

Institutions are at the center of OIE theory and analyses. They are "systems of established and embedded social rules that structure social interactions" (Hodgson 2006, 18). Walter Neale (1987) sees institutions as repeated patterns of behavior, guided by rules that give order to the behaviors, and justified by folkways. The rules can be explicit, such as an established and enforced environmental regulation, or implicit, such as a handshake. Institutions involve habits of thought that tie social behaviors to past circumstances (Dutraive 2012). At a given time, a set of social criteria (folkways) exists to align institutionalized behaviors and rules to deeply held cultural criteria.

OIE worldview: cultural values

Economists often highlight exchange value. Relative prices reflect relative social value and guide the (market) economy to produce the goods and services most valued by society. Here, the focus is on cultural values. Cultural values "are the basic and primary prescriptive forces that circumscribe societal norms, which in turn serve as criteria for institutional patterns" (Hayden 1988, 417). People or societies don't choose their culture, they receive it. The values themselves are discernible, but their underlying cultural anchors are seldom obvious:

> Culture is man's medium; there is not one aspect of human life that is not touched and altered by culture. This means personality, how people express themselves (including shows of emotion), the way they think, how they move, how problems are solved, how their cities are planned and laid out, how transportation systems function and are organized, as well as how economic and government systems are put together and function. However, like the purloined letter, *it is frequently the most obvious and taken-for-granted and therefore the least studied aspects of culture that influence behavior in the deepest and most subtle ways.*
>
> *(Hall 1989, 16–17, emphasis added)*

Once established, cultural values are very slow to change. Social beliefs are more malleable and serve to align institutionalized rules and behaviors with cultural values. When changing conditions call for institutional change, the change will require society to adjust its social beliefs and folkways to realign the new rules or behaviors with their cultural anchors (Dolfsma and Verburg 2008). Institutional change slows as social beliefs adjust or vested interests resist the needed change.

Researchers work to identify cultural values and how they vary across social groups. Only a few broad values are evident. According to F. Gregory Hayden:

> Some Western values that have been the same for centuries include: (1) strong domination of nature by humans, (2) atomistic conceptualization, (3) extensive hierarchical relationships, (4) flowing time, (5) dualistic thought, (6) dynamic expansiveness and (7) universalism.
>
> *(Hayden 2006, 77)*

Hayden's list is conceptually consistent with the findings of other researchers (Adkisson 2014; Doran and Littrell 2013). Table 6.1 assigns working definitions to the cultural values based on Hayden's comments and insights provided by other culture researchers. Alternative values at the opposite extreme of the value spectrum follow each working definition. There will be regional, subgroup, and individual variations in cultural orientations. However, even considering the diversity of modern Western societies, there is consistency in cultural values (Spindler and Spindler 1983: Spindler et al. 1990). These values are accepted as representative of dominant American cultural values.

OIE worldview: methodology

OIE methodology is pluralistic. It uses many methods including those of disciplines other than economics. Stanfield (1999) describes OIE's overall method as the "comparative method," which itself includes several methods: field studies, case studies, pattern modeling, storytelling, instrumental reasoning, participant observation, and historical criticism, among others. Original institutionalists observe and analyze quantitative data, but their holistic worldview invites them to incorporate a wide range of evidence, much of which is not easily quantifiable (Wilber and Harrison 1978). Institutionalists use abductive as well as deductive or inductive reasoning (Webb 2007). What follows is an example of historical case analysis.

Case studies of institutional adjustment in support of sustainability

Building on OIE, this three-part section examines real-world cases where environmental/sustainability issues called for institutional change. These literature-based cases reveal the roles of culture and social beliefs in institutional adjustment via policy change. The case studies span nearly two centuries.

Use and regulation of pesticides: arsenic and DDT

In nineteenth-century America, the development of turnpikes, canals, steamboats, barges, and railroads tied the nation together creating opportunities for farmers to grow crops for sale in distant and growing urban markets. The United States was long on land and short on labor, inviting the use of labor-saving tools in American agriculture. Jointly, these changes led to the adoption of large-scale,

TABLE 6.1 Western cultural values.

Western cultural values Hayden (1988, 2006)	*Synthesized working definitions (Alternative/contrasting values in parentheses)*	*Sources contributing to syntheses*
Strong domination of nature by man (Domination)	The natural environment exists to be subdued. Humans can control nature or their environment to achieve goals. (Submission to nature; external control.)	Hayden (1988; 2006); Trompenaars and Hampden-Turner (1998)
Atomistic conceptualization (Atomism)	Reality is fundamentally divisible into units with enough independence that interactions between the pieces can be ignored. Closely related to individualism. People value personal freedom, achievement, independent decision-making, and responsibility for one's own care. (Organic conceptualization; holism; communitarianism; collectivism.)	Hofstede (2001); Trompenaars and Hampden-Turner (1998); Usinier (1996); Strauss (2008)
Extensive hierarchical relationships (Hierarchy)	Authority and power are widely, though not necessarily equally, distributed. This is related to low power distance. Power and authority tend to be situational and not extend beyond the specific situations where power and authority are assigned. (High power distance; diffusive culture.)	Hayden (1988; 2006); Hofstede (2001); Trompenaars and Hampden-Turner (1998)
Flowing time	Time exists. It has a beginning and an end. It flows by and can be wasted; therefore, time is a scarce commodity with value. The past, present, and future have different values. Flowing time suggests that the present is more valuable than the future. (Cyclical time; synchronous time; past or future time orientation.)	Hayden (1987; 1988; 2006); Hofstede (2001); Trompenaars and Hampden-Turner (1998)
Dualistic thought (Dualism)	Thought is organized into mutually exclusive categories with fixed meanings. Dualisms provide a means of imposing order on ideas or perceptions of reality; they involve drawing distinctions, such as good and evil, heaven and hell, labor and capital, demand and supply, profit and cost. (Pluralistic thought.)	Hayden (1988; 2006); Dow (2012); Robinson (2020)

(Continued)

TABLE 6.1 Continued

Western cultural values Hayden (1988, 2006)	*Synthesized working definitions (Alternative/contrasting values in parentheses)*	*Sources contributing to syntheses*
Dynamic expansiveness (Dynamism)	Agents operate in a dynamic world where the existence of growth and creation is good. Things will work out. Technology will develop and evolve in response to emerging problems. (Fatalism.)	Hayden (1988, 2006); Trompenaars and Hampden-Turner (1998); Saha 1998
Universalism	Values apply to all of humankind and to the natural environment. People place a high importance on laws, rules, values, and obligations. They try to deal fairly with people based on these rules, but rules trump relationships. (Moral exclusiveness; particularism.)	Schwartz (2007); Trompenaars and Hampden-Turner (1998)

Source: Compiled by the author.

monocrop agriculture. Transporting crops over long distances also moved hitchhiking insects from one region to other regions where they had few natural predators. Together, these changes created conditions conducive to severe insect depredations by potato beetles, locusts, gypsy moths, cotton army worms, etc. If the newly industrialized agriculture was to be successful, pests needed to be controlled (Graham 2019). James Whorton (1974) labeled this "the insect emergency."

Responses to the insect emergency fell into three categories: biological, physical, and chemical methods. Biological methods involved the encouragement or introduction of natural predators. Physical methods involved mechanical or hand harvesting and destruction of the offending pests. Chemical methods involved the application of various organic compounds, tobacco or pyrethrum flower, for example. By mid-century, these methods had proven less than satisfactory, and attention turned to inorganic substances, especially arsenic (Whorton 1974).

Arsenic is "a naturally occurring element … [as it] is widely distributed in the Earth's crust. It is found in water, air, food, and soil" (Arsenic n.d.) Long-term exposure threatens human health. High-level exposure can cause acute symptoms and, at the extreme, death (Arsenic 2018). Arsenic has been used in poisons, medicines, chemical weapons, and cosmetics (Frith 2013).

Paris green, an arsenic-containing pigment, came into use as an insecticide in 1867. In the 1890s, the use of lead arsenate began. Other arsenical compounds were used as insecticides well into the twentieth century (Hughes et al. 2011). A major concern was the arsenic and lead residues left on fruit as it went to market.

State and local governments attempted to regulate insecticide residues on fruit, but lack of resources and varying enthusiasm rendered regulation very weak. Federal action was slow to come. As the residue issue simmered, "nearly 100 bills had been introduced in Congress to regulate food and drugs" (United States Food and Drug Administration 2019). As a response to muckraking journalism and the arousal of public attention, a federal regulatory structure emerged with the 1906 Food and Drug Act. It passed. As Marc Law and Gary Libecap (2006) write:

> Concerns about food quality generated demand for food regulation among advocates for consumers. Progressive reform groups—most notably women's groups like the General Federation of Women's Clubs (GFWC), The Women's Christian Temperance Union (WTCU), as well as leaders of the home economics movement and public health officials—lobbied for regulations that banned the sale of adulterated and misbranded food products.
>
> *(Law and Libecap 2006, 326–327)*

The Insecticide Act of 1910 followed. It prohibited "the manufacture, sale, or transport of adulterated or misbranded pesticides [and] protected farmers and ranchers from marketing of ineffective products" (Fernandez-Cornejo et al. 2014, 3).

The 1906 and 1910 Acts focused on the adulteration of food and drugs. The emphasis was on labeling. Producers could add things at will, if the label notified buyers. The Acts allowed condemnation of tainted products and prosecution of violators, but they provided little useful guidance as to specific definitions of foods and drugs and failed to define safe and acceptable levels of contamination. Arsenic residues became a federal issue in 1919 when Boston's health commissioner notified the United States Department of Agriculture (USDA) that tainted fruit had been transported across state lines. Responsibility fell to the Bureau of Chemistry, housed in the USDA. This created conflicts between the Bureau's charge to regulate insecticide residues and the USDA's interests in promoting agricultural production. Regulation remained weak and enforcement often led to protracted court battles (Whorton 1974).

The Federal Food, Drug, and Cosmetic Act of 1938 (FFDCA) "[p]rovided that safe tolerances be set for residues of unavoidable poisonous substances, such as pesticides, in food" (Fernandez-Cornejo et al. 2014, 3). The residue issue languished as various interests debated the appropriate maximum residue levels. By 1950, the US Food and Drug Administration (FDA) accepted the administrative residue tolerances imposed immediately after passage of the FFDCA. Because producers could easily meet these tolerances and perhaps because producers had already responded to European threats to boycott American fruit, seizures of produce declined precipitously throughout the 1940s (Whorton 1974). Thus, the "added power [the FDA] received was in a sense unneeded, for by 1938 the FDA considered the residue problem of arsenic, lead, and fluorine [(another toxic insecticide introduced in the early 1930s)] to be declining" (Whorton 1974, 243).

Arsenic is no longer widely used as an insecticide (IARC Working Group 2012) but land contaminated with arsenic remains an issue of concern (Hughes et al. 2011). Policy actions had done little to control arsenic use or reduce residues. According to Whorton (1974, 247), "The decline did not mean...that spray residues would no longer be a hazard; rather, arsenic and lead were simply being replaced by residue from insecticides whose dangers were even less clear."

Meanwhile, DDT (dichloro-diphenyl-trichloroethane) and other synthetic pesticides developed before and during World War II were on the ascendency in the mid-twentieth century. DDT was synthesized in 1874, but its usefulness as an insecticide was not immediately known (Turusov, Rakitsky, and Tomatis 2002). In 1939, Paul Müller, a researcher working for Geigy, a Swiss company, developed DDT as an insecticide. DDT met the contemporary ideal qualities for an insecticide, but Müller overlooked the fact that DDT did not degrade quickly in the environment and thus accumulated in the biota (Jarman and Ballschmiter 2012).

World War II loomed large in the eventual prominence of DDT. That war required that military personnel move into areas where threats of disease were as great as those of battle. Military planners sought effective means to fight disease-carrying insects. DDT was used to kill mites, mosquitos, flies, fleas, and other potentially disease-carrying pests, with great success. Writing toward the end of the war on military use of DDT and other insecticides, USDA entomologist F.C. Bishopp (1945, 378) reported: "The incidence of malaria … has been brought to a commendable low; typhus outbreaks have been avoided; and typhoid, plague, and yellow fever … have been banished from our armed forces." Reports from the war front, combined with effusive praise for DDT and other insecticides in the popular press, inspired a love story involving Americans and their pesticides (Mart 2015).

The military recognized that DDT exposure carried risks, but continued its use because the benefits of disease prevention outweighed the perceived costs of short-term exposure to DDT. The public was enthusiastic about DDT, in part because of its effectiveness in the war, but also because it was largely unaware of, or ignored, potential risks.

Producers could initially sell DDT only to the federal government. As the war ended, government scientists expressed concern about releasing DDT for civilian use, recommending that DDT's release be delayed until safety concerns could be addressed (Russell 1999). As the postwar surplus of DDT grew, pressure to allow civilian sales grew. Some DDT producers asked the War Production Board to maintain control of DDT until a larger surplus accumulated (thereby ensuring a sufficient quantity of the product would be available for national defense purposes) and guidelines for safe and effective use developed. Others "wanted the freedom to sell to civilians all the DDT they could make beyond military requirements" (Russell 1999, 791). The second preference won the day, leaving DDT regulation largely to the market.

After civilian release, DDT regulation reverted to prewar rules:

> Under the pre-World War II regulatory system, no government agency had the authority to keep pesticides off the market. The Department of Agriculture had the power to enforce labeling requirements, and the Food and Drug Administration had the authority to seize foods with pesticide residues above specified levels. But neither agency had the power to stop a company from selling an accurately labeled chemical.
>
> *(Russell 1999, 791)*

Congress rescinded the Insecticide Act and replaced it with the Federal Insecticide, Fungicide, and Rodenticide Act of 1947. It "established the basic framework for pesticide regulation that is still in effect today" (Graham 2019, 103–104) but, like the 1910 Act, it focused on pesticide purchasers rather than others facing potential exposure to pesticides.

Lacking effective federal regulation, DDT would be subject only to regulation by market forces for the next 27 years. DDT production and sales grew. The United States used approximately 1.35 billion pounds of DDT between 1945 and 1972 (United States Environmental Protection Agency 1975). However, evidence mounted suggesting that, beyond its impacts on human health, DDT caused significant environmental disruption. Rachel Carson (1962) is credited with bringing the issue of insecticide overuse to the general public. Citing extensive research on the impact of pesticides, especially DDT, her book, *Silent Spring*, garnered widespread attention.[2] Carson's was not the only call to action. "Scientists and activists gathered knowledge, mobilized citizen groups, lobbied Congress, and used the legal system to influence policy" (Russell 1999, 793). These activities led to the eventual ban of DDT sales in the United States in 1972. Once again, the Federal government took control of DDT.

The arsenic/DDT story documents a slow change in America's dominant worldview. In the beginning, the "quiescent Earth" worldview dominated. The fact that the insects died and helped farmers make a profit was enough to justify liberal insecticide use. Talks of human health concerns were countered by arguments that removing residues before taking fruit to market would drive costs up and hurt farmers. Nascent regulatory efforts to control residues stalled over the definition of acceptable residue amounts. Arsenic and DDT advocates downplayed scientific research findings, discounted non-acute impacts on human health, or claimed Europeans or Eastern US farmers were pushing residue reductions to strengthen their own competitive position. Conflicting governmental goals and the federalist structure of the US government blurred lines of regulatory authority. Yet, by the 1960s, the dominant worldview had evolved to acknowledge human impacts on the natural environment, enabling the US government to outlaw the use of a popular and effective insecticide (DDT) in the early 1970s. The dominant American perspective on nature had changed (Marx 2008).

The insecticide case nests well in the broader history of environmental actions (Rinfret and Pautz 2019). Institutions evolved. Rules regarding insecticides changed. Responsibility for insecticide regulations moved among governmental levels and from agency to agency. Knowledge and technology evolved. Solutions to problems led to other problems.

The case also teaches something about the impact of social context on environmental problem-solving. The behavior of individuals and institutions revealed several underlying beliefs. Table 6.2 identifies the social beliefs that seemed to guide the use and regulation of insecticides during the period. It also briefly summarizes the behaviors related to each belief, and lists the cultural values (from Table 6.1) likely to be satisfied by the beliefs and behaviors.

By the end of the period, the environmental view of nature had come to dominate decision-making. Feedback from the environment, accumulated toxins, dead birds, etc., signaled the need to turn from the quiescent Earth view of nature. The environmental protection (or "nature as environment" in Table 6.1) view allows humans and the rest of nature to coexist in a hierarchy of sorts with humans still dominating nature, although in different ways. Meanwhile, individualism and laissez-faire beliefs survived, but attitudes changed as to what government interventions were warranted. The emerging environmental view of nature helped justify the move toward environmental regulation.

The turn to environmental regulation: the Clean Air Act

During the period 1969–1990, at least 19 major federal environmental laws emerged (Rinfret and Pautz, 2019). The United States Environmental Protection Agency (EPA) came into existence in early December 1970, launching a new era of environmental policy in the United States. For example, later that same month, Congress passed the Clean Air Act of 1970 (CAA), a substantial amendment to the Clean Air Act of 1963 (United States Environmental Protection Agency n.d.). Under the CAA, the EPA aimed programs toward:

- Reducing outdoor, or ambient, concentrations of air pollutants that cause smog, haze, acid rain, and other problems;
- Reducing emissions of toxic air pollutants that are known to, or are suspected of, causing cancer or other serious health effects; and
- Phasing out production and use of chemicals that destroy stratospheric ozone.

These pollutants "come from stationary sources (like chemical plants, gas stations, and powerplants) and mobile sources (like cars, trucks, and planes)" (United States Environmental Protection Agency 2007, 4).

The National Ambient Air Quality Standards (NAAQS) provide the foundation for air pollution reduction in the United States. The EPA maintains a list of criteria pollutants (specific pollutants with target levels) shown to "have an

TABLE 6.2 Social beliefs revealed in the insecticide case.

Social belief	*Related behavior(s)*	*Supporting cultural value(s)*
Nature as quiescent Earth	Early on, little attention was given to pesticide impacts beyond the killing of pests. Collateral damage to the environment was largely overlooked.	Domination Atomism
Econocentrism	Suggestions that producers should reduce pesticide application or remove excess residues were met with arguments that it would cost too much, limit production, and threaten the incomes of producers. A cost–benefit calculus dominated thinking and discussions. The desire for DDT profits pushed DDT to market before its time.	Atomism Dualism
Anthropocentrism	Early discussions of pesticide residues focused on possible harm to humans but not to the environment. Pests are defined by their impact on human endeavors.	Domination Hierarchy
The proof is in the pudding	Because arsenic occurs in nature, it could not be proven that insecticides were the source of arsenic related problems. Scientists produced conflicting evidence on health effects, but arsenic (and DDT) clearly killed insects. In producers' experience, acute symptoms were rare, so they discounted scientific evidence.	Atomism Dualism
More is better	Insecticides were presumed necessary to maintain or increase production. Overapplication was common because "if a little insecticide was good, a lot would be better."	Domination Dynamism
Don't tread on me (individual sovereignty)	Western producers argued that producers in the Eastern US, Europeans, and government bureaucrats were trying to protect their own interests at the expense of Western producers who faced different production challenges.	Atomism Universalism
There's no time like the present	Current needs to kill pests took precedence over hypothetical future health issues.	Atomism Flowing time
States' rights (federalism)	Initial regulation varied across states. National government could not intervene until residues became an interstate commerce issue.	Atomism Hierarchy

(Continued)

TABLE 6.2 Continued

Social belief	*Related behavior(s)*	*Supporting cultural value(s)*
Laissez-faire	The whole process was marked by a fear of government power being centralized and usurping producer rights. Early regulation focused on providing consumers with information and then allowing consumers to decide whether to use potentially dangerous products.	Atomism Hierarchy
The squeaky wheel gets the grease (majority rules)	A representative democracy must respond to many demands. It was only after muckraking journalists, scientists, and the general public demanded change that the national government began to give public health and environmental issues serious attention.	Hierarchy Universalism
Nature as environment	By 1970, the dominant quiescent Earth view gave way to the view of nature as the environment system that had to be considered more carefully as humans work to provide for themselves.	Domination Hierarchy
Where there's a will, there's a way	When the insect emergency arose, humans developed means to fight the insects. When arsenic use was fading, DDT and other insecticides were developed to replace them. When the United States banned DDT, it was replaced by yet-newer insecticides. (And, beyond the story here, genetic engineering developed to modify plants and insects to supplement the use of pesticides.)	Domination Dynamism
Majority rules	Congressional action on regulation stalled until the tide of public opinion turned in favor of federal environmental action.	Atomism Universalism

Source: Author's summary.

adverse effect on public health or welfare and that are present in the ambient air" (Boyd 2019, 28). The current list includes carbon monoxide (CO), lead (Pb), nitrogen dioxide (NO_2), ozone (O_3), sulfur dioxide (SO_2) and particulate matter (NAAQS Table n.d.).

For each air pollutant, the EPA identifies target (maximum) thresholds, monitors and reports actual levels, identifies and regulates both stationary and mobile pollution sources, and works with states and tribes to manage, regulate, and reduce pollutant levels. Primary standards are "set to protect public health with an adequate margin of safety … . Secondary standards are set to protect public welfare, including protection against visibility impairment and damage to animals, crops, vegetation and buildings" (Boyd 2019, 29). The list of criteria pollutants and their target levels face regular review and change as new scientific knowledge emerges. Similarly, methods of mitigation change as pollution reduction technologies evolve.

The CAA has several design features that influence the development and enforcement of the NAAQS (Boyd 2019; National Research Council 2004; Patashnik 2019; United States Environmental Protection Agency 2007; Wiseman 2019). They include:

- The 1970 CAA amendments passed by a vote of 73 to 0 in the Senate and 374 to 1 in the House (Kenworthy 1970). Bipartisan support endured through 1990. The program has proven durable, though some signs of discontent have arisen recently.
- The EPA sets the standards, monitors and reports pollution levels, reviews scientific and technological changes, evaluates state and tribal implementation plans addressing non-compliant counties, and assists states and tribes by providing research and technological information through its technology clearinghouse.
- States and tribes develop and enforce implementation plans for stationary sources, monitor air quality, and provide feedback to the EPA on their efforts. Mobile source regulation occurs at the federal level.
- The CAA encourages/requires outside input on the EPA and the NAAQS. Independent scientific review supplements the EPA's scientific efforts. The CAA allows civil actions against "the EPA administrator for failure to discharge any nondiscretionary duty" and petitions to review specific EPA actions (Boyd 2019, 37).
- The NAAQS face regular review and adjustment. State and tribal implementation plans face periodic reviews, and new polluting facilities in non-compliant counties are generally required to adopt the best available control technology.
- The CAA treats major and minor sources differently with major sources generally facing more stringent controls.
- Existing sources built under previous standards can be grandfathered under older standards.
- Regulation of hazardous air pollutants (beyond criteria pollutants) occurs at the federal level. States can implement more stringent standards if they so choose.
- The EPA uses market-based mechanisms when possible, for example, trading of pollution credits to deal with acid rain, cross-border pollution, and the reduction of lead in gasoline.

Since 1970, US air quality has improved substantially (Boyd 2019). Beyond notably cleaner air, US residents experienced the CAA through the switch from leaded to unleaded gasoline, the move away from freon use as a refrigerant, a change in propellants used in aerosol cans, and increasingly sophisticated emission systems in cars.

The success of the CAA and NAAQS is evident although lingering issues have slowed or prevented even greater success. Some of the issues identified in Carlson and Burtraw (2019) are:

- The distinction between major and minor sources encourages some sources to operate under the major/minor threshold to avoid regulation;
- Flexibility allows some states to write substandard implementation plans and then to litigate for years while continuing to operate below standards;
- Some grandfathered sources can operate for years without improving their pollution performance;
- The focus on criteria pollutants draws states' attention and resources away from other, potentially more important, local pollutant problems, for example wood stoves, paint shops, dry cleaners, and restaurants (Adelman 2014);
- Overall attainment has improved with substantial local/regional variation, leaving significant portions of the population (for example in southern California) living in areas of non-attainment; and
- Cross-border issues continue to be a problem.

The CAA and NAAQS story differs from the insecticide story in one important way. Efforts to regulate air quality arose during a period of widespread public (and bipartisan political) support for environmental action. In other ways, the air and insecticide stories seem to have been shaped by the same social beliefs. The quiescent Earth belief and technological change gave birth to the air pollution problem. Anthropocentrism led to primary standards (human focused) taking priority over secondary standards (non-human issues). Laissez-faire and individual sovereignty beliefs led to the need to be flexible, accommodate public input, and identify primary and secondary sources which ultimately allowed some important air pollution sources to go unchecked. Federalism required that subnational governments be involved in regulation and enforcement processes. Econocentrism and laissez-faire beliefs required heavy reliance on market-based (rather than direct regulatory) mechanisms.

The CAA and NAAQS brought much success, but success came in part because the chosen regulatory structure satisfied social beliefs reasonably well. The turn to environmental regulation also created tensions with the result that the 1990 amendments to the Clean Air Act were the last major environmental laws passed by Congress:

> [D]uring the first major efforts regarding environmental protection in the 1970s, we saw legislative action to determine environmental outcomes.

> Over time, however, with the evolving role of Congress, the increasing power of the presidency and its influence on executive branch agencies, and the growing partisan divide, environmental concerns have been crowded out of the legislative agenda of Congress.
>
> *(Rinfet and Pautz 2019, 49)*

The growing dominance of the "nature as environment" belief did not relieve all social tension on environmental issues. Air quality improved, but industries saw increased costs; industrial structure and job patterns changed, and the urgency of environmental change became less obvious as environmental conditions improved. Since 1990, environmentalism has become more and more a partisan issue. Also, other issues, such as terrorism, war, political scandal, and economic crises, often overshadow environmental issues.

Climate change—global warming

There is substantial scientific evidence that global temperatures have been rising, at an increasing rate, for well over a century. In 1988, the World Meteorological Organization and the United Nations Environment Program joined to create the Intergovernmental Panel on Climate Change (IPCC). The IPCC monitors and assesses climate change science and provides regular assessment reports to members, currently 195 nations. The 2014 report concludes that the evidence for global warming is unequivocal and that it is extremely likely that anthropogenic carbon (CO_2) and other greenhouse gas emissions are the dominant cause of warming observed since the mid-twentieth century (IPCC 2014). In 2018, the United States emitted 15 percent of the world's greenhouse gases, second to China with 28 percent. On a per-capita basis, the United States contributed 16.56 metric tons, over twice that of China (Union of Concerned Scientists 2020).

As in the previous cases, the issues of concern would exist, in some form, even in the absence of human activity. Arsenic occurs in the natural environment. Volcanic activity, forest fires, and wind dirty the air. Likewise, there are natural climate cycles driven by astronomical and geological phenomena. The eccentricity of Earth's orbit around the sun, variations in the tilt of Earth's axis, and variations in the direction to which its axis points (Milankovitch cycles) vary over geologic time, resulting in cyclical variation in the intensity of solar radiation on the planet (Bennett, 1990; Buis 2020). On a shorter timescale, changes in ocean currents affect regional climates and there are regular annual weather cycles that mask long-term changes (National Oceanic and Atmospheric Administration 2011). During any hour, day, week, or season, individual people experience normal, above normal, or below normal temperatures. Thus, even facing substantial evidence of global warming, there is room for reasonable disagreement on the details (Long 2011).

Whether natural or human-caused, significant global warming promises to upset current patterns of human behavior and warrants action in response. Yet, despite the growing consensus that human activities cause, or at least aggravate, global warming, there are disagreements as to how and whether to respond. It is a global issue that relies on national responses, yet effective and durable public policies and actions have not emerged, at least in the United States. In part, the reason is that public opinion on climate change is still too diverse to inspire political consensus. It is a complex issue that involves uncertainty and competes with many other issues for attention. The public relies on at least three methods to deal with the crowded issue space and to process the specifics of climate change: reliance on intermediaries, bundling of multiple issues, and neglect or denial.

Influence of intermediaries

Public opinion on climate change "is *directly* influenced by media coverage, extreme drought conditions, and economic conditions [and the] most important driver of media [coverage] remains elite cues from politicians and movement actors" (Carmichael and Brulle 2017, 245). However, intermediaries, politicians, and movement actors, do not always provide the same cues.

Nordhaus (2013) identifies three major approaches to global warming. Adaptation, mitigation, and geoengineering. Adaptation implies actions to adjust to climate change, rather than trying to control the changes. Mitigation promotes actions to slow or reverse global warming by reducing greenhouse gas emissions. Geoengineering involves the introduction of cooling elements into the environment to reflect sunlight and heat back into space, or technologies to remove carbon dioxide from the environment and store it. Mitigation has been at the core of climate change discussions to date. Possible approaches to mitigation include slowing overall economic growth, reducing energy consumption, and reducing the carbon intensity of production.

Nisbet (2014) identifies three groups of "public intellectuals" involved in the climate change debate that "have sparked wider debate through their popular books, essays, and commentaries" (Nisbet 2014, 811). These groups, along with other activists, help shape public knowledge and opinions on climate change.[3] Their approaches differ substantially. "Ecological activists" see global warming as a failure of capitalism and consumerism. They call for strong regulation, rationing of energy, and localization of economies. "Smart growth reformers" see global warming as a market failure. They advocate putting a price on carbon and making government investments in innovation. "Ecomodernists" advocate reframing the problem as an energy innovation and social resilience challenge. They promote government investments in energy technologies and resilience strategies.

Issue bundling

A 2019 Pew Research Center survey found that 44 percent of respondents thought climate change should be a top priority for the President and Congress. However, in the ranking of priorities, climate change ranked only seventeenth. The top five priorities were: the economy, health care costs, education, terrorism, and Social Security. The broader category "environment" came in eighth, at 56 percent (Bialik 2019). The abundance of issues forces individuals to choose their battles.

Issue bundling involves "tying together the co-benefits of previously distinct public concerns" (Koehn 2008, 54). Focusing on the Peoples Republic of China and the United States, Koehn (2008) advocates bundling proposed actions on climate change with other, perhaps more salient, policy issues. Prospects include other local environmental concerns, health issues, and economic co-benefits including "economic-development, employment opportunities, and cost savings" (Koehn 2008, 69). Bergquist, Mildenberger, and Stokes (2020) posed a variety of alternative issue/policy bundles to a sample of Americans to see which combinations enhance support for the included climate change action. They found that:

> climate change policy bundles that include social and economic reforms such as affordable housing, a $15 minimum wage, or a job guarantee increase US public support for climate mitigation. Clean energy standards, regardless of what technologies are included, also make climate policies more popular.
>
> *(Bergquist, Mildenberger, and Stokes 2020, 2)*

A US example of issue bundling at the national level is House Resolution 109 (HR 109), introduced in the first session of the 116th Congress on February 7, 2019 (H. Res. 109, 116th Congress 2019). HR 109 calls for the creation of a Green New Deal. The resolution bundles action on climate change with job creation, infrastructure investments, and social justice. The proposal is controversial, but still under consideration.

Over recent decades, issue bundling has taken another form in the United States and around the world: the bundling of issues under ideological banners. The bipartisan support for environmental policy evident in the early 1970s was already beginning to fall apart in the 1980s. The political winds shifted toward fiscal conservatism. The 1994 Republican "Contract with America" pressured Republican candidates for national office to pledge their support for a bundle of ten specific actions. Later, (in 2009) the anti-tax Tea Party movement gained strength. It has been difficult to have civil discussions about fiscal matters, especially taxes, ever since (Adkisson and Mohammed 2012). The political divide over fiscal matters has expanded to include many controversial issues such as reproductive rights, immigration, international relations, COVID-19, and climate change, among others. In this political environment, to call oneself a Republican or Democrat, conservative or liberal, implies adherence to specific positions on these issues. The divide is exaggerated by social media "echo chambers," where communities of like-minded individuals avoid opinion challenges and filter information (Barberá 2020).

In this charged cultural atmosphere, positions on environmentalism have become nearly inseparable from ideological positions. Since 1970, the partisan divide in congressional environmental voting scores and in the acceptance of global warming as a real, important, and scientifically supported issue has grown substantially. Republican and conservative support for action on global warming has decreased, while it has increased among Democrats and liberals (Dunlap, McCright, and Yarosh 2016). Shao (2017) studies the relationships between demographic attributes, political predisposition, religiosity, attentiveness to news sources, and weather/climate factors on perceptions of global warming. Shao found that identification as a Republican or conservative (especially if supportive of Tea Party ideas) and identification as an evangelical fundamentalist (not all Christian or other religions) are associated with negative perceptions of global warming. Weather conditions, ten-year, seasonal temperature trends, had limited explanatory power. The bundling of moral and fiscal issues with climate change has made moderation and bipartisan cooperation difficult.

Neglect/denial

Neglect and denial of the global warming issue are closely related to issue bundling. People face many challenges in their daily lives. Concerns about earning a living, raising families, caring for elderly parents, maintaining health, and myriad other things leave little room for broader and less immediate issues such as climate change. Of those who engage in the climate change issue, some deny that it exists, or that it is a problem. Deniers make many claims (Skeptical Science n.d.). Those on the more reasonable end of the spectrum refer to natural climate cycles as discussed above. Others rely on factual, but irrelevant, issues such as contrary short-term weather trends. Some seek to discredit the scientific evidence.

Climate change denial is part of a broader trend in the search for simple answers. Issue bundling, especially where issues are bundled under political, religious, or other ideological umbrellas, simplifies the lives of busy people. Without exploring evidence, listening to counterarguments, or considering issues in their broader context, one can simply adopt the positions associated with their preferred ideology, liberal or conservative. It is rather like children who, when facing questions about their religion, turn and ask their parent for the answer. Once an issue becomes tied to an ideological position, the "parent" can easily manipulate the "child." In a "post-truth" era, the repetition of a spurious claim may be enough to establish it as a fact, independent of evidence or rationality (Lewandowsky, Ecker, and Cook 2017).

Values, beliefs, and global warming

As in the cases of insecticides and air pollution, it is social beliefs and, ultimately culture, that shapes global warming actions and reactions. Proposals by ecological activists, who see global warming as a failure of capitalism and consumerism, bump against econocentrism as well as beliefs such as "more is better" and "don't tread on me." Smart growth reformers are more econocentric, but face challenges from those with laissez-faire, "don't tread on me," and perhaps states' rights beliefs. And geoengineering proposals appeal especially to the "where there's a will, there's a way" belief because such proposals are grounded in faith in technological solutions.

Beyond social beliefs, whether a person prefers mitigation or adaptation likely varies with the probability that they will personally experience the damaging effects of global warming. Meanwhile, those who oppose action or deny global warming have several social beliefs on their side: anthropocentrism, "the proof is in the pudding," "more is better," "don't tread on me," "there's no time like the present," laissez-faire, and perhaps a lingering quiescent Earth belief. Carmichael and Brulle (2017) summarize the apparent reason why national action on global warming has been difficult to achieve: there is a wide range of opinion surrounding climate change, and while various information campaigns and media messages "may be persuasive to individuals exposed to them," a shift in the beliefs of a significant portion of the public is required "to be detectable in the aggregate level of public opinion" (Carmichael and Brulle 2017, 236–237). Social beliefs must move toward convergence to allow consensus on climate change policy.

Summary and conclusion

The three cases above demonstrate several OIE concepts. There were patterns of human activity, governed by sets of rules (some implicit, some explicit), that reflected the existing states of technology, nature, and folkways. Over time, human-driven changes, especially evolving technologies coming out of the industrial revolution, called for changes in other patterns of behavior. Better transportation and growing industrial output improved living standards for many, but, in doing so, created other problems, for example, the insect emergency, air pollution, and seemingly, global warming. In each case, perceived threats to the environment and the long-term sustainability of modern ways of life inspired efforts to address the environmental issues.

Improving sustainability will require collective action through public policy. Although the cases above understate some very important influences on public policy, especially power and vested interests, they show that cultural values, beliefs, and folkways shape the policy process. To achieve success, advocates on any side of an issue need either to satisfy dominant social beliefs or successfully inspire the adoption of alternative social beliefs to align the behaviors they advocate with dominant underlying cultural values. The apparent shift from the "quiescent Earth" to the "nature as environment" belief demonstrates this. It is almost certain that the belief shift was not complete, but it was enough to open the door to substantial action on environmental issues in the 1970s and 1980s.

Assuming, as the scientific evidence suggests, that global warming is happening and human activities are the dominant cause, addressing the problem will require more than effective and durable public policies that change human behavior patterns. Social beliefs will first need to evolve, creating folkways appropriate to the new behaviors.

Acknowledgments

The author thanks Jim Peach, Tom Kemp, Lawrence LaPlue, Greg Hayden, Charles Whalen, Stephen Adkisson, and Justine Adkisson for comments and suggestions on earlier versions.

Notes

1 According to the OIE, Veblen and Commons provide the underpinnings of a rich tradition continued by Wesley C. Mitchell, Clarence Ayres, John Kenneth Galbraith, and many others; see Adkisson (2009; 2010).
2 Carson's title, *Silent Spring*, is a reference to the lack of bird song in areas where DDT had been used.
3 See Table 1 in Nisbet (2014, 814).

References

Adelman, David E. 2014. "Environmental Federalism When Numbers Matter More than Size." *UCLA Journal of Environmental Law and Policy* 32 (2): 238–328. https://doi.org/10.2139/ssrn.2316294

Adkisson, Richard V. 2009. "The Economy as an Open System: An Institutionalist Framework for Economic Development." In *Institutional Analysis and Praxis*, edited by Tara Natarajan, Wolfram Elsner, and Scott Fullwiler, 25–38. New York: Springer. https://doi.org/10.1007/978-0-387-88741-8_2

———. 2010. "The Original Institutionalist Perspective on Economy and Its Place in a Pluralist Paradigm." *International Journal of Pluralism and Economics Education* 1 (4): 356–371. https://doi.org/10.1504/ijpee.2010.037976

———. 2014. "Quantifying Culture: Problems and Promises." *Journal of Economic Issues* 48 (1): 89–108. https://doi.org/10.2753/jei0021-3624480104

Adkisson, Richard V. and Mikidadu Mohammed. 2012. "Pragmatism to Dogmatism: The Laissez Faire Myth and the Disabling of the American Fisc." *Review of Social Economy* 70 (4): 421–450. https://doi.org/10.1080/00346764.2012.690606

Arsenic. n.d. National Institute of Environmental Health Sciences. https://www.niehs.nih.gov/health/topics/agents/arsenic/index.cfm. Accessed July 17, 2020.

Arsenic 2018. World Health Organization. February 15. https://www.who.int/news-room/fact-sheets/detail/arsenic. Accessed July 17, 2020.

Ayres, Clarence E. (1944) 1962. "Foreword." *The Theory of Economic Progress: A Study of the Fundamentals of Economic Development and Cultural Change*. New York: Shocken Books.

Bennett, Keith D. 1990. "Milankovitch Cycles and their Effects on Species in Ecological and Evolutionary Time." *Paleobiology* 16 (1): 11–21. https://doi.org/10.1017/s0094837300009684

Barberá, Pablo. 2020. "Social Media, Echo Chambers, and Political Polarization." *Social Media and Democracy: The State of the Field, Prospects for Reform*, edited by Nathaniel Persily and Joshua A. Tucker, 34–55. Cambridge: Cambridge University Press. https://doi.org/10.1017/9781108890960.004

Bergquist, Parrish, Matto Mildenberger, and Leah C. Stokes. 2020. "Combining Climate, Economic, and Social Policy Builds Public Support for Climate Action in the US." *Environmental Research Letters* 15 (5): 054019. https://doi.org/10.1088/1748-9326/ab81c1https://iopscience.iop.org/article/10.1088/1748-9326/ab81c1. Accessed November 22, 2020.

Bialik, Kristen. 2019. "State of the Union 2019: How Americans See Major National Issues." Pew Research Center, Fact Tank. https://www.pewresearch.org/fact-tank/2019/02/04/state-of-the-union-2019-how-americans-see-major-national-issues/. Accessed August 15, 2020.

Bishopp, F.C. 1945. "Insect Problems in World War II with Special References to the Insecticide DDT." *American Journal of Public Health and the Nation's Health* 35 (4): 373–378. https://doi.org/10.2105/ajph.35.4.373

Block, Fred. 2001. "Introduction." In *The Great Transformation: The Political and Economic Origins of Our Time*, by Karl Polanyi, xviii–xxxviii. Boston, MA: Beacon Press.

Boyd, William. 2019. "The Clean Air Act's National Ambient Air Quality Standards: A Case Study of Durability and Flexibility in Program Design and Implementation." In *Lessons from the Clean Air Act: Building Durability and Adaptability into US Climate and Energy Policy*, edited by Ann Carlson and Dallas Burtraw, 19–34. Cambridge: Cambridge University Press. https://doi.org/10.1017/9781108377195.002

Buis, Alan. 2020. "Milankovitch (Orbital) Cycles and Their Role in Earth's Climate." NASA Global Climate Change: Vital Signs of the Planet." https://climate.nasa.gov/news/2948/milankovitch-orbital-cycles-and-their-role-in-earths-climate/. Accessed August 13, 2020.

Carlson, Ann, and Dallas Burtraw, eds. 2019. *Lessons from the Clean Air Act: Building Durability and Adaptability into US Climate and Energy Policy*. Cambridge: Cambridge University Press. https://doi.org/10.1017/9781108377195

Carmichael, Jason T., and Robert J. Brulle. 2017. "Elite Cues, Media Coverage, and Public Concern: An Integrated Path Analysis of Public Opinion on Climate Change, 2001–2013." *Environmental Politics* 26 (2): 232–252. https://doi.org/10.1080/09644016.2016.1263433

Carson, Rachel. 1962. *Silent Spring*. Boston, MA: Houghton Mifflin.

Colby, Michael E. 1989. *The Evolution of Paradigms of Environmental Management in Development* (Vol. 313). Washington, DC: Strategic Planning and Review Department, World Bank.

Dolfsma, Wilfred, and Rudi Verburg. 2008. "Structure, Agency and the Role of Values in Processes of Institutional Change." *Journal of Economic Issues* 42 (4): 1031–1054. https://doi.org/10.1080/00213624.2008.11507201

Doran, Caroline Josephine, and Romie Frederick Littrell. 2013. "Measuring Mainstream US Cultural Values." *Journal of Business Ethics* 117 (2): 261–280. https://doi.org/10.1007/s10551-012-1515-z

Dow, Sheila. 2012. "Beyond Dualism." In *Foundations for New Economic Thinking: A Collection of Essays*, edited by Sheila Dow, 52–71. Basingstoke, UK: Palgrave Macmillan. https://doi.org/10.1057/9781137000729_4

Dunlap, Riley E., Aaron M. McCright, and Jerrod H. Yarosh. 2016. "The Political Divide on Climate Change: Partisan Polarization Widens in the US." *Environment: Science and Policy for Sustainable Development* 58 (5): 4–23. https://doi.org/10.1080/00139157.2016.1208995

Dutraive, Véroique. 2012. "The Pragmatist View of Knowledge and Beliefs in Institutional Economics: The Significance of Habits and Thought, Transactions and Institutions in the Conception of Economic Behaviour." *Handbook of Knowledge and Economics*, edited by Richard Arena, Agnés Festré and Nathalie Lazaric, 99–120. Cheltenham, UK: Edward Elgar. https://doi.org/10.4337/9781781001028.00011

Fernandez-Cornejo, Jorge, Richard Nehring, Craig Osteen, Seth James Wechsler, Andrew Martin, and Alex Vialou. 2014. "Pesticide Use in US Agriculture: 21 Selected Crops, 1960–2008." *Economic Information Bulletin No. 124*. United States Department of Agriculture, Economic Research Service. https://doi.org/10.2139/ssrn.2502986

Frith, John. 2013. "Arsenic—The 'Poison of Kings' and the 'Saviour of Syphilis.'" *Journal of Military and Veterans Health* 21 (43): 11–17.

Graham, Kate Z. 2019. "Federal Regulation of Pesticide Residues: A Brief History and Analysis." *Journal of Food Law & Policy* 15 (1): 98–130.

H. Res. 109, 116th Congress. 2019. https://www.congress.gov/116/bills/hres109/BILLS-116hres109ih.pdf. Accessed August 21, 2020

Hall, Edward Twitchell. 1989. *Beyond Culture*. New York: Anchor Books.

Hayden, F. Gregory. 1987. "Evolution of Time Constructs and their Impact on Socioeconomic Planning." *Journal of Economic Issues* 21 (3): 1281–1312. https://doi.org/10.1080/00213624.1987.11504704

———. 1988. "Values, Beliefs, and Attitudes in a Sociotechnical Setting." *Journal of Economic Issues* 22 (2): 415–426. https://doi.org/10.1080/00213624.1988.11504771

———. 2006. *Policymaking for a Good Society: The Social Fabric Matrix Approach to Policy Analysis and Program Evaluation*. New York: Springer Science & Business Media. https://doi.org/10.1007/0-387-29370-1

Heilbroner, Robert L. and William Milberg. 2012. *The Making of Economic Society, 13th ed.* Upper Saddle River, NJ: Pearson Education Company.

Hobbes, Thomas. 1651. *Leviathan*, prepared for the McMaster University Archive of the History of Economic Thought by Rod Hay. https://socialsciences.mcmaster.ca/econ/ugcm/3ll3/hobbes/Leviathan.pdf. Accessed April 10, 2020.

Hodgson, Geoffrey M., 2006. "What are Institutions?" *Journal of Economic Issues* 40 (1): 1–25. https://doi.org/10.1080/00213624.2006.11506879

———. 2014. "On Fuzzy Frontiers and Fragmented Foundations: Some Reflections on the Original and New Institutional Economics." *Journal of Institutional Economics* 10 (4): 591–611. https://doi.org/10.1017/s1744137414000307

Hofstede, Geert. 2001. *Culture's Consequences: Comparing Values, Behaviors, Institutions and Organizations Across Nations*. Newbury Park, CA: Sage.

Hughes, Michael F., Barbara D. Beck, Yu Chen, Ari S. Lewis, and David J. Thomas. 2011. "Arsenic Exposure and Toxicology: A Historical Perspective." *Toxicological Sciences* 123 (2): 305–332. https://doi.org/10.1093/toxsci/kfr184

IARC Working Group on the Evaluation of Carcinogenic Risk to Humans. 2012. "Arsenic and Arsenic Compounds." In *Arsenic, Metals, Fibres and Dusts*. Lyon, France: International Agency for Research on Cancer. https://www.ncbi.nlm.nih.gov/books/NBK304380/. Accessed July 17, 2020.

IPCC. 2014. *Climate Change 2014: Synthesis Report. Contribution of Working Groups I, II and III to the Fifth Assessment Report of the Intergovernmental Panel on Climate Change* [Core Writing Team, R.K. Pachauri and L.A. Meyer (eds.)]. Geneva, Switzerland: Intergovernmental Panel on Climate Change.

Jarman, Walter M., and Karlheinz Ballschmiter. 2012. "From Coal to DDT: The History of the Development of the Pesticide DDT from Synthetic Dyes till Silent Spring." *Endeavour* 36 (4): 131–142. https://doi.org/10.1016/j.endeavour.2012.10.003

Kenworthy, E.W. 1970. "Tough New Clean-Air Bill Passed by Senate, 73 to 0." *New York Times*, September 23, 1970.

Koehn, Peter H. 2008. "Underneath Kyoto: Emerging Subnational Government Initiatives and Incipient Issue-Bundling Opportunities in China and the United States." *Global Environmental Politics* 8 (1): 53–77. https://doi.org/10.1162/glep.2008.8.1.53

Law, Marc, and Gary D. Libecap. 2006. "The Determinants of Progressive Era Reform. The Pure Food and Drugs Act of 1906." In *Corruption and Reform: Lessons from America's Economic History*, edited by Edward L. Glaeser and Claudia Goldin, 319–342. Chicago, IL: University of Chicago Press.

Lewandowsky, Stephan, Ullrich K.H. Ecker, and John Cook. 2017. "Beyond Misinformation: Understanding and Coping with the 'Post-Truth' Era." *Journal of Applied Research in Memory and Cognition* 6 (4): 353–369. https://doi.org/10.1016/j.jarmac.2017.07.008

Lewis, Simon L. and Mark A. Maslin. 2015. "Defining the Anthropocene." *Nature* 519 (7542): 171–180. https://doi.org/10.1038/nature14258

Long, Graham. 2011. "Disagreement and Responses to Climate Change." *Environmental Values* 20 (4): 503–525. https://doi.org/10.3197/096327111x13150367351294

Mart, Michelle. 2015. *Pesticides, a Love Story: America's Enduring Embrace of Dangerous Chemicals*. Lawrence, Kansas: University Press of Kansas.

Marx, Leo. 2008. "The Idea of Nature in America." *Daedalus* 137 (2): 8–21. https://doi.org/10.1162/daed.2008.137.2.8

Matutinović, Igor. 2007. "An Institutional Approach to Sustainability: Historical Interplay of Worldviews, Institutions and Technology." *Journal of Economic Issues* 41 (4): 1109–1137. https://doi.org/10.1080/00213624.2007.11507089

National Ambient Air Quality Standards (NAAQS). n.d. "NAAQS Table." https://www.epa.gov/criteria-air-pollutants/naaqs-table. Accessed November 22, 2020.

National Oceanic and Atmospheric Administration. 2011. "Ocean Currents." https://www.noaa.gov/education/resource-collections/ocean-coasts/ocean-currents. Accessed August 13, 2020.

National Research Council. 2004. *Air Quality Management in the United States*. Washington, DC: National Academies Press. https://www.nap.edu/catalog/10728/air-quality-management-in-the-united-states. Accessed May 29, 2020. https://doi.org/10.17226/10728

Neale, Walter C. 1987. "Institutions." *Journal of Economic Issues* 21 (3): 1177–1206. https://doi.org/10.1080/00213624.1987.11504700

Nisbet, Matthew C. 2014. "Disruptive Ideas: Public Intellectuals and their Arguments for Action on Climate Change." *Wiley Interdisciplinary Reviews: Climate Change* 5 (6): 809–823. https://doi.org/10.1002/wcc.317

Nordhaus, William D. 2013. *The Climate Casino: Risk, Uncertainty, and Economics for a Warming World*. New Haven, CT: Yale University Press.

Patashink, Erik M. 2019. "The Clean Air Act's Use of Market Mechanisms." In *Lessons from the Clean Air Act: Building Durability and Adaptability into US Climate and Energy Policy*, edited by Ann Carlson and Dallas Burtraw, 201–224. Cambridge: Cambridge University Press. https://doi.org/10.1017/9781108377195.006

Petr, Jerry L. 1987. "The Nature and Necessity of the Mixed Economy." *Journal of Economic Issues* 21 (4): 1445–1468. https://doi.org/10.1080/00213624.1987.11504711

Rinfret, Sara R., and Michelle C. Pautz. 2019. *US Environmental Policy in Action, 2nd ed.* Cham, Switzerland: Springer. https://doi.org/10.1007/978-3-030-11316-2

Robinson, Howard. 2020. "Dualism." *The Stanford Encyclopedia of Philosophy,* Fall 2020 Edition, edited by Edward N. Zalta. https://plato.stanford.edu/archives/fall2020/entries/dualism. Accessed November 22, 2020.

Russell, Edmund P. 1999. "The Strange Career of DDT: Experts, Federal Capacity, and Environmentalism in World War II." *Technology and Culture* 40 (4): 770–796. https://doi.org/10.1353/tech.1999.0192

Saha, Arunoday. 1998. "Technological Innovation and Western Values." *Technology in Society* 20 (4): 499–520. https://doi.org/10.1016/s0160-791x(98)00030-x

Schwartz, Shalom H. 2007. "Universalism Values and the Inclusiveness of our Moral Universe." *Journal of Cross-Cultural Psychology* 38 (6): 711–728. https://doi.org/10.1177/0022022107308992

Shao, Wanyun. 2017. "Weather, Climate, Politics, or God? Determinants of American Public Opinions toward Global Warming." *Environmental Politics* 26 (1): 71–96. https://doi.org/10.1080/09644016.2016.1223190

Skeptical Science. n.d. "Global Warming & Climate Change Myths." https://www.skepticalscience.com/argument.php. Accessed August 22, 2020.

Spindler, George D. and Louise Spindler. 1983. "Anthropologists View American Culture." *Annual Review of Anthropology* 12 (1): 49–78. https://doi.org/10.1146/annurev.an.12.100183.000405

Spindler, George D., Louise S. Spindler, Henry T. Trueba, and Melvin D. Williams. 1990. *The American Cultural Dialogue and Its Transmission*. Bristol, PA, The Falmer Press.

Stanfield, James Ronald. 1999. "The Scope, Method, and Significance of Original Institutional Economics." *Journal of Economic Issues* 33 (2): 231–255. https://doi.org/10.1080/00213624.1999.11506154

Strauss, Daniel F.M. 2008. "Atomism and Holism in the Understanding of Society and Social Systems." *Koers* 73 (2): 187–206. https://doi.org/10.4102/koers.v73i2.159

Swaney, James A. 1987. "Elements of a Neoinstitutional Environmental Economics." *Journal of Economic Issues* 21 (4): 1739–1779. https://doi.org/10.1080/00213624.1987.11504721

Tromenaars, Fons and Charles Hampden-Turner. 1998. *Riding the Waves of Culture: Understanding Diversity in Global Business, 2nd Ed.* New York: McGraw-Hill.

Turusov, Vladimir, Valery Rakitsky, and Lorenzo Tomatis. 2002. "Dichlorodiphenyltrichloroethane (DDT): Ubiquity, Persistence, and Risks." *Environmental Health Perspectives* 110 (2): 125–128. https://doi.org/10.1289/ehp.02110125

Union of Concerned Scientists. 2020. "Each Country's Share of CO2 Emissions." August 12. https://www.ucsusa.org/resources/each-countrys-share-co2-emissions. Accessed August 15, 2020.

United States Environmental Protection Agency. n.d. "Milestones in EPA and Environmental History." https://www.epa.gov/history/milestones-epa-and-environmental-history. Accessed August 10, 2020.

———. 1975. "DDT Regulatory History: A Brief Survey (to 1975)." https://archive.epa.gov/epa/aboutepa/ddt-regulatory-history-brief-survey-1975.html. Accessed July 28, 2020.

———. 2007. "The Plain English Guide to the Clean Air Act." Office of Air Quality Planning and Standards Publication No. EPA-456/K-07-001. https://www.epa.gov/sites/production/files/2015-08/documents/peg.pdf. Accessed May 20, 2020.

United States Food and Drug Administration. 2019. "The 1906 Food and Drugs Act and its Enforcement." https://www.fda.gov/about-fda/fdas-evolving-regulatory-powers/part-i-1906-food-and-drugs-act-and-its-enforcement. Accessed July 20, 2020.

Usunier, Jean-Claude. 1996. "Atomistic versus Organic Approaches: An Illustration through Cross-National Differences in Market Research." *International Studies of*

Management & Organization 26 (4): 90–112. https://doi.org/10.1080/00208825.1996.11656696
Webb, James L. 2007. "Pragmatisms (plural) Part 1: Classical Pragmatism and some Implications for Empirical Inquiry." *Journal of Economic Issues* 41 (4): 1063–1086. https://doi.org/10.1080/00213624.2007.11507087
Whorton, James C. 1974. *Before Silent Spring: Pesticides and Public Health in Pre-DDT America*. Princeton, New Jersey: Princeton University Press.
Wilber, Charles K., and Robert S. Harrison. 1978. "The Methodological Basis of Institutional Economics: Pattern Model, Storytelling, and Holism." *Journal of Economic Issues* 12 (1): 61–89. https://doi.org/10.1080/00213624.1978.11503505
Wiseman, Hannah J. 2019. "Stationary Sources, Movable Rules: Intransigence and Innovation under the Clean Air Act." In *Lessons from the Clean Air Act: Building Durability and Adaptability into US Climate and Energy Policy*, edited by Ann Carlson and Dallas Burtraw, 57–112. Cambridge: Cambridge University Press. https://doi.org/10.1017/9781108377195.003

PART II

Methods

7

INVESTIGATIONAL ECONOMICS

A practitioner's guide to economics in the tradition of John R. Commons

Thomas Kemp

Introduction

Much of what follows is based on the experiences of the author working as an economist in academia, government, and consulting. About 15 years ago, after having spent several years in academia, I found myself thrust into government work, first as an elected official, and later as a policy advisor and regional development commissioner. (The advisory and commission work continue to the present.) From that applied work, I learned—more slowly than I would like to admit—that much, if not most, of the conventional formal education in economics has little applicability to reality.

Since returning full-time to the classroom, I have attempted to integrate into my teaching, and my university's economics curriculum in general, what I learned outside academia. This has meant bringing some of my more advanced students into private consulting projects and returning the methodologies of that applied work into my classes. Although time will tell what long-run student success comes of this, I have found that motivated students respond well to a more applied, but also more intellectually and technologically strenuous, education. So far, former students report that the training has served them well in their occupations and other contexts.

One constant throughout my professional work is the influence of the methods and processes of John R. Commons. Although I read nearly all of his written work for my PhD dissertation more than 20 years ago, my appreciation of the wisdom in his approach continues to grow as I gain additional experience. Commons referred to that approach as "investigational economics."[1] It emphasizes scientific neutrality in investigation, methodology, and research dissemination, combined with participatory development of any subsequent public policy. The role of the economist and economics is to investigate, inform, and assist.

DOI: 10.4324/9781003160434-7

The end in view is the facilitation of conflict resolution and better-informed participants in the socioeconomic system. It is, therefore, a highly applied take on the role of economists and economics as a field of study.

Commons is generally recognized as one of the founders of institutional economics. As such, his work is invariably bound up with that school of thought. While many, if not most, of the modern economists sympathetic to the "institutionalist" label have been active as "applied" economists, none of their efforts have been as carefully documented as those of Commons and his students. In his writings—spread over several books, dozens of published articles, and personal correspondence—we find an approach to "doing" economics that differs significantly from the policy advice and advocacy of textbook positive economics.

Although nearly all of the early institutionalists were actively involved in the development and design of economic policy, it is arguable that Commons directly and indirectly (through his students) had the most prolonged contact with those in policymaking circles and had the most significant influence on policy design and implementation. From enactment of the Wisconsin civil service law (1905), through establishment of the Milwaukee Bureau of Economy and Efficiency (1910) and Wisconsin's ratification of the first state unemployment insurance plan (1932), to passage of the federal Social Security Act (1935), Commons and his students were heavily involved in advising and developing economic policies at all levels of government during the first half of the twentieth century.

Institutional economics has always emphasized how society creates, structures, and restructures the economy. Indeed, this may be the one thread running through all the work of the tradition's founders. Central to the works of Thorstein Veblen (1857–1929), Commons (1862–1945), Wesley Mitchell (1874–1948) and other early institutionalist pioneers is the notion that the social framework structures the economic framework—a view of the economy as a socially instituted process. What has been less discussed within the institutionalist literature is the role of economists as educators, policy advisors, and policy advocates. That is, to what extent is the economist a part of this socially instituted process? How do we "do," rather than "talk" about, institutional economics?

Those questions are the subject of this chapter. But why bother? What's wrong with conventional, textbook economics? Although it is hazardous to generalize, the textbook approach can be seen as proceeding unquestioningly from core precepts (such as the assumptions of profit-maximization by firms and utility-maximization by consumers) placed at the center of a formal model and then concluding, in a rather "back door" manner, with a call for expanding or correcting the market structure. That is, conventional economics nearly always leads to an attempt to "get the prices right" through the institutionalization of markets. In short, the policy intent of textbook economics is either to eliminate institutional obstacles that stand in the way of achieving something approaching a perfectly competitive market, or, when that is not possible, to implement policy changes that will most effectively mimic the outcomes of such a market.

To be sure, there is often merit to the "textbook" approach. Where social institutions may be stable and relied upon, and where market failures are limited, conventional economic approaches can yield results that may be described as "instrumental" in the Deweyan sense (that is, where the approach contributes to achieving the end in view) as well as *reasonably* consistent, in terms of outcomes, with the investigational process of institutional economics outlined here. For example, in many cases we can use estimated hedonic values to estimate damages resulting from certain negative externalities; that is, we can use such estimates to "get the price right."

In other cases, however, the textbook approach falls flat. When institutional structures are weak, indeterminate, or in flux—that is, when there is social conflict—the reliance on simple motivational precepts can, at best, lead economists astray. At worst, the conventional approach can turn economists into political hacks—ideological advocates masquerading in lab coats.

I suspect that many (perhaps even most) economists would concede that a weakness of textbook economics is the underlying idea that markets, and markets alone, can—if structured properly—resolve all questions of production and distribution. Yet, a problem without a solution is not helpful, and that is where Commons becomes most relevant. In this chapter, I show that Commons's investigational approach not only contains a more modest and neutral set of processes that can be used to practice economics, but also represents an opportunity to gain new insight into how society operates. As a result, his approach offers a vehicle for improving economics education and enhancing the policymaking process.

In short, this chapter brings together the essential aspects of Commons's applied institutionalism to show how one goes about "doing" economics in the Commons tradition, and to illustrate how such economics is better suited to the needs of our students and communities.

The discussion that follows is divided into four sections, followed by a brief conclusion. The first three sections outline Commons's investigative method; the fourth section discusses recent examples of that method at work. The first section focuses on the economist as a civil servant, and on the *structure* of Commons's method, highlighting a few legislative areas to which Commons and his students gave special attention. The second section addresses the matter of policy administration, emphasizing the role of administrative commissions. In Commons's framework, administration refers to desirable characteristics of the *process* of his method; in administration, we glimpse the economist as a facilitator in the mitigation of social conflict. Third, we turn to the economist as an academic and researcher, and to economics as a field of academic inquiry. This is the economist as an *investigator* of facts, *observer* of the unfolding socioeconomic process, and *translator* of data. In the fourth section, I review two projects completed by my faculty-student research team, which I believe are solid examples of "doing" economics in the Commons tradition. Although they are modest in approach, scope, and audience, my students and I have found such work to be highly rewarding. The projects have attracted significant community discussion, and more importantly, have played a constructive role (in the view of their intended audience) in policymaking and resolution of ongoing conflicts.

The institutional foundations of investigational economics

The role of economic data and the civil service

The story of Wisconsin's civil service system, enacted into law very early in the twentieth century, is a book unto itself.[2] In brief, the law established several requirements, terms, and conditions for individuals seeking employment in that state's civil service. For example, the law covers competency testing for individuals appointed to the civil service and the Civil Service Commission; sets terms for members of the Civil Service Commission; includes a salary schedule; spells out a set of Commission duties; describes conditions and processes for the removal of commissioners and civil servants; addresses notices of vacancies; and details punishments for violating the public trust (see Wisconsin 1905). In sum, the legislation makes it difficult to appoint individuals of questionable qualifications to either the civil service or the Civil Service Commission. The underlying motivations for the law were twofold: to depoliticize the civil service, and to establish an institution capable of not only gathering, recording, and disseminating reliable information, but also assisting in the search for fact-based solutions to conflicts within the state of Wisconsin.

The work of the civil service forms the institutional foundation of Commons's method. That's because the state and its agents must be able to provide the basic data and research that can be relied upon as facts, which, when agreed upon by all parties, serve as the basis for resolving conflict. Whereas textbook economics generally takes "the market" as the channel through which information is disseminated, Commons viewed provision of basic information and facts as at least partly a responsibility of the democratic state. Although this may sound unconventional, when one considers simple weights and measures, the centrality of state-defined facts becomes fairly obvious. It is not "the market" that tells us what is a kilogram—it is "the state." It is not the market that determines what is annual real Gross Domestic Product (GDP)—it is the state (in this case, the federal government).

Commons repeatedly stressed that a reliable civil service was central and critical to his idea of successful policy design. To his way of thinking, the unimpeachability of the civil service is required so that the process associated with effective procedure (administration) might lead to lasting conflict resolution. In other words, "buy-in" of conflicting parties to policy actions can be achieved only when the agents of the state are impartial seekers of facts and relentless guardians of those facts.

From Commons's perspective, facts form the *foundation* upon which social conflict might be resolved. Without that foundation, no stable resolution would be possible. Writing the dissenting opinion to the final report of the national

Commission on Industrial Relations (1916, 193), Commons stated in no uncertain terms: "No matter whatever else may be recommended, no recommendation can be depended upon that does not provide fully for the integrity, reliability, and complete inclusion of all material facts in every publication of official statistics and investigations."

I came to fully understand this some years ago when I had the good fortune to visit the statistical bureau in a developing nation. At that time, the statistical agency was just beginning to develop its industrial data (among other series) along with conventional International Standard Industrial Classification (ISIC) standards.[3] As a result, the publicly available data was limited to single-digit codes. As I had been employed to conduct an economic impact analysis, those codes would not be sufficient to understand inter-industry linkages and construct the input-output tables my work required. To learn what data might not be available to the public, I requested a meeting at the statistical agency. It took some "string-pulling," but I was eventually granted the meeting.

Upon arriving at the agency, I found myself at the entryway to a fortress—something like a medieval castle. The entrance was guarded by several well-armed soldiers, accompanied by a tank, several supporting vehicles, and dual portcullises. The car we arrived in could not enter the area, and our credentials were checked by phone in the few meters of space between the two portcullises. Once inside, and after the pleasantries were completed, I asked: Why all the security? I was told I had seen only a small part of it. The directors were proud of the fact that their compound operated on its own power grid with built-in redundancies, and that their computers operated independent of the wider internet, protected by all sorts of additional security that I did not even attempt to understand.

I was told that security was needed for a variety of reasons, but perhaps the most important was to build trust in the agency. The bureau had experienced a great unwillingness of private firms to share data with the agency. Although the bureau directors had repeatedly told business owners that their data was secure, the agency had not yet built sufficient trust. Business owners were wary that the agency would cause them economic harm by sharing their data with competitors.

Though the law compelled the release of a certain amount of business data, the agency found that this was insufficient and that evasion was commonplace. The agency's leadership discovered it was necessary for everyone to fully believe in the impartiality and total discretion of the organization; establishing trust was essential to fashioning the sort of industrial data that economists have access to in developed nations such as the United States. Thus, the agency treated seriously the matter of trust and impartiality; and viewed building that trust as an ongoing matter.

This was clearly what Commons's was getting at by stressing the centrality of civil service reform. To resolve a conflict without resort to power, there would need to be "something we can all agree on." Commons's civil service reforms ensured facts that all parties can agree on. Without "above the fray" civil servants and reliable, publicly available data, the only way the public sector could be an effective part of conflict resolution would be through coercive or violent action. That is, if the state cannot convince or persuade, it will be driven to use force to resolve social conflict. For obvious reasons, coercive or violent solutions would be not only undesirable, but also unstable. This was well understood by Commons, who wrote:

> One of the most important facts to be recognized is that governments, whether State or Federal, cannot be looked to alone for remedying conditions. As soon as people come to look upon the coercive power of government as the only means of remedying abuses, then the struggle of control of the government is substituted for the private initiative through private associations, from which the real substantial improvements must come. We must look for the greatest improvement to come through cooperation [of those associations] with the government to promote their private interests.
> *(Commission on Industrial Relations 1916, 172)*

A neutral and effective civil service can serve as a foundation for stable and effective conflict resolution in two ways. First, by acting as a trusted source of data, the civil service is the provider of "truth" (lower case "t") in the sense that the facts of a situation are a resolved matter, a foundation upon which negotiation can occur. Second, by being impartial observers of economic conflict, civil servants may effectively develop and implement a process that might lead all parties to arrive at an agreeable solution. This is the investigational approach of the economist in civil service.

Settled law and conflict resolution: minimum wages as a case study

Conflict resolution does not occur in a vacuum, nor does it proceed from "ground zero" with each new event. The case Commons built for minimum-wage laws is illustrative because it complements his explanation of an effective civil service. A minimum wage is not a participant-driven process of conflict resolution mediated by the state. Indeed, the idea of a minimum wage would seem to run contrary to the principles laid out in the previous section: Minimum-wage laws externally force price conditions onto specific markets without negotiation. But workable minimum-wage laws are the result of historical negotiated processes. Today, one might say that such laws represent "settled law"; yet, in the early decades of the twentieth century, when Commons was writing, this was not the case.

Writing in the 1936 edition of *Principles of Labor Legislation*, Commons and co-author John Andrews (his former student) lay out the case-law history that brought society to the then-current question of the legality of minimum-wage legislation (Commons and Andrews 1936, 43–82). Starting from a provision of the US Constitution that gives the federal government responsibility to provide for the health and welfare of society, Commons and Andrews (1936, 43–44) review first existing laws mandating standards for the health and well-being of employees and then laws dealing with wage payment. Their point is to establish what has already been negotiated, what has been decided through democratic processes. Having presented the settled status of those matters, Commons and Andrews (1936, 44–47) then turn to the available evidence regarding wages and conditions of health and welfare, and ultimately to what has been done regarding minimum wages and what outcomes have resulted.

In short, Commons and Andrews performed what they saw as the role of the academic economist in ongoing social debates. They traced what is known about the issue at hand as it relates to what has already been decided as in the public interest. A sophisticated understanding of legal evolution emerges: The structure and limits of economic activity are the subjects of an ongoing discussion that occurs "at the margin" of what that society has already determined to be in the public interest.

Human communities have already come to a large number of conclusions about how society and economy should and should not, must and must not, be organized. For society to function effectively, all of these must not be up for renegotiation at the same time—some "ground rules" must be considered settled. How we proceed from these depends on the nature of the society, however, and in any case the facts and the procedure must be both clear and factual. Commons's treatment of the minimum wage outlines "what we have all agreed on," "what has been tried," and "what is known about the outcomes of our actions to date." It is informative; it does not advocate. It does not build a theoretical argument suggesting minimum wages "should" cause unemployment owing to market interference. It does not highlight an expenditure multiplier that will improve overall economic performance. Indeed, one is hard-pressed to find such arguments anywhere in Commons's work. What one finds instead are modest inferences based upon the available data.

Thus, in addition to the importance of impartial data, one other lesson stands out as a foundation of Commons's investigational economics: the practicing institutional economist is versed in the legal environment of her work. She reads the existing regulations and relevant law before considering, much less crafting, new policies.

The administrative process of investigational economics

Administering "utilitarian idealism"

Commons once described his approach to economics as being one of "utilitarian idealism" (Commons 1913). Philosophically speaking, this combination of terms is not very helpful. Like so many of the terms he coined for his ideas, they seem to direct the reader down poorly illuminated corridors of thought. However, if we drop the philosophical baggage of each of the terms and focus instead on the most literal meaning of each, we can see the interesting idea that Commons is driving at. Before delving into three pages of superficial Greek history, he states, "By idealism seems to be meant the yearning for perfection above and beyond the mere grind and hustle for necessities, luxuries and wealth" (Commons 1913, 1). Several paragraphs later we get the rest of the story: "To combine idealism and utilitarianism, our modern worker asks that we combine leisure and work in the same person. This means shorter hours of work and more opportunity for education" (Commons 1913, 3).

What we arrive at is the seemingly obvious but often overlooked notion that economics must remain focused on the dual tasks of solving real-world problems while also looking towards what might be considered the "ideal." By ideal, however, Commons (1913, 5–6) is referring to the best example of a thing. For example, what is "the ideal cow" or the "the perfect ear of corn?" This utilitarian ideal is a very specific sort—the best of a given thing that can be envisioned. It is not a global ideal; and it is *not* unobtainable: it is not a winged cow or an ear of corn that cures cancer. It is instead a product of the *process* of envisioning the best obtainable outcome.

Thus, for the economist the task is to investigate what has occurred and what the associated outcomes of those events have been, thereby shedding light on what are the best obtainable practices to address a particular end. Economists must then present their findings to the public, so that those who make up society might choose the policy they want. Of course, this is a simplification. "Society" is generally a large set of people with diverse perspectives, knowledge, and interest in any given conflict; we will return to this below.

What, then, is *not* the role of the economist or economics? What is beyond economics? Commons's written work gives us a very clear and useful delineation (discussed below). That said, it is not easy to uncover where the line lies. His inclination to use specific terminology across opposing sets of ideas can easily lead to confusion. In this case, that word is "administration." Commons puts a great deal of emphasis on the word—going so far as to title his 1913 book *Labor and Administration*. It is scattered throughout his early Wisconsin era work and assigned to a variety of topics. Like utilitarian idealism, his usage is conflicted but also illustrative. Consider the following two quotes, from the same text, a few dozen pages apart:

> Administration is more than a mechanism. It is the means of getting and keeping competent officials. It is the method of determining what authority or powers the officials shall have, how they shall execute the laws, what procedure they shall follow in court, what facts they shall investigate for the use of the court in its duty of interpretation. Administration is legislation in action.
>
> *(Commons and Andrews 1936, 448)*

> Here is exactly where the field of administration lies. A labor department, with a representation of interests, can do what the legislature cannot do. If it is given leeway in drafting rules and regulations, it can call upon the more advanced employers then enforce these standards on the more backward ones. … [I]t can assist the best in setting the standards for the worst.
>
> *(Commons and Andrews 1936, 479)*

Does administration refer to the civil service itself—for example, a government department of labor? Does administration refer to the operating procedures of the commission—as in the investigations of the federal and state industrial commissions on which Commons served? Does administration refer to desirable human resources practices (how to keep competent officials)? Or, does administration refer to the research agenda of the academic? Certainly, any of these interpretations could be read into the above quotes. To some extent, they are all correct readings of Commons's writings. This is because by "administration" Commons is referring to a set of operating principles and processes that are broadly appropriate for a given individual within a particular organization or environment. (Here the word "appropriate" is used within the context of achieving Commons's "reasonable" economic outcomes.)[4] In other words, administration has broad meaning that includes the process of being an economist and conveying economic information. In this way, the centrality of administration becomes clear as it simultaneously gives us the role of the economist, commissioner, and civil servant.

The commission

The "commission," which is repeatedly discussed in Commons's works, can be described as a set of processes. These processes apply to any specific commission—whether it be a public service, public utilities, or industrial commission. That Commons was repeatedly drawn to this organizational form is likely a consequence of his extensive experiences in public service. Commons uses the commission as a proxy for a desirable set of processes for the reception of conflict-related information and the mitigation of ongoing conflict. Seen in this way, Commons used the term because, in the interest of conflict resolution, it combines expertise, participation, and the balance of power among various groups.

For the unacquainted, Commons's attention to commissions may seem strange, but most people likely have some experience with public utility commissions. Then again, many people have probably known little except that such institutions have some bearing on the electric bill or other utility bills they receive every month; and Commons (and many commentators on his work) seldom gives his reader many operational details. In practice, commissions are a sort of intermediary between the state (government) and the general population—quasi-public groups of project managers tasked with the gathering of information as well as the design and implementation of policy.

Commissions are usually given a charge, from elected officials or the civil service, detailing their mission, scope, and duration. Their membership is then appointed by either elected officials or the civil service; and commissioners and their staff of civil servants turn to experts and affected citizens for assistance and information (often provided in the form of testimony) as needed. Commissions are not subservient to the civil service or elected officials; they are the operationalization of the public purpose as embodied by the legal structure. The description of the Wisconsin Public Service Commission is typical of their legal structure:

> The Public Service Commission is headed by three commissioners who serve six-year terms, one of whom the Governor designates to serve as the chairperson. [s. 15.79 (1), Stats.] Commissioners are nominated by the Governor and are appointed with Senate approval. [s. 15.06 (1) (c) 1., Stats.] Reflecting on the need for technical expertise that had been found lacking in municipal governments, the commissioners are supported in their work by a professional staff of auditors, accountants, engineers, attorneys, planners, and economists.
>
> *(Wisconsin Legislative Council 2017, 3)*

That Commons only speaks in the most general terms regarding the organizational or structural specifics of the commission is no accident. Exactly how many people should serve on a commission involves tradeoffs. In the experience of the author, additional membership provides an opportunity for broader representation of interests, but also increases the risk of diminished organizational effectiveness as well as the possibility that internal coalitions will form and run counter to the commission's mission and credibility. Similarly, the appropriate duration and scope of the commission also involve tradeoffs. These tradeoffs illustrate the broader point that the essence of a commission is found more in its processes than its form or structure.

Instead of focusing on the structure of commissions, Commons devotes considerable attention to their desired operational characteristics. His thoughts can be summed up in a word: credibility. Like the civil service, the commission must be seen as credible by all affected parties.[5] The reasoning, however, is different. Whereas the civil service must be credible as a provider of facts, the commission must provide a credible *process* of conflict resolution. Commons (1913, 178) put it directly: "It is intended that the members of the commission itself should not be representative of either the employers or employees, but that they should have the confidence of both sides." He continues: "They must be men [*sic*] not only competent but having the respect of the great opposing interests." These two quotes also point to the intermediate place of the commission between the state and at least two competing private interests. As such, the commission may have a method for appointed membership, such as one member from party X, one from party Y, and a third from the civil service or similar neutral body to ensure a broad representation of interests. The only structural specifics are the limitations of what will allow for a successful process. The *structure* is subservient to the *process* of conflict resolution.

Addressing the qualifications of the various advisories to the commission, Commons also stresses the necessity of responsibility and credibility: "Wisconsin has had for seven years a Civil Service Commission, and nearly all of the employees of the Industrial Commission were placed under the civil service law." He continues: "The Civil Service Commission of Wisconsin adapts its examinations to these conditions so that through cooperation of the commissions, the deputies of the Industrial Commission are coming to have the full confidence of employers and employees as *practical men* [*sic*]" (Commons 1913, 404–405, italics added).[6]

The investigative work of the commission, according to Commons, is not the same as the work of the academic engaged in pure theory or laboratory sciences, or even the work of the civil service. In *Labor and Administration,* he states:

> The real distinction which entitles the commission to its position as a fourth branch of government is not administration, but investigation and research. But its investigations are not the academic research of the laboratory study, nor the journalistic investigation of the agitator, but the constructive investigation of the administrator. It is this constructive investigation that gives to the commission its lawful position in government and its effective position in the enforcement of law.
>
> *(Commons 1913, 396)*

The following line of questioning from Commons, speaking as a member of the US Commission on Industrial Relations, with John Frey, an officer in the International Molders' Union, illustrates the method of investigation that Commons believed necessary for a commission to be seen as credible. In this case, the subject was a particular labor dispute:

Commissioner Commons: "On this question that Mr. Weinstock asked, with reference to the establishment of a permanent national body, you answered it under the impression that he meant that that body should be given the power to arbitrate … . Now, supposing that body was given power of only mediation or using conciliation in a different sense, a conciliatory or mediating power, or endeavoring to get—"

Mr. Frey: "I would be heartily in favor of anything that would increase the application of mediation and conciliation, because in my opinion it is not the conciliation of the labor trouble, but it is the only thing that maintains the largest degree of peaceable relations."

Commissioner Commons: "Does your organization have any contact with the State boards of arbitration and mediation and conciliation?"

Mr. Frey: "We have had the members of such boards talk to us, but whenever they have offered their good services and tried to do something, we have never seen any practical results, or many practical results. We have not found them effective in our trade."

Commissioner Commons: "Can you give any particular reasons why they have not been effective?"

Mr. Frey: "The foundry men generally decline to have anything to do with them."

Commissioner Commons: "You think the foundry men would not listen to them?"

Mr. Frey: "We would gladly have taken advantage of anything they could do to assist to bring about a settlement of the question."

Commissioner Commons: "That is, if they could have arranged a conference with the foundry men you would have accepted it?"

Mr. Frey: "Why, yes; because we find that when we can meet the foundry men and talk matters over, we generally reach a settlement, and as I read from that circular the members of the National Founders' Association were advised not to meet with us in conference because of the danger of reaching a settlement of their strike. They were afraid to talk with us because it would lead to a settlement of the strike."

Commissioner Commons: "In arranging such a conference, should there exist such an opportunity, naturally that board would be represented at the conference?"

Mr. Frey: "Yes."

Commissioner Commons: "But only in a mediating capacity?"

Mr. Frey: "Only in a mediating capacity."

Commissioner Commons: "Attempting to bring them together?"

Mr. Frey: "Not as a party with arbitrary right to cast a third vote and determine what should be done."

(Commission on Industrial Relations 1916, 549)

When questioning Frey, Commons has two aims. First, he attempts to understand the culture of Frey's union and the Founders' union. (What are the prevailing attitudes and desire for resolution of the conflict? And what are the attitudes toward conventional channels of dispute resolution?) Second, Commons attempts to understand the nature of the conflict. (What are the impediments to a resolution?) What is absent is equally noteworthy. There is no advice to Mr. Frey as to what should be done. Commons does not attempt to lecture Mr. Frey about the equalization of bargaining power, much less about the textbook notion of "rational" economic beings. He is there primarily to listen and learn—not to teach, lecture, or profess. This is Commons's application of "administration" to the commission. It illustrates the process of the economist dealing with the public in the recovery of facts and for the purpose of moving toward the mitigation of social conflict.

The *place* of elected officials, the civil service, the commission, the economic advisor or expert witness, and the affected population can be summarized as follows: The elected officials or the civil service provide the mandate of the commission (conflict to be resolved); the advisor or witness conveys information to the commission, and the affected parties must see the commission as credible and just.

Thus, we have laid out the place and process (i.e., "administration") of the commission as advocated by Commons. As in the case of the economist as civil servant, the economist as commissioner must be widely seen as having credibility and impartiality. But the roles also contain some differences: Where the role of the economist in the civil service is to provide value-free data and the neutral execution of policy, the role of the economist on a commission is to uncover the social facts of the matter, use those facts to work toward agreeable solutions, and achieve broad community "buy-in." The role of the commission is to understand conflict and to seek out its resolution, not to mandate solutions but to remove the obstacles to them. In this way, a stable solution to social conflict is achieved. In the next section, we will consider the role of the economist as an academic.

The role of economics and the academic economist

Commons and the "fool friends of labor": the role of the economist

As the previous sections make clear, Commons did not believe it was the place of the economist to take a leadership role in constructing or implementing economic policy. His reasoning was straightforward: The economist does not have any "skin in the game." As Commons (1934, 88) put it, "I learned … that the place of the economist was that of advisor to the leaders if they wanted him [*sic*], and not that of propagandist to the masses." He continued: "Hence I always accepted philosophically what they [representative leaders] rejected of my hard work, and stuck to them nevertheless."

Commons contrasted the economist as an advisor with what he referred to as the "fool friends of labor," a phrase he borrowed from labor leader Samuel Gompers. Of those individuals, Commons (1934, 87) writes: "They started the strike without funds, or organization, or negotiational leadership, or any attempts at a trade agreement. … It was here that I first learned to distrust the intellectuals as leaders in labor movements." Commons referred to such economists and intellectuals as being "class conscious," but not "wage conscious." According to Commons's investigative method, the reasonable economist should offer information and advice, but should not be the policy decision-maker or advocate.

It is difficult to say where "the line" is between advisor and advocate, between researcher and polemicist. It seems likely that one has crossed "it" when one believes they have the Truth (with a capital "T") on a matter and that they need only to convey this truth to others (and then for the community to act on it) for an optimal outcome to occur. In practice, I have found it very easy to walk over this line and have paid a price for doing so more than once. It is easy to slip from advisor to advocate, to let our ego and passion take a front seat.

Indeed, it is clear that Commons, on several occasions, slipped into the role of advocacy (see for example, Chasse 1991). It is also true that there is both a need and a place for advocacy. Yet Commons had good instincts (reinforced, of course, by considerable practical experience): the neutrality of academic experts is often critical in enabling parties to reach negotiated solutions, since such experts can uncover and present the facts that parties need to resolve their disputes. Similarly, it is also true that the academic or even the policy advisor will usually not be the one primarily affected by policy action. As Commons (1913, 8) put it,

> The regulation of public utilities, the revision of currency and tariff laws, the relations of capital and labor, are economic as well as legal or political questions. On these and other subjects the science of economics remains academic after it has been summoned to the work of construction.

He continued:

> But in the arrangement finally decided upon, the scientist, the engineer, the physician, the sanitarian, who are the technical experts, are called in and utilized, just as they are in private employment, when their services are needed and when the practical men have problems beyond their technical knowledge. If however, the scientists dominated the investigation, their results, however brilliant and conclusive, might not be reasonable.
>
> *(Commons 1913, 406–407)*[7]

Thus, economic advice and advocacy must be kept separate. The economist is there to convey what has been already "settled" (including, for example, data, history, and institutional facts) in a manner similar to settled law. According to Commons, the economist is there to inform and, where helpful, to guide, not to decide or advocate. In a similar manner, there is economic research, and there is the work of achieving a negotiated solution, with advocates on all sides; from Commons's perspective, economists should stick to the research and let practitioners representing the disputants fashion their own solutions.

Constructive research: the role of economics as a field of study

Never shy about creating new terms to label his ideas, Commons referred to his approach to academic research as "constructive research." John D. Chasse, writing on the work of the American Association for Labor Legislation—of which Commons was a leading member and researcher—explains constructive research as that which is "aimed at solving social problems rather than advancing academic disciplines. This 'constructive research' included scholarship—historical studies, worldwide surveys of existing practices, statistical analyses, and sponsored conferences" (Chasse 1991, 800). Commons (1913, 12–13) stated grandly that constructive research "reduces the coercive functions of government and increases the part played by persuasion. ... It analyses the facts and reduces them to the point where the public can use them." He continued: "To the constructive investigator, research is absorbing. He [*sic*] shares in that gradual reconstruction of society that, on occasion, arouses the orator, lawyer, preacher or politician."

Here we can see where the economist fits in Commons's broader process. A review of Commons's peer-reviewed publications from the 1900s through the mid-1920s also points the way.[8] What we find in this work is a reporting of economic facts and events. They collectively represent an attempt to understand the set of socially negotiated rules and norms that structure economic activity. His work takes these facts as they are. There is no attempt to impose an outside order on them in the form of behavioral assumptions. Instead, in somewhat clinical terms, the data are allowed to speak for themselves. This again is Commons's investigational method—to seek out the facts of economic organization, to organize those facts, and to present them so that society might reach better-informed solutions to economic problems.

We can contrast this with the approach taken by the majority of modern introductory texts. The first-year economics student is invariably exposed to the merits of the "economic way of thinking." (Given the normative bent and a priori reasoning, it is not clear why this is not simply referred to as the social philosophy of economics.) In this way, the student of economics learns to see events of the world through the lenses of marginal analysis, individual utility maximization, and the corresponding maximization of profits (and minimization of costs) by businesses.

The foregoing is, of course, an oversimplification of the methodological approach of economics. It is after all, only what we find in first-year texts. Still, it is enough to illustrate a significant difference in approach between conventional economics and Commons.[9]

Before turning to recent applications of Commons's method, it is worth briefly considering how Commons's constructive research squares with a classic statement on the fundamentals of institutionalist economic policy. That statement, by Jerry Petr (1984), lists ten attributes to the institutionalist approach to policy. Most of those attributes are unquestionably in line with Commons's constructive research. They include: (1) a holistic conception of economics, which sees all social disciplines as interconnected and all real-world problems as interdisciplinary; (2) an appreciation of ongoing socioeconomic evolution; (3) an emphasis on the social and policymaking processes that move us from "here to there"; (4) a focus on fact-based analyses; (5) a recognition of the socioeconomic significance of technological change (broadly defined to include all science, human skill, and knowledge); (6) an experimental or instrumental method that's not afraid to develop and test policies "with the intention of influencing social processes in a positive direction" and is committed to using human intelligence to work out "the problems of social conduct"; and (7) a non-dogmatic or pragmatic orientation that seeks not universal truths, but instead "humanity's best stab at societal improvement given the factual basis of a particular situation" (Petr 1984, 4–9). But Petr's list also includes three other attributes that might not be so obvious in their alignment with Commons's constructive research: (8) values-driven, (9) activist, and (10) democratic (Petr 1984, 4).

Let's begin with the attributes of *values-driven* and *activist* economics. For Petr (1984, 4), the "values-driven" nature of institutionalism is offered as an alternative to the "price-motivated" orientation of conventional economics; thus, institutionalism seeks a solution in the public interest that is not wedded, a priori, to "getting the prices right." And "activist" economics means merely that institutionalism is "an economics of control—in which the attempt is made to channel the ever-present [social] flux into serviceable channels for humanity" (Petr 1984, 7). Taken together, what these mean to Petr is that society should drive and shape the economy, not the reverse. All of this is consistent with Commons's constructive research. Moreover, all economics—orthodox and heterodox—is fundamentally values-driven and activist, since all good-faith research and policy is designed to improve the state of the world; what separates institutionalism from textbook economics is willingness to look beyond "getting prices right" and to acknowledge that economics can never be value free.[10]

Petr's attention to *democracy* can also be reconciled with Commons's method. On the grounds of "economic efficiency," conventional economists often call for elimination of the minimum wage; Commons would have countered by demonstrating that minimum wages improve the general well-being of the community and result in improved economic performance. Conventional economists expect the benevolence of the market to produce a net gain for society; in Commons's view, it is instead through participatory, democratic governance and policymaking that social improvement occurs. Commons's perspective is fully consistent with Petr's view of democracy as an attribute of the institutionalist approach to policy, which he summarizes as follows: "The community … provide[s] the ultimate policy evaluation" (Petr 1984, 10).

Putting Commons's method to practice

This section presents a pair of stories on how I have maintained the line between investigation and advocacy. Although these research projects were useful to the intended audiences and in both cases assisted in conflict resolution, they would not be publishable in their current form in today's leading economics journal. The work does not *prove* anything. It does not convey or uncover "Truth." It does not tell anybody what they should or should not do. It only lays out the facts and gives some basic inferences that may be drawn from them. Indeed, in some ways, it is similar to a good deal of Commons's work during the early years of the twentieth century, work that he often published in the *American Economic Review*, but that would never get published there or in similar journals today.[11]

These examples illustrate how we might better serve local communities while simultaneously enhancing our skill sets as economists as well as improving the quality of our academic programs.

Tax increment financing

The first project outlined here was completed roughly five years ago at the request of a few members of the Wisconsin Legislature (Kemp, Ng and Jones 2016). As such, those in the intended audience (that is, state legislators and their diverse constituents) would have varying levels of familiarity with the subject, "tax increment financing" (TIF), a common method of financing municipal economic development in the United States.[12] The original report contained many pictures, graphs, and tables—visual displays all designed to drive home the points made in the text. Key points were highlighted in bold text, and sections were short and clearly delineated, allowing readers to skip ahead according to their particular knowledge and interests. The purpose of the work was not to convince or persuade, but to inform—to assess the state of affairs, provide data, and offer some of the more obvious inferences that could be drawn from the work. This report contributed to changes in a municipal ordinance and has informed debate at the state level.[13]

After opening with a discussion that establishes a baseline of information on TIF projects, the report evaluates the data along the lines of questioning from previous TIF debates. These include, but are not limited to: type of TIF project (in previous policy discussions, much was made of the "correct" types, while early legislation was highly restrictive), size of the issuing municipality (initially only communities legally designated as cities could use TIF), and size of the project relative to the total municipal debt load. The overall goal was not to prove or disprove any specific hypothesis; instead, the research problem was based on the known fault lines of the policy conflict. The goal was to provide information, based on available and widely agreed-upon data, to enable better-informed TIF policy debates.

A concluding section of the report attempts to move the discussion forward, highlighting the main inferences drawn from the analysis. There is also a call for more data, presented as necessary to address questions that residents of local communities have already shown a desire to see answered. Since answers to those questions are of interest to all parties, the request for data does not aid one side of matter at the expense of others. In this way, the integrity of the data and the civil service can be maintained going forward. Although this certainly walks close to the line of "advocacy," the investigation only seeks to *assist*, not shape, the policy development process.

Rural economic development

Over the past several years, I have worked with a number of governmental entities on rural economic development projects.[14] They have been especially challenging: the nature of the "problem" or research question is not well defined; the social and economic difficulties are many; and the "solutions" are rarely what people wish to hear. The outcomes of these projects have varied, but I have never experienced what could be considered a wholesale "success" in the form community socioeconomic revitalization. Instead, I have had to be content with improving the quality of development discussions and helping people understand that their local problems are not unique.

Although not a significant problem in Commons's time, the slow but constant decline of rural communities is perhaps one of the most pressing current economic problems in the central United States. Indeed, the problems of these communities go beyond a lack of jobs; challenges also often include population decline as well as substance abuse and mental-health issues, although job loss is usually seen as the source of all the other problems. Today, however, it is rare for large firms to locate in rural areas and provide thousands, or even hundreds, of jobs. Thus, it is important to have realistic discussions, focused on specific preferences, available resources, and achievable outcomes.

In my experience, an effective way to untangle community preferences is to engage in "benchmarking" with community stakeholders. My approach—based on Commons's thinking regarding stakeholder participation, scientific neutrality, and informed decision-making—involves the following steps. First, I facilitate a discussion with community stakeholders on desired economic and social outcomes, and their vision of the ideal community. When the issue of new "jobs" comes up, I ask how much the jobs should pay and what types of working conditions they might involve. When the question of "affordable housing" is raised, I ask how big the living space should be and what sort of amenities are expected. What exactly does it mean to have "good schools" or a "low crime rate?" By focusing on economic and sociological factors, we sketch a specific picture of what the affected parties mean by economic development.

Then, armed with that profile, we begin an investigation of what is known about communities with that desired set of characteristics. Within the United States, the Census Bureau regularly collects and publishes a large amount of community data and, in my experience, such data is widely regarded as credible. Using that data and sifting through community characteristics to ensure relevant comparisons, we arrive at a set of communities with the desired characteristics; this serves as a first step toward the "achievable ideal." Next, we investigate what events have occurred and strategies have been employed to achieve those communities' outcomes. That information is then shared with the community undertaking the benchmarking, enabling a discussion about what might be possible and what might be done to improve matters.

In this way, economic development becomes a conversation among the affected parties. To some extent, this produces "buy-in" from the start. People have some knowledge and agreement about what goals they are looking to achieve. They also understand what policies and actions have been used elsewhere to get where they want to be. Economic development is not something imposed on the community, and its strategies are not drawn from an economics textbook (or worse, from the mind of an economist!). Instead, what emerges is a stakeholder-designed plan, based on the expressed preferences of those same individuals. The role of the economist is to provide the necessary information and data to know what has been achieved, what has worked, and what has not worked. The community decides what to do with that information.

Concluding summary

In this chapter, I have laid out the essentials of John R. Commons's investigational economics. These include a belief in the critical value of neutral scientific research and the need for participatory policy design and implementation. Neutral scientific research refers to the investigation of socioeconomic events and the presentation of socioeconomic data as facts. This is different from applying data and events to a priori behavioral assumptions with the aim of deriving the economic "Truth" underlying those events. Participatory development is seen as the path to socially stable—and socially desirable—policy actions. This is to be contrasted with both so-called "power politics," where political leverage is used to shift policy in favor of one interest group or another, as well as technocratic reform based on purely academic research projects.

I have also shown the role of the economist in the various structures and processes associated with investigation and policy design. The role of the economist in the civil service is invariably different from that of the economist serving as a commissioner, and from that of the academic economist. As such, an economist's investigations will take different forms in different contexts. At the same time, I have shown how the procedural method known as a "commission" resolves social conflict by bringing together these different investigational forms.

Finally, using examples of my own work, I have shown how Commons's investigational economics might be put into practice by academic economists. Similar work is being completed daily within many public agencies and business firms around the world. Indeed, for those of us who teach undergraduates, it is likely that many of our former students are doing such work. I hope that these examples might lead not only to an improved economic science, but also to more effective economics curricula and superior service to our communities.

Acknowledgments

The author wishes to thank Kota Kitagawa, Timothy Wunder, and Charles Whalen for helpful comments on drafts of this chapter.

Notes

1 "Investigational Economics" was the original title of Commons's final book *The Economics of Collective Action*, published five years after his death in 1950 (see Samuels 1998).
2 Fortunately, that book has been written, and is available as a free download; see Wisconsin Office of State Employment Relations (2005).
3 International Standard Industrial Classification (ISIC) refers to the method by which economists and lawmakers define industries. ISIC code meanings can be downloaded at https://tinyurl.com/yysp42mu.
4 For an explanation of Commons's "reasonable value," see Chapter 2 of this volume (by Charles Whalen); see also Ramstad (2001).
5 Malcolm Rutherford, who also emphasizes the role of commissions in Commons's process, underscores the importance of credibility. According to Rutherford (2015, 95), "The economist experts who staff these agencies are seen by Commons as engaging in applied social science and as very different from purely political appointees subject to bias and corruption....[T]his highly optimistic (almost utopian) view of commissions relies on commissions remaining objective and nonpartisan."
6 Although Commons does not make it clear, it must be the case that he is writing above not of the civil service directly, but instead of the members of the general public who are called upon to participate in and advise the commission. They must be confidently "practical men"—individuals who believe in fair process. In particular, they must be seen as practical by those who will be affected by the process. We can see this in his contribution to the final report of the US Commission on Industrial Relations (1916, 178), where he writes:

> [The advisories'] purpose is not only to give...the commission the benefit of advice and to bring together for conference the representative labor man and employees, but to guarantee as far as possible that all appointments, all publications, and all rules and regulations, and other acts of the commission, shall, before they are published or become valid, be under the continuous supervision of the recognized leaders of organized capital and organized labor, and public representatives.

7 By "reasonable," Commons meant practicable (Commons 1913, 407).
8 See, for example, Commons (1909; 1911; 1923); Commons et al. (1921).
9 To the extent that Commons represents the approach of institutional economics in general, or the degree to which his approach approximates what is commonly referred to as "The Scientific Method" is, I think, more difficult to argue and I shall not undertake that project. However, Malcolm Rutherford (2013) does look at institutionalism in general, and his work suggests that institutional economics—at least in its interwar heyday—operated in a manner that appreciated scientific objectivity. For example, Rutherford (2013, 8) writes: "Institutionalists as a group saw the scientific method as one that emphasized empirical investigation, the development of theories based upon assumptions that confirmed real-world conditions, and the critical examination of theories based upon empirical findings."
10 As Gunnar Myrdal (1978, 778–779) wrote, "Valuations are always with us. Disinterested research there has never been and can never be. Prior to answers there must be questions. There can be no view except from a viewpoint. In the questions raised and the viewpoint chosen, valuations are implied."
11 I believe the closed nature of conventional economic journals to be a significant flaw in contemporary economics, perhaps one that would even be agreed upon by many mainstream economists. I also believe that this flaw misdirects academic resources away from more productive places, especially small, regional academic institutions.

12 It is worth noting that although TIF is easily the most common method through which municipalities in the United States finance economic development, I was not able to find a single mention of it in economics textbooks.
13 One of the students who assisted in this work, Irene Ng, is currently pursuing her MBA.
14 See, for example, Kemp (2019).

References

Chasse, John Dennis. 1991. "The American Association for Labor Legislation: An Episode in Institutional Policy Analysis." *Journal of Economic Issues* 25 (3): 799–828. https://doi.org/10.1080/00213624.1991.11505202

Commission on Industrial Relations. 1916. *Final Report and Testimony Submitted to Congress by the Commission on Industrial Relations.* Washington DC: Government Printing Office.

Commons, John R. 1909. "American Shoemakers, 1648–1895." *Quarterly Journal of Economics* 24 (1): 39–84. https://doi.org/10.2307/1886057

———. 1911. "Organized Labor's Attitude Toward Industrial Efficiency." *American Economic Review* 1 (3): 463–472.

———. 1913. *Labor and Administration*, New York: Macmillan.

———. 1923. "Wage Theories and Wage Policies." *American Economic Review* 13 (1): 110–117.

———. 1934. *Myself.* New York: Macmillan.

Commons, John R., and John B. Andrews. 1936. *Principles of Labor Legislation*, fourth ed. New York: Harper and Brothers.

Commons, John R., Willis Wisler, Alfred P. Haake, O. F. Carpenter, Jennie McMullin Turner and others. 1921. *Industrial Government.* New York: Macmillan.

Kemp, Thomas A., Irene Ng, and Peter Jones. 2016. "A Statistical Assessment of Wisconsin's Open Tax Increment District Projects." Submitted to the City of Eau Clair, Wisconsin and Wisconsin General Assembly, January 2016. Available from the author upon request.

———. 2019. "Integrating Applied Fieldwork into the Undergraduate Economic Curriculum." *Journal of Economic Issues* 53 (2): 471–477. https://doi.org/10.1080/00213624.2019.1594539

Myrdal, Gunnar. 1978. "Institutional Economics." *Journal of Economic Issues* 12 (4): 771–784. https://doi.org/10.1080/00213624.1978.11503577

Ramstad, Yngve. 2001. "John R. Commons's Reasonable Value and the Problem of Just Price." *Journal of Economic Issues* 35 (2): 253–277. https://doi.org/10.1080/00213624.2001.11506360

Rutherford, Malcolm. 2013. *The Institutionalist Movement in American Economics, 1918–1947.* Cambridge: Cambridge University Press. https://doi.org/10.1017/CBO9780511977046

———. 2015. "Institutionalism and the Social Control of Business." *History of Political Economy* 47 (annual supplement): 77–98. https://doi.org/10.1215/00182702-3130451

Samuels, Warren J. 1998. "John R. Commons's Investigational Economics." *Research in the History of Economic Thought and Methodology: A Research Annual*, Archival Supplement 7, edited by Warren J. Samuels and Jeff E. Biddle, 37–326. London: JAI Press.

Petr, Jerry L. 1984. "Fundamentals of an Institutionalist Perspective on Economic Policy." *Journal of Economic Issues* 18 (1): 1–17. https://doi.org/10.1080/00213624.1984.11504216

Wisconsin Legislative Council. 2017. *Overview of Wisconsin's Public Utility Regulatory System*. https://tinyurl.com/y2l8rmq6. Accessed July 6, 2020.

Wisconsin, State of. 1905. Wisconsin Civil Service Law, Chapter 363 (June 16, 1905). Available at https://tinyurl.com/y6lzumwf. Accessed July 6, 2020.

Wisconsin Office of State Employment Relations. 2005. *The History of Wisconsin Civil Service*, 1905–2005. Madison: Wisconsin Office of State Employment Relations. https://tinyurl.com/y3ckdgnp. Accessed August 10, 2020.

8

INSTITUTIONAL IMPACT ANALYSIS

The situation, structure, and performance framework

Sarah S.H. Klammer, Eric A. Scorsone, and Charles J. Whalen

> The Institutional Problem is not only transaction costs—how to grease the wheels of commerce to minimize friction—but also who has the wheels and cart in the first place.
>
> —A. Allan Schmid[1]

Introduction

A. Allan Schmid (1935–2017) was a University Distinguished Professor in the Department of Agricultural, Food, and Resource Economics at Michigan State University (MSU). From the late 1950s until his retirement in 2006, Schmid worked to develop and refine what he called the "situation, structure, and performance" (SSP) framework of institutional analysis. The framework was first introduced in 1978, in Schmid's *Property, Power, and Public Choice: An Inquiry into Law and Economics*.[2]

Adapted from a paradigm developed in the field of industrial organization, SSP reframes the way we think about the fundamental issues of human conflict and cooperation, their root sources, and the consequences of the methods we choose to address such human interdependence. Schmid ([1978] 1987, xiv) developed SSP to be a constructive approach to institutional impact analysis, focused on how alternative institutional structures affect interdependence in substantive terms of *who gets what*—including the "impact" of institutional choices on economic outcomes such as wealth and its distribution. While SSP was well received for its thought-provoking aspects and for enabling researchers to tackle tough economic issues in a new light, Schmid's framework and subsequent work remain relatively obscure, especially outside the community of agricultural economists. With that in mind, this chapter seeks to sketch and explore his way of thinking about issues of institutional (or policy) choice.[3]

DOI: 10.4324/9781003160434-8

The chapter begins with a brief look at the origin and development of SSP. Schmid obtained his graduate degrees in agricultural economics at the University of Wisconsin, Madison, where he studied with students of John R. Commons, the pioneering institutional economist. Those Madison professors, including Kenneth Parsons and Edwin Witte, introduced him to Common's idea of the transaction as the basic unit of economic analysis, a building block that would later underscore Schmid's conception of human interdependence as the source of all human conflict (or cooperation).[4] In 1959, Schmid joined the faculty at MSU, his home base for the rest of his career, drawing on what he learned in Wisconsin to conduct applied research on water systems and other topics involving agriculture and the environment. In Michigan, many of his colleagues engaged in research involving production economics and industrial organization using the "structure-conduct-performance" (SCP) paradigm.[5] Schmid's SSP framework builds on the SCP paradigm but adds the key issue of interdependence. The first section of the chapter traces the roots of his framework and summarizes not only what Schmid believed he accomplished, but also how he thought SSP would be useful in anticipating and evaluating the impact of institutional alternatives.

The second section outlines key elements of the SSP framework and describes how they are connected and interact. *Situation* identifies the characteristics of the goods and/or services under consideration, as well as the nature of interdependence involved in the associated transactions. Central to the analysis of the situation is Schmid's conception of inherent characteristics of goods, or "good types," described in that section.[6] *Structure* refers to the institutional rules of the game that determine who has rights versus duties in light of that interdependence. *Performance* outlines the distributional outcomes of the rules as currently expressed (or as expressed under the institutional change to be introduced). Schmid ([1978] 1987, 23) argued that SSP may be more useful than conventional economics because it emphasizes the measurement of performance "in terms of who gets what," rather than in abstract, aggregate welfare terms.

The third section focuses on applications of the SSP framework. It includes a discussion of how Schmid applied the framework as well as how others have used it. Beyond Schmid's own work, the framework has been applied to a variety of issues including, for example, airspace regulation in the United States, payday lending in Tennessee, and protection of drinking water in Costa Rica.

The fourth section—which is followed by a brief chapter summary and conclusion—discusses ongoing research to bolster and extend the SSP approach. Particular attention will be given to ongoing efforts to incorporate into SSP insight from legal scholar Wesley N. Hohfeld.

The central aim of this chapter is to shine a light on Schmid's development of a promising analytical framework. We highlight the spirit of his research, how it has been used by others, and how we hope it may be further developed and more widely used going forward, thereby helping to advance not just institutional economics, but also economic thinking in general.

Origins

The inception and evolution of a model can be difficult to trace. When the model in question develops over the course of an entire career, and is influenced by many teachers and colleagues along the way, this task becomes even greater. Schmid's approach to institutional analysis, the SSP framework, is one such model.

Nebraska, Wisconsin, and Michigan State University

Schmid began building his model of institutional analysis as a graduate student in the Department of Agricultural Economics at the University of Wisconsin in the 1950s, earning a PhD in 1959, and continuing to refine the framework until the publication of his final academic text and subsequent retirement from MSU in 2006. His publications in the period of the early 1970s through the 1980s contain the first presentations of his approach to institutional analysis, known today as the SSP framework (Schmid 1974; 1978; [1978] 1987). The roots of the model, however, date much further back.

Growing up in the rural plains, Schmid became keenly interested in land and water issues, including land-use policy and water development. This curiosity and drive to learn led him to pursue a university education, and at that time there was no better place to learn about the most pressing agricultural and land issues of the day than at the land-grant universities of the United States (and few majors were more relevant than agricultural economics). While he was an undergraduate at the University of Nebraska, Schmid's intellectual influences (via books and articles) ranged from Elmer Davis, Charles M. Hardin, and Jerome Frank, to economists John Kenneth Galbraith and Gunnar Myrdal. He was also influenced in the direction of institutional economics by Wisconsin graduates Don Kanel and Kris Kristjanson, members of the Nebraska faculty of agricultural economics (Schmid 2003).[7] In 1956, because of these interests and influences, Schmid began a graduate program in agricultural economics at the University of Wisconsin, Madison.

Schmid's interests in water and land-use policy were well suited to Madison. As one of the nation's original land-grant universities, the university had a well-established agricultural economics department that emphasized extension work. This matched Schmid's early research interests and the "get out of your armchair" approach to economics that he practiced and advocated throughout his career (Schmid 2008).

Madison also boasted a strong legacy of research into institutions, law, and policy, which Schmid found essential to his understanding of economic issues. He took courses from Selig Perlman on economic systems, Martin Glaser on public utilities, Walter Morton on monetary policy, W.R. Parks on government and agriculture, Karl Bogholt on the philosophy of John Dewey, Jacob Beuscher on legal issues, and Witte on public policy (Schmid 2003; Scorsone

2017). This interdisciplinary approach to scholarly pursuits would continue throughout his life.

When Schmid retired, he reflected on the steady influence of philosophy—including a network of philosophically inclined colleagues—on his career. He enjoyed discussing economists' philosophical approaches as well as reviewing colleagues' philosophy-oriented work (Schmid 1978). With regard to the role of values in academic research, he favored the perspective of Gunnar Myrdal, which Schmid called the "naked normativist," who "puts his personal value judgements up front for all to see" (Schmid 2008). This was in contrast to taking the role of the "deceptive normativist" (associated with much of conventional economics). Schmid's emphasis on the unavoidably normative nature of economics, especially the role of ethics in shaping policy, was a key influence on how he designed and taught SSP.

Commons' institutionalism also had a major influence on the SSP framework. It was in Witte's course that Schmid is likely to have first come into contact with the ideas of Commons, particularly Commons's contributions to institutional analysis, including insight into how institutions (manifested as rights) shape power in the economy, and how transactions serve as the basic unit of economic analysis.[8] Schmid's (1959) dissertation, "Water Allocation and Development in Wisconsin," was a vintage form of institutional economics analysis in this vein.[9]

In his dissertation, Schmid assessed the distribution of water rights and duties among the various parties in Wisconsin. Specifically, he examined how the rules and customs of the Wisconsin Water Commission evolved to address conflicts between agricultural, industrial, and municipal users. He wrote, "[A]ll is fine until the numbers of each group (water users) create a conflict and interdependence becomes obvious; … now that the outline of a theory which recognizes the conjectural interdependence has been traced, its essential nature may be spelled out" (Schmid 1959, 302). Human Interdependence, tied to Common's idea of the transaction, eventually became a formal part of Schmid's SSP.

Following his graduate work, Schmid joined the Department of Agricultural Economics at MSU. He began working closely with fellow Wisconsin graduate Warren Samuels (who had served as Witte's teaching assistant) as well as with other colleagues conducting research in the area of organizational and production economics. Much of that work included explorations of institutional and legal-economic issues (Schmid 2003).[10] At that time, MSU extension faculty used the SCP and related frameworks to investigate emerging state and local land-use policy questions. In a 1964 edited book, Schmid and colleague James Shaffer wrote a chapter about the potential implications of different marketing systems in agriculture, laying out a general framework for studying interconnections between physical performance results and variations in intangible social relationships (Schmid and Schaffer 1964, 24). In that chapter, we get an early glimpse at Schmid's idea of a connection between interdependence and performance.

Where colleagues like Samuels concentrated on describing the relationship between (1) the conduct and behavior of individuals and groups, and (2) legal-economic performance (Mercuro 2001; Samuels 1992), Schmid focused on human interdependence. Upon inheriting Raleigh Barlowe's "Advanced Land Economics" course, which Schmid eventually transformed into the renamed "Institutional and Behavioral Economics," he began formally developing key concepts of the SSP framework. In a draft of his classroom textbook from the early 1970s entitled, "The Economics of Property, Power and Public Choice," Schmid identified the inherent characteristics of goods, or *good types*, as key to interdependence and institutional structural choice (Schmid 1974). This early text would later become his 1978 book, *Property, Power, and Public Choice.*

Inherent characteristics of goods

Schmid's work on SSP evolved over two decades of exploring how old concepts could be recast and used to advance economic analysis. He was particularly keen on changing economists' use of the language of market failures, externalities, and public goods. Because of his attention to land and water uses and markets, Schmid understood the grip of the conventional language of market failure. He also understood that land and water cannot be treated like the private goods (and services) typically analyzed by economists. According to Schmid (1981, 79), this traditional language obscures the nature of the interdependence at the core of these situations:

> The language of welfare economic theory has crept into popular speech. Everyone talks about externalities and the divergence of private and social costs. Some of this language is unfortunate and confuses public discussion and [interferes with] learning from experience with past resource controls.

Schmid believed the term "public good" was problematic because it inferred that the good in question had to be provided by government action. He argued that this wasn't the case. In a 1961 publication on water allocation in Wisconsin, Schmid wrote of the mix of public and private gains and losses that policymakers always confront, requiring decisions that economists' labels don't make any easier:

> One particular use cannot be stamped with the label "public" to the exclusion of all others. Even the right of fishing in a navigable stream is not a single interest. This is illustrated by the 1959 amendment [to state law], which prevents diversion from trout streams. Are trout fishermen more "public" than bass fishermen? All uses including irrigation contribute to the public benefit and some procedure should be employed which attempts to weigh the gains of one group against the loss to others.
>
> *(Schmid 1961, 187)*

What Schmid believed really mattered were the physical, biological, or other innate characteristics that define our idea of public goods. In his courses, Schmid noted that changes in land use are often *non-marginal* in character, which means they don't fit neoclassical theory very well. He asked: What are the characteristics of goods (or services) that make collective action particularly important? In the case of the public good, these were most often the characteristics of non-exclusion and non-rivalry. His approach was to take each characteristic separately and then examine the potential impacts of institutional alternatives and performance.

Using real-world cases, Schmid conducted that sort of examination not only in the classroom, but also in his research, eventually introducing additional features of public goods including economies of scale and information and transaction costs (Schmid 2003; 2008). The development of his ideas was informed by a variety of practical projects, ranging from research supported by the environmental nonprofit Resources for the Future (Schmid 1968) to work for the US Army Corps of Engineers Systems Analysis Group (Schmid 1969).

Analytical institutionalism

Schmid's early practical experiences contributed to his thinking about the character of goods; they also marked the beginning of his crusade for what he called an "analytical institutional economics." Responding to arguments over public provision of (or failure to provide) environmental services, Schmid wrote:

> One gets the feeling that [certain new policies and institutions] are preferred more out of recognition that what exists has failed some of the environmental interest groups rather than any solid prediction that the alternative will produce a given new result when actually implemented in detail. Before we can improve our predictive powers we will need to develop further an analytical institutional economics.
>
> *(Schmid 1972, 893)*

In addition, he wrote: "Institutions shape the goods which shape men [and women], and they also directly affect men [and women] … . The need for behavioral data to link institutions to actual conduct should be clear. We need theories of behavior and not just advantage" (Schmid 1972, 900).

It has long been asserted that institutional economics has no body of theory. While Schmid (1986) refuted this, he recognized the need for a cohesive applied model linking institutions and the characteristics of goods responsible for human interdependence. The SCP model of other economists recognized the importance of institutions but was missing explicit mention of the character of the goods (and thus the nature of the underlying interdependence) that policies and institutional changes aim to reallocate.[11] Schmid firmly believed: "You can't design policy (institutions) if you do not know where human interdependence is coming from" (Schmid 2008, 137).

Drawing on Common's notion of the transaction as the basic unit of economic analysis, Schmid created the SSP framework, connecting the characteristics of goods, the institutions that inform them, and human interdependence (which he also called "the matter to be sorted out"). It appeared first in his *Property, Power, and Public Choice* (Schmid [1978] 1987) and, in its final form, in *Conflict and Cooperation: Institutional and Behavioral Economics* (Schmid 2004). Toward the end of his career, documenting various contributions to the MSU tradition or "Spartan School" of institutionalism, Schmid described his contribution as follows:

> Instead of the structure, conduct, performance framework of industrial organization, Schmid made the character (situation) of the good being produced explicit in a framework of Situation, Structure and Performance. Structure included many more institutional variables than market structure. The market is not a single entity, but rather alternative detailed market rules matter. The market and the law unavoidably form a nexus rather than being separate alternatives. Here the influence of Warren Samuels is evident as expressed in his article, "The Legal-Economic Nexus."
>
> *(Schmid 2003, 210)*

The situation-structure-performance framework

Schmid used institutional analysis to shed light on how institutions change, grow, and affect the way people interact with each other. His SSP model offers a specific type of institutional analysis, explaining how alternative institutional structures affect instances of human interdependence and substantive economic outcomes of wealth and its distribution. What are the economic performance consequences of alternative rules? Who are the parties affected? SSP theory is rooted in the proposition that if you understand how the characteristics of goods (or services) cause one person's actions to affect others, then you can find ways to mediate that interdependence through changes in the institutional structure, thereby enabling predictions about economic performance and the distributional consequences (Schmid 1986).

Interdependence

SSP begins with institutions. Schmid defined institutions as "sets (networks) of ordered relationships (connections) among people that define their rights, their exposure to the rights of others, their privileges, and their responsibilities" (Schmid 2004, 6). Those relationships form a complex system, not easily understood or unraveled, but integral to the way things work. Moreover, institutions are more than rules of the game, and they do more than provide constraints: "They are also enablement to do what the individual cannot do alone" (Schmid

2004, 7–8). This view of institutions follows Commons (1950, 21), who wrote: "An institution is collective action in control, liberation, and expansion of individual action."

Because Schmid viewed institutions as a system of the relationships of individuals, he did not see them as something separate from individuals (Schmid 2004, 9). He also traced the source of social conflict or cooperation not to institutions, but instead to the inherent characteristics of goods and services. He wrote:

> Different kinds of goods and services create different kinds of interdependencies, and thus it takes different institutions to control and direct them. Institutions define the opportunity sets of interdependent transacting parties. When one party's choices affect another party, Alpha's opportunity is Beta's constraint and vice versa. There are opportunities for cooperation and conflict.
>
> *(Schmid 2004, 1)*

Thus, Schmid's focus was on the interactions of individuals (consistent with Commons's focus on transactions), which occur in the context of goods and services with particular characteristics.

Since the character of human interaction (or interdependence) stems from the characteristics of various goods and services, Schmid's "good types" play a crucial role in the SSP framework. Characteristics highlighted by Schmid include the degree of incompatibility (scarcity and/or rivalry), exclusion cost, economies of scale, the effect of another user on cost, the cost to produce another physical unit, and various information and transaction costs (Schmid 2004, 16, 90). These are aspects of a given technology that, combined with the current institutions that inform them, are taken as a given (at least in the near term) as independent variables. Table 8.1 includes a list of good types and examples of each.

Situation

When using the SSP framework, the first step in institutional impact analysis is to identify the true source of interdependence or interdependencies under investigation. This is the key to what Schmid calls the *situation*, which often appears in the form of a problem or conflict between individuals or groups. The situation encompasses the inherent characteristics of a particular good, the parties connected by the interdependence that the good generates, and the existing institutional and technological setting.

Sometimes identifying the situation is straightforward, as in the case of a dispute over who gets to use a physical, incompatible-use good such as a computer (that is, persons A and B are interdependent because they cannot use the computer simultaneously). But often the source of interdependence is less clear, as in the case of goods with multiple characteristics. Even when a case is seemingly

TABLE 8.1 Inherent characteristics of goods (good types).

Characteristic	*Definition*	*Examples*
High exclusion cost	A good that, if made available to Alpha, entails a high cost of excluding consumption/use by Beta. The exclusion cost is greater than net revenue.	1. Cleaner air 2. Union benefits Who pays? Who is a free-rider? An unwilling rider?
Economies of scale	A good characterized by declining marginal cost for an additional physical unit of production.	1. Tap water 2. Airlines Who pays fixed cost and who pays only marginal cost?
Incompatible use	A good with two or more uses and/or users which are at odds: If Alpha (Beta) consumes/uses it for activity 1 (2), then Beta (Alpha) cannot consume/use it for activity 2 (1).	1. Air (between industry and breather) 2. Land (between farmer A and B)
Non-rival	A good for which there is zero marginal cost per additional use or user: One person can consume/use the good without decreasing the amount available for consumption/use by another (consumption/use is non-rival).	1. National defense (within physical boundaries) 2. Cable TV
Transaction costs	Cost of executing transaction, including cost of: • establishing a transaction position • locating a transaction partner • negotiating an agreement • monitoring and enforcing the agreement	1. Buying/selling a home 2. Buying/selling a car
High information cost	A good which requires cost > 0 to measure quality of its attribute(s), beyond minimal use of the five senses. In its most extreme form, quality can only be measured/known by consumption of the good (Nelson's experience good).	1. Liability of accidents 2. Product attributes (organic, non-genetically modi fied, etc.)

Source: Authors' interpretation, based on Schmid (2004) and Schweikhardt (2016).

straightforward, however, interdependence must be clarified by identifying the set of background variables that inform the situation. These variables include existing embedded institutions, habits, and other cultural and physical features of the setting that condition the interdependence—and can even include constitutional or other legal limits on individuals and transactions.

The situational element of SSP is arguably one of Schmid's most important contributions to institutional analysis. Most institutional approaches start with a variety of institutional alternatives to be explored. In so doing, they typically hold a series of unstated assumptions in the background, including assumptions about the nature of the interdependence forcing the search for institutional change. Schmid's goal was to bring such interdependence to the forefront and use it to shape the analysis.

Structure

Structure refers to the institutional alternatives that people consider to address the interdependencies of a given situation (Schmid 2004, 17). Structure is the independent variable of the SSP framework, and Schmid uses structure to describe the relationships between people that define their relative opportunity sets. While such relationships are sometimes informal, available institutional alternatives can often be written as a list of legal relationships between parties (spelling out, for example, a party's liability or someone's right to seek an injunction or damages).

In Schmid's analyses, two or more alternative structures (which may range, for example, from contractual arrangements to organizational structures) are put forth as possible ways of dealing with interdependence. Each alternative is then evaluated according to how it addresses the interdependence at the center of the analysis, giving particular attention to the fact that each alternative may have different outcomes for the parties involved. This focus differs sharply from other modes of choosing between institutional alternatives—such as the market-focused "Chicago School" of law and economics—that would seek merely to identify the most "efficient" structural alternative. In contrast, the SSP approach aims to first identify the source of interdependence (the situation), and then identify the various, case-based performance characteristics of each structural alternative, without using a preconceived notion of *efficiency* as a point of reference.

Performance

The final dimension of impact analysis involves creating hypotheses for how alternative institutions affect economic *performance*. This is the dependent variable of impact analysis and can be examined in many ways. Performance measures might include estimates of monetary gains or losses; calculations of costs associated with making or enforcing the institutional change; enumeration of rights granted or taken; projections of the number of complaints filed by the parties; or assessment against an ethical yardstick.

A key feature of Schmid's approach to institutional analysis is that there is no feature of a good that determines what is either the "right" institutional change or the "appropriate" form of economic performance. Instead, SSP emphasizes the need to define performance in substantive terms of who gets what (Schmid 2008). In Schmid's economics, the institutional resolution of human interdependence requires a normative judgment about whose interests (should) count.

Figure 8.1 depicts the conceptual framework for conducting analyses using SSP. Stated as a functional relationship, Performance is a function of Structural or Institutional Alternative A, or B (or perhaps even C), holding the Situation (characteristics of a good, technology, other institutional features, etc.) constant.

It is important to note that SSP impact analysis is tied to a specific situation, at a specific time (Schmid 2004, 138). If the situation changes, then the analysis and its results will also change. Moreover, an institutional change introduced because of findings produced by impact analysis may have consequences (affecting technology, economic outcomes, or even how people think about the economy) that alter the socioeconomic environment, thus creating a very different situational starting point for the next time period (Schmid 2004, 14). A new situation leads to examinations of new structural alternatives and the possibility of further substantive changes in economic performance.

In Table 8.2, we borrow a simplified example that derives from Schmid (2004). It begins with a situation involving a good characterized by the trait of incompatible use, and then traces the analysis through the analytical dimensions of structure and performance. While space prevents us from examining a variety

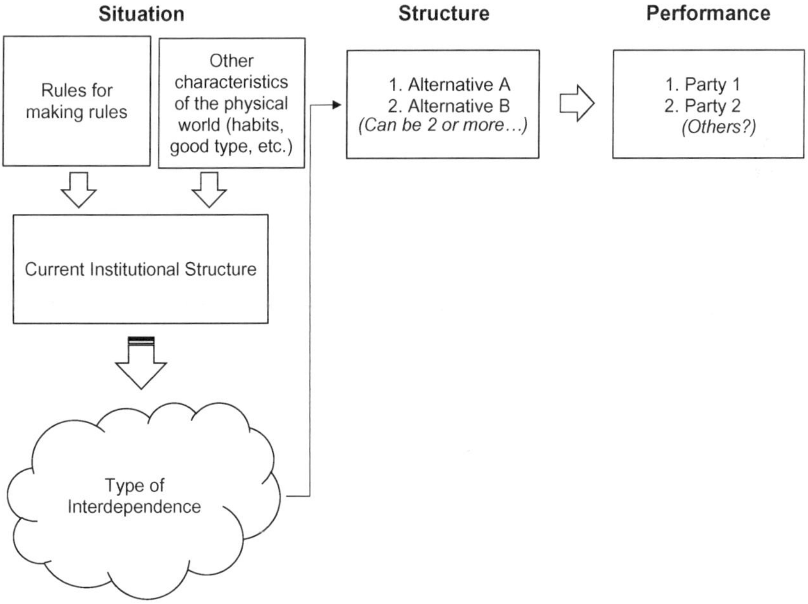

FIGURE 8.1 A visual guide to situation, structure, and performance (used with permission of Sarah Klammer).

TABLE 8.2 Incompatible-use good type: situation, structure, performance.

Situation	*Structure*	*Performance*
Air – a conflict between Industry (which emits wastes) and Breather (who needs air that won't make them sick)	1. Breather has right to use air but may trade with industry that needs to emit wastes 2. Industry has right to emit (use air) 3. Breather has right to use air to some point (or quality level) x, as determined by a regulating body	1. Breather gets clean air or sells (profits) to Industry whose bid > Breather's reservation price. High transaction costs for trade likely; industry pays 2. Industry pollutes (profits); breather likely suffers (incurs medical costs, etc.) 3. Breather likely to have cleaner air than in (2); Industry likely to pollute less. Transaction costs (maintaining the regulating body) dispersed between breathers and industry (yet another matter to be sorted out)

Source: Authors' interpretation, based on Schmid (2004).

of types of goods here, we encourage interested readers to see Schmid (2004) for additional examples; the next section also illustrates the real-world applicability of Schmid's SSP framework.

Only some of the performance measures mentioned above are included in the example presented in Table 8.2. Also, other structural alternatives might be available, or the researcher might be asked to compare an alternative to the current status quo. In addition, enforcement costs could be included in various ways, or ethical sentiments could be the focus. In any event, at the heart of such analyses is, again, an effort to highlight the consequential impact of decisions about whose interests count.

Applications

Schmid used the SSP framework in a variety of contexts and applications. His approach has also been used by other economists investigating topics ranging from regulation of airspace to protection of drinking water. It has even received attention in an environmental economics textbook (Vatn 2007) and a law-school casebook on public policy (Dallas 2005). This section reviews some of the applications by Schmid and others, with special attention to a water study conducted by Michael Kaplowitz, Daniel Ortega-Pacheco, and Frank Lupi (2008).

Schmid

As mentioned earlier in this chapter, Schmid introduced his framework in *Property, Power, and Public Choice* and gave it considerable attention in his follow-up volume, *Conflict and Cooperation* (Schmid [1978] 1987; 2004). In the latter, he worked through numerous examples of human interdependence, showing either how they were dealt with in the past (with performance outcomes already known) or how they could be addressed in light of the inherent characteristics of the goods in question. His examples range from a comparison of the political institutions adopted in England and France in the seventeenth century to a discussion of policy alternatives that can be used to address air pollution (Schmid 2004, 90–96, 240–242).

Schmid also drew on the SSP framework and concepts in many other publications. For instance, in an article on public choice in local judicial systems, Schmid and his coauthor identified the court decisions that shape a community's "law and order environment" as *joint impact goods*. Looking at such decisions from that perspective enabled the authors to frame and analyze issues including community dissatisfaction with rural–urban court consolidation (Broder and Schmid 1983). Another example can be found in a report Schmid wrote for the Office of Technology Assessment of the US Congress. In that report, which developed a conceptual framework for congressional thinking on intellectual property, Schmid used his SSP approach to work through a variety of interdependencies and alternative institutional structures that could be used to address matters such as the notion of "fair use" (Schmid 1985).[12]

Others

Other economists have applied the SSP framework to analyze a wide range of topics. For example, Glen Atkinson (1990) used the framework to analyze interdependence that necessitates airspace regulation, noting that characteristics of airspace include incompatible use, poorly defined property rights, and high exclusion costs. According to Atkinson (1990, 475), a key strength of Schmid's approach is that it offers "a taxonomy of the varieties of interdependence caused by a particular situation."

Patricia Aust Sterns and Lawrence Busch (2002) used Schmid's framework to examine two different approaches to setting standards on exports of fruits, vegetables, and flowers.[13] Starting with a *situation* characterized by inherent interdependencies in horticultural markets—stemming from high information costs and the impracticality of producing goods of varying quality for different consumers—Sterns and Busch considered two different institutional *structures* used to set industry standards: the top-down (retailer-initiated) approach adopted for horticultural markets in Europe, and the bottom-up (producer-initiated) approach employed in Africa and the Caribbean. Their analysis demonstrated that these structures led to different economic performance outcomes in three areas: participation of stakeholders, market access for small growers, and distribution of the costs of standards. In particular, they found that the bottom-up approach provided small growers with more opportunity for participating in the making of regulatory decisions, greater market access, and a slightly smaller cost burden (owing to training and assistance provided by the standard-setting organization).

More recent examples of the SSP framework's applications can be found in work on casino gambling in Macao, the provision of environmental services in Ecuador, and financial regulation in the United States. Here is a brief summary of such work:

- Ricardo C.S. Siu (2006) applied the framework to examine a decision, implemented in 2002, to replace the monopolistic structure of Macao's casino industry with an oligopolistic structure. Among his findings (regarding economic performance) were an increase in that industry's employment and property development, but also shortages of skilled labor and rising labor costs in other industries.
- Daniel Ortega-Pacheco and Inéz Manzano-Torres (2009) used the SSP framework to examine new constitutional reforms affecting the provision of environmental services in Ecuador and to evaluate their likely effect on the generation of land-based carbon credits. They concluded that the reforms might prevent landowners from participating effectively in the international carbon market and that alternative institutional structures might, therefore, be warranted.
- David Zalewski (2014) and Sherry Davis Kasper (2014) relied on Schmid's framework to examine the US subprime mortgage crisis of 2007–2010 and the growth of payday lending in Tennessee, respectively. A key conclusion of Zalewski (2014, 496) was that more than a dozen years of shifting financial risk and burdens from lenders to borrowers underscores "the need for structural changes in the US housing finance system," while Kasper (2014, 922) closed with a similar conclusion, arguing in favor of federal protection for borrowers because payday lenders "have clearly affected the distribution of rights to remain profitable at the expense of consumers."

SSP and drinking water in Costa Rica

The SSP framework is best illustrated with an example. The work of Kaplowitz, Ortega-Pacheco, and Lupi (2008) shows how the framework might be applied to tackle real-world issues. The authors used the SSP approach to evaluate two policy instruments for protecting drinking water in eastern Costa Rica. These two very different instruments are (1) a local program that offers payments to landowners for providing environmental services and (2) a national watershed conservation tax. A brief summary of their analysis and main findings follows.

Situation

The authors begin their analysis by describing threats to Costa Rica's potable water sector—such as changes in rural land use—and attempts to address them. They then describe the drinking water systems in two sets of case study communities (each with clusters of four similar communities) in eastern Costa Rica. This part of their analysis highlights background characteristics of the situation, such as the fact that revenue from water bills is the primary source of funds supporting the operation and maintenance of local aqueduct systems.

In addition to background characteristics, that portion of the analysis also identifies the situation's main sources of interdependence. The authors write:

> Three main interdependencies arise from characteristics of drinking water and the actors involved in drinking water transactions in eastern Costa Rica. They are: 1) potential incompatible use of the land adversely impacting water quality; 2) pricing issues associated with the provision of potable water where the marginal cost of additional users in the system may be very low; and 3) lack of information concerning transaction costs.
>
> *(Kaplowitz, Ortega-Pacheco, and Lupi 2008, 388)*

To end the situational discussion, the authors identify possible institutional changes to address the characteristics of the goods in question. For example, on incompatible land use, they write:

> Solutions to the issue of incompatible use of the land, once factor ownership is given, would depend essentially on whether the continued or proposed use of the land adds more to the landowners' incomes than it subtracts from the water users' incomes. Consequently, landowners may be willing to receive payments to discontinue a particular land use or adopt certain practices to protect water sources and secure the provision of the service.
>
> *(Kaplowitz, Ortega-Pacheco, and Lupi 2008, 388)*

Structure

In their analysis of institutional structure, the authors discuss elements of two policy arrangements they selected for close scrutiny. As mentioned above, one involves paying landowners to provide environmental services, an approach that has been used in some parts of Costa Rica; the other involves a conservation tax, which was enacted in 2006, to be implemented over a seven-year period. The authors examine various aspects of each of these policies, including instrument type (contractual agreements versus regulation), enabling institutions (the existing "rules for making rules" that allow the change), and administration and implementation (which spell out "who has to do what") (Kaplowitz, Ortega-Pacheco, and Lupi 2008, 389–391).

Performance

The authors then offer predictions about the economic performance likely to result from the two different policy arrangements, evaluating those predictions using evidence from field research, previous experience, and other data sources.

The authors conclude that joint use of both the payments to landowners and the conservation tax might be the best way forward. Their results suggest that the water tax on its own would not generate sufficient revenue for rural communities to purchase the land needed to protect drinking water sources; the results also indicate that the tax would involve considerable implementation and enforcement costs. They conclude that communities could draw on a combination of Costa Rica's formal (legal) and informal (social) institutions to implement both policy changes as complementary initiatives, resulting in "viable and reasonable approaches for protection of drinking water sources" (Kaplowitz, Ortega-Pacheco, and Lupi 2008, 396). They even suggest practical ways that the nation's regulatory framework could be modified to help ensure the success of this mixed-policy strategy.

Summarizing their work, Kaplowitz, Ortega-Pacheco, and Lupi (2008, 382) write that the SSP framework allowed them to "specify relationships, describe the attributes of the goods and services that create human independencies (situation), explore the characteristics of the alternative institutional arrangements (structures), and evaluate the alternatives' relative efficacy (performance)." In particular, the framework provided insight by highlighting different sources of interdependence, contributing to greater awareness of the varying needs of the affected communities, and underscoring the unique challenges of each existing institutional environment.

Theoretical frontiers

Critics of institutionalism often maintain that the school's analyses suffer from a general lack of functionality and a proclivity toward seemingly tautological issues. Schmid combated that argument in his institutional impact framework through the creation of a specific taxonomy of types of interdependencies between people, defined by good types that highlight "the inherent characteristics" of the good in question. But other ways to address the issue of interdependence extend beyond Schmid's use of good types. This section describes some ongoing work to advance the SSP approach by incorporating legal insight into Schmid's analytical framework.

The underlying legal framework

Economic relationships are almost always defined by an underlying legal framework that informs the nature of interdependence between transacting parties, whether it is the Uniform Commercial Code, common law, statutory law, constitutional law, or even international law. Commons (1924), Ronald Coase (1960), and more recently Elinor Ostrom (1990) and others have explored the implications of the law for economic transactions and performance. Legal structures define the relationships of parties engaging in a transaction, including who has what rights or duties.

While economists such as those just mentioned have often provided new insight into the law, legal theory can also provide new insight into economic relations and performance. The SSP framework, with its built-in awareness of human interdependence as it relates to the law and other institutions, as well as its decades of use as a tool of applied institutionalism, is uniquely positioned to work well with legal theory. In particular, Schmid's framework can be enhanced by incorporating the legal analysis of Wesley N. Hohfeld (1917) to further define and clarify both the *situation* and the *structure* components of the SSP model.

Legal analysis as applied to SSP

Hohfeld, who taught law at Stanford and Yale, observed that there was no clear or universally agreed-upon meaning for "right" and other critical words used to describe legal relations. To address this, he developed a set of relationships (entitlements and disablements) that he saw as the "common denominators" of all legal relations. He also offered three rules that each legal relation must meet (Schlag 2015, 188–189):

1. Each relation has its unique correlative (each conception is another way of stating its correlative).
2. Each relation has its unique opposite (opposites cannot be accorded to the same party for the same act).
3. Each relation is *never* any of the others (holding parties and actions constant).

With his "common denominator" relations and three rules, Hohfeld provided a way to distinguish clearly between legal and nonlegal relations (Schlag 2015). Later, Commons adjusted some of Hohfeld's model to make it better suited for the field of economics, giving it more of a behavioral, rather than logical, perspective (Fiorito 2010). The subsequent analytical framework, which can be referred to as the Hohfeld legal framework of jural correlatives, is presented in Table 8.3.

Key to the Hohfeldian discussion of jural correlatives is that there is *always* a person (or party) on *each* end of a legal matter. In this way, Hohfeld's idea of legal relations is highly compatible with Schmid's idea of interdependence. In work currently in progress, Scorsone and Klammer are incorporating Hohfeld's legal taxonomy into the SSP model and applying it to real-world examples. Through that work, they hope to show not only that the *structures* of various institutional alternatives are more clearly defined, but also that the *performance* of those alternatives is more thoroughly explored.

Conclusion

Toward the end of his career, Schmid (2003, 207) reflected on institutional economics at MSU. He described the Spartan School as rooted in the work of Commons

TABLE 8.3 Hohfeld's jural relations.

Person or Party A	*Person or Party B*
Right: A claim by one party, enforceable by state power, that others act in a certain manner in relation to the stakeholder. *A's right means that B has a duty to do/not do something.*	Duty: An obligation, enforceable by state power, that requires B to act or precludes action in relation to the right held by A.
Privilege: Permission for A to act in a certain manner without being held liable for damages to others.	Exposure: B is exposed to A's action without legal protection against A for exercising their privilege.
Power: A can change legal relations between A and B.	Liability: B is subject to having the legal relationship with A changed.
Immunity: A is not subject to the power of B.	Disability: B is unable to avoid changes in legal relations made by A.

Source: Authors' interpretation, based on Hohfeld (1917).

and his Wisconsin students, informed by many other scholars and sources (including the field of industrial organization), and animated by an "originality of its own." This is also a succinct characterization of Schmid's own institutionalism, and each of those contributing elements is evident in his SSP framework. The usefulness of that innovative framework has been demonstrated in Schmid's work and in the work of others; indeed, as we have shown, the framework has been used to study a wide range of economic issues beyond his primary field of land and resource economics, including industry regulation and financial economics.

Despite its demonstrated usefulness, the SSP approach to institutional analysis has what some might see as a considerable drawback: It requires researchers to start by clearly articulating assumptions and end by relying on value judgments to draw policy conclusions. Using the SSP framework does not provide ready-made answers to policy questions; it will not reveal an objective "best" or "most efficient" institutional structure. In Schmid's economics, there is no value-free analysis; answering policy questions requires value judgments, and those judgments must be made explicit for all to see.

Of course, Schmid did not consider the need for value judgments to be a shortcoming. On the contrary, he sided with Myrdal on the inherently normative nature of economic policy—and with Joan Robinson (1970, 122), who argued that economists' attempts to be purely objective "must necessarily be either self-deception or a device to deceive others." Today, in an era of climate change, pandemics, financial instability, and acute inequality, it is increasingly apparent that society needs clear thinking on the distributional consequences of policy alternatives, not simple answers that conceal more than they reveal. The SSP framework can facilitate such thinking, thus advancing institutional economics and helping us make the world a better place in which to live.

Acknowledgments

The authors wish to thank Patricia Norris and Tom Kemp for comments on a chapter draft.

Notes

1 From: *Alternative Economic Structures: Evolution and Impact*, edited by Sandra Batie and Nicholas Mercuro, © 2008, Routledge, p. 22. Reproduced by permission of Taylor and Francis Group.
2 The second edition of *Property, Power, and Public Choice* (Schmid [1978] 1987) is the most widely cited.
3 Schmid ([1978] 1987; 2004) also intended for his SSP framework to enable what he called "institutional *change* analysis," involving longer-term analyses in which institutions are dependent variables, rather than the independent variables that they are in *impact* analysis. Schmid's change analysis is not addressed in this chapter.
4 Schmid (2008) mentions the influence of both Parsons and Witte. For some of their relevant work, see Parsons (1942); Parsons (1985); and Witte (1954).
5 The SCP model depicts the influence of an industry's structure (such as barriers to entry and other more fixed conditions) on the conduct of producers (such as pricing) and the resulting performance of enterprises and the industry overall; see, for example, Bain (1959).
6 Schmid's terminology emphasizes *goods*, but his framework and analysis apply to goods and services.
7 The genesis of much of Schmid's thinking and work in the mid-1950s can be traced to the work of teachers like Don Kanel. See Kanel (1955, 1156).
8 See Commons (1931; 1934); also see Chapter 2 (by Charles Whalen) in this volume.
9 In his earliest works, Schmid did not focus on the transaction; instead, he constructed analyses around Common's view of how contracts and property rights shape power in the economy. See, for example Schmid (1965).
10 See, for example, Samuels and Schmid (2012); Samuels, Schmid, and Shaffer (1994); and Samuels, Medema, and Schmid (1997).
11 Similar to SCP is the "strategy-structure-performance" paradigm of organizational economics, which also had an effect on Schmid's thinking; see Rumelt (1974).
12 Schmid's MSU students have also used the SSP framework as the basis for countless research papers, theses, and dissertations; see, for example: Beedy (2005); Cormier (2001); Duprey (2000); Singh (2000); and Wessen (1998).
13 When their article was published, Sterns was a doctoral candidate in agricultural economics at MSU and Busch (who passed away in 2019) was a MSU professor.

References

Atkinson, Glen. 1990. "Airspace Regulation: Redefining the Public Domain." *Journal of Economic Issues* 23 (2): 473–480. https://doi.org/10.1080/00213624.1990.11505046

Bain, John S. 1959. *Industrial Organization*. New York: John Wiley and Sons.

Beedy, Tracy. 2005. "The Evolution of Global Institutions Governing the Movement of Plant Genetic Resources." Plan B paper. East Lansing, MI: Michigan State University. https://doi.org/10.22004/ag.econ.11011. Accessed November 23, 2020.

Broder, Josef M. and A. Allan Schmid. 1983. "Public Choice in Local Judicial Systems." *Public Choice* 40 (1): 7–19. https://doi.org/10.1007/bf00174993

Coase, Ronald. 1960. "The Problem of Social Cost." *The Journal of Law and Economics* 3 (October): 1–44. https://doi.org/10.1086/466560

Commons, John R. 1924. *Legal Foundations of Capitalism*. New York: Macmillan.
———. 1931. “Institutional Economics.” *American Economic Review* 21 (4): 648–657.
———. 1934. *Institutional Economics*. New York: Macmillan.
———. 1950. *The Economics of Collective Action*, edited by Kenneth H. Parsons. New York: Macmillan.
Cormier, Kelley. 2001. “Farm Restructuring in Kazakhstan: An Institutional Economics Approach.” Agricultural Economics Report No. 612. East Lansing, MI: Michigan State University. https://doi.org/10.22004/ag.econ.10949. Accessed November 23, 2020.
Dallas, Lynne L. 2005. *Law and Public Policy: A Socioeconomic Approach*. Durham, NC: Carolina Academic Press.
Duprey, Steven B. 2000. “Solid Waste Collection: Institutional Analysis and Case Study—Delhi Charter Township, MI.” M.S. thesis, Michigan State University. https://doi.org/10.25335/M5697017H. Accessed November 23, 2020.
Fiorito, Luca. 2010. “John R. Commons, Wesley N. Hohfeld, and the Origins of Transactional Economics.” *History of Political Economy* 42 (2): 267–295. https://doi.org/10.1215/00182702-2010-003
Hohfeld, Wesley N. 1917. “Fundamental Legal Conceptions as Applied in Judicial Reasoning.” *Yale Law Journal* 26 (8): 710–770. https://doi.org/10.2307/786270
Kanel, Don.1955. “Discussion: Integration of Research in Law and Economics as Applied to Agriculture.” *American Journal of Agricultural Economics* 37 (5): 1153–1157. https://doi.org/10.2307/1234009
Kaplowitz, Michael D., Daniel V. Ortega-Pacheco, and Frank Lupi. 2008. “Payment for Environmental Services and Other Institutions for Protecting Drinking Water in Eastern Costa Rica.” In *Alternative Institutional Structures: Evolution and Impact*, edited by Sandra Batie and Nicholas Mercuro, 380–401. London: Routledge. https://doi.org/10.4324/9780203894439-21
Kasper, Sherry D. 2014. “Payday Lending: The Case of Tennessee.” *Journal of Economic Issues* 48 (4): 905–925.
Mercuro, Nicholas. 2001. “Output Categories for a Comparative Institutional Approach to Law and Economics.” In *Economics Broadly Considered: Essays in Honor of Warren J. Samuels*, ed. Jeff Biddle John Davis, and Steven Medema, 217–249. New York: Routledge. https://doi.org/10.4324/9780203469118_chapter_12
Ortega-Pacheco, Daniel V. and Inés M. Manzano-Torres. 2009. “Institutional Change and Climate Policy in Ecuador.” In *Implementing the Clean Development Mechanism: Legal and Institutional Challenges*, edited by Michael Mehling, Amy Merrill, Karl Upston-Hooper, 185–205. Berlin: Lexxion.
Ostrom, Elinor. 1990. *Governing the Commons*. Cambridge: Cambridge University Press. https://doi.org/10.1017/cbo9781316423936
Parsons, Kenneth H. 1942. “John R. Commons’ Point of View.” *Journal of Land and Public Utility Economics* 18 (3): 245–266. https://doi.org/10.2307/3159056
———. 1985. “John R. Commons: His Relevance to Contemporary Economics.” *Journal of Economic Issues* 19 (3): 755–778. https://doi.org/10.1080/00213624.1985.11504414
Robinson, Joan. 1970. *Freedom and Necessity*. London: George Allen and Unwin.
Rumelt, Richard P. 1974. *Strategy, Structure, and Economic Performance*. Cambridge: Harvard Univ. Press.
Samuels, Warren J. 1992. “The Legal-Economic Nexus.” In *Essays on the Economic Role of Government*, edited by Warren J. Samuels, 162–186. Basingstoke, UK: Macmillan. https://doi.org/10.1007/978-1-349-12374-2_5

Samuels, Warren J., Steven G. Medema, and A. Allan Schmid. 1997. *The Economy as a Process of Valuation*. Cheltenham, UK: Edward Elgar Publishing.
Samuels, Warren J. and A. Allan Schmid. 2012. *Law and Economics: An Institutional Perspective*. Boston, MA: Kluwer.
Samuels, Warren J., A. Allan Schmid, and James D. Shaffer. 1994. "An Evolutionary Approach to Law and Economics." In *Evolutionary Concepts in Contemporary Economics*, edited by Richard England, 93–110. Ann Arbor, MI: University of Michigan Press.
Schlag, Pierre. 2015. "How to Do Things with Hohfeld." *Law and Contemporary Problems* 78 (1): 186–234. https://doi.org/10.2139/ssrn.2465148
Schmid, A. Allan. 1959. "Water Allocation and Development in Wisconsin." Ph.D. dissertation, Department of Agricultural Economics, University of Wisconsin, Madison, WI.
———. 1961. "Water Allocation by Permit in Wisconsin." *Land Economics* 37 (2): 182–187. https://doi.org/10.2307/3159564
———. 1965. "Property, Power and Progress." *Land Economics* 41 (3): 275–279. https://doi.org/10.2307/3144861
———. 1968. *Converting Land from Rural to Urban Uses*. Baltimore, MD: John Hopkins Press. https://doi.org/10.4324/9781315718699
———. 1969. "Effective Public Policy and the Government Budget: A Uniform Treatment of Public Expenditures and Public Rules." In *Analysis and Evaluation of Public Expenditures: The PPBS System, a Compendium of Papers for the Joint Economic Committee of the U.S. Congress, Volume 1*, 579–591. Washington, DC: US Congress.
———. 1972. "Analytical Institutional Economics." *American Journal of Agricultural Economics* 54 (5): 893–901. https://doi.org/10.2307/1239236
———. 1974. "The Economics of Property, Power and Public Choice." East Lansing, MI: Michigan State University. Photocopy.
———. 1978. "A Review of 'Philosophic Foundations of Agricultural Economic Thought' by Glenn Johnson." East Lansing, MI: Michigan State University, Department of Agricultural Economics Staff Paper, No. 78-9.
———. 1981. "Predicting the Performance of Alternative Institutions." In *Law and Economics: An Institutional Perspective*, edited by Warren J. Samuels and A. Allan Schmid, 76–94. Boston, MA: Kluwer. https://doi.org/10.1007/978-94-009-8766-1_3
———. 1985. *A Conceptual Framework for Organizing Observations on Intellectual Property Stakeholders*. Washington DC: Office of Technology Assessment, U.S Congress.
———. 1986. "Neo-institutional Economic Theories." Parsons Lecture, delivered at University of Wisconsin, Madison. Photocopy.
———. (1978) 1987. *Property, Power, and Public Choice: An Inquiry into Law and Economics, 2nd Edition*. New York: Praeger.
———. 2003 "The Spartan School of Institutional Economics at Michigan State University." In *Research in the History of Economic Thought and Methodology*, Volume 22, edited by Warren J. Samuels, 207–243. Bingley, UK: Emerald. https://doi.org/10.1016/s0743-4154(03)22051-4
———. 2004. *Conflict and Cooperation: Institutional and Behavioral Economics*. Malden, MA: Blackwell. https://doi.org/10.1002/9780470773833
———. 2008. "My Work as an Institutional Economist." https://msu.edu/user/schmid/My work.htm#_ftn7. Accessed July 4, 2020.
Schmid, A. Allan. and James Shaffer. 1964. "Marketing in Social Perspective." In *Agricultural Market Analysis: Development, Performance, Process*, edited by Vernon L. Sorenson, 11–34. East Lansing, MI: Bureau of Business and Economics Research, Michigan State University.

Schweikhardt, David. 2016. "Institutional and Behavioral Economics Course Slides." East Lansing, MI: Michigan State University. Photocopy.

Scorsone, Eric. 2017. "In Memoriam: A. Allan Schmid (1935–2017)." *Journal of Economic Issues* 51 (3): 881–888.

Singh, Meenu. 2000. "An Analysis of Common-Pool-Resource in an Institutional Economics Framework: Evidence from Tank Irrigation and Group-Owned Wells in South India." Plan B paper, Michigan State University, East Lansing, MI. https://doi.org/10.22004/ag.econ.11255. Accessed November 23, 2020.

Siu, Ricardo C.S. 2006. "Evolution of Macao's Casino Industry from Monopoly to Oligopoly: Social and Economic Reconsideration." *Journal of Economic Issues* 40 (4): 967–990. https://doi.org/10.1080/00213624.2006.11506970

Sterns, Patricia A. and Lawrence Busch. 2002. "Standard Setting in the African Horticultural Export Market: A Bottom-Up or Top-Down Approach?" *Journal of Economic Issues* 36 (2): 527–537. https://doi.org/10.1080/00213624.2002.11506497

Vatn, Arild. 2007. *Institutions and the Environment*. Cheltenham, UK: Edward Elgar.

Wessen, Paul D. 1998. "Institutional Economics of Arabica Coffee Marketing in Cameroon." Ph.D. dissertation, Michigan State University, East Lansing, MI. https://doi.org/10.25335/pv3d-3g83. Accessed November 23, 2020.

Witte, Edwin E. 1954. "Institutional Economics as Seen by an Institutional Economist." *Southern Economic Journal* 21 (2): 131–140. https://doi.org/10.2307/1054737

Zalewski, David A. 2014. "Collective Action and Economic Justice: A Structural Approach." *Journal of Economic Issues* 48 (2): 493–500. https://doi.org/10.2753/jei0021-3624480224

9

MYTH BUSTING

Institutional economics and mythopoetics

Mary V. Wrenn

Introduction

All societies are bound together by shared cultural beliefs—mythical understandings and interpretations of the world—which serve to maintain cohesion and reduce uncertainty about the fragility of human existence. As cultures evolve, technology develops and new social institutions emerge. Meanwhile, the mythopoetic (myth-making) tendency of humans continues to serve as the connective tissue in the web of culture, ever evolving but consistently defining and redefining patterns of human behavior. A society's myths justify and sustain prescriptive patterns of behavior; taken together, these myths create the rationale for a system of social norms.

This chapter demonstrates that the study of mythopoetics has long been part of the tools and methods of institutional economics.[1] In particular, the chapter traces such institutionalist research, with particular attention to the function as well as the form of enabling myths. The research examined includes that of Thorstein Veblen, John Kenneth Galbraith, and William Dugger. The chapter shows that the study of mythopoetics reveals, and thus institutional economists must keep in mind, that myths are both structurally determined and socially transformative.

The chapter gives special attention to explaining the mythological nature and character of neoliberalism. Neoliberal myths are structurally determined in that they reflect the interests and values of society's dominant power structure. They also serve to build support for adoption of neoliberal policy prescriptions, paving the way for social transformation that further advances neoliberal interests. Neoliberalism's enabling myths—allowing the status quo to go unchallenged in addition to facilitating enactment of neoliberal policies—are highly effective because they get people to buy into both the worldview and

DOI: 10.4324/9781003160434-9

behavioral norms that underlie and sustain neoliberal institutions and policy prescriptions. Indeed, according to the neoliberal mythology, such norms are not merely reflective of what's normal; they are, more importantly, *natural conditions of humankind.*

Veblen, Galbraith, and the mythopoetic foundations of economics

Veblen

In writings from the end of the nineteenth century through the early decades of the twentieth century, Veblen's analyses of the mythology within any given society considered two basic overlapping functions: myths contribute to social continuity and material progress, but myths and ceremonial behaviors also maintain the status quo and prevailing power relations.

Social reproduction: social continuity and epistemic evolution

Contrary to the early descriptions of the Veblenian dichotomy (see Chapter 1 of this volume, by William Waller, for a closer examination), Veblen did not see myths or ceremonial impulses as inherently in conflict with industry, technology, or progress. Veblen (1906; 1908) compared the mythological systems of belief of non-Western and Western societies and found in many cases that the former, both historically and during his time, had surpassed the latter in complexity, metaphysical conceits, and evolutionary development. For Veblen (1906), "primitive" individuals shared with the individuals of Western civilization the natural state of idle curiosity and exploration of the unknown, albeit tempered by the surrounding cultural milieu and pragmatic necessities of their respective time period.[2]

Veblen (1908) noted that in non-Western, "primitive" societies, the development of the local epistemological set was based on lived experience that fit into a broader mythological structure reflecting the local cultural milieu. He also maintained that in such settled and peaceful societies, there was less likely to be a hierarchy rooted in invidious distinctions, less likelihood of property rights, and a higher probability of matriarchal lineage.[3] In these peaceful societies, the overarching mythological structure containing the local knowledge would focus on nurturance and growth. Living in accordance with nature was more likely than domination over nature, and the theistic system looser, tied to the living world (as opposed to fiat), and populated by many (mostly female) deities who were not hostile to humans. Veblen also noted that non-peaceful—"predatory"—societies would, by contrast, create monotheistic, male deities unconnected to specific phenomena. In addition, they were more likely to be patriarchal; more likely to treat nature as something to be controlled and harnessed rather than as something in which to live in accord; and the deity more likely to act punitively.

Veblen (1906) carefully noted, however, that these complex systems of mythology did not serve as a replacement for practical systems of knowledge—instead, the mythology of many non-Western societies existed alongside sophisticated systems of knowledge and served an entertainment purpose for the society rather than an epistemological one. Veblen found this to be especially true of more peaceful societies that did not have to rely on supernatural narratives to instigate the otherwise latent impulse to war. Early, non-Western societies' versions of the natural sciences were based on lived experiences and thus did not require the technological development of the laboratory—nature itself was the natural science laboratory. Moreover, the non-Western societies' natural science knowledge was born out of idle curiosity rather than pursuit of mastery, acquisition, or profit. "Testing" within non-Western natural science was born out of consistency of experience through living with nature without a general aim toward a practical end, though pragmatic discovery had its place. Knowledge developed by way of aimless, dialectical testing—unstandardized and largely consistent with the spiritual worldview of the society or of the individual, rather than with the results of other inquiry.

In *The Instinct of Workmanship*, Veblen (1914) noted that mythical beliefs entered into the habitual routines of the worker and thus into the evolution of technology, but were not necessarily influential in the application or development of technology; myths didn't contribute, but they also did not hinder. The damage of myths in the development of the industrial arts was limited; supernatural beliefs undermined workers' belief in themselves and in their own individual craft. As technology advanced and as the skill in applying that technology developed, the less the worker credited supernatural beliefs with their product and craft. The more advanced the technology and the greater the required technical skill, the more the supernatural forces once attributed to production became detached from the material world and were instead credited with influencing the worker's "initiative and self-direction"—the workmanship itself (Veblen 1914).

Even in the employment of magic, inanimate objects and tools did not contain or perform magical acts by themselves—it was the wielder of magic who channeled supernatural forces into these inanimate objects; without the magician and the supernatural incantations, the tools remained as lifeless as they ever were. Inanimate objects were thus not the source of magic, but merely instruments used temporarily to expedite magical effects. Inanimate objects or tools were epiphenomenal, ancillary to the magic worked. Veblen further noted that even natural phenomena such as weather, seasons, or fire were ascribed to the workings of a god, demon, or magic practitioner rather than imbued directly with supernatural powers or considerations. After all, Prometheus gave fire—an inanimate tool—to humans (Veblen 1914).

Veblen (1914) noted that if the worker were to attach mythos to the technical aspects of workmanship, then this attachment would indeed hinder the evolution and progress of technology; but it was not a usual practice for the worker to do so. Veblen contrasted the attachment of myth to mechanics against the attachment of myth to the natural world, where he argued that mythological interpretation had an indifferent impact on the development of understanding. To illustrate the difference, Veblen discussed the art of storytelling, noting that in most cultures, animas assigned to the natural world through plant or animal behavior were accepted more readily than animas imbued to tools or technical application. "Witness the relative barrenness of primitive folk-tales on this inanimate side, as compared with the exuberance of the myths and legends that interpret the life of plants and animals," wrote Veblen (1914, 75).

Veblen argued that scientists could benefit from the mythology surrounding the natural world by sparking creative thought and interest, while the non-animated application of the tools of their scientific trade left their objective findings on nature uncontaminated by folklore or myth. According to Veblen (1906), the science of his time marked the first application of the mechanistically causal and impersonal manners of thinking to the idle curiosity driving science inquiry. He also noted the mechanistic development of modern science using technological advances within the laboratory. For Veblen, this embrace of technology removed from the development of the natural sciences the purview of the lived experiences of all individuals, sequestering scientists and creating a clique of individuals with barriers to entry. The result was the development of a corpus of Western, natural science knowledge which was clinical, abstruse, and utilitarian.

According to Veblen, scientific inquiry driven by pursuit of practical ends did not advance knowledge. Moreover, vocational training in practical areas of study, such as law or business, is extrinsic and inhibitive to general and genuine scientific study. When disciplines (like economics) made the artificial reach to respectability by superimposing scientific jargon and methods on to their areas of study, the subjects lost meaning and their efforts became wasteful (Veblen 1906).

Veblen was specifically referencing the way in which natural sciences in the Western world began to gain legitimacy in societies previously dominated by religious belief. The accepted subjects initially considered as part of science—astrology and alchemy, for instance—do not exist (except as systems of belief to be studied) in academia today, but were initially considered serious subjects of study. The reason astrology and alchemy were originally taken seriously is that both subjects corresponded with the prevailing canons of truth and were adjacent to the ascendancy of status dictated by the religious socialization dominant at the time (Veblen 1900).

The saving grace of the modern, Western natural sciences of that time was that technology could not completely disabuse the scientist of their sense of wonder. As a result, the motivation of scientific inquiry remained as open and "idle" as that of non-Western societies. Curiosity without a specific objective or aim remained; practical uses were serendipitous. However, Veblen also pointed out that the standards of scientific inquiries—"canons of validity"—were shaped by both modern technology and cultural context; and Veblen made special note of the increasing influence of the former on the latter: "Hence men have learned to think in the terms in which the technological processes act" (Veblen 1906).

Status reproduction: maintenance of the status quo and power relations

Socialization is a powerful force. It digs the forward path for individuals; provides their measures of success; and serves as the standard against which inquiry is driven and knowledge is acquired. In other words, socialization and the established habits that grow out of it condition the individual toward confirmation bias, such that when that which confirms or correlates with what one already understands as truth is reached, the individual pushes no further and accepts what has been discovered. In addition, Veblen (1900) adds that individuals rely on habits that have previously served them well even when they undertake new and different activities.

However, Veblen (1900) also argues that the tendency toward confirmation bias can only exist within a society wherein the hierarchy and associated esteems of status are generally accepted as true and the highest rungs of the hierarchy are generally accepted as aspirational—the highest standard to which one can aspire. The hierarchy of status thus tacitly informs the individual's pursuits of inquiry and as such operates as a universalizing norm under which the individual acts and assimilates or discards new information. The hierarchy of status is thus a quasi-religious system, with settled truths and natural laws which are said to exist outside of and over any given society (Veblen 1900). An example of such an institutional setup is that of the military—heavily reliant on rank and ceremony—which valorizes imperial impulses and lethal force through an almost superstitious adherence to the chain of command and established rule.

The circumscription of social circles and their ordering in rank of respectability is mediated by consumption and ceremonial displays which—out of the reach of inferiors—further vests the irrefutable mythos with the naturalness of hierarchy. In Veblen's 1894 piece, "The Economic Theory of Woman's Dress," he comments on costuming upper-class women to display the conspicuous expense associated with apparel design and construction. The baldest example of this practice according to Veblen (1894) is the dress designed for ceremonial events, such as an evening gown, which is excessive in its expense but can only be worn once in polite society.

Within any social circle, the intra-reproduction of status continues through the adherence to long-established mythological rituals and ceremonies, even when that adherence—as a result of overall societal and technological change—culminates in a simulacrum of the original. Indeed, marriage rites serve as an example that Veblen uses to examine and discuss the ceremonies and myths constructed initially to preserve the configuration of social relations within a social circle, but that are later replicated throughout the whole of society (1899). He writes:

> It follows logically, as a matter of course, that if once the motions leading to a desired consummation have been rehearsed in the accredited form and

> sequence, the same substantial result will be attained as that produced by the process imitated.
>
> *(Veblen 1899)*

What is remarkable about this particular quote is that although Veblen is discussing marriage rituals, it could also apply to the practices engaged in by economists.

Veblen (1900) pointed out that when the foundations of a hierarchy consist of canons of truth animated by belief, it becomes all the more difficult for either superstition or material conditions to provide a countervailing force. Further, the more a given society buys into those generally accepted truths, the more entrenched that hierarchy and associated networks of power become. This analysis of status reproduction applies to the economics discipline as well.

The economics discipline's tendency toward myth can be traced to the classical economics that began in the late eighteenth century. The theoretical foundations created and assembled by the classicals are what Veblen (1898) refers to as "ceremonial adequacy." Built from a priori assumptions and speculative accounts of economic history, these theories slid toward an acceptable conclusion for that historical time. What emerged from the founders of the discipline were thus foundational principles, mechanisms by which markets worked conducive to the behavior expectations of the time. These foundational principles then transformed into what Veblen (1898) referred to as the "ceremonial canon of knowledge."

Veblen's analysis (1900) of Adam Smith's work points out that the internal mechanics of his theories appear conclusive and undeniable, with an internal causal sequence that is logically consistent and lends the overall analysis a sense of authority—of settled science. Veblen argues that this air of settled science is entirely ceremonial, that the overall frame of Smith's work is itself entirely teleological—an economic ouroboros—that bears only coincidental resemblance to material reality. The occasional coincidence, however, lends further credibility to the authority of the system. That coincidence of reality and theory was generalized and, in turn, formalized so that when material reality departed from theory, it was cast as an abnormal divergence.

A half-century before Milton Friedman would write his infamous "as if" paper justifying the use of unrealistic assumptions as metaphor, Veblen (1898) condemned what he called "the convenient use of metaphor" as contributing to the standardization, universalization, and canonization of the foundational principles set out by the classical economists. This reliance on assumptions and metaphor proved useful to the classicals as a heuristic device—an efficient system of shorthand—and, most of all, it saved them from the messiness of reality. Building up from those foundational principles and laws was also made easier by these accepted canons of truth, since new concepts and theories needed only to stick to the internal logic of the foundational concepts, rather than reflect the economy of the time.

With an internally consistent logic and specialized jargon, the economics discipline could then derive any required "ceremonially consistent formula … [via] the deductive method." The result, according to Veblen (1900, 379) was a nascent discipline with "ceremonial" legitimation—a discipline that that amounted, in reality, to "a taxonomic science." Moreover, Veblen marks this as the beginning of the discipline of economic mythology, upon which further mythological concepts, principles, and laws would be built, and with which the discipline's hierarchy and status would be maintained.

Galbraith

Veblen died just a couple of months shy of the Great Crash of 1929 (after already having lost money in the market). We can only speculate on what he might have thought of the economics discipline as that financial crisis amplified the already unfolding Great Depression and economists stubbornly stuck to their prevailing paradigm. However, John Kenneth Galbraith, who came to prominence in the 1950s and published consistently until shortly before his death in 2006, continued Veblen's line of thinking in his critique of economics as a "system of belief."

Power

According to Galbraith (1970), economics is a "system of belief" that cordons off acceptable and unacceptable doctrine. Moreover, its limits have political consequences. For example, Galbraith cites the refusal of economists at the start of the twentieth century to engage in theoretical discussion about the tendency toward monopoly. Refusal on the part of economists to incorporate that tendency into their theories of competition meant the political sphere also failed to enact policies or protections to limit the scope and power of monopolistic enterprises. In addition, the ideological bias of pre-Depression economics in favor of limited government served to constraint political intervention for social needs writ large. Since World War II, the system of belief within economics has likewise been cordoned around the theoretical lodestone of the neoclassical synthesis, and the only acceptable clergy have been its believers, who, of course, preach the theology of economics as scientific.

The neoclassical synthesis did not substantially change the dominant edifices of theory within the economics discipline. Instead, it merely made room for narrowly prescribed political intervention, primarily on the supply side of the economy. The conventional economic wisdom continued (and continues) to perpetuate the myth of scarcity, which further fueled (and fuels) the myth that production must continue unabetted—for how else might scarcity be ameliorated (Galbraith [1958] 1998)? The price mechanism—first presented in economic theory during the Victorian era, and so carefully explained, plotted, and mathematized in modern economics courses—perpetuates the myth that markets are passively responsive to internal logics and external shocks. The reality consists of firms acting to safeguard themselves from the vicissitudes of the market by securing inputs at desired prices (through a supply chain over which they seek to exert control) and selling final goods and services to consumers at prices determined administratively by means of a mark-up over the costs of production (designed to cover factor costs, provide for enterprise investment needs, and ensure a desired rate of return for shareholders) (Galbraith [1967] 2007).

At the heart of the mythology of economics is the individual (or individual household) who acts with complete autonomy, makes rational decisions, and exists in an atomistic bubble (Galbraith [1967] 2007). From this folkloric individual extend further myths, which sustain the internal logic of the economics discipline's system of belief. The strongest prevailing myth about the individual in economics—both before and after the Keynesian Revolution—is that of consumer sovereignty.

Galbraith describes the myth of consumer sovereignty as the myth of individual demand, which is held to be largely (with some acknowledgment to the persuasiveness of producers) independent from, and external to, supply. Galbraith also argues that the myth of consumer sovereignty is particularly dangerous as it imbues the individual with a false sense of agency. Moreover, consumer sovereignty is a necessary myth for the continued functioning of capitalism. The people of the United States, so heavily socialized with the ideals of freedom and the power of democracy, would not participate willingly in a system in which they, their tastes and preferences, and their economic choices were so obviously managed (Galbraith [1967] 2007). It is a myth taught in every principles of economics course, securing its place in the wider culture.

With consumer sovereignty, consumers control the market, and the market, in turn, controls corporate interests, subordinating corporate efforts to maximize profit to the needs and desires of consumers. With consumer sovereignty, power relationships don't factor into economic activity (Galbraith [1967] 2007). Indeed, the greatest trick economics ever pulled was convincing the world that power doesn't exist. By excluding power from the discipline, economics was and is able to contribute to the critical social replication of the enabling myth of indifferent free markets, an invention that sustains the passive, producer-centric understanding of capitalism.

Galbraith notes that teaching the myth of consumer sovereignty has the long-term adverse consequence of creating cognitive dissonance in a world where power actually rests with producers; that dissonance undermines the social sciences and education writ large. At the same time, consumer sovereignty acts as a convenient protection for industry; for example, under consumer sovereignty, producers are not to blame for not offering climate-friendly options to the consumer because after all, producers are just passively responding to what consumers want. The exclusion of power from economics is not necessarily an overt or deliberate omission—economists do not gather to conspire to leave power outside their classrooms or scholarly work. Instead (as Veblen might note) the status reproduction within economics suffocates any chance of epistemic evolution; the culture of the discipline does the excluding on its own (Galbraith [1967] 2007).

Galbraith (1973, 218–220) identifies four mechanisms by which the enabling myths of economics are replicated and sustained. The first is the standard economics curriculum taught in most universities. Economics courses, especially the introductory courses taught to fulfill students' general education needs across a wide range of majors, continue to emphasize markets as passively reacting, according to their own internal logic, to externals shocks. From this paradigmatic frame, which is not itself examined, markets appear amoral and their machinations mechanical. There remains no discussion of power relationships in the standard economics curriculum.

The second mechanism is education writ large. Public school systems in the United States are consistently underfunded and, when cutbacks are necessary, arts programs and other curricula not deemed vital to the generation of income are the first to get squeezed. At the university level, the same scenario is played out, but in much starker terms. Those majors which appear pragmatic and in service to an easily recognizable professional path—such as business, law, medicine, and engineering—are held in higher esteem by administrators and parents alike. Subjects that are more self-fulfilling than professionally useful are consistently framed as an unnecessary extravagance. The result is a university system transformed into vocational training in service to the interests of capitalism; the bifurcation of education into useful and wasteful categories feeds the enabling myths of capitalism.

The other mechanisms identified by Galbraith as perpetuating enabling myths involve advertising and public policy, respectively. In particular, the third mechanism is passive acquiescence to ever-encroaching advertising efforts. Galbraith (1973, 219) writes: "Anyone who without thought yields to persuasion as to purchases, behavior or belief yields something of himself [*sic*] to the purposes of the [corporate] planning system" that promotes capitalism's dominant enabling myths. The final mechanism is public policy: specifically, policies that emerge from the cajoling of professional advocates—lawyers and lobbyists—who work on behalf of corporate interests.

For Galbraith, the core enabling belief outside academia is that what benefits capitalism also benefits the individual: the notion that individual needs are best met when capitalism, which is considered to be a self-correcting system, is secure and functioning according to plan. As such, individuals are believed best-served in a world where both consumption and production are, as a consequence of the price system, reliably growing and in balance. This core enabling myth is buttressed by what Galbraith calls (1973, 217) "convenient social virtue"—those virtues, such as relentless hard work and choosing to pursue income-generating activities over leisure pursuits, are valorized and put into the service of capitalism. In fact, the core enabling myth of the beneficence of capitalism serves as a veil that shrouds the identity of those (corporate leaders, in particular) to whom the spoils of these virtues actually redound (Galbraith 1973).

There is endless variety in the ways and means with which corporations perpetuate their myths and exercise their power (Galbraith 1977). Through marketing, advertising, and carefully produced and placed news releases, corporations shape consumer perceptions, manufacture wants, and manipulate consumer demand. Corporations also manipulate markets by administering prices and manipulating inventory by means including stockpiling and creating illusions of shortage, scarcity, or limited offers (Galbraith 1977).

During turbulent economic times, corporations have an emergency cord to pull: the health of "the economy" and the emotional state of "the markets." Politicians are fearful of any policy or government action that might tip the economy into recession or make the stock market volatile. This perpetual paranoia is largely the result of a different myth repeatedly reported in corporate media—that the stock market is the oracle of the economic health of the nation.

Corporations are not the victims of clumsy or ill-informed government interference. To the contrary, corporations possess and execute considerable leverage and discipline over politicians. Corporations rely on the state for their continued existence, but they also control the levers of power of the state, by lobbying elected officials and contributing to candidates for public office (and re-election efforts are a constant background hum for politicians, even from their first days in office). These efforts ensure access and influence for the corporation to the political process and decision-making, smoothing out wrinkles and greasing wheels to ensure continued corporate success and growth (Galbraith 1977).

Corporate myths enable corporate power. Those myths—of corporate servitude to the consumer, of corporations as beneficent contributors to the public good, and of the private sector as a victim of feckless political machinations—conceal the direct power corporations have in the operations of the state. This is not to say that the public wholly trust corporate decrees or activities; there exists (as mentioned above in the discussion of consumer sovereignty) a latent cognitive dissonance spawned by the corporate mythological universe. And in that suspicion, dissatisfaction, and unease with corporate socialization lies the potential for constructive change (Galbraith 1977).

The dismantling of enabling myths

To even envision a society where all might flourish, one must first dismantle the enabling myths that keep the current system in place. This is no simple feat. Enabling myths work because they emerge from voices of authority—from those currently seated in power and who have a vested interest in remaining there. Enabling myths are also comforting; they create a world of knowns and clear paths for action, rather than the uncertainty that actually surrounds critical decisions that need be made as a society evolves.

Galbraith (1973) believed the university could play a significant role in undermining the current system. Higher education that teaches students to challenge conventional thinking would go a long way toward dismantling the conventional enabling myths required to keep the gears of capitalism going. At a minimum, Galbraith ([1967] 2007) argued that universities should not transform into willing partners for the capitalist system by offering a supply of fresh recruits trained for positions in the technocracy or managerial tracks, nor should they become further entangled with corporations by forming strategic partnerships that provide business funding for research and graduate studies that suit specific corporate needs. As early as 1973, Galbraith explained that resistance to prevailing beliefs emerges from critique—including criticism of the economics curriculum as it is currently taught, disapproval of the demeaning of the arts and humanities and exaltation of hard sciences and "professional" vocational training, and rejection of ever-enlarging, ever-encroaching business marketing efforts (Galbraith 1973, 218–220).

According to Galbraith (1973), the power relationships that keep the current system in place are rooted in belief, and to change or replace the current system our efforts should aim to challenge those beliefs—that is, to unmask the enabling myths—rather than to attack the system itself. Moreover, the manner in which belief systems are held in place and replicated differs between countries and is primarily predicated on the type of political system in place. Dictatorships, for instance, use coercion and force, while Western-style liberalism uses Enlightenment-type assurances that responsible and well-informed adults are making reasonable, scientifically based decisions and are not, in fact, ignoring or debasing beliefs contrary to those which support capitalism.

In countries such as the United States, the difficulty in dismantling the social virtues and enabling myths of the present system begins with the assumption that we cannot be fooled—that our agency and our wits cannot be subsumed or subordinated to the dictates of any system. People at the bottom of the financial hierarchy, who see the machinations of capitalism and the state bearing down on them daily, are the most likely to accept that the system is flawed and that the virtues that allegedly allow one to climb up from the bottom rungs lack meaning. Unfortunately, without income and power, those individuals lack the gravitas for an audience; moreover, material reality and the relentless pursuit of the basic needs of life already exhaust them. In addition, as individuals ascend the financial hierarchy, more needs appear on the horizon and add—rather than ease—material pressures (Galbraith 1973).

To counter the current system, the prevailing myths must be dismantled and the mechanisms by which they have historically been socially replicated must be exposed. In addition, the human and communal needs that the current system ignores or neglects must be front and center in the discussion of what should come next (Galbraith [1967] 2007). If we are able to dismantle the enabling myths of capitalism, then people would be freed from the collective effort required to keep capitalism—a social structure prone to crisis—afloat. Freed from that collective effort to sustain what Galbraith refers to as the capitalist "planning system," people would then be able to thrive as individuals and charge the state with the welfare of all its constituents (Galbraith 1973).

The dismantling of enabling myths is made somewhat easier by the incongruity of those myths with the lived experience and material reality of individuals. The more inequality, financial precarity, environmental degradation, incarceration, imperial militarism, and cultural malaise produced by capitalism, the flimsier the enabling myths seem. The starker reality grows, the more transparent the enabling myths become (Galbraith 1973).

Dugger's analysis of myths in the time of neoliberalism

Dugger, a prominent contemporary institutionalist, began his career in the mid-1970s, just as neoliberalism began to take hold in the United States. His analysis of enabling myths identifies two basic types: those that blame some omnipotent, uncontrollable force for socioeconomic outcomes, and those that blame the individual for her own socioeconomic outcomes. The uncontrollable force might take the form of destiny, government, the generic "they/them," or that seemingly autonomous and natural constellation called "the market." In fact, the omnipotence of the market is the prevailing enabling myth of this first type: at its heart is the notion that the market—a non-human and natural force of nature—makes decisions blindly, but not arbitrarily, based on the contribution of an individual or firm to that other mythical force, the economy. The only human that is ever to blame in the totality of all of these myths is the individual worker or consumer; all other blame is attributed to the twists and turns of fate (Dugger 1987; 1989a). The myth of the omnipotent market masks the individual responsibility of those in positions of power, while the responsibility placed on workers and consumers masks the responsibility of institutions.

Dugger uses the adjective "enabling" when discussing the myths that support capitalism because the primary purpose of those myths is to enable capitalism to persist despite the grotesqueries it produces. The omnipotent myth of the market as a natural force sustains capitalism, just as it also sustains the second-order agent-centric myths of meritocracy and individualism (Dugger 1989b). The enabling myth of individual responsibility reinforces the enabling myth that has been a constant throughout all stages of capitalism: that people in poverty deserve to be there (Dugger and Sherman 2000).

The omnipotent

The myth of the market as a force of nature, unencumbered by the considerations of the people within it and following only the amoral course of its own logic, is the dominant omnipotent myth of capitalism writ large (Dugger 1989a). This myth is reinforced by the standard university economics curriculum. Indeed, many of the core principles of the economics discipline are entirely mythical and supportive of fictive market spontaneity, including the positive/normative distinction, the "natural" rate of unemployment, the marginal productivity of wages, and Adam Smith's invisible hand. Say's Law states that markets adjust automatically; an imbalance in production within one market is said to cause an adjustment in a related market that brings the original market back to balance: disruptions in production—whether surpluses or shortages—are thus temporary and will smooth over time.

The same logic of Say's Law applies to markets involving people as well as goods: if an individual is unemployed for an extended period of time, it is the result of the individual failing to adapt to a changing labor market. According to conventional economics, the surplus of workers in one market is temporary because it will be met with an adjustment in another job market. Although the Great Depression revealed on a large scale Say's Law as a myth, it remains part of the general economics curriculum in spirit if not in name (Dugger and Sherman 2000; Galbraith [1958] 1998). While supply and demand do interact and determine the market clearing price, such interaction only occurs at the most superficial level. The forces that push and pull on supply and demand are determined by power relationships and serve the interests of those with power (Dugger 1987).

By contrast, institutional economists are market atheists; we do not believe in the supernatural forces—or spontaneous ordering—of markets or price systems (Dugger 1989a). The market is not an autonomous, uninterested force. Rather, it is the culmination of decisions of those with power and authority, combined with technological developments (which are also funded and developed by those with power, authority, and means) against the resistance of those who have no power or authority and therefore are subject to exploitation. The resistance by those without power or authority is tempered and suffocated by the market myth, which suggests that one cannot argue against the market system's logical machinations (Dugger 1987). Divisions within the bottom strata of society further diminish the potential of social redress for disenfranchised groups by weakening social bonds and attempts at collective action (Dugger and Sherman 2000).

The reality, as Dugger (1989a) clearly lays out, is that the market is the outcome, not the genesis, of existing social relations, power differentials, class positioning, and political decisions. Markets are not organic; they do not represent a spontaneous ordering of exchange. Rather, they are the result of processes instituted by the political decisions of those in power (Dugger 1989b). As well, market outcomes are cumulative in nature; those at the top of the financial hierarchy possess the means to influence further political decisions that allow the market to persist (Dugger 1989b). Moreover, enabling myths are backed by the power of the state, which maintains the monopoly on force, upholds property rights, and is dependent upon the coffers of those at the top of the financial hierarchy (Dugger 2000).

The market myth veils the political decisions and private maneuverings that are the real determinants of market outcomes (Dugger 1987). Framing the market as a natural occurrence, which is assumed to generate a process that cannot be stopped, absolves those with the power to make political changes of any responsibility for its failings (Dugger 1989b). If market outcomes are inevitable and without prejudice, then anyone with power is absolved of its machinations

(Dugger 1989b). This myth of the market as a naturally occurring force reinforces its immutability and casts attempts at market corrections as foolhardy and futile (Dugger 1989b). That the market myth so completely veils the levers of power is what makes this particular enabling myth so dangerous. Veiled power is unaccountable power; it is tyranny (Dugger 1989a).

The individual

If the market is a natural force as the omnipotent enabling myth instructs, then it is not subject to the social conditioning of racist and sexist impulses; according to this logic, market outcomes are race and sex neutral (Dugger 1987). Discrimination in any form, be it sexism, racism, or any other -ism, is composed of a set of enabling myths which justify power imbalances as of no ultimate consequence; the enabling myth of meritocracy negates the impact of discrimination even if it were admitted. Instead, individuals are instructed and socialized that they and only they are to blame for their economic precarity, their marginalized positions in society (Dugger 1994). The enabling myth of individual responsibility deftly neutralizes arguments of racism and sexism (Dugger 1987).

The inequality produced by capitalism is justified through enabling myths that are tacit expressions of a belief in natural supremacy based on some demographic, such as sex, gender, race, ethnicity, sexual orientation, or class. Rather than overt expressions of hate for any particular group, enabling myths are embedded in the institutions of society and are reinforced through what Dugger refers to as the "vicious cycle" of cumulative causation. Those at the top of the financial hierarchy have access to the best education, health care, and early childhood development care, so early in life they have advantages that will be carried into adulthood. Those at the bottom of the financial hierarchy go to the local, often underfunded, schools (which rely on the proceeds from a lower property-tax base), might not have access to health care (which depends on their parents' employment), and might not have access to early childhood development care, which is not provided by government in the United States. From the start, children from low-income families are set on a path to economic insecurity based on what they lack; then, when they later lack resources of their own, the original enabling myths seem reaffirmed and are strengthened. Inequality is thus a path-dependent process, established early in life (Dugger 2000).

Accordingly, those at the top of the financial hierarchy need to feel no guilt or shame—the market rewarded them according to the natural, Newtonian-like mechanics of the market in this most efficient and beneficent system of capitalism. Inequality, exploitation, and discrimination are thus turned into myths of projected blame and are framed as convenient excuses for those who lack the work ethic, ambition, or intellect to succeed (Dugger 1989b).

There is, in fact, a causal link between enabling myths and inequality: enabling myths justify inequality, and inequality further distances people in their social relationships. That increasing social distance between the different groups of people who find themselves at the bottom of the financial hierarchy—people who, collectively, represent the majority of society—allows the amplification and deeper embedding of enabling myths into culture (Dugger 1994). For example, Dugger (2000) outlines six enabling myths which have become deeply embedded into the institutions of the United States: class, race, sexism, jingoism, homophobia, and anti-Semitism.

Dugger (2000) also identifies four mechanisms by which those enabling myths work: double standards, blind spots, stereotypes, and "otherness." Double standards become strikingly obvious when contrasting the ways in which police interact with white individuals versus people of color. Or in the way that women are critiqued as shrill, bitchy, or cut-throat, when the same qualities in men are heralded as evidence of ambition or decisiveness. Blind spots are essentially spurious correlations erroneously credited: the wealthy white man believes hard work and dedication rewarded him fairly, rather than crediting his financial success to initial advantages or privilege. Stereotypes bestow the benefit of the doubt to those in the top social strata and shadows of doubt to those below. Otherness is embodied in the adage "history is written by the victors"—the lives, struggles, and contributions of the underlying population are not taught, celebrated, or even documented (Dugger 2000). Otherness might manifest in a variety of ways, such as emulation or scapegoating, both of which perform important social control functions—if those in the lower social strata have something to which they aspire and some other group to blame when those aspirations remain unmet, then the enabling myths remain instructive and institutionalized (Dugger and Sherman 2000).[4]

Both kinds of enabling myths—the myth of individual responsibility and the myth of the market as a natural force—reinforce the narrative that there is nothing that can be done or need be done at a systemic level. Accordingly, the only human who is to blame for exploitation or poverty is the individual herself (Dugger 1987). This framing allows the government and society writ large to shirk their responsibilities in social reproduction and the progression of civilization.

For example, the lack of universally available childcare, the lack of family leave, the general lack of a social safety net, and, of course, the absence of a broader social support system are all the result of the enabling myths surrounding individual responsibility and the post–World War II mythology of the nuclear family unit. The enabling myth of the nuclear family as the social ideal is one that hinges on the related enabling myth of (biological) motherhood as the most important nurturance and care relationship in a young person's life, what Dugger (1994, 11) refers to as the "myth of exclusive maternal care." The enabling myth of the need for a woman to be "supermom" means that young people and adults with problems that were the result of unmet needs during childhood have only their mothers to blame, which relieves the state of both the expense and responsibility in social reproduction: problematic children who become problematic adults have only themselves to blame, but failing that, they can blame their irresponsible mothers (Dugger 1994).

Neoliberalism: myth versus mechanics

Dugger's framework

The difference between the rhetoric and reality of neoliberalism can be measured by the efficacy and size of what Dugger termed "enabling myths." Indeed, Dugger's work on enabling myths is foundational to understanding the mythos of neoliberalism—and the fact that much of his work was conducted in the midst of the rising momentum of neoliberalism indicates a remarkable perspicacity. By applying the *omnipotent* and *individual* mythology distinction of Dugger's framework, we are able to see not only the separate qualities and processes of these two categories of enabling myths, but also how these mythopoetic types interact and reinforce one another within neoliberalism.

Neoliberalism is itself an omnipotent myth. It is a myth of systemic force propelled by its own internal logic, autonomous and indifferent to the people within it. The neoliberal market is simply the latest incarnation of the omnipotent myth of the market as a natural force.

Neoliberalism embodies an ideological shift in the purpose of the state: from one that ensures full employment and protects its citizens against the exigencies of the market, to one that ensures individual responsibility and protects the market itself. The neoliberal narrative—the mythological story of its own omnipotence—is woven from enabling myths that are essential not only to its continued survival, but also to its assistance from the polity and to its popular, cultural support.

The neoliberal narrative consists of three core enabling myths that distinguish it from earlier stages of capitalism: privatization of currently state-provided goods and services; deregulation of industry; and retrenchment of the welfare state. The enabling myths of privatization and deregulation are themselves omnipotent, auxiliary myths, which have evolved and adapted under neoliberalism to support the overarching, omnipotent myth of the neoliberal market as an organic force. Accordingly, privatization and deregulation are each neutral and autonomous systemic processes that ensure the continued indifferent and independent operation of the neoliberal market as a whole. Advocates of privatization and deregulation both argue that erecting a wall between government and business creates a more efficient (albeit mythical) neoliberal market, while private industry is brought to heel by natural market forces. The interactive reciprocity between these omnipotent myths further institutionalizes the functioning and mythos of each—and simultaneously insulates them from any challenges to the system.

The neoliberal market is constituted entirely of the aggregation of mythical autonomous individuals, and as such it remains unconstrained by any one individual or group; there is no power which might—or even could—exploit it according to its own omnipotent mythology. The myth of the individual and individualism reinforces the omnipotence of neoliberalism, while the autonomous and apolitical neoliberal market ideology reinforces the complete agency of the individual. Indeed, the retrenchment of the welfare state, specifically through attrition or elimination of social programs designed to help the poor, erects a wall between the individual and the state, which "frees" the individual to exercise her correspondingly mythical agency and decide for herself how to navigate the omnipotent neoliberal market system. Within neoliberalism, the locus of control is the mythical, autonomous individual—freely exercising her agency within the mythical omnipotent neoliberal market system.

Galbraith's practical application

The "disguising myth" of the state, as Galbraith (1973, 232) calls it, is one which suggests that the needs of producers are not prioritized over the needs of individuals. Under neoliberalism, the underlying (actual) priority remains the same, but the belief has transformed. Given the access to information through the Internet generally and the 24-hour news cycle specifically, it is no surprise that the priorities of the state can no longer remain as veiled as in the past. Instead, the prevailing belief which continues to support corporate interests writ large is that the health of the economy is imperative to the health of the general public. Instead of attempting to obfuscate the power that corporate interests have over the state, the enabling myth suggests that it is in the individual's best interest that this is so.

Galbraith discusses the myth that the health of the economy resides in protecting, at highest priority, the supply side of the economy. The importance of production in capitalist society resides in generating income (jobs!) for the people employed by capitalists—not in the survival per se of any particular capitalist endeavor. Moreover, the mythical importance of production naturally tilts the economy toward *overproduction*, and it is in the attempts to eliminate that overproduction that we see corporate manipulation of consumers, rampant and environmentally unsustainable consumerism, and use of political pressure to stave off the stagnation looming at the horizon of overproduction (Galbraith [1958] 1998).

Corporations had and continue to have direct access to the legislative and executive branches of government; any public policies as well as any admonitions about adherence to social norms or shared ethics that emerge from these sources should automatically be assumed to serve the interests of capital rather than those of the public (Galbraith 1973). During elections, corporations can easily arrange for unlimited amounts of funds to flow to or against candidates through political action committees and events sponsorship. Once an official is in office, corporations maintain access to politicians through lobbying efforts—indeed, more money is spent on the latter than the former by orders of magnitude (Galbraith 1977; Wrenn 2020). Politicians are held hostage by corporations when the economy appears headed toward a contraction or crisis, and the ransom is always paid in the form of government contracts, tax breaks or credits, and, when necessary, government bailouts (Galbraith 1977; Wrenn 2020).

Writing in the mid-1970s, Galbraith (1973) had hope that change was on the horizon; he found encouragement in rejection by the young of the conventions of the day and in their skepticism of the established order. Nearly 50 years have passed since the initial publication of that work, and instead we've endured a half-century of the neoliberal project. Galbraith was not Panglossian in his hope, however; he recognized that challenging the beliefs of the planning system involves an uphill battle to expose the power relationships that perpetuate those beliefs as well as the mechanisms by which society's powerful institutions operate. In addition, the general public lacked an imagination of possibilities—of other, more humane and equitable ways of organizing the economy and society. These are the challenges we have yet to meet in the intervening decades.

Veblen's socialization practices and processes

According to Veblen, social myths serve two essential purposes in reproducing a society: to explain and to teach. In early human civilizations, myths helped explain natural phenomena before humans had the scientific apparatuses and knowledge to explain why those natural phenomena occurred. Myths also served the function of warnings against specific behaviors—cautionary tales, for example, about the perils of hubris or the virtues of honesty. As societies grow and knowledge of the natural world accumulates, technology grows alongside it and mythology becomes a less useful tool, except in seemingly complex systems.

As witness to the acceleration of technological advance and material intensification at the start of the twentieth century, Veblen observed and postulated that the growing mystification in increasingly complex production processes would sever the connection for consumers between workers and the material objects they produce—that is, the human element in production would be lost. Indeed, as material progress has continued to amplify since Veblen's time, so too has the overall complexity of capitalism. With greater complexity comes less transparency and individuals slip further out of touch with the totality. This disrupted orientation grows as capitalism evolves and mystification thus deepens: what was not known in the material production of objects in the early stages of capitalism has grown into a complete disconnection with the way in which evermore abstract markets for intangible assets operate within this latest stage of capitalism called neoliberalism (Wrenn 2014). Mystification fertilizes and nurtures mythology, and when it is the economic system that is mystifying, the mythology of its machinations and its operators enlarges and further embeds.

Neoliberal socialization processes teach the neoliberal market myth and the myth of the superiority of the individual. Through socialization, neoliberalism reinforces individual responsibility: each individual should be accountable only to herself. Under neoliberalism, society is thus comprised entirely and solely of self-interested, atomistic individuals seeking to forward their own agendas.

The emphasis on individual accountability and responsibility naturally segues into the power of the individual acting alone (Wrenn 2015). Within neoliberalism, agents are taught not just the ethos of individual responsibility, but also—indeed, more importantly—that they are the drivers of destiny. Within neoliberalism, the individual can, through the democratic process (via votes or money), determine the structure, composition, and path of the state. Individuals acting alone, however, have no power over systemic forces. Therefore, according to the internal logic of the neoliberal mythological set, there is no locus of power which might be blamed for system failings. The myth of the individual in neoliberalism thus reproduces and further entrenches hierarchy and status.

As the mystification of neoliberalism adapts and assimilates existing and new institutions into its greater mythical totality, individuals become increasingly disconnected from one another, their social relationships, and their old social structures.[5] That the omnipotent neoliberal myth answers to no one and that the individual stands completely alone and alienated from any greater social safety net or means of recourse, compels her to create social moorings and continuity through investment in the seemingly natural order of the socioeconomic hierarchy of neoliberalism. As a result, Veblen's conclusions—of the natural law of hierarchy becoming more difficult and irrefutable the more it is rooted in foundations which are animated by belief—thus become all the more ominous.

Conclusion

Veblen's critique of the mythology of economics remains painfully relevant. Out of convenient analytical metaphor grows myth, and out of myth grows methodology that remains, at its core, committed to the "ceremony of settled science" of the late eighteenth and nineteenth centuries. Over the course of the twentieth century, economics refined its internal logic with greater, more specialized jargon, which has only further canonized its teleology.

Galbraith's exposition of economics as a system of belief helps to encapsulate the macrocosm of the mythology of the discipline, while his methodical examination of its foundational myths—including scarcity, consumer sovereignty, and the passive price mechanism—reveal their shakiness. By exposing this system of belief, Galbraith demonstrates the complicity of the economics discipline in the exclusion, and thus veiling, of power within capitalism—what he called the discipline's disguising myth.

Dugger expands and elucidates the connection between the mythology of the economics discipline and Galbraith's disguising myth of power within capitalism. Power relationships more accurately define the economies of the Western world than does the current (which is also the past) general economics curriculum. The hidden nature of these power relationships, Dugger shows, reinforces the omnipotent myth of the market as a spontaneous and dispassionate systemic force.

The myths that encompass and enable neoliberalism cannot be understood without Veblen's socialization practices, Galbraith's practical application, and Dugger's framework of mythological types. The overarching myth of neoliberalism as humanity's best hope in resource allocation is supported by the core myth of the market as a naturally occurring phenomenon.[6] The omnipotent neoliberal mythology—which shapes US (and other Western) institutions, embeds itself in our socialization practices, and becomes codified through the ancillary myths of deregulation, privatization, and the retrenchment of the welfare state—is based, at its core, on the myth of individualism.

The growth of corporate power feeds the assertion of the myths about markets and individualism through direct influence within the political sphere; that growth also further entrenches the myth of neoliberalism as the crowning human achievement in resource allocation and efficiency. In addition, mystification produces and promulgates the supporting myths that maintain the social continuity and epistemic evolution in the social reproduction of neoliberalism. Within neoliberalism, our mythological cosmos does not exist alongside our practical and material realities; instead, the mythology of neoliberalism wraps around our practical and material realities, shifting focus from the omnipotent mythological forces that (we are socialized to believe) cannot and should not be controlled, to the individual with her mythological agency and accountability.

Enabling myths are not simply swallowed by a gullible, uneducated public; enabling myths are so deeply ingrained in our institutions that they remain hidden. The endurance of enabling myths speaks to their power, but not to their invincibility. The enabling myths of neoliberalism are ultimately betrayed by their contradictions. The corporate extortion of the political sphere, allegedly motivated by concerns about the health of the economy, unmasks the lie of neoliberalism's omnipotence. The absurdity of the scale of inequality reveals the incongruity between the neoliberal myth of individualism and material circumstance. The persistence of economic crises undermines the sterile, chimerical curriculum of economics. Institutionalists bear the solemn, and at times quixotic, responsibility of myth busting.

Acknowledgments

The author would like to extend her thanks to the editor of this volume, Charles Whalen, and to Bill Waller and Janice Peterson for all of their helpful comments.

Notes

1 In particular, I refer above to what many call "original" institutional economics, which is rooted in the work of Thorstein Veblen and John R. Commons and has continued through the work of more recent economists including John Kenneth Galbraith, William Dugger, Anne Mayhew, and other members of the Association for Evolutionary Economics.

2 Veblen (1906) noted that the technological progression in early societies was usually less interesting and dramatic than their mythical system, but both elements of society nevertheless existed alongside each other.

3 Jennings (1998) and Camic (2020) both suggest Veblen and his contemporaries did not have substantial evidence for his remarks about matriarchal lineage.

4 See Myrdal's (1944) *American Dilemma* for a treatise on scapegoating.
5 This process of disconnection is what Polanyi (1944) termed "disembedding."
6 See, for example, Margaret Thatcher's (1997) insistence that "there is no alternative," not only to the Conservative Party, but also to market-oriented (neoliberal) policies, which, she argues, are grounded in "the basic truths" about markets—and human nature.

References

Camic, Charles. 2020. *Veblen: The Making of an Economist Who Unmade Economics*. Cambridge, MA: Harvard University Press.

Dugger, William M. 1987. "Corporate Hegemony and Market Mythology." *Challenge* 29 (6): 55–58. https://doi.org/10.1080/05775132.1987.11471136

———. editor. 1989a. *Radical Institutionalism: Contemporary Voices*. New York: Greenwood Press.

———. 1989b. "Instituted Process and Enabling Myth: The Two Faces of the Market." *Journal of Economic Issues* 23 (2): 607–615. https://doi.org/10.1080/00213624.1989.11504927

———. 1994. "Institutionalism and Feminism." In *The Economic Status of Women Under Capitalism*, edited by Janice Peterson and Doug Brown, 3–18. Aldershot, UK: Edward Elgar.

———. 2000. "Deception and Inequality: The Enabling Myth Concept." In *Capitalism, Socialism, and Radical Political Economy: Essays in Honor of Howard J. Sherman*, edited by Robert Pollin, 66–80. Aldershot, UK: Edward Elgar.

Dugger, William M. and Howard J. Sherman. 2000. *Reclaiming Evolution: A Dialogue between Marxism and Institutionalism on Social Change*. London: Routledge. https://doi.org/10.4324/9780203160589

Galbraith, John Kenneth. (1958) 1998. *The Affluent Society*. Fortieth Anniversary Edition. New York: Houghton Mifflin.

———. (1967) 2007. *The New Industrial State*. Princeton, NJ: Princeton University Press. https://doi.org/10.1515/9781400873180

———. 1970. "Economics as a System of Belief." *American Economic Review* 60 (2): 469–478.

———. 1973. *Economics and the Public Purpose*. Boston, MA: Houghton Mifflin.

———. 1977. *The Age of Uncertainty*. Boston, MA: Houghton Mifflin.

Jennings, Ann. 1998. "Veblen's Feminism in Historical Perspective." In *The Founding of Institutional Economics*, edited by Warren J. Samuels, 201–233. London: Routledge. https://doi.org/10.4324/9780203021927-17

Myrdal, Gunnar. 1944. *An American Dilemma*. New York: Harper and Brothers.

Polanyi, Karl. 1944. *The Great Transformation*. New York: Farrar and Rinehart.

Thatcher, Margaret. 1997. "The Boneless Wonder of New Labour." *Daily Telegraph* 1 April 1997.

Veblen, Thorstein. 1894. "The Economic Theory of Woman's Dress." *Popular Science Monthly* 46 (2): 198–205.

———. 1898. "Why is Economics Not an Evolutionary Science?" *Quarterly Journal of Economics* 12 (4): 373–397. https://doi.org/10.2307/1882952

———. 1899. "The Barbarian Status of Women." *American Journal of Sociology* 4 (4): 503–514. https://doi.org/10.1086/210824

——— 1900. "The Preconceptions of Economic Science." *Quarterly Journal of Economics* 14 (2): 240–269. https://doi.org/10.2307/1883770

———. 1906. "The Place of Science in Modern Civilization." *American Journal of Sociology* 11 (5): 585–609. https://doi.org/10.1086/211429

———. 1908. "The Evolution of the Scientific Point of View." *University of California Chronicle* 10 (4): 395–416.

———. 1914. *The Instinct of Workmanship and the State of the Industrial Arts*. New York: Macmillan.

Wrenn, Mary V. 2014. "The Social Ontology of Fear and Neoliberalism." *Review of Social Economy* 72 (3): 337–353. https://doi.org/10.1080/00346764.2014.927726

———. 2015. "Agency and Neoliberalism." *Cambridge Journal of Economics* 39 (5): 1231–1243.

———. 2020. "On Veblenian Waste and Polanyian Protective Responses: Evidence from the United States." *Panoeconomicus* 67 (4): 449–464. https://doi.org/10.2298/pan170925002w

10

STORYTELLING AND INSTITUTIONAL CHANGE

The power and pitfalls of economic narratives

Charles J. Whalen

Introduction

Nearly a half-century ago, heterodox economist Benjamin Ward (1972, 179) expressed the mainstream economists' view of storytelling as follows:

> Storytelling is the output of the soft parts of economics. It is not taken seriously, in the sense that a formalist-positivist [aka mainstream economist] believes that the only parts of storytelling that are really a part of economics are the parts that can be formalized into [a] mathematical-statistical framework.

A decade later, Deirdre McCloskey (1983, 505), also critical of the mainstream on stories, made a similar observation: "When engaging in verbal economics we are more or less loose, it is said, taking literary license with our 'story;' but when we do mathematics we put away childish things." Although both Ward and McCloskey opposed such mainstream thinking and held out hope for greater attention to, and appreciation of, storytelling in economics, it's also clear that the profession has remained obsessed with mathematical models and quantitative techniques, often at the expense of shedding better light on economic reality, even in the aftermath of the global financial crisis of 2007–2009.

In the past few years, however, there has been a flurry of interest, across academic disciplines, in the importance of stories. A common thread of that recent research, including some within economics, is a heightened awareness of the power of *narrative* as a form of communication and persuasion.[1] This chapter examines the nature and role of storytelling in institutional economics, a school of thought long associated with use of narratives and whose practitioners

DOI: 10.4324/9781003160434-10

in recent decades have often expressed skepticism toward mathematical models and methods.

The discussion that follows is divided into six parts. The first section places storytelling in the context of the goals and methods of economics. Then three sections consider, in turn, the attention given to storytelling in institutionalist research on economic methodology, theory, and real-world cases of institutional change. The final two sections, taken together, provide an overview of the power and pitfalls of economic narratives, a short discussion of a strategy for improving storytelling robustness, and a brief conclusion.

Storytelling in economics

Placing storytelling in the context of the goals and methods of economics isn't easy. There's a huge risk of becoming either swept away by the swift current of literature on methods or stuck in a weedy tributary such as rhetoric or the philosophy of science. The challenge is all the greater when one considers the definition of economics attributed long ago to Jacob Viner: "Economics is what economists do."[2]

As it turns out, though, Viner's definition can actually serve as a useful starting point. Economists do lots of different types of work—in fact, there's extraordinary variety in the *what*, *how*, and *why* of economics. So, instead of looking at storytelling through the lens of a kaleidoscope, my aim here is to place storytelling in the context of the science of economics as I see it.

The definition and purpose of economics

I borrow my preferred definition of economics from institutionalist Allan Gruchy (1987, 21), who described economics as "the science of social provisioning." Such a science includes the study of how societies decide what to produce, as well as how to produce, and for whom. But it also includes the study of want creation, which institutionalists recognize as shaped in large part by one's culture and the influence of existing social institutions. In addition, markets are understood as only one type of human institution involved in social provisioning—other institutions, including the state, the family, and indeed culture in its totality, are also significant and within the scope of economics. As a result, a science of social provisioning gives attention not only to market (or exchange) value, but also to other types of valuation affecting the provisioning process, such as use value and societal value (decided through a social process such as democratic decision-making, for example).[3]

Gruchy's definition of economics leads to a threefold purpose. In particular, the goals of economics are to understand social provisioning, communicate that understanding to others, and apply that understanding with the aim of making the world a better place in which to live. To be sure, achieving these goals involves a great deal of research, but it also requires thoughtful judgments and effective explanations.

From research to theory

When it comes to seeking an understanding of socioeconomic reality, I take an eclectic and pluralistic perspective: understanding requires not only visits to the library to learn from others who have studied the same or similar phenomena, but also explorations into the real world. Research should be thorough, and everything available should be fair game; all sources—texts, direct observations, interviews, and quantitative and qualitative data—provide an opportunity to learn. To be sure, not everything can be studied, and all investigations require being on the lookout for the explicit and hidden assumptions contained in every type of research material: judgment calls and critical thinking are essential to understanding economic life.[4]

To communicate an understanding of how an economy works (in whole or in part) and then use that understanding to address socioeconomic problems, an economist needs to first have a framework for her/his own understanding. We must be able to explain the economy to ourselves before we can explain it to others. Thus, *explanation* is at the heart of economics—and while effective explanations do not guarantee success in economics or any other discipline, ineffective explanations are rarely useful (except, of course, to those who believe they benefit from keeping matters obscure).[5]

Since explanation is at the heart of economics, then so too is theory. An explanation of an event, object, or phenomenon provides an account of not just *what* happens, but also *why* it happens.[6] However, in economics, as with all other sciences, we rarely (if ever) have complete certainty about what happens and why, so our explanations (even in the realm of economic history) are provisional, and we call them *theories*. At bottom, though, a theory is nothing more than an explanation, as indicated by this dictionary definition: "a coherent group of general propositions used as principles of explanation for a class of phenomena."[7]

Sentences versus equations

Economics textbooks show there are three main ways to communicate the content of economic theory: words, diagrams (including tables, graphs, and other visual displays of information), and mathematical equations. Within economics, there has long been a preference for, and emphasis on, the latter. As suggested in this chapter's introduction, mathematical formalism in economics is seen as "rigorous" and "precise," while mere words are considered "vague" and "sloppy" (McCloskey 1983, 510).

Presenting economic theory by means of words, sentences, and paragraphs (with numbers and other quantitative data added as a complement, not the main means of communication) might be derided by many economists, but it is usually where economic theory begins—and ends. On narrative as a starting point, take, for example, Hyman Minsky's (non-mainstream) financial instability hypothesis and his associated investment theory of business cycles. What was presented mostly in words—as a story or narrative—in the 1970s (see, for example, Minsky

1982, 14–70), was formalized in the 1990s by Keen (1995) and Delli Gatti, Gallegati, and Minsky (1996).[8] Words are also largely where economic theory ends, and not just because mathematical conclusions must be summarized in words: As Leontief (1971, 2) stated in his presidential address to the American Economic Association (AEA), the usefulness of a mathematical economic model, no matter how complex and sophisticated, depends entirely on the validity of its initial assumptions.[9]

There is actually an extensive literature demonstrating that the precision and rigor of mathematical economics and econometrics are often oversold. For example, McCloskey (1983) uses examples including "human capital," "marginal productivity," and the "production function," to argue that economic theory in mathematical garb is no less metaphorical than when expressed in plain English. McCloskey (1996) also argues that "statistical significance" and mathematical economic proofs fall short of being either meaningful science or relevant to understanding (and shaping policies for) the real world. Mayer (1993, ix) devotes an entire book to the argument that economists have erred by choosing the "rigor, precision, and elegance" of mathematical economics over the example of empirical sciences such as biology, which would enable it to say much more about the real world.[10] Another book, a classic work on economic methodology by Blaug (1980, 256–257), argues that much econometric work is "like playing tennis with the net down"—it doesn't seriously attempt to refute testable predictions or discriminate between competing explanations.[11]

In the 1970s, in a series of lectures, a number of high-profile mainstream economists in the United States and England argued that economists had sacrificed too much real-world relevance in the pursuit of rigor.[12] Their message was not that economists should cast aside all rigor, but that the profession needed a new commitment to observation, real-world data, realistic theories, and attention to practical problems. Much of what these distinguished economists had to say could be boiled down to the statement traceable to Carveth Read, an eighteenth-century philosopher, "It is better to be approximately right than precisely wrong" (Sauro 2016). A decade later, however, one of these economists argued that academic economics was in a state of "splendid isolation" and that he did not expect any change to come from within the profession (Leontief 1982, 107).

The global financial crisis that began in the United States in 2007 led to a similar set of calls (for greater attention to economic realism) by prominent economists on both sides of the Atlantic Ocean.[13] This time, the bottom-line message was that economics must address the fact that the global crisis was unimaginable to most economists because they had become enamored of rigorous models and elegant theories without room for economic crises.[14] "It's not just that they missed it; they positively denied it would happen," says Franklin Allen of the Wharton School (quoted in Whalen 2013, 13). However, while it would be wrong to say the crisis had no effect at all on economic research conducted by mainstream economists, today most academic economic scholarship remains tied to "the same self-contained, abstract art form" that dominated the profession for decades before the crisis (Mason 2018).[15]

Storytelling and economic narratives

Ward's (1972) *What's Wrong with Economics?* includes a chapter-long discussion of (and case for) storytelling in economics. According to Ward (1972, 180), "Storytelling is an attempt to give an account of an interrelated set of phenomena in which fact, theory, and values are all mixed together in the telling." He adds:

> Historians of course are the archetypal storytellers, especially when the historian has some coherent purpose. He [*sic*] then tries to get the facts to fit his purpose, without misstating them. But much of the connective material for his story is not really factual historical material, but theory about human behavior, the impact of the environment on the actors, and so forth. This is woven into the story, and one of the major tests of storytelling historians is their ability to make the facts support the theory and vice versa.
>
> *(Ward 1972, 180)*

Reviewing Ward's book, Robert Solow writes that storytelling is "exactly" what the modern economist does. In fact, according to Solow (1973, 697), economists use "exactly the same words: 'The story I'm trying to tell is this … ,' only the story is told in calculus." At one level, Ward and Solow agree. In fact, Ward (1972, 181) writes that "storytelling is ubiquitous … because only with storytelling can one tie research to the uses to which economics is put." But Ward means that storytelling is ubiquitous because economists must at some point step back from their blackboards and use *words* to explain what's going on in their analyses (and why it matters), whereas Solow seems to suggest calculus speaks for itself.

In the preface to the latest edition of David Colander's textbook, *Economics*, Colander (2020) offers a view that sides with Ward. "Recent economic pedagogy has shifted away from seeing textbooks as a narrative, to seeing them as a compilation of models that can be presented in separable building blocks or modules," Colander (2020, vi) writes. He accepts the current trend, but only with a huge caveat:

> This modularization of the teaching of economic principles … makes a lot of sense *as long as one remembers that you also need mortar and architectural blueprints to hold the building blocks together.* That mortar and those blueprints are embedded in the text's narrative. Unfortunately, mortar and blueprints don't fit nicely into building block modules captured by learning objectives. Mortar and blueprints require conceptualization that goes beyond the standard models—conceptualization that brings the big picture into focus.

> And, because there are a variety of architectural blueprints, there … [are] a variety of big pictures; models highlight only one of those blueprints.
> *(Colander 2020, vi, emphasis added)*

In short, Colander (2020, vi) believes economics is about *ideas*—about the way the economy works, and how to make the economy work better—*not models*. Storytelling—in the form of a word-based narrative—is not only ubiquitous; it's also *indispensable* to a meaningful economics.

Of course, Solow would agree that economics is ultimately about ideas. In fact, in his review of Ward's book, Solow (1973, 697–698) argues that economists—indeed, scientists in all fields—are really aiming to convey a narrative: "[T]he positivist apparatus may be a rationalization of the process [in that it dresses attempts at persuasion in scientific garb], but it does not describe what actually happens," which is simply an attempt to develop and tell a compelling story. But unless the story is presented in words, many assumptions remain implicit and hidden, relayed only "by the selection of topics and emphases" (Ward 1972, 183).

In a direct counter to the economics profession's bias in favor of formalism over stories or economic narratives, Ward (1972, 179–188) highlights the strengths of narratives and their development relative to economic formalism. For example, storytelling forces an explicit expression of "priors." Whereas formalized economics makes "central parts of the story implicit," storytelling brings them out.[16] Ward also argues that developing stories (narratives) allows for: drawing on information-rich data (such as direct observation via fieldwork, not just sampling data, for example); giving attention to real-world interdependencies and nuance; and changing stories to reflect new information during an investigation. To be sure, statistical analyses can constructively sort out patterns and relationships not apparent through observation alone—indeed, the early institutionalists were strong advocates of empirical methods precisely for this reason (see, for example, Commons 1925, 75–94). But the key point is that narratives also have strengths, for both theory construction and communication, and should not be dismissed. In some cases, formalism is a "crude, second best" to storytelling, rather than the reverse.

Narrative economics

A trio of mainstream economists has recently received considerable attention for addressing the role of narratives in economics. Two of them are George Akerlof and Dennis Snower, whose joint article begins with the observation that "standard economics omits the role of narratives" in economic decision-making (Akerlof and Snower 2016, 58). They suggest this omission is a mistake because people are actually influenced by narratives in a variety of circumstances. In fact, Akerlof and Snower (2016, 58) argue narratives play a role in "understanding the environment; focusing attention; predicting events; motivating action; assigning social roles and identities; defining power relations; and establishing and conveying social norms." In particular, their article examines these various aspects of the role of narratives in the context of an account of the history of Russia and the Soviet Union in the twentieth century. Robert Shiller is the other notable contributor to this sort of research. "Narrative Economics" is the title of both his recent presidential address to the AEA and his latest book, published in 2019 with the subtitle: *How Stories Go Viral and Drive Major Economic Events* (Shiller 2017; 2019).

Akerlof, Snower, and Shiller have similar notions of an economic narrative. Akerlof and Snower (2016, 58) describe a narrative "as a sequence of causally linked events and their underlying sources, unfolding through time, which may be used as a template for interpreting our ongoing experience." They also describe economic narratives as "the stories that people tell themselves and others" when they make economic decisions (or decisions with economic consequences). Shiller (2019, 3) defines such narratives as contagious stories that "have the potential to change how people make economic decisions."

In his presidential address, Shiller (2017, 968) uses the term "narrative"

> to mean a simple story or easily expressed explanation of events that many people want to bring up in conversation or on news or social media because it can be used to stimulate the concerns or emotions of others, and/or because it appears to advance self-interest.

He adds:

> As I (and others) use the term, a narrative is a gem for conversation, and may take the form of an extraordinary or heroic tale or even a joke. It is not generally a researched story, and may have glaring holes, as in urban legends.

In addition, Shiller (2017, 967) describes *narrative economics* as "the study of the spread and dynamics of popular narratives, the stories, particularly those of human interest and emotion, and how these change through time, to understand economic fluctuations." Then, in the preface to his book, Shiller (2019, xi) boils down that field of study to the following: "First and foremost, I want to examine how narrative contagion affects economic events."

The mainstream's research on narratives has certainly produced important insight—see, for example, Akerlof and Snower's (2016, 59) discussion of the "interrelated roles of narratives in decision formation" and Shiller's (2019, 87–103) "seven propositions of narrative economics"—but its perspective also has two important implications. One is that we cannot look to the mainstream's "narrative economics" for advances in the development and use of economic narratives as a form of scientific presentation and communication. For them, a narrative is an object of study, created by others, not something to be constructed.[17]

The other implication is that although Shiller (2019, xi) mentions that a narrative can be a "theory, explanation, or plan," we should not expect narrative economists to turn their attention toward the real-world consequences of their own, mainstream economic theories. The Laffer Curve (a graphical description of Arthur Laffer's notion that you can cut taxes without also cutting government expenditures) is, of course, fair game for investigation and analysis (see Shiller 2019, 42–47). But the equally simplistic notions that free-market capitalism produces the best of all possible worlds and that competitive markets generate optimal outcomes for all economic participants—both of which can be considered reasonable "narrative" interpretations of standard economics—have so far escaped scrutiny (despite their far-reaching economic consequences) and are likely to remain unexamined.[18] The statement that a narrative is not generally "a researched story" seems to imply that standard economic theory doesn't qualify and is, therefore, off limits.

Storytelling and methodology

Having provided a look at storytelling in the context of economics overall, this section and the two that follow it examine the attention given to storytelling in institutionalist research. This section focuses on research in the area of economic methodology, with special attention to the notion of a pattern model as well as to the matter of theory assessment. It discusses an article by Charles Wilber and Robert Harrison (1978) and a book by Wilber and Kenneth Jameson (1983). It also stresses that facts alone are no substitute for economic interpretation.

Pattern models

Wilber and Harrison's (1978) article is a classic on institutionalist methodology, set against the backdrop of a critical look at conventional economic theory. It describes the worldview of mainstream economic theory as centered on an "atomistic" society of independent economic agents (people and businesses) in an economy separable from the larger social whole. To be sure, structural changes are allowed, but even they must ideally be isolated for the purposes of economic analysis, rather than occurring all at once. The mainstream's formal modeling fits with its worldview, but the real world has not been so accommodating. According to Wilber and Harrison (1978, 69), modeling of mainstream theory has led to a body of thought insulated from refutation (since attempts at falsification are routinely said to be inconclusive) but also incapable of providing a useful description of our interrelated and dynamic social reality. Still, the mainstream persists, and much of its work involves using formal models to defend storytelling (narratives) about a competitive economy that could or should exist, even if it doesn't exist today (Wilber and Harrison 1978, 70).

While Wilber and Harrison (1978) view mainstream storytelling as subordinate to economic orthodoxy's primary aim of mathematical modeling, they personally treat storytelling as essential to all the work of economists, from theory-building through pursuit of economic reform. They also see the economy through a different lens: they view the world from a more holistic and evolutionary perspective than the economic mainstream, and that causes them to reject the mainstream's formal models in favor of what institutionalists call *pattern models*. Unlike mainstream models, which rest on economic laws and are constructed by relying heavily on deduction, pattern models are constructed by building up from observations and data.[19] Builders of pattern models use the comparative method to highlight common patterns and themes, as well as to identify working hypotheses. Their results are presented most often in narrative form (at least initially, especially since economists' traditional modeling tools are best suited for an atomistic world).

Pattern models focus on part–whole relations, which is just another way of saying, as did Thorstein Veblen, that what institutionalists have in mind is a "systems economics" (quoted in Wilber and Harrison 1978, 83). Interdependence of the various elements of the socioeconomic system, including the people who participate in that system, is a key feature of any pattern model. But so too is socioeconomic evolution. As Wilber and Harrison (1978, 80) write: "Reality for holists is viewed as a process of evolutionary change driven by the dynamic interaction between the parts and whole." In fact, they argue that "changes in the pattern of relations are ... the very essence of social reality" (Wilber and Harrison 1978, 71).[20]

Wilber and Harrison (1978, 78–79, 88, n. 42) identify over a dozen institutionalist journal articles that each create a pattern model to explain economic behavior on topics ranging from economic development to industrial organization. Most are based on a few case studies, but the authors also mention some institutionalists who have drawn on a larger number of sources "to construct more general theory from the pattern model approach." In particular, they mention Veblen's stage theory of capitalism, John R. Commons's theory of "reasonable capitalism," John Kenneth Galbraith's theory of the "planning system" in post–World War II advanced industrial democracies, and Gunnar Myrdal's theory of circular causation.[21]

Post-Keynesian institutionalism: pattern modeling applied

A few years following publication of the article by Wilber and Harrison, Wilber and Jameson (1983) published *An Inquiry into the Poverty of Economics*, which presents a pattern model of the US economy and applies it to address the problem of stagflation. That book begins by highlighting shortcomings of Keynesian, monetarist, and Marxist analyses of the US economy. Then it offers an alternative economic narrative they call post-Keynesian institutionalism (PKI), a blend of insights from institutionalism and the economics of Keynes. The authors' discussion of PKI gives attention to methodology, theory, and policy analysis, but at the heart of the book is an effort to tell a story, "by means of a pattern model," that explains the structure and operation of the US economy as it existed at that time (Wilber and Jameson 1983, 155).

Wilber and Jameson's post-Keynesian institutionalist analysis incorporates an extensive array of studies and sources, but relies heavily on Galbraith's notion of a bimodal economy. According to Galbraith, US economic activity in the first few decades following World War II was driven by powerful, oligopolistic firms in what he called the economy's "planning" sector, while countless small firms operated in a much more competitive part of the economy called the "market" sector. Planning-sector firms had considerable discretion over a wide range of business decisions, including the setting of wages and prices, and, according to Wilber and Jameson, that discretion played a crucial role in the economy's simultaneous generation of inflation and unemployment (Wilber and Jameson 1983, 167–229).[22]

Theory assessment: back to storytelling

In a world of competing theories, how can we evaluate the alternatives (including, for example, mainstream economics and PKI) and choose one over another? Wilber and Jameson (1983, 146–151) demonstrate that there are a number of econometric difficulties standing in the way of theory assessment and choice, and that adverse statistical results can always be explained away.[23] The choice among alternative theories "cannot be made solely on empirical grounds," they write.

According to Wilber and Jameson (1983, 150–151), evaluating theories is actually determined largely "by one's own vision of the economic process and attendant policy implications … .Economists would do better to drop the 'scientific' pretensions and accept the fact that they are 'storytellers.'" In fact, Wilber and Jameson (1983, 151) see this as an *opportunity* for the economics profession:

> In that case, statistical testing would become merely one more piece of evidence contributing to the reality and coherence of the "story." At the minimum, this methodological approach would generate caution and humility. It might also direct the economist's attention to questions of institutional structure that have been neglected by standard economists because they have not been amenable to econometric investigation.

Beyond facts?

It's clear that Wilber and Jameson saw a role for facts (including facts generated through statistical analyses) and encouraged investigations that would produce even more of them. But is it really the case that economics must also go beyond collecting and even arranging facts? Alas, yes; and this is not a new realization. In fact, it was not new when Joseph Schumpeter (1949) devoted his AEA presidential address to the subject of ideology in economics. Indeed, as Hugh Fletcher (1932, 1078–108), a critic of institutionalism, stressed in the early 1930s, "Facts as facts are of no significance … . Facts … are significant—whether for economic reform or for the construction of a system of economic theory—only in so far as they can be formulated into generalizations."[24] Schumpeter and Fletcher approached the matter differently, but whether we call the added element ideology (Schumpeter) or avoid naming it at all (Fletcher), economists have long recognized we need more than facts.

Facts are necessary for economic theory and analysis; absolutely. But facts alone don't tell a story. We also need to know how facts came about, and how they relate to other facts. And having even more facts and arranging them in an orderly manner (which itself requires going beyond facts and into the realm of judgment) is not sufficient. The key, as Veblen (1898, 377) stressed long ago, is the *interpretation* of facts; economists often agree on the facts but still disagree strongly over their meaning.[25] To summarize: an examination of attention to storytelling in institutionalist research on economic methodology highlights the importance of pattern models, but it also underscores the need for economists—when fashioning theories and when choosing among them—to go beyond facts and into the realm of interpretation.

Storytelling and theory

The work of John Watkins illustrates the role of storytelling in institutionalist teaching and research on economic theory. In the first chapter of his recent introductory textbook, Watkins (2013, 1) stresses that economics is an "interpretive science" and that, because economics is often used to justify public policy choices and other real-world decisions, its interpretations have important real-world consequences. Watkins (2013, 5) also stresses that storytelling, which combines facts and interpretation, is the key to teaching economics. Building on those two emphases, his book introduces all the concepts and models found in conventional introductory texts, but also presents heterodox as well as mainstream economic perspectives.

Stories of consumers and macroeconomics

Some of Watkins's contributions to academic journals also focus on economists' stories. We look here at one of those contributions, an article published as "The Stories that Economists Tell: Mainstream, Hyman Minsky, and Institutional Views of Consumer Behavior" (Watkins 2018).[26] It provides an illuminating comparison of analyses of consumer behavior and its macroeconomic significance, but the article also helps shed further light on the question of theory assessment.

Watkins begins with the mainstream view of consumer behavior and macroeconomics, which incorporates the permanent-income and rational-expectations hypotheses into dynamic stochastic general equilibrium models. In those models, consumers are assumed to maximize utility over their lifespan and to have the prescience necessary to smooth out their consumption accordingly. As Charles Goodhart of the London School of Economics observed when the global financial crisis was still ongoing, mainstream theory assumed "the existence of representative agents who never default … . This makes *all* agents [households and firms] perfectly creditworthy." That observation, in a nutshell, answers Queen Elizabeth's question: "Why had nobody noticed that the credit crunch was on its way?" (both Goodhart and the Queen are quoted in Watkins 2018, 535–536). The crisis was, from the perspective of standard theory, inconceivable.

Watkins then turns to the economics of Minsky, whose heterodox financial instability hypothesis was "widely used" to explain the crisis. Watkins (2018, 536–537) describes the Minskyan analysis as follows:

> Over time, businesses seek riskier investments such that cash inflows (total revenue less variable costs) are insufficient to pay the interest payments on debts. The refusal of creditors to refinance forces institutions to sell assets, potentially precipitating a debt-deflation depression. In the crisis of 2008, the decline in cash inflows stemmed from consumers' failure to make payments [to banks and businesses].

Watkins also highlights a number of Minsky's observations and insights on consumer behavior, all of which were contained in a book Hy wrote in the mid-1970s, yet remain relevant to shaping a realistic theoretical understanding of such behavior and its effects on businesses and the economy overall. They can be summarized as follows: (1) the consumer preferences of society in general are shaped by business advertising and the culturally driven desire for conspicuous consumption; (2) the affluent have trained their wealth gains on consumption of capital-intensive goods (private jets, yachts, luxury homes, etc.), not less–capital-intensive pursuits (such as poetry and philosophy), and sharp income inequality has fueled that capital intensity and buoyed the return to capital; and (3) government spending in the post–World War II era has also tended toward capital-intensive expenditures (such as those that purchase extraordinarily expensive weapons systems).

The rest of Watkins's (2018, 538–539) article draws on more than a half-dozen institutionalist research articles. They shed light on how corporations have promoted private- and public-sector institutional changes to mold consumer behavior in ways that increase business cash inflows (mainly by increasing consumer indebtedness and ensuring that businesses and banks are protected from downside risk). He concludes that a genuine commitment to making economics more realistic must move in the direction of Minsky and the institutionalists.

Theory assessment revisited

Watkins's article provides an illuminating comparison of economic analyses, but also sheds further light on the matter of theory assessment. When evaluating alternative theories and choosing one over another, a key question must, of course, be: how effectively does each theory meet our needs? And, of course, if a theory doesn't shed light on the real-world phenomenon we're trying to understand, then that theory can't possibly fare well in such an assessment.

As it turns out, when the global financial crisis unfolded, even prominent mainstream economists recognized that standard theory did not measure up. For example, Ricardo Caballero, of the Massachusetts Institute of Technology, wasn't willing to mention Minsky by name, but, in 2010, he conceded: "[U]p to now the insight-building mode (both past and present) of the periphery of macroeconomics has proven to be more useful than the macro-machine-building mode of the core to help our understanding of significant macroeconomic events" (quoted in Watkins 2018, 536). Willem Buiter, chief economist at Citigroup in London, had a similar observation: Conventional theory had become a "severe handicap" to central bankers trying to cope with the crisis; the theories of mainstream economists "not only did not allow questions about insolvency and illiquidity to be answered; they did not allow such questions to be asked" (quoted in Whalen 2013, 14).

Minsky and other institutionalists on the "periphery" of the profession might not have used high-powered, machine-driven mathematical models (which is, of course, the reason Caballero defines them as outside the professional "core"), but history shows that only their storytelling could provide valuable real-world insight at a time when such insight was needed most. Complex and elegant models are nice, but are not inherently superior to solidly grounded and coherent narratives. Watkins's article helps drive home two of this chapter's main points: economics is ultimately about ideas—not model complexity—and storytelling (narrative) is ultimately the way those ideas are conveyed to others.[27]

Storytelling and institutional change

Deborah Figart's (2017a) recent book, *Stories of Progressive Institutional Change*, provides an excellent illustration of attention to storytelling in institutionalist research on institutional change. Building explicitly on Wilber and Harrison's (1978) approach to storytelling, Figart's book uses a wide range of sources to present eight short stories of progressive change.[28] She describes how people envisioned alternative realities to a "neoliberal" economy shaped by the mythical notion of laissez-faire and banded together to form social movements, attack institutional rigidities, overcome discrimination and unjust treatment, and transform "values, habits, and customs" (Figart 2017a, 7).[29] In this section, we look briefly at Figart's cases and conclusions, as well as at the role of prediction in institutionalism.

Cases of progressive change

The cases presented by Figart demonstrate the broad scope of the social provisioning process examined by institutional economists. Three chapters explore specific instances of institutional change aimed at improving wages and working conditions "for some of the lowest paid workers" in the United States: migrant farm laborers, restaurant workers, and retail employees (Figart 2017a, 8). Two chapters provide accounts from the finance sector: one focuses on students who refused to repay loans taken out to attend a for-profit college that they assert had defrauded them, thereby pressuring regulators to curb abusive practices by such colleges and associated lenders and loan servicers; and another finance-related chapter centers on the public banking movement in the United States, "a grassroots effort that offers an innovative strategy for reversing the dearth of funds for public infrastructure projects and local economic development" (Figart 2017a, 7).

The other three chapters address topics that affect many, many people at a personal level, yet also have national and even global consequences. One chapter describes a decade-long effort to estimate and incorporate unpaid work in the home within measures of US economic activity. Another considers "the amazing shift in laws and regulations brought about by the movement to advance marriage equality in the United States" (Figart 2017a, 9). Figart's final chapter analyzes consumption and production of coffee and its implications for environmental sustainability, with a focus on certifications that aim toward "global sustainable agriculture and development practices" (Figart 2017a, 10).

Conflict, change, and the big picture

Figart's book leads to a few overarching conclusions. The first two are that the process of institutional change is not necessarily harmonious and that it is always ongoing. While there may be times that institutional change occurs in response to a persuasive argument showing how such change will result in mutual gains for all stakeholders, Figart's (2017a, 10) stories emphasize the more typical situation in which collective action is required to challenge and unseat vested interests. She also emphasizes that her stories, like all stories of social change, are unfinished. Despite the social progress she describes in each of her eight cases, Figart also emphasizes that "there is a long way to go" for each of the movements highlighted: "The stories are [still] evolving" (Figart 2017a, 10; 2017b, 282).

In addition to underscoring social conflict and constant change, Figart also concludes by stressing that institutionalists' stories are vital not only for what they teach us about individual cases but also for helping us understand society as a whole. She writes: "Institutional economists are particularly adept at uncovering and analyzing … the small or individual picture … in order to weave themes together and understand the bigger one" (Figart 2017a, 10–11). In his AEA presidential address nearly a half-century ago, Robert Gordon (1976, 1) criticized his fellow economists for shying away "from the big questions about how and why the institutional structure is changing—and where it is taking us." Figart demonstrates not only that institutionalists are not shy, but also that storytelling—by shedding light on the big picture—plays an indispensable role in moving economics forward.

Prediction, working hypotheses, and scenarios

Figart's short stories often end with a brief discussion of challenges and possibilities ahead, but she does not offer predictions of the sort found in conventional economics. Mainstream economics offers predictions for two reasons: to test their theories and to offer policy guidance. The first sort of predictions leads to results, as has been discussed, that are most often inconclusive. The second is usually of limited use because conventional economic predictions depend on limited changes, imposed by assuming *ceteris paribus* (all other things being the same), whereas multiple behavioral and institutional changes occur simultaneously in the real world (Wilber and Harrison 1978, 67). Institutional economics places much less emphasis on prediction.

Instead of focusing on making and/or testing predictions, institutionalists rely on working hypotheses and scenarios. Institutionalists adopt working hypotheses as components and products of their theorizing, recognizing always that such hypotheses are provisional (which means they should be subject to constant review and revision in light of the available evidence; see, for example, Epstein 1999).[30] Meanwhile, sketching out alternative scenarios is an important way that institutionalists can offer policy guidance in a world of complex, simultaneous change. Each scenario can highlight changes in one or more strategic variables and provide a narrative of various considerations and likely consequences, and a full set of scenarios offers decision-makers useful information about a range of options and possibilities (see, for example, Kochan, Katz, and McKersie 1986; and Whalen 2011).[31]

Narrative power and pitfalls

This section provides an overview of the power and pitfalls of economic narratives as well as a brief discussion of how to improve storytelling robustness. To sketch the power of narratives, we summarize the key points presented above. The discussion of pitfalls and robustness returns us to Ward (1972).

The power of narratives

Economics is about understanding social provisioning and then communicating that understanding to others as well as applying it to help make the world a better place. Explanation—what happens and why—is at the heart of economics. Storytelling, via narratives, is a solid way of organizing and communicating our economic understanding. Narratives offer a valuable way of developing, presenting, and sharing our theories—narratives are not facts without theory.

The suggestion that narratives are inherently less scientific than mathematical models is nonsense. After all, theories begin and end with words, not just as a practical matter but also in that their usefulness depends on initial assumptions. The scientific rigor of formal economics is often oversold, and many mainstream economists have recognized—for many decades, but especially in the unfolding of the global financial crisis of 2007–2009—that conventional economics has often sacrificed far too much relevance in pursuit of that rigor.

Economic storytelling is not merely ubiquitous (all economists must step away from their whiteboard at some point); it is also indispensable to a meaningful economics. Economics is about ideas, and the blueprints, mortar, and big picture in economics require a narrative. Storytelling helps bring assumptions to the surface and makes central parts of the story explicit; allows us to draw on information-rich (quantitative, qualitative, and observational) data; equips us to give attention to interdependencies and nuances; and enables us to change our theories as new information arises. Narratives are no crude "second best" to formalism.[32]

Mainstream economists have recently recognized the importance of narratives in economic life. But they still fail to appreciate economics as a science of narrative construction and delivery. The mainstream's "narrative economics" is useful, but it is not a substitute for (indeed, only underscores the importance of) economic narratives.

Recognizing that storytelling is an essential part of economics, institutionalists emphasize stories when constructing theories, analyzing economic events, and investigating institutional change. In large part because institutionalist methodology appreciates the role of storytelling, institutional economists often construct theories via pattern models, usually presented in narrative form. Those models have time and again explored practical questions that conventional economics wouldn't even ask, and offered insightful analyses of real-world socioeconomic activity. Moreover, storytelling is a powerful tool enabling institutionalists not only to analyze individual cases of institutional change and to sketch useful alternative scenarios as a guide to further change, but also to simultaneously bring social provisioning's important questions and "big picture" into clearer view.

Storytelling pitfalls—and what to do about them

The biggest difficulty with economic narratives is that we can never be sure they are accurate. Does our narrative incorporate vital elements of the real-world economy and convey a solid grasp of how that economy operates, or is it merely a bundle of mistakes, misinformation, or outright myths? Also, if we can't disprove our story (which is our theory in narrative form), how can we be sure (and demonstrate to others) that we're serious about questioning its validity and not just hiding behind an "ample store of immunizing stratagems" (which is the charge often leveled at an opponent's camp in an academic dispute; see Blaug 1980, 259)? In addition, since all stories are based on preconceptions and preanalytic judgments, how do we know we're not missing important questions; are we only carrying around the analytical equivalent of a hammer and seeing nails in need of a whack wherever we look?

There are no easy answers to these questions, and the fact that the same questions can be asked of all schools of thought and modes of analysis provides only limited comfort. Myrdal (1969) would suggest we begin by making our assumptions, judgments, and values as explicit as possible. To be sure, that is a useful start, as is adopting—and working to push the whole of the profession toward adopting—a pluralistic approach to methods and analysis. All methods have usefulness, and all theories provide insight into certain aspects of the economy. Yes, the task is to find the approach—or combination of approaches—most useful for a particular problem; but only a pluralistic economics can both offer the full array of tools and insights we need and ensure we're not overlooking questions that desperately need to be asked and answered.

Just as stories of the real world must always be evolving, stories created by institutionalism's pattern modeling approach are never complete or fully conclusive (Ramstad 1986, 1073; Wilber and Harrison 1978, 76). Nevertheless, since it's obvious that narratives "can be based on varying degrees of truth" (Shiller 2017, 968), it's useful to consider Ward's (1972, 189–190) strategy for improving storytelling robustness. In particular, he offers a "checklist of questions which must be given a serious answer as part of the storytelling process." According to Ward, "The stronger the 'Yes' to each of these questions, the stronger is the verification of the story." The questions are:

1. Are the facts and theories correctly stated?
2. Are [no] important facts or theories omitted?[33]
3. Can one find other stories [on related questions or topics] which use the facts and theories employed in the given story? [In other words, can the story be situated in or connected to a body of related stories?]
4. Are the facts and theories relevant or essential to the story: that is, can no other hypotheses be used to tell as good a story about the facts?[34]
5. Do experts in the various parts of the story believe the story itself?
6. Are values [and all pre-analytic judgments and assumptions] correctly stated?
7. Are all relevant values [and other judgments and assumptions] included? (Ward 1972, 189)

Conclusion: taking stories seriously

This chapter does not argue that mathematical models or empirical analyses are useless or unimportant. Instead, it calls for a recognition that, like it or not, storytelling—or, if you prefer, the fashioning and presentation of narratives—has a central place in economics and that we need to appreciate its role and take it seriously.

In 1973, Robert Solow acknowledged there was "much truth" in Benjamin Ward's observation that mainstream economics has a tendency "to judge the merit of a particular piece of work by the cleverness of its technique and not the social value, not even the intrinsic scientific value, of its results." In fact, Solow (1973, 698) continued: "Students absorb this standard of professional quality and the accompanying definition of what constitutes a good research topic. They look for theorems, not solutions to problems." Little has changed in the several decades since then.[35]

Some, including Solow (1973, 698), have suggested economists don't know how to "move to something better." Others, including Leontief (1982, 107), have argued the mainstream has simply no interest in changing. But we must—and can—do better.

Serious real-world economic problems need addressing. Socioeconomic evolution and ongoing institutional change are inescapable facts of life. Economic narratives are ubiquitous, indispensable, and powerful. By embracing storytelling, institutionalists are showing the way forward.

Acknowledgments

The author wishes to thank Deb Figart, Jim Peach, John Watkins, and Linda Whalen for comments and suggestions.

Notes

1 In economics, key recent contributions on narratives include Shiller (2017; 2019) and Akerlof and Snower (2016). For recent contributions and evidence of interest in narratives beyond economics, see, for example, Department of Journalism (2020); Hagström and Gustafsson (2019); Meekhof (2018); Polletta and Callahan (2017); and Yang and Hobbs (2020).

2 For an attempt to trace the origins of the quote attributed to Viner, see Backhouse, Middleton, and Tribe (1997, 2, n. 1).

3 Among contemporary textbook definitions, David Colander's (2020, 5) probably comes closest to the one offered by Gruchy: "Economics is the study of how human beings coordinate their wants and desires, given the decision-making mechanisms, social customs, and political realities of the society." But inquiries into the sources of wants and desires are not explicitly within the scope of that definition. For a discussion of alternative definitions of economics, see Backhouse and Medema (2009), who recognize: "Whether or not economists are conscious of it happening, adhering to a specific definition may constrain the problems that economists believe it is legitimate to tackle and the methods by which they choose to tackle them" (Backhouse and Medema 2009, 231).

4 On the role of judgments in economics, including value judgments and even ideology, see, for example, Schumpeter (1949) and Myrdal (1969); on critical thinking, see Colander (2020, vi–ix, 20). As these authors recognize, even identifying and selecting a problem to study involves value judgments.

5 On the perverse value of keeping matters obscure, Galbraith (1979, 293) writes: "Complexity and obscurity...have professional value....They exclude the outsiders, keep down the competition, [and] preserve the image of a privileged or priestly class." Mayer (1993, 153) suggests the same perverse outlook shapes the profession's internal scoring system: all too often a paper is admired "just because it is so technical that few can understand it."

6 Because it addresses *why*, an explanation is more than description. Of course, an explanation is also less than a comprehensive description, but, in fact, few (if any) descriptions are ever comprehensive. In most cases, a description instead highlights what a person considers something's most essential features.

7 See Theory (n.d.).

8 Two points are worthwhile here. One is that I am using "story" and "narrative" as synonyms. The other is that, in the mid-1990s, economist Peter Albin was planning to take up residence at the Levy Economics Institute with Hyman Minsky and help infuse Hy's analyses with cutting-edge modeling techniques appropriate to complex, adaptive systems. Then Albin had a stroke, and that work never happened; not too long thereafter, Minsky became gravely ill and died within a year. It is intriguing to consider what Minsky and Albin would have produced.

9 Resisting the temptation to make a side trip into the muddy waters of the literature on unrealistic assumptions, I refer readers to Caldwell (1980) and Musgrave (1981).

10 Mayer (1993, 29) suggests that even physics is a more empirical science than economics.

11 On testing, see also Mayer (1993, 132–151); and Leamer (1983) is a classic on the limitations of econometrics. To be sure, there is much that could be discussed here, including economists' tendency to resort to "verification by theory" (Ward 1972, 173–177) and the use of econometrics for purposes that include "showing that our theory *might* be right," taking a technique "for a walk," and engaging in "ceremonial activity" valued by the economics profession (Mayer 1993, 148). But space is limited, so this temptation to stray off course will also be resisted.

12 See, for example: Leontief (1971); Phelps Brown (1972); Worswick (1972); and Gordon (1976). Of course, there is also economic theory (such as Arrow–Debreu general equilibrium theory) that represents merely "solving puzzles that we have ourselves created"—devoid of any connection to reality, except perhaps as a mental exercise or warm-up (Blaug 1980, 256).

13 For the views of these economists (including, for example, Ricardo Caballero, Paul Krugman, Lawrence Summers, and William Buiter), see Whalen (2013, 13–14).

14 Examples include macroeconomics's dynamic stochastic general-equilibrium model and finance's efficient-market hypothesis.

15 While some economists troubled by the global financial crisis argue that the way forward is to develop better mathematical economic models, others, such as Lawson (2009, 763) warn that "the nature and conditions of social reality are such that the forms of mathematical deductivist reasoning favored by modern economists are almost entirely inadequate as tools of insightful social analysis." In particular, Lawson (2009, 764) stresses that the real world often lacks the regularities and behavioral independence that are essential to conventional modeling.

16 To be sure, storytelling requires judgments—including value judgments—but so too does constructing formal theory; storytelling provides an opportunity to make those judgments explicit. Of course, much is explicit in formal economic models, but, as Colander's remarks on mortar and blueprints suggest, one element regularly overlooked in presentations based on formal models is attention to a key question that economics should answer: *Why*?

17 Shiller is clear that he sees narrative economics as the study of other peoples' narratives and their consequences for economic activity (a view in line with Akerlof and Snower 2016), not as an area of economics devoted to creating and presenting narratives of economic life (see Cummings 2019; and Shiller 2019, xi).

18 The same can be said of the narratives that the macroeconomy is always at full employment (part of real business cycle-theory) and that financial-market participants do not, as a group, make systematic errors when predicting the future (which is the efficient-market hypothesis that shaped the study of financial markets even as the global financial crisis unfolded).

19 One is tempted to suggest that institutionalist pattern modeling stresses induction, while the conventional formal economic modeling stresses deduction, but, in fact,

pattern modeling is part of institutionalist theory construction and all theorizing is a mix of induction and deduction (Blaug 1980, 14–17). As it turns out, Wilber and Harrison do not use the term (induction or inductive) in their article.

20 Cumulative causation, for example, is a phenomenon that often gets particular attention in the dynamic economics of institutionalism (Wilber and Harrison 1978, 73–74).

21 Another excellent example of pattern modeling is Commons's (1909) theory of the US labor movement and how it evolved with industrial development. Also, for a discussion that illustrates how pattern modeling actually takes place, see Ramstad (1986), who applies that concept to explain the development of Commons's theory of reasonable value (which is roughly equivalent to what Wilber and Jameson call "reasonable capitalism").

22 The development and details of PKI are discussed in Chapter 4 (by Whalen) of this edited volume.

23 On econometric difficulties affecting theory choice, see also Blaug (1980, 256–258).

24 The economic mainstream's "economic laws" are one type of generalization, but institutionalism's pattern models, an important source of institutionalist stories, also involve generalization.

25 In fact, James Ronald Stanfield (1999, 236), an adherent to "original" institutional economics, quotes Douglass North, a leader of (mainstream-oriented) "new" institutional economics, to underscore the point that both institutionalist camps agree on the vital role of interpretation since "there are no objective facts in the world." For a similar perspective from the vantage point of philosophy of science, see Feyerabend (1993, 11).

26 The role of storytelling in economic theory is also examined in Watkins (2010).

27 The proposition that storytelling is vital to conveying information to others extends beyond economists as theory communicators and should also be fully appreciated by economists as theory-builders. This chapter has already mentioned that interviews and observations (site visits or even engagement as a participant observer, for example) should be used as part of the raw material of theory construction. In fact, such methods have been essential to development of institutionalist contributions on a wide range of matters including administered pricing, labor-market segmentation and wage setting, and even financial-market operations. For example, Minsky's familiarity with bankers was essential to the development of his innovative and insightful financial theories. But to fully appreciate this point one must also recognize that the women and men we are interviewing *also* have stories, and telling those stories is often also the best way for *them* to convey information. Labor economist Michael Piore (1979) learned that early in his career. He entered factories with official data and interview questions, but soon learned that the most essential information came from letting each interviewee tell their own story (which they were actually far more willing to do than respond to formal questionnaires). Making time to listen to the stories of others is vital to high-quality institutionalist storytelling.

28 Three of these stories also can be found in Figart (2017b).

29 According to Figart (2017a, 6), neoliberalism is characterized by globalization, deregulation, financialization, and erosion of protections for workers.

30 It's important to note, however, that mainstream theories constructed via formal modeling are no more certain than institutionalist theories constructed via pattern modeling. The scientific methodology of conventional economics can, at best, only falsify predictions; it cannot confirm or verify theories. The only certainty science provides is "the certainty of ignorance" (Blaug 1980, 12).

31 The situation-structure-performance framework in Chapter 8 of this book also can be viewed as an approach to presenting scenarios.

32 Recognizing that the inclusivity of economic narratives is the inverse of the exclusivity of economic formalism (see note 5 above), Watkins observes (in recent correspondence with this author) that yet another strength of storytelling is it makes

economics "more accessible and, therefore, more democratic; …stories invite more people to the conversation." In a similar manner, McCloskey (1990; 20–21; 1996, 130) argues that formalism stands in the way of more "open discussion" in economics, and that less attention to mathematics and more openness to stories would bring economics "back in the conversation" of humankind.

33 Blaug's (1980, 127) discussion of Ward's chapter suggests a complementary question: are we confident there are no counterexamples to the low-level generalizations on which our story is constructed?

34 Like Ward, both Watkins (2013, 5) and Wilber and Harrison (1978, 76) also stress that fashioning a story provides insight into theory assessment. Watkins refers to this as "mapping" theory to reality, which provides a chance to show whether facts can be interpreted in a way "that adheres to the story"; and Wilber and Harrison emphasize that interpretations offered by narratives "are continually tested by how well they fit together in a pattern and to what extent new evidence can be explained within the pattern."

35 See, for example, Atkinson and Oleson (1996: 708); Lawson (2009); Caballero (2010: 85); and Mason (2018).

References

Akerlof, George A. and Dennis J. Snower. 2016. "Bread and Bullets." *Journal of Economic Behavior and Organization* 126 (Part B): 58–71. https://doi.org/10.1016/j.jebo.2015.10.021

Atkinson, Glen and Ted Oleson. 1996. "Institutional Inquiry: The Search for Similarities and Differences." *Journal of Economic Issues* 30 (3): 701–718. https://doi.org/10.1080/00213624.1996.11505832

Backhouse, Roger and Steven Medema. 2009. "On the Definition of Economics." *Journal of Economic Perspectives* 23 (1): 221–233. https://doi.org/10.1257/jep.23.1.221

Backhouse, Roger, Roger Middleton, and Keith Tribe. 1997. "Economics Is What Economists Do, But What Do the Numbers Tell Us?" Paper presented at the Annual History of Economic Thought Conference, University of Bristol, 3–5 September. https://tinyurl.com/yxvr4cth. Accessed November 23, 2020.

Blaug, Mark. 1980. *The Methodology of Economics*. Cambridge: Cambridge University Press.

Caballero, Ricardo J. 2010. "Macroeconomics after the Crisis: Time to Deal with the Pretense-of-Knowledge Syndrome." *Journal of Economic Perspectives* 24 (4): 85–102. https://doi.org/10.1257/jep.24.4.85

Caldwell, Bruce. 1980. "A Critique of Friedman's Methodological Instrumentalism." *Southern Economic Journal* 47 (2): 366–374. https://doi.org/10.2307/1057529

Colander, David C. 2020. *Economics*, 11th edition. New York: McGraw Hill.

Commons, J. R. 1909. "American Shoemakers, 1648–1895: A Sketch of Industrial Evolution." *Quarterly Journal of Economics* 24 (1): 39–84. https://doi.org/10.2307/1886057

———. 1925. *Reasonable Value*. Ann Arbor, MI: Edwards Brothers.

Cummings, Mike. 2019. "Robert Shiller on the Power of Narratives." *Yale News* (November 4). https://tinyurl.com/yyrvfdgy. Accessed September 28, 2020.

Delli Gatti, Domenico, Mauro Gallegati, and Hyman Minsky. 1996. "Financial Institutions, Economic Policy, and the Dynamic Behavior of the Economy." In *Behavioral Norms, Technological Progress, and Economic Dynamics*, edited by Ernst Helmstadter and Mark Perlman, 393–412. Ann Arbor, MI: University of Michigan Press.

Department of Journalism. 2020. "The Power of Narrative: Telling True Stories in Turbulent Times." Information on a conference organized by the Department of Journalism, College of Communication, Boston University, Boston, MA (scheduled for March 20–22, 2020). https://www.bu.edu/com/narrative/about.html. Accessed September 25, 2020.

Epstein, Philip. 1999. "Wesley Mitchell's Grand Design and Its Critics." *Journal of Economic Issues* 33 (3): 525–553. https://doi.org/10.1080/00213624.1999.11506185

Feyerabend, Paul. 1993. *Against Method*, third edition. London: Verso.

Figart, Deborah M. 2017a. *Stories of Progressive Institutional Change: Challenges to the Neoliberal Economy*. Cham, Switzerland: Palgrave Macmillan. https://doi.org/10.1007/978-3-319-59779-9

———. 2017b. "Three Short Stories of Progressive Institutional Change." *Journal of Economic Issues* 51 (2): 263–284. https://doi.org/10.1080/00213624.2017.1320503

Fletcher, Hugh M. 1932. "Institutional Economics." *American Economic Review* 22 (1-Supplement): 107–109.

Galbraith, John Kenneth. 1979. "Writing and Typing." In *Annals of an Abiding Liberal*, edited by Andrea D. Williams. New York: Meridian.

Gordon, Robert A. 1976. "Rigor and Relevance in a Changing Institutional Setting." *American Economic Review* 76 (1): 1–14.

Gruchy, Allan G. 1987. *The Reconstruction of Economics*. New York: Greenwood Press.

Hagström, Linus and Karl Gustafsson. 2019. "Narrative Power: How Storytelling Shapes East Asian International Politics." *Cambridge Review of International Affairs* 32 (4): 387–406. https://doi.org/10.1080/09557571.2019.1623498

Keen, Steve. 1995. "Finance and Economic Breakdown: Modeling Minsky's 'Financial Instability Hypothesis.'" *Journal of Post Keynesian Economics* 17 (4): 607–635. https://doi.org/10.1080/01603477.1995.11490053

Kochan, Thomas A., Harry C. Katz, and Robert B. McKersie. 1986. *The Transformation of American Industrial Relations*. New York: Basic Books. https://doi.org/10.7591/9781501731693

Lawson, Tony. 2009. "The Current Economic Crisis: Its Nature and the Course of Academic Economics." *Cambridge Journal of Economics* 33 (4): 759–777. https://doi.org/10.1093/cje/bep035

Leamer, Edward. 1983. "Let's Take the Con Out of Econometrics." *American Economic Review* 73 (1): 31–43.

Leontief, Wassily. 1971. "Theoretical Assumptions and Nonobserved Facts." *American Economic Review* 61 (1): 1–7.

———. 1982. "Letter to the Editor." *Science* 217 (4555): 104, 107.

Mason, J. W. 2018. "Pulling Rabbits Out of Hats." *Jacobin* November 29. https://tinyurl.com/y4bfs6tb. Accessed September 27, 2020.

Mayer, Thomas. 1993. *Truth versus Precision in Economics*. Aldershot: Edward Elgar.

McCloskey, Deirdre. 1983. "The Rhetoric of Economics." *Journal of Economic Literature* 21 (2): 481–517.

———. 1990. "Storytelling in Economics." In *Narrative in Culture*, edited by Christopher Warner, 5–22. London: Routledge.

———. 1996. *The Vices of Economists—The Virtues of the Bourgeoise*. Amsterdam: Amsterdam University Press.

Meekhof, Kristin. 2018. "The Power of the Narrative." Psychology Today (February). https://tinyurl.com/yxezjdnh. Accessed September 25, 2020.

Minsky, Hyman P. 1982. *Can "It" Happen Again*? Armonk, NY: M.E. Sharpe.

Musgrave, Alan. 1981. "'Unreal Assumptions' in Economic Theory." *Kyklos* 34 (3): 377–387. https://doi.org/10.1111/j.1467-6435.1981.tb01195.x

Myrdal, Gunnar. 1969. *Objectivity in Social Research*. Middletown, CT: Wesleyan University Press.

Phelps Brown, E. A. 1972. "The Underdevelopment of Economics." *Economic Journal* 82 (325): 1–10.

Piore, Michael J. 1979. "Qualitative Research Techniques in Economics." *Administrative Science Quarterly* 24 (4): 560–569. https://doi.org/10.2307/2392362

Polletta, Francesca and Jessica Callahan. 2017. "Deep Stories, Nostalgia Narratives, and Fake News: Storytelling in the Trump Era." *American Journal of Cultural Sociology* 5 (3): 392–408. https://doi.org/10.1057/s41290-017-0037-7

Ramstad, Yngve. 1986. "A Pragmatist's Quest for Holistic Knowledge: The Scientific Methodology of John R. Commons." *Journal of Economic Issues* 20 (4): 1067–1105. https://doi.org/10.1080/00213624.1986.11504576

Sauro, Jeff. 2016. "Better to be Approximately Right than Exactly Wrong." MeasuringU .com. April 12. https://measuringu.com/approx-right/. Accessed September 27, 2020.

Schumpeter, Joseph A. 1949. "Science and Ideology." *American Economic Review* 39 (2): 346–359.

Shiller, Robert J. 2017. "Narrative Economics." *American Economic Review* 107 (4): 967–1004. https://doi.org/10.1257/aer.107.4.967

———. 2019. *Narrative Economics: How Stories Go Viral and Drive Economic Events*. Princeton, NJ: Princeton University Press. https://doi.org/10.1515/9780691189970

Solow, Robert M. 1973. "What's Wrong with Economics?" *Journal of Economic Issues* 7 (4): 694–698. https://doi.org/10.1080/00213624.1973.11503142

Stanfield, James Ronald. 1999. "The Scope, Method, and Significance of Original Institutional Economics." *Journal of Economic Issues* 33 (2): 231–255. https://doi.org /10.1080/00213624.1999.11506154

Theory (n.d.). *Random House Kernerman Webster's College Dictionary*. 2010. Retrieved September 26, 2020, from https://www.thefreedictionary.com/theory.

Veblen, Thorstein. 1898. "Why Is Economics Not an Evolutionary Science? *Quarterly Journal of Economics* 12 (4): 373–397. https://doi.org/10.2307/1882952

Ward, Benjamin. 1972. *What's Wrong with Economics?* New York: Basic Books. https://do i.org/10.1007/978-1-349-01806-2

Watkins, John P. 2010. "Mainstream Efforts to Tell a Better Story: Natural Selection as a Misplaced Metaphor: The Problem of Corporate Power." *Journal of Economic Issues* 44 (4): 991–1008. https://doi.org/10.2753/jei0021-3624440407

———. 2013. *An Introduction to Economics as an Interpretive Science: Mainstream and Heterodox Views*. Published by the author; printed by CreateSpace.

———. 2018. "The Stories that Economists Tell: Mainstream, Hyman Minsky, and Institutional Views of Consumer Behavior." *Journal of Economic Issues* 52 (2): 534–540. https://doi.org/10.1080/00213624.2018.1469933

Wilber, Charles K. and Robert S. Harrison. 1978. "The Methodological Basis of Institutional Economics: Pattern Model, Storytelling, and Holism." *Journal of Economic Issues* 12 (1): 61–89. https://doi.org/10.1080/00213624.1978.11503505

Wilber, Charles K. and Kenneth P. Jameson. 1983. *An Inquiry into the Poverty of Economics*. Notre Dame, IN: University of Notre Dame Press.

Whalen, Charles J. 2011. "Union Engagement in Western New York Economic Development." In *Advances in Industrial and Labor Relations, Volume 18*, edited by David

Lewin, Bruce Kaufman, and Paul Gollan, 177–213. Bingley, UK: Emerald. https://doi.org/10.1108/s0742-6186(2011)0000018009

———. 2013. "Post-Keynesian Institutionalism after the Great Recession." *European Journal of Economics and Economic Policies: Intervention* 10 (1): 12–27. https://doi.org/10.2139/ssrn.2062469

Worswick, G. D. N. 1972. "Is Progress in Economics Possible?" *Economic Journal* 82 (325): 73–86. https://doi.org/10.2307/2230207

Yang, Yang and Jill Hobbs. 2020. "The Power of Stories: Narratives and Information Framing Effects in Science Communication." *American Journal of Agricultural Economics* 102 (4): 1271–1296. https://doi.org/10.1002/ajae.12078

11

SYSTEM DYNAMICS, DATA SCIENCE, AND INSTITUTIONAL ANALYSIS

Michael J. Radzicki

Introduction

In his enormously influential economics textbook, Noble laureate Paul Samuelson wrote a passage well known to institutional economists:

> [Forty] years ago Institutionalism withered away as an effective counterforce in economics. Who can explain it when a movement turns sterile? Perhaps it was the case that mainstream American economics had always been more pragmatic and empirical than mainstream English or French economics; it was therefore able, so to speak, to absorb and take over with superior analytical and econometric tools the descriptive tasks and policy formulations of the Institutionalists.
>
> *(Samuelson 1976, 847)*

Of course, Samuelson led the movement to bring mathematical rigor and the approach of the natural sciences into the economics profession, and his views were consistent with the consensus among mainstream economists during the second half of the twentieth century. To the institutionalists, however, the mainstream perspective meant that many of the things they found fundamental to their method of analysis (e.g., cultural and psychological factors, the details associated with specific times and places, and the inherent conflict between ceremonial and technological forces) were deemed irrelevant to modern economic research. In response, institutional economists fought back with two main arguments: (1) that their approach to scientific explanation utilizes inductive logic, which is significantly different from the deductive approach employed by mainstream economists; and (2) that the mathematical tools of the day were inadequate for institutional analysis.[1]

DOI: 10.4324/9781003160434-11

While the institutionalists' counterarguments were legitimate, they did very little to change the mainstream's views on the "proper" way to do economic analysis. The good news is that today modern tools from the fields of simulation and data science can be used by institutional economists to add mathematical rigor and insight to their traditional approach to economic analysis. These tools either did not exist or were not widely understood by economists during the second half of the twentieth century. The purpose of this chapter, therefore, is to provide an overview of how these tools can be used to add value to institutional economic analysis.

Pattern modeling and system dynamics

According to Wilber and Harrison (1978), and following Diesing (1971), institutional economists commonly employ a pattern modeling approach to economic analysis. To produce a pattern model, an institutional economist acts like a detective at a crime scene, searching for clues in order to assemble a holistic explanation or pattern for the problem at hand. The economist detective collects all available information (numerical, written, "eye witness" interviews, focus group engagements, direct observation, etc.) and uses a systems approach to pull the clues or pieces of the puzzle together into a coherent whole or mosaic that yields important insights into the problem or question motivating the analysis.

Over time, institutional economists accumulate a variety of pattern models. Any regularities that are identified among the patterns are collected into sets of *real typologies*, and any regularities that are identified among the real typologies are collected into *fundamental principles of economics*. Kapp (1976) has argued that the most important fundamental principle of institutional economics is Gunnar Myrdal's (1957) concept of circular and cumulative causation, which is thought to provide the underlying explanation for the nonequilibrium dynamics of economic systems.

Of importance is that pattern modeling is primarily a bottom-up approach that goes from specific instances to general principles—i.e., from real-world experience and observation to theory. Indeed, to engage in pattern modeling institutional economists have to literally get out from behind their desks and find out what is going on in the economy. That said, the detective economist also turns to the profession's collection of real typologies and fundamental principles for guidance at the next "crime scene." In other words, s/he does not try to solve problems in a vacuum, devoid of any reference points or theoretical framework.

System dynamics modeling is pattern modeling

In a series of papers some years ago Radzicki (1988; 1990; 2003) pointed out that system dynamics employs a method of analysis that is strikingly similar to the approach employed by institutional economics. In other words, system dynamics modeling *is* pattern modeling.

System dynamicists do not try to model systems; instead, they model problems from a systems perspective.[2] Like an institutional economist, a system dynamicist utilizes all available sources of information in order to piece together a pattern or explanation (i.e., a simulation model) for a particular problem.[3] Information is deemed relevant, and hence included in the model, if and only if it directly contributes to an understanding of the problem to which the modeling effort is being directed.[4] That said, in practice system dynamics modeling is an iterative activity in which the steps in the process (including the identification of relevant information) are routinely revisited, and the model revised, as the act of modeling itself generates new insights into the problem.[5]

The creator of system dynamics, Jay W. Forrester, often argued that a good system dynamics model should be a *generic structure* that is applicable to any problem in its class or "family" when properly modified to fit a specific situation. For example, although Forrester's (1969) urban dynamics model was originally created by working with city officials from Boston, he felt that it could mimic the dynamics of *any* city when properly parameterized for a particular urban setting. Similarly, Homer's (1987) model of the diffusion of new medical technologies into the marketplace was able to mimic the (significantly different) dynamics of both cardiac pacemakers, and the antibiotic clindamycin, with only a handful of changes to its parameters and table functions.[6] Finally, in his later years Forrester (2003) began to see his system dynamics macroeconomic model not as a pattern model of the US economy, but rather as a generic macroeconomic structure. In sum, generic structures in system dynamics modeling are equivalent to real typologies in institutional analysis.[7]

Principles of system dynamics modeling

At the highest level of generality, system dynamics modeling is based on a number of fundamental *principles of systems*. Among the most important principles are:

1) Principle of accumulation—this principle asserts that all dynamic behavior in the world occurs when flows accumulate in stocks.[8]
2) Ubiquitous nature of feedback—this principle asserts that stocks and flows do not exist in isolation but are instead almost always part of feedback loops.
3) Structure causes behavior—this principle implies that, to change a system's behavior, the system's structure must be redesigned.

Several observations surrounding those three principles are noteworthy. First, the principle of accumulation is in alignment with Boulding's (1950) attempt to reconstruct economics around the concept of the balance sheet, as well as the more recent movement by post-Keynesian economists to construct "stock-flow–consistent" models.[9] More to the point, system dynamicists have been building stock-flow–consistent models since the mid-1950s.

Second, the importance of feedback loops in a system dynamics model, and in the real world, cannot be overemphasized. Indeed, an old system-dynamics thought experiment involves asking someone who disputes this principle to think about the consequences of driving a car at 70 miles per hour on the highway blindfolded, while wearing noise-canceling headphones, thus cutting off the feedback of information!

Feedback is the transmission and return of information about the amount of "stuff" that has accumulated in each of a system's stocks over time. For example, the distance in miles a car has traveled on the highway from a starting point over any interval of time would represent the accumulation of the car's speed. This information flows throughout the system and either directly or indirectly returns to the system's flows causing them to adjust and adapt, which, in turn, changes the state of the system. Continuing with the automotive example, the driver may drop the speed of the car to zero and stop at a filling station when s/he receives feedback indicating that the number of miles driven is close to the car's maximum on one tank of gas. This, in turn, stops the accumulation of speed in the distance stock, which defines the state of the automotive system (e.g., the distance the car has traveled from the time it left its starting point).

Two types of feedback loops exist: positive loops and negative loops. Positive loops represent self-reinforcing processes such as population growth, wage-price spirals, speculative bubbles, or compound interest. They typically cause systems to move away from their present position. Negative loops, on the other hand, represent goal-seeking behavior in which corrective action tries to keep the amount of "stuff" in a stock at a desired level. Examples of negative feedback-loop processes include "invisible hand" market structures, labor hiring and separation decisions, administered price strategies, and capital acquisition activities. Negative loops typically work to stabilize systems, although they can cause a system to oscillate if the corrective actions they motivate are delayed. Over time, positive and negative loops fight to control a system and determine its time path. At the macroeconomic level, positive feedback loops determine the economy's trend and negative feedback loops determine its cycle(s).

Third, the combination of principles one and two corresponds directly to Myrdal's principle of circular and cumulative causation. O'Hara (2008), however, notes that circular and cumulative causation really only applies to positive feedback loops and hence to nonequilibrium processes such as economic hysteresis and path dependence.[10] On the other hand, engineers who turned their attention to economic modeling such as Arnold Tustin (1953), Bill Phillips (1954),[11] and Jay W. Forrester (1956),[12] as well as economists who adopted a servomechanism/control engineering approach to economic analyses such as R.G.D. Allen (1959), Axel Leijonhufvud (1968),[13] and Steve Keen (1995),[14] utilize both positive and negative feedback loops in their modeling.

Fourth, the principle that structure causes behavior explains the difficulty policymakers have in solving socioeconomic problems. Forrester (1993) notes that, if the ancient Greeks were magically transported to the present day, they would understand absolutely nothing about modern technology, but would understand nearly everything about many modern socioeconomic problems, as these problems haven't changed very much over the millennia. Forrester attributes the persistence of socioeconomic problems to the failure of policymakers to view socioeconomic entities as *systems* and to evaluate them from this perspective.[15]

Complex socioeconomic systems have a number of structural characteristics that make them difficult to understand and control. These characteristics include:

- Components that are embedded in complex networks of interconnected feedback loops, within which relationships of cause and effect are separated (and obscured) by time and space, making it difficult to understand the relationship between system structure and system behavior;
- Structures that typically arise via evolutionary forces, rather than conscious design, which means that they frequently lack robust architectures that can mitigate their vulnerability to major external shocks (e.g., black swan events) that can significantly disrupt their normal behavior; and
- Feedback structures that can often produce robust and persistent behavior that is *undesirable*.

System dynamicists believe that in order to improve the dynamics of modern socioeconomic systems, their structures must be redesigned so that: stakeholder goals are aligned; vicious circle relationships are mitigated; leverage points are identified; long-run/short-run trade-offs are evaluated; the likely actions of other actors in the system are taken into account; robustness and resiliency become the norm; and policy implementation via intuition and experience is enhanced with insights from the application of modern tools of simulation and data science.[16] Forrester has argued that the process is similar to that of designing an airplane. A properly designed plane can be flown "well" (smoothly, efficiently) by pilots of many different skill levels, while a poorly designed plane can only be flown well by the most skilled pilots.

The principle that structure causes behavior also begs the question as to what system dynamicists look for when they map out the structure of a socioeconomic system that is performing poorly. Components of system structure that are typically considered by system dynamicists include: the *physical structure* of a system (e.g., physical stocks and flows of people, machines, money, natural and other resources; constraints and limiting factors; and technological innovations); the *institutional structure* of a system (e.g., organizational units and hierarchy,[17] lines of authority, formal and informal laws and "rules of the game," and information availability and quality); and the *psychological decision-making structure* of a system (e.g., the mental models of the decision-makers, which are cognitively limited and biased, and shaped by things such as culture and tradition, habits, routines, standard operating procedures, incentives, values, rewards and goals, heuristics, perceptions, and forecasts).

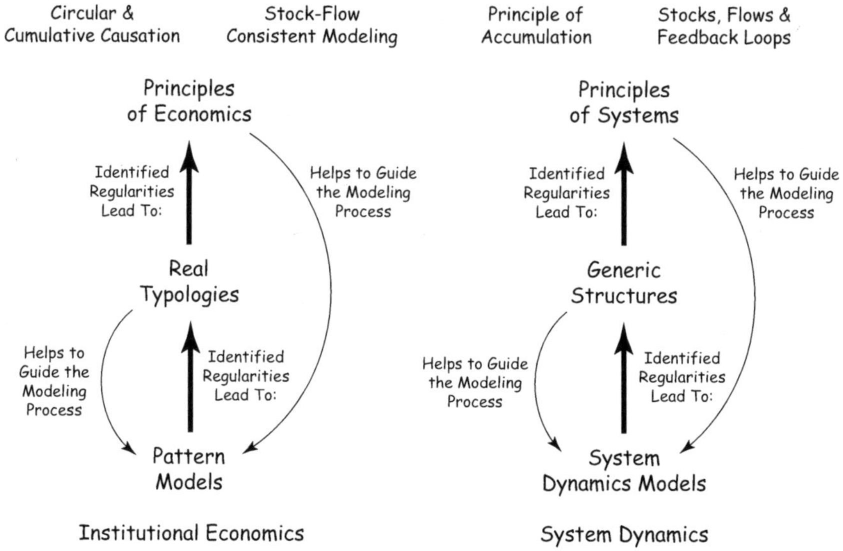

FIGURE 11.1 Explanation in institutional economics and system dynamics.

Institutional economists should find the elements of system structure that are deemed relevant by system dynamicists to be quite familiar. Figure 11.1 presents the parallel nature of the institutionalist and system dynamics pattern modeling processes. Moreover, Hayden (1982) developed a tool for methodically identifying the important elements of a socioeconomic system's structure and laying out their causal interactions, known as the social fabric matrix.[18] Social fabric matrices have been used at times by system dynamicists to bring order and discipline to the conceptualization stage of the pattern modeling process, and it is a tool that should arguably be utilized more frequently for this purpose.[19]

Model builders and model users

Forrester (1985) long argued that the true value created by system dynamics comes, not from any particular model, but from the modeling process itself, as it is the iterative struggle to understand the problematic dynamics of a system (i.e., the iterative struggle to assemble the pattern) that generates insight and understanding.

Over the years, system dynamicists have found it is often valuable to involve future model users, who are often domain experts and stakeholders, in the modeling process. This not only enables valuable, firsthand, information to be embedded in a model; it also helps users achieve a sense of model ownership and hence confidence in model results. Of course, experts and stakeholders frequently disagree, and typically offer multiple solutions to a problem, all of which are logical and thought to have worked elsewhere. The beauty of a system dynamics model is that it can be used to evaluate which proposed solutions (or combinations of solutions), implemented in what order, are likely to yield desired results and which ones will not. By testing assumptions, running proposed scenarios, and identifying specific areas of agreement and disagreement, model users can *learn* about a system's structure and behavior and develop a consensus with respect to the sorts of structural redesigns that are necessary to achieve goals and reach desirable (or at least acceptable) solutions.[20] In an effort to bring some order to what can be a rather complicated process, system dynamicists have developed *group model-building techniques* to help identify and incorporate expert knowledge into a model.[21]

Pushing the preceding points further, it is quite common for a future model user to not have participated *at all* in a model's creation. As such, s/he frequently does not understand the model or believe its results. This almost guarantees that s/he will not enthusiastically embrace any counterintuitive system redesigns discovered by interacting with the model. In this rather typical situation, system dynamicists have found that turning a model into a game—within which users can interact with the underlying model in a rigorous, yet user-friendly, environment and learn about its structural dynamics in an orderly and engaging fashion—can lead to insight, understanding, and confidence in proposed policy changes.

Although a variety of techniques for turning system dynamics models into games have been created over the years, Meadows (1989) has developed a method that frequently leads to successful outcomes and can thus be considered the current "best practice" in the field. According to Meadows (1989, 636–637):

> The games of interest to me always: involve more than one player, force participants to interact in decision making, include physical pieces (boards, markers, etc.) and use a System Dynamics model as the referee or environment for the simulation. These games always involve several iterations of a basic decision sequence, ranging from five one-year cycles in my AIDS game to the ten five-year cycles that are required in STRATAGEM. After each cycle the decisions are entered into a System Dynamics model which calculates out the consequences of players' action and specifies the starting condition for the beginning of the next cycle. This is very different from video games in which one person alone interacts with the computer.

Finally, according to Wilber and Harrison (1978), *storytelling* is a hallmark of traditional institutional analysis. The good news is that storytelling is also used quite frequently by system dynamicists to help those who did not participate in a model's construction understand how its structure causes its behavior. Modern system dynamics software literally has a storytelling feature that enables a model creator to lead an audience through a step-by step recreation of a model's pattern, and to show the impact of each additional pattern component on the model's behavior. Brick-by-brick, additional structure is revealed and additional simulations are run, until the full pattern is revealed and the base run mimicking the reference mode is presented. Other tools that enhance the story, including reality checks, causal tracing, and feedback-loop dominance algorithms help the stakeholders relate model structure to model behavior.[22]

Econometrics, reference modes, and a role for data science

As noted by Samuelson, econometric modeling rose to prominence within the economics profession during the second half of the twentieth century. Empirical work in economics evolved away from observation in the field to applying statistical techniques to numerical data sets in order to estimate the parameters of a model whose mathematical structure was derived directly from economic theory. For example, economists were taught to set up a multiple regression model, run it once, and evaluate the resulting t and F statistics, R2, etc., and then decide whether or not the data supported the theory from which the econometric model was derived. If the data and/or the model's structure violated one of the assumptions necessary for a best linear unbiased estimator (BLUE), a correction procedure was applied so that a better set of parameter estimates could be obtained. Data mining, however, was discouraged, if not downright forbidden. Running, say, a stepwise regression procedure that iterated until it yielded a regression that best fit a large data set, and then pretending it was the first and only regression that was run, was considered scientific malfeasance.[23]

Historically, system dynamics modeling was seen as a direct competitor to econometric modeling.[24] One of the early methodological debates between economists and system dynamicists involved the alleged *requirement* that models be statistically fit to time series data, both for the purposes of estimating parameter values and instilling confidence that the model could mimic, and hence explain, the behavior of the actual system. Although statistically fitting a model to a dataset is the raison d'être of econometric modeling, it was originally seen as unnecessary in system dynamics modeling.

Fitting a model to a data set

A system dynamics modeling project begins with the definition of the problem to which the model will be directed. The problem is typically first stated in words and then converted into a dynamic picture known as a reference mode. A reference mode is a time series graph(s) that reveals the time shapes (in absolute terms and relative to one another) of important system variables that visually tell the story of the system's problems. The reference mode specifies the relevant units of time over which the model will be simulated, and the length of time necessary to see the dynamics of the problem unfold. The time series plots can portray hard or soft variables and be created from numerical data and/or qualitatively from the mental models of experts and stakeholders.[25] The system dynamics model (i.e., the pattern) is constructed so that its base run mimics the reference mode to an acceptable degree of fidelity. An acceptable fit often means a qualitative, rather than a point-by-point, match to the data. When this has been accomplished, the model is thought to offer an explanation for the problem. "What-if" simulation experiments can then be run and compared to the base run so that proposed system re-designs can be evaluated.[26]

There are several reasons why system dynamicists originally did not feel the need to statistically fit their models to data. The first was that a series of synthetic data experiments undertaken by the System Dynamics Group at the Massachusetts Institute of Technology showed convincingly that traditional econometric techniques could not consistently recover the known parameters of a system dynamics model under anything approaching realistic conditions.[27] This view changed somewhat in the mid-1970s when Peterson (1980) devised a way to use techniques from electrical engineering to accurately estimate the parameters of a system dynamics model under a variety of challenging real world conditions.[28]

The second reason system dynamicists did not feel the need to fit their models to data is that the ability to fit a model to a particular time series was not seen by system dynamicists as a strong test of model validity. For example, when describing his system dynamics model of the macroeconomy, which he ultimately considered to be a generic structure, Forrester (2003, 5) wrote:

> There is no reason that a generic model should reproduce any specific historical time series. Instead, it should generate the kind of dynamic behavior that is observed in the systems that are being represented … . I believe there is much too much attention given in economics, and in system dynamics, to reproducing a specific historical time series. The dynamic character of past behavior is very important, but the specific values at exact points in historical time are not. Different random sequences in the past in the real economy would have produced different historical data sequences all with the same general character, just as would happen in a series of model simulations using different random inputs.

Finally, the third reason is the traditional paradigm of system dynamics contains no reason to fit a model to time series data. According to Peterson (2005), if best practices are followed during the construction of a system dynamics model, which includes the identification of all relevant feedback loops and nonlinear relationships, the results will be a very robust model that can be used to develop a set of *simple-to-follow* policies leading to a more robust system redesign. The deliverable to the model users, therefore, is not so much a model, but rather a set of robust feedback rules that can be followed by policymakers to compute decisions from incoming data. The feedback rules act as a type of guidance system that keeps the actual system on a favorable time path, irrespective of the system's specific state or particular parameter values. As a consequence, there is no need to estimate precise parameter values, no need to fit the model to historical data, and no need to forecast anything. This original perspective was inspired by a 1950s view of servomechanism technology: applications required light weight, high speed, and low power while, at the same time, computers were heavy, slow, and power-hungry. Hence robust feedback policies had to be made as simple as possible.

Notwithstanding Forrester's skepticism about the need to fit system dynamics models to historical data, today most system dynamicists hold a different view. In a provocative paper Sterman (2018, 29) argues:

> Today, data have never been more abundant. Methods to reliably measure previously unquantified concepts, unavailable to [Forrester], are now essential. Rigorous data collection, both qualitative and quantitative, opens up new opportunities for formal estimation of model parameters, relationships and structure, to assess the ability of models to replicate the historical data, and to characterize the sensitivity of results to uncertainty, providing more reliable and useful insights and policy recommendations.

Modern techniques from data science

Although the list of modern techniques from the field of data science is huge and growing larger every day, a few of them that might be appealing to institutional economists who may wish to apply system dynamics to a problem are worth mentioning here. These techniques can be reasonably divided into two broad categories: techniques for developing better reference modes, and techniques for identifying patterns in data sets that are difficult for humans to detect with the unaided mind.

Economist and system dynamicist Khalid Saeed (1992) has long argued that a complex dynamic problem, as defined by a reference mode, should be "sliced" into simple pieces to make the modeling process more manageable. For example, an economic system exhibiting an interacting trend, a long-term cycle, a short-term cycle, and noise might have its behavior smoothed and disaggregated into a separate trend and separate cycles. The modeler can then select which of the modes of behavior s/he wishes to initially address with a model.

The good news is that modern techniques from data science can be used to identify reference modes and facilitate Saeed's slicing process. For example, modern data-visualization tools can be used to help modelers recognize problematic behaviors in large data sets, and many formal techniques, such as Holt-Winters exponential smoothing, can be used to break down time-series data into its component modes of behavior.[29]

In terms of inductive logic, modern data-science techniques can be used to find patterns in large datasets that were previously undiscoverable with the unaided human mind. For example, cluster analysis can be used to find natural groups of entities (e.g., people, firms, industries, locations, machines, etc.) such that, within each group the entities are very similar, and among the groups the entities are very different. These groups or clusters can often be used at the model conceptualization stage to help identify model sectors. Additionally, network analysis techniques can be applied to large data sets to find interconnections for a system dynamics model that are not obvious to the economist detective at a crime scene. And finally, association rule techniques can be used to find events in large data sets that usually happen together. The classic example is purchases of "beer and diapers"—i.e., those who buy diapers tend to also buy beer![30]

"If my only tool is a hammer ..."

As with all tools, system dynamics has its strengths and weaknesses. As such, it may or may not be the most appropriate tool to use when addressing any particular problem. Since many of the strengths of system dynamics have already been described, this section will describe its weaknesses and suggest fixes or other tools that may, at times, be more appropriate for institutional economic analysis.

The first weakness of system dynamics models is that they tend to have poor user interfaces. This is really not a characteristic of the underlying technique but rather a result of inattention to the topic by the producers of system dynamics software. As younger scholars, who grew up playing sophisticated computer games that enable them to essentially "be inside" a simulation, begin to take over the economics profession, the need for superior user interfaces is becoming ever more crucial. The good news is that some system dynamics software developers have recently made significant advances in this area.[31]

The second weakness of system dynamics is that it is awkward to apply to problems that have significant spatial aspects. As such, if a problem has significant dynamic *and* spatial aspects to it, another simulation tool such as agent-based modeling should be considered.[32] Along these lines, post-Keynesian economists are beginning to build stock-flow–consistent agent-based models.[33]

The third issue associated with system dynamics is that it is a continuous-time modeling technique that is implemented on a discrete machine (i.e., a digital computer). Since a digital computer cannot take infinitesimally small steps forward in simulated time, the numerical solutions to system dynamics models are only approximate and result in non-integer values being generated for stock and flow variables. As models are (by definition) not real, this should not be a problem per se. However, when actual stock and flow data are compared to synthetic stock and flow data, the integer/non-integer distinction becomes obvious and can cause a loss of confidence among some model users. Moreover, synthetic flow data from a system dynamics model represents, theoretically, *instantaneous* rates of change (i.e., change at a *point* in time), while actual flow data from a real system are measured over discrete chunks of time and represent change over a *span* of time (e.g., quarterly sales, which are the *sum* of all sales for a three month period).[34] As such, even when a modeler possesses a comprehensive database of actual stock and flow data that correspond directly to the stock and flow concepts in a system dynamics model, the actual values from the database will almost certainly not match their synthetic counterparts on a point-by-point basis.

The fourth weakness associated with system dynamics modeling is that the order at which entities enter each of a system's stocks is not preserved. Instead, the entities that are accumulated in each of a system's stocks are "stirred and mixed" and flow out of each stock according to a probability distribution. As a consequence, concepts that require order of entry to be preserved within a stock (e.g., situations requiring FIFO—first-in-first-out—and/or LIFO—last-in-first-out—accounting) are at times difficult to implement in system dynamics models.[35]

The fifth issue associated with system dynamics modeling is that everything that accumulates in each of a system's stocks is assumed to be identical. In some cases, this is not a problem, but in other cases it can be a significant problem. For example, if a system stock contains "cash," it is legitimate to assume that all of the currency units are identical. On the other hand, if a system's stock contains "people," and the differences among people (gender, educational attainment, income level, etc.) are important to the problem that is motivating the creation of the model, it is not legitimate to simply assume that all of the people are the same. System dynamicists have some solutions to this dilemma, including both the use of co-flow structures that calculate the average attribute of the entities in a stock (e.g., the average level of educational attainment for a stock of people) and the replication of stock-flow structure for each attribute (e.g., replacing a single stock of "people" with a stock of "rich people" and a stock of "poor people"). Unfortunately, these solutions can quickly become unwieldy and, at some point, the problem essentially turns into an agent-based modeling problem.

The final issue associated with system dynamics models is that, although they are dynamic, they are *not* "evolutionary." In other words, they are ergodic and move in Newtonian time, rather than non-ergodic and moving in Darwinian time, and the agents they represent do not make decisions that are fundamentally uncertain. This weakness is of particular importance to heterodox economists such as institutionalists, post-Keynesians, Marxists, and neo-Schumpeterians.

The debate surrounding whether or not system dynamics models can evolve is actually quite old.[36] As noted by Schieritz and Grosler (2002), in order for a dynamic simulation model to evolve, its structure must cause its behavior *and* its behavior must feed back to alter its structure (i.e., its equations). In economics, the typical way that an evolutionary model alters its structure in response to its behavior is via learning, imitation, and rule adaptation/mutation by its agents. System dynamics models that are built according to the original paradigm developed by Forrester possess structures that cause their behaviors, but do not alter their structures in response to their unfolding dynamics.[37]

There are essentially four counterarguments offered by system dynamicists to the claim that their models are dynamic but not evolutionary. The first is that the issue is irrelevant as, although models that generate truly evolutionary behavior may be more "realistic," they won't necessarily yield superior insight into the proper policies that should be implemented to improve system behavior.

The second argument is that although the structure of a system dynamics model may not change in response to its behavior during any given simulation run, its structure *does* change during the iterative *modeling process* in response to its simulated behavior. This is significant because, as noted before, system dynamicists believe that it is the (pattern) modeling *process* that is key, not *the model*.

The third argument is that although a system dynamics model doesn't endogenously change its *actual* structure during a simulation run, it does change its *active* structure during a simulation run, owing to shifts in feedback-loop dominance. In other words, in the case of nonlinear systems, the strength of their feedback loops can change as a simulation unfolds and this can cause dramatic alterations in their time paths that are often unpredictable.[38]

The final argument offered by system dynamicists has been put forth by Radzicki and Sterman (1994). They point out that there are a number of different definitions of evolutionary change, as well as a number of different characteristics of models that enable them to be classified as evolutionary. They further point out that system dynamics models can generate behavior that meets some of the definitions for evolutionary change and possess some characteristics that enable them to be classified as evolutionary.[39] As a consequence, Radzicki and Sterman argue that it is simplistic to conclude that system dynamics models are dynamic but not evolutionary, and provide an example model to support their claim.[40]

Future directions

Institutional (and other heterodox) economists have the opportunity to begin using modern tools of simulation and data science, where appropriate, in unprecedented levels to add both rigor and additional insight to their analyses. For those who are interested, some places to begin include the following[41]

- Identify pattern recognition tools and techniques from the field of data science that can be useful for institutional analysis: These inductive, logic-based algorithms might be able to add value to the traditional pattern modeling approach in and of themselves, and can most certainly add value, where appropriate, to the system dynamics modeling process.
- Identify modern methods for eliciting and analyzing qualitative data for use in institutional analyses and system dynamics modeling: Many techniques have been created since Forrester began stressing the importance of integrating the mental models of system participants into a system dynamics model. Ford (2009, Chapter 16), for example, has done extensive work on bringing Daniel McFadden's discrete choice survey and modeling techniques into system dynamics models. More generally, Sterman (2018, 22–23) notes:

"Protocols for eliciting people's knowledge, beliefs and preferences include interviews, ethnographic study, survey methods, focus groups, conjoint analysis, nominal group technique, concurrent verbal protocols, and many others … . [T]he literature is vast … . Convenience samples and just 'talking to people' are no longer acceptable."

- Add insights from behavioral and experimental economics to system dynamics models: Since the flow equations in system dynamics models often represent human decision-making structures, working with behavioral economists to make these structures consistent with what is known about human cognition and judgment (warts and all) can, in principle, greatly enrich these models. Moreover, games based on system dynamics models that have been enriched with behavioral insights can, in principle, be used to test human subjects in experimental economics settings.
- Bring a continuous-time perspective into the stock-flow consistent modeling paradigm of post-Keynesian institutionalists: There is no reason, in principle, that traditional stock-flow consistent modeling can't benefit, where appropriate, from the use of a continuous-time perspective. Indeed, system dynamicists and post-Keynesian institutionalists can, in principle, share information and determine how and when to best use each representation of time.
- Bring a multi-method modeling perspective into institutional analysis and dynamic modeling: Borshchev (2015) has done extensive work in developing software and procedures for building multi-method dynamic simulation models. The idea here is to select the correct type of dynamic modeling technique for the problem at hand and, if necessary, blend elements of several techniques (such as system dynamics modeling, agent-based modeling, and discrete event modeling) together in a single model. This approach can, in principle, overcome some of the limitations associated with any one traditional simulation modeling technique.

Conclusion

The modern tools of simulation and data science, and the methods used to blend them together, have advanced spectacularly over the last 20 years. Heterodox economists should consider using them where appropriate. As Sterman (2018, 32) writes:

> Robust methods for parameter estimation, identification, assessment of goodness of fit, and parametric and structural sensitivity analysis are now available, not only in econometrics but also in engineering, artificial intelligence and machine learning … . Following [Forrester's] example, system dynamics modelers should master the state of the art and use these tools, follow new developments as the tools continue to evolve, and innovate to develop new methods appropriate for the models we build. The advent of

"big data" and analytics including machine learning, various artificial intelligence methods and the ability to process data sets of previously unimaginable size also create unprecedented opportunities for dynamic modelers.

In short, if institutional economists begin to apply, where appropriate, modern tools from the fields of simulation and data science in their research, they will generate new insight into the socioeconomic challenges of the day and inoculate themselves from Samuelson's charge that mainstream economists conduct economic research with "superior analytical and econometric tools."

Acknowledgments

The author thanks Charles Whalen, Saeed Langarudi, and Rafaat Zaini for insightful comments on an earlier draft of this chapter.

Notes

1 These tools consisted primarily of closed-form, analytical modeling techniques and (mostly linear) statistical procedures.
2 Trying to model "the system" that is experiencing a problem—i.e., trying to produce a digital twin of the system—is, generally speaking, a bad idea as it typically leads to giant models that are extremely difficult to understand and control, and that are falsely seen as capable of answering all questions related to the system. Indeed, some system dynamicists believe it's simply impossible in principle to produce an identical digital twin of any actual system. Instead, system dynamicists believe—as do most institutionalists—that a better approach is to focus a model on a particular problem and ruthlessly leave out those parts of the actual system that are deemed irrelevant for this purpose.
3 Forrester (1980a, 10) frequently described system dynamics modeling as "an extension of the case study approach."
4 Langarudi and Radzicki (2015) present a large-scale system dynamics model that contains a significant number of interacting "soft" socio-political-economic variables that is quite different from a traditional development economics model.
5 See the discussions in Randers (1980); Forrester (1980b); and Forrester (1985).
6 Thompson (1985) modified Homer's model for the case of artificial skin.
7 See the discussion in Forrester and Senge (1980) and Paich (1985).
8 Forrester frequently quipped that "nature integrates, it doesn't take derivatives."
9 For more on reconstructing economics around the balance sheet, see the discussion in Mass (1980). On stock-flow–consistent models, see for example, Godley and Lavoie (2007); see also Radzicki (2019), which contains a system dynamics representation of one of Godley and Lavoie's models. For evidence that many post-Keynesian economists consider themselves to be post-Keynesian institutionalists, see, for example, Whalen (2020).
10 See for example Kaldor (1972), David (1985), Davidson (1993), and Belke et al. (2014), as well as the work of János Kornai (see Haggard 2018).
11 Ryder and Cavana (2021) present a system dynamics representation of the Phillips machine.
12 See Saeed (2015).
13 Cochrane and Graham (1976) note that "Axel Leijonhufvud has referred to the introduction of control engineering into [macroeconomic] analysis by Tustin, Phillips, and others in the 1950s as 'the Keynesian Revolution which did not come off.'"

14 Rammelt (2019) presents a modified system dynamics version of Keen's model.

15 Sterman (2000, Chapter 1) attributes the persistence of socioeconomic problems to, among other things, "policy resistance," which is quite common in complex systems whose structures contain lots of goal-seeking, negative feedback loops.

16 If a socioeconomic system already exists (e.g., the US health care insurance system), system dynamics is used to examine the implications of alternative system *re-designs*. If a system only exists in the minds of policymakers, system dynamics is used to examine the implications of alternative original system *designs*. A US infrastructure bank, or Keynes's notion of the bancor, are examples of systems that currently only exist as ideas.

17 Modern system dynamics software makes representing institutional hierarchies with modules quite easy. For example, see isee systems' STELLA Architect (https://www.iseesystems.com).

18 See also Natarajan, Elsner, and Fullwiler (2009).

19 See Gill (1996) and Radzicki (2009).

20 For an actual case study illustrating this process, see Sterman (2000, 743–755). Sterman changed the name of the firm in the study to Fast Growth Electronics for proprietary reasons. Page 745 of that case study lists all the solutions proposed by the experts and stakeholders.

21 See the survey of group model-building techniques and results in Scott et al. (2016), McCardle-Keurentjes et. al (2018), and Rouwette and Vennix (2020).

22 An algorithm example is STELLA's "Loops the Matter" algorithm. For details see Schoenberg, Pál Davidsen, and Eberlein (2020).

23 The proper procedure in this case would be to take the "best" regression found by the stepwise procedure and run it one time on a new sample, and then report the results.

24 See the extensive discussions in Greenberger et. al (1976) and Sommer (1984).

25 Of course, written information can be used as well. Sterman (2018) provides a detailed discussion of Forrester's use of observation and interviews to capture the mental models of experts and stakeholders, as well as modern techniques for incorporating qualitative and quantitative data into system dynamics models.

26 During the construction of a reference mode, it is also common to specify the time shapes for "best case," "worst case," and "most likely case" outcomes, as well what "solved" or "improved" means to model users. As there are inevitably trade-offs associated with any system redesign, a multi-attribute "scoring metric" may also be specified so that it's possible to rank the efficacy of proposed policy changes.

27 See, for example, Senge (1977).

28 Graham (1980) provides an overview of simple parameter estimation techniques that utilize data below the level of a system dynamics model's aggregation. For a more contemporary survey of modern parameter estimation techniques for use in system dynamics modeling, see Rahmandad et al. (2015).

29 For a succinct overview of Holt-Winters exponential smoothing, see Goodwin (2010).

30 Of course, care must always be taken to avoid spurious correlations (see Vigen 2015). See also the cautionary tales in Smith (2020).

31 Again, see isee systems' STELLA Architect (https://www.iseesystems.com).

32 A comprehensive overview of agent-based modeling and its relationship to institutional economics is beyond the scope of this chapter. However, it should be noted that system dynamics and agent-based modeling are similar in that they both are nonlinear, dynamic, simulation modeling techniques that utilize a systems perspective. Although they differ in many respects, the most fundamental dissimilarity involves their methodological starting points. A system dynamics modeler starts by identifying a reference mode that describes a system's problematic behavior that is known, but not well understood. An agent-based modeler, on the other hand, starts by identifying the rules that are followed by individual system agents. The system's aggregate behavior is initially unknown and is said to "emerge" during a simulation run. Indeed, if an agent-based modeler can successfully predict a system's aggregate

behavior from knowledge of the rules given to its individual agents, the system's behavior is not considered to be "emergent." For more information on agent-based modeling and its relationship to heterodox economics see Potts (2000) and Carrillo-Hermosilla and Unruh (2006).

33 See Caiani et al. (2016).

34 In other words, creating actual flow data requires the use of a stock or accumulation process that does not exist in the corresponding flow variable in the system dynamics model.

35 Solutions to this problem have been developed and are routinely used, but their implementation starts to push a model away from the "pure" system dynamics paradigm.

36 See the discussions in Perlman (1980) and Radzicki and Sterman (1994).

37 Richardson (2000), however, makes a valiant attempt to see if he can make a system dynamics model "learn."

38 Of note is that recent advancements in nonlinear science have yielded software solutions that enable system dynamicists to better understand the impact of shifting feedback-loop dominance on model behavior. See, for example, Schoenberg et al. (2020).

39 In response to Wittenberg's (1992) criticism that Sterman's (1985) model of Thomas Kuhn's *Structure of Scientific Revolutions* does not adequately capture the revolutionary nature of paradigmatic change, Sterman worked with Witenberg to produce a new model of Kuhnian paradigm change that generated path-dependent dynamics and self-organizing behavior via circular and cumulative causal relationships. See Sterman and Wittenberg (1999).

40 In an insightful paper, Atkinson (2004, 282) suggests that a good test of the ability of a system dynamics model to capture evolutionary behavior at an acceptable level would be to model the evolution of the shoemaking industry from 1648 to 1895 as described by John Commons in 1909.

41 For examples of institutionalist research using system dynamics and other modern tools of simulation and data science, see: Saeed (2004); Harvey (2013); and Lewis and Dangerfield (2021).

Bibliography

Allen, R. G. D. 1959. *Mathematical Economics*. 2nd Edition. London: Macmillan and Company Limited. https://doi.org/10.1007/978-1-349-81547-0

Atkinson, Glen. 2004. "Common Ground for Institutional Economics and System Dynamics Modeling." *System Dynamics Review* 20 (4): 275–286. https://doi.org/10.1002/sdr.300

Belke, Ansgar, Matthias Göcke, and Laura Werner. 2014. "Hysteresis Effects in Economics – Different Methods for Describing Economic Path-Dependence." in *Hysteresis: Types, Applications and Behavior Patterns in Complex Systems*, edited by José Carlos Diaz, 19–42. New York: Nova Science Publishers.

Berger, Sebastian. 2008. "Circular and Cumulative Causation (CCC) à la Myrdal and Kapp - Political Institutionalism for Minimizing Social Costs." *Journal of Economic Issues* 42 (2): 357–365. https://doi.org/10.1080/00213624.2008.11507144

———. 2009. *The Foundations of Non-Equilibrium Economics: The Principle of Circular and Cumulative Causation*. London: Routledge. https://doi.org/10.4324/9780203873731

Borshchev, Andrei. 2015. *The Big Book of Simulation Modeling: Multimethod Modeling with AnyLogic 6*. Chicago, IL: AnyLogic North America.

Boulding, Kenneth E. 1950. *A Reconstruction of Economics*. New York: John Wiley & Sons.

Caiani, Alessandro, Antoine Godin, Eugenio Caverzasi, Mauro Gallegati, Stephen Kinsella, and Joseph E. Stiglitz. 2016. "Agent Based-Stock Flow Consistent

Macroeconomics: Towards a Benchmark Model." *Journal of Economic Dynamics and Control* 69 (August): 375–408. https://doi.org/10.1016/j.jedc.2016.06.001

Carrillo-Hermosilla, Javier and Gregory Unruh. 2006. "Technological Stability and Change: An Integrated and Evolutionary Approach." *Journal of Economic Issues* 40 (3): 707–742. https://doi.org/10.1080/00213624.2006.11506942

Cochrane, James and John Graham. 1976. "Cybernetics and Macroeconomics." *Economic Inquiry* 14 (2): 241–250. https://doi.org/10.1111/j.1465-7295.1976.tb00390.x

David, Paul. 1985. "Clio and the Economics of QWERTY." *American Economic Review* 75 (2): 332–337.

Davidson, Paul. 1993. "The Elephant and the Butterfly: Or Hysteresis and Post Keynesian Economics." *Journal of Post Keynesian Economics* 15 (3): 309–322. https://doi.org/10.1080/01603477.1993.11489946

Diesing, Paul. 1971. *Patterns of Discovery in the Social Sciences.* Chicago, IL: Aldine-Atherton. https://doi.org/10.4324/9781315126142

Ford, Andrew. 2009. *Modeling the Environment.* 2nd Edition. Washington, D.C.: Island Press.

Forrester, Jay W. 1956. "Dynamic Models of Economic Systems and Industrial Organizations." System Dynamics Group Memo D-0000. Alfred P. Sloan School of Management, Massachusetts Institute of Technology. Cambridge, Massachusetts.

———. 1961. *Industrial Dynamics.* Cambridge, MA: The MIT Press.

———. 1968. *Principles of Systems.* Cambridge, MA: The MIT Press.

———. 1969. *Urban Dynamics.* Cambridge, MA: The MIT Press.

———. 1980a. "System Dynamics - Future Opportunities." In *System Dynamics.* TIMS Studies in the Management Sciences, Volume 14, edited by Augusto Legasto, Jay Forrester, and James Lyneis, 7–21. New York: North Holland.

———. 1980b. "Information Sources for Modeling the National Economy." *Journal of the American Statistical Association* 75 (371): 555–574. https://doi.org/10.2307/2287647

———. 1985. "'The' Model versus a Modeling 'Process'." *System Dynamics Review* 1 (1): 133–134. https://doi.org/10.1002/sdr.4260010112

———. 1993. "System Dynamics and the Lessons of 35 Years." In *Systems-Based Approach to Policymaking,* edited by Kenyon De Greene, 199–240. Norwell, MA: Kluwer Academic Publishers. https://doi.org/10.1007/978-1-4615-3226-2_7

———. 2003. "Economic Theory for the New Millennium." Plenary Address to the 2003 International System Dynamics Conference. New York. July 21st. System Dynamics Group Memo D-4886-1. Massachusetts Institute of Technology.

Forrester, Jay and Peter Senge. 1980. "Tests for Building Confidence in System Dynamics Models." In *System Dynamics.* TIMS Studies in the Management Sciences. Volume 14, edited by Augusto Legasto, Jay Forrester, and James Lyneis, 209–228. New York: North Holland.

Gill, Roderic. 1996. "An Integrated Social Fabric Matrix/System Dynamics Approach to Policy Analysis." *System Dynamics Review* 14 (2): 554–580. https://doi.org/10.1002/(sici)1099-1727(199623)12:3%3C167::aid-sdr100%3E3.0.co;2-3

Godley, Wynne and Marc Lavoie. 2007. *Monetary Economics: An Integrated Approach to Credit, Money, Income, Production and Wealth.* London: Palgrave MacMillan.

Goodwin, Peter. 2010. "The Holt-Winters Approach to Exponential Smoothing: 50 Years Old and Going Strong." *Foresight* (Fall) available at www.forecasters.org/foresight

Graham, Alan. 1980. "Parameter Estimation in System Dynamics Modeling." In *Elements of the System Dynamics Method,* edited by Jørgen Randers, 143–161. Cambridge, MA: MIT Press.

Greenberger, Martin, Matthew Crenson, and Brian Crissey. 1976. *Models in the Policy Process: Public Decision Making in the Computer Era*. New York: Russell Sage Foundation.

Haggard, Stephen. 2018. "Janos Kornai as Political Economist." *Acta Oeconomica* 68 (S): 9–25. https://doi.org/10.1556/032.2018.68.s.3

Harvey, John T. 2013. "Keynes's Trade Cycle: A System Dynamics Model." *Journal of Post Keynesian Economics* 36 (1): 105–130. https://doi.org/10.2753/pke0160-3477360106

Hayden, Gregory. 1982. "Social Fabric Matrix: From Perspective to Analytical Tool" *Journal of Economic Issues* 16 (3): 637–662. https://doi.org/10.1080/00213624.1982.11504025

Homer, Jack 1987. "A Diffusion Model with Application to Evolving Medical Technologies." *Technological Forecasting and Social Change* 31 (3): 197–218. https://doi.org/10.1016/0040-1625(87)90011-4

Kaldor, Nicholas. 1972. "The Irrelevance of Equilibrium Economics." *The Economic Journal* 82 (328): 1237–1255. https://doi.org/10.2307/2231304

Kapp, K. William. 1976. "The Nature and Significance of Institutional Economics." *Kyklos* 29 (June): 209–230. https://doi.org/10.1111/j.1467-6435.1976.tb01971.x

Steve, Keen. 1995. "Finance and Economic Breakdown: Modeling Minsky's Financial Instability Hypothesis." *Journal of Post Keynesian Economics* 17 (4): 607–635. https://doi.org/10.1080/01603477.1995.11490053

Langrudi, Saeed and Michael Radzicki. 2015. "A Simulation Model of Katouzian's Theory of Arbitrary State and Society." *Forum for Social Economics* 47 (1): 1–38. https://doi.org/10.1080/07360932.2015.1051076

Leijonhufvud, Axel. 1968. *On Keynesian Economics and the Economics of Keynes: A Study in Monetary Theory*. New York: Oxford University Press.

Lewis, Jide and Brian Dangerfield. 2021. "Policy Responses to Sovereign Debt Induced Banking Crises: A Model-Based Evaluation of Alternatives." In *Feedback Economics: Economic Modeling with System Dynamics*, edited by Robert Y. Cavana, Brian Dangerfield, Oleg V. Pavlov, Michael J. Radzicki, and I. David Wheat, Chapter 13. Heidelberg: Springer-Berlin.

Mass, Nathaniel 1980. "Stock and Flow Variables and the Dynamics of Supply and Demand." In *Elements of the System Dynamics Method*, edited by Jørgen Randers, 95–114. Cambridge, MA: MIT Press.

McCardle-Keurentjes, Marleen, Etiënne Rouwette, Jac Vennix, and Eric Jacobs. 2018. "Potential Benefits of Model Use in Group Model Building: Insights from an Experimental Investigation." *System Dynamics Review* 34 (1–2): 354–384. https://doi.org/10.1002/sdr.1603

Meadows, Dennis 1989. "Gaming to Implement System Dynamics Models." In *Computer-Based Management of Complex Systems*, edited by Peter Milling and Erich Zahn, 635–640. Berlin: Springer-Verlag. https://doi.org/10.1007/978-3-642-74946-9_69

Myrdal, Gunnar. 1957. "The Principle of Circular and Cumulative Causation." In *Economic Theory and Underdeveloped Regions*, edited by Gunnar Myrdal, 11–22. London: Methuen and Co., Ltd.

Natarajan, Tara, Wolfram Elsner, and Scott Fullwiler. 2009. *Institutional Analysis and Praxis: The Social Fabric Matrix Approach*. New York: Springer. https://doi.org/10.1007/978-0-387-88741-8

O'Hara, Phillip. 2008. "Principle of Circular and Cumulative Causation: Fusing Myrdalian and Kaldorian Growth and Development Dynamics." *Journal of Economic Issues* 42 (2): 375–387. https://doi.org/10.1080/00213624.2008.11507146

Paich, Mark. 1985. "Generic Structures." *System Dynamics Review* 1 (1): 126–132. https://doi.org/10.1002/sdr.4260010111

Perlman, Louis J. 1980. "Time in System Dynamics Models." In *System Dynamics. TIMS Studies in the Management Sciences.* Volume 14, edited by Augusto Legasto, Jr., Jay Forrester, and James Lyneis, 75–89. New York: North Holland.

Peterson, David 1980. "Statistical Tools for System Dynamics." In *Elements of the System Dynamics Method*, edited by Jørgen Randers, 226–245. Cambridge, MA: MIT Press.

———. 2005. "Optimal Stochastic System Dynamics: How to Improve an Uncertain, Nonlinear World." Powerpoint Slides. Ph.D. Seminar. Worcester Polytechnic Institute. April 13th.

Phillips, A. W. 1954. "Stabilisation Policy in a Closed Economy." *Economic Journal* 64 (254): 290–323.

Potts, Jason. 2000. *The New Evolutionary Microeconomics: Complexity, Competence and Adaptive Behavior.* Northampton, MA: Edward Elgar.

Radzicki, Michael. 1988. "Institutional Dynamics: An Extension of the Institutionalist Approach to Socioeconomic Analysis." *Journal of Economic Issues* 22 (3): 633–666. https://doi.org/10.1080/00213624.1988.11504801

———. 1990. "Methodologia Oeconomiae et Systematis Dynamis." *System Dynamics Review* 6 (2): 123–147. https://doi.org/10.1002/sdr.4260060202

———. 2003. "Mr. Hamilton, Mr. Forrester and a Foundation for Evolutionary Economics." *Journal of Economic Issues* 37 (1): 133–173. https://doi.org/10.1080/00213624.2003.11506561

———. 2009. "Convergence of the Social Fabric Matrix and Complex Modelling." In *Institutional Analysis and Praxis: The Social Fabric Matrix Approach*, edited by Tara Natarajan, Wolfram Elsner, and Scott T. Fullwiler, 69–85. Berlin: Springer-Verlag. https://doi.org/10.1007/978-0-387-88741-8_5

———. 2019. "System Dynamics and its Contribution to Economics/Economic Modeling." *Encyclopedia of Complexity and Systems Science*, edited by Robert Meyers. Berlin: Springer-Berlin, Heidelberg. https://doi.org/10.1007/978-3-642-27737-5_539-2

Radzicki, Michael and John Sterman. 1994. "Evolutionary Economics and System Dynamics." In *Evolutionary Concepts in Contemporary Economics*, edited by Richard England, 61–89. Ann Arbor, MI: University of Michigan Press.

Rammelt, Crelis. 2019. "The Dynamics of Financial Instability: Simplifying Keen's Goodwin–Minsky Model." *System Dynamics Review* 35 (2): 140–159. https://doi.org/10.1002/sdr.1627

Randers, Jørgen. 1980. "Guidelines for Model Conceptualization." In *Elements of the System Dynamics Method*, edited by Jørgen Randers, 117–139. Cambridge, MA: MIT Press.

Hazhir, Rahmandad, Rogelio Oliva, and Nathaniel Osgood. 2015. *Analytical Methods for Dynamic Modelers.* Cambridge, MA: MIT Press. https://doi.org/10.7551/mitpress/9927.001.0001

Richardson, George. 2000. "Can System Dynamics Models Learn?" Powerpoint Slides and Model Code. Available at https://www.albany.edu/~gpr/Can%20SD%20models%20learn.pdf. Accessed December 21, 2020.

Rouwette, Etiënne and Jac Vennix. 2020. "Group Model Building." In *System Dynamics. Encyclopedia of Complexity and Systems Science Series*, edited by Brian Dangerfield, 91–107. Springer, New York, NY. https://doi.org/10.1007/978-1-4939-8790-0_264

Ryder, William and Robert Cavana. 2021. "A System Dynamics View of the Phillips Machine: 'Chasing Some Hares!'" In *Feedback Economics: Economic Modeling with System Dynamics*, edited by Robert Cavana, Brian Dangerfield, Oleg Pavlov, Michael Radzicki, and David Wheat, Chapter 5. Heidelberg: Springer-Berlin.

Saeed, Khalid. 1992. "Slicing a Complex Problem for System Dynamics Modeling." *System Dynamics Review* 8 (3): 251–261. https://doi.org/10.1002/sdr.4260080305

———. 2004. "Designing an Environmental Mitigation Banking Institution for Linking the Size of Economic Activity to Environmental Capacity." *Journal of Economic Issues* 38 (4): 909–937. https://doi.org/10.1080/00213624.2004.11506749

———. 2015. "Jay Forrester's Operational Approach to Economics." *System Dynamics Review* 30 (4): 233–261. https://doi.org/10.1002/sdr.1525

Samuelson, Paul. 1976. *Economics*. 10th Edition. New York: McGraw-Hill.

Schieritz, Nadine and Andreas Grosler. 2002. "Emergent Structures in Supply Chains – A Study Integrating Agent-Based and System Dynamics Modeling." *Proceedings of the 36th Hawaii International Conference on System Sciences*. IEEE Computer Society. https://doi.org/10.1109/hicss.2003.1174226

Schoenberg, William, Pál Davidsen, and Robert Eberlein. 2020. "Understanding Model Behavior Using the Loops the Matter Method." *System Dynamics Review* 36 (2): 158–190. https://doi.org/10.1002/sdr.1658

Scott, Rodney, Robert Cavana, and Donald Cameron. 2016. "Recent Evidence on the Effectiveness of Group Model Building." *European Journal of Operational Research* 249 (3): 908–918. https://doi.org/10.1016/j.ejor.2015.06.078

Senge, Peter. 1977. "Statistical Estimation of Feedback Models." *Simulation* 28 (6): 177–184. https://doi.org/10.1177/003754977702800606

Smith, Gary. 2020. "Data Mining Fool's Gold." *Journal of Information Technology* 35 (3): 182–194. https://doi.org/10.1177/0268396220915600

Sommer, Manfred. 1984. "The Econometric Challenge to System Dynamics and Vice Versa: Some Future Perspectives." *Technological Forecasting and Social Change* 25 (3): 263–280. https://doi.org/10.1016/0040-1625(84)90005-2

Sterman, John. 1985. "The Growth of Knowledge: Testing A Theory of Scientific Revolutions with a Formal Model." *Technological Forecasting and Social Change* 28 (2): 93–122. https://doi.org/10.1016/0040-1625(85)90009-5

———. 2018. "System Dynamics at Sixty: The Path Forward." *System Dynamics Review* 34 (1–2): 5–47. https://doi.org/10.1002/sdr.1601

———. 2000. *Business Dynamics: Systems Thinking and Modeling for a Complex World*. New York: Irwin McGraw-Hill.

Sterman, John and Jason Wittenberg. 1999. "Path Dependence, Competition, and Succession in the Dynamics of Scientific Revolution." *Organization Science* 10 (3): 322–341. https://doi.org/10.1287/orsc.10.3.322

Thompson, Elizabeth. 1985. "Artificial Skin: Its Path to Adoption." Senior Thesis. Massachusetts Institute of Technology.

Tustin, Arnold. 1953. *The Mechanism of Economic Systems*. Cambridge, MA.: Harvard Univ. Press.

Vigen, Tyler. 2015. *Spurious Correlations*. New York: Hachette Books.

Whalen, Charles. 2020. "Post-Keynesian Institutionalism: Past, Present, and Future." *Evolutionary and Institutional Economics Review* 17 (1): 71–92. https://doi.org/10.1007/s40844-019-00150-4

Wilber, Charles and Robert Harrison. 1978. "The Methodological Basis of Institutional Economics: Pattern Model, Storytelling, and Holism." *Journal of Economic Issues* 12 (1): 61–89. https://doi.org/10.1080/00213624.1978.11503505

Wittenberg, Jason. 1992. "On the Very Idea of a System Dynamics Model of Kuhnian Science." *System Dynamics Review* 8 (1): 21–33. https://doi.org/10.1002/sdr.4260080103

INDEX

Note: Page numbers in *italics* indicate figures, **bold** indicate tables and page numbers with "n" indicates the end notes in the text.

Made in the USA
Las Vegas, NV
31 October 2024

5b6e06b7-9b7d-41a8-aed9-348d6290f60fR01